The Profit-Taker

The proven
rapid money-maker
in good and bad markets

The Profit-Taker

The proven
rapid money-maker
in good and bad markets

Don Abrams

John Wiley & Sons

New York • Chichester • Brisbane • Toronto

Library of Congress Cataloging in Publication Data:

Abrams, Don, 1931-
  The profit-taker.

  1. Speculation.   2. Investments.   I. Title.

HG6041.A25   1980   332.6'78   79-22695
ISBN 0-471-06228-6

Printed in the United States of America

10 9 8 7 6 5 4 3 2 1

"The only gift is a portion of thyself."

Emerson

Contents

1. A Truly Unique and Loveable Strategy

What makes this book different from the thousands of other "money-making" books?

Every great new tune is made up of the same basic musical notes that underlie any musical composition. This book is based on the same investment principles that many sensible investors have been using for years. What makes it different is the way it combines these old investment strategies with new and exciting techniques designed to pluck profits from the stock market *no matter how it moves — up or down.*

Most investment plans depend on predicting the way the market will move. This book does not. It plays a brand new tune on an old piano.

Much of my life has been a search for an ultra-conservative yet highly profitable investment strategy. I have found it in the Profit-Taker, and in this book I want to share it with you. As Ralph Waldo Emerson said, "Rings and other jewels are not gifts, but apologies for gifts. The only gift is a portion of thyself." An important part of my life culminates in the Profit-Taker.

This book is not merely a theory for making money if you happen to predict the correct movement of the stock market. It is a practical course of action that shows you how to make money *no matter how the market moves.*

It will give you all the fascinating fundamentals you need to understand and apply the Profit-Taker technique. It will free you forever from having to rely on "hot tips" and the advice of often contradictory "experts."

Allegedly sound stock market strategies, when analyzed, are often only marginally profitable. They are too sluggish, too lethargic, too dull, to produce any substantial profit. If for no other reason, sheer boredom will compel you to abandon these strategies.

This book is different. It does not simply tantalize you with the prospect of making "big money." It provides the necessary blueprint to accomplish this objective. The goal of this book is not "Let's talk about how to make a million," but "Let's do it —starting right now."

What is the Profit-Taker?

The Profit-Taker is an investment strategy I have built out of my own experience as an investor. It is a sophisticated strategy, but its approach is straightforward. In this book I have made every effort to simplify or discard the often discouraging and unnecessary financial jargon of the investment world.

The Profit-Taker combines ultra-conservative investment techniques with huge profit potential. Once you understand it and start to implement it, you will be able to play the stock market with none of the usual attendant anxieties of the ordinary investor.

The Profit-Taker incorporates many of the investment concepts already frequently used by investors, among them the technique known as "hedging," which combines investments in convertible securities with the short sale of the common stock underlying them. *Do not let these terms disconcert you.* They will be carefully and simply explained at the appropriate time. The Profit-Taker goes far beyond the use of these "hedge" techniques. Through a series of short- and long-term goals, carefully planned in advance, this extraordinary, wonder-working technique can deliver considerable profits through only small fluctuations in the price of common stock, regardless of whether the fluctuations take place on the downside or the upside. The recommended strategy is not theoretical. It is functional, demonstrated by personal trades.

This book is presented in a question and answer format to allow investors with varying degrees of experience to read and learn at different speeds.

A serious beginner will easily be able to follow the book's reasoning and, as a result, be in command of a strategy both highly profitable and highly protective of the initial investment.

The already experienced investor will value the Profit-Taker technique, especially if he has lost money in any kind of investment — mining stock, options, commodities or even real estate.

If money or "money power" is one of your major personal goals then the skilful application of the concepts presented here will provide you with the necessary knowledge to accomplish your objectives.

The practical and exciting techniques examined in sequence in this book culminate in the concept I fortunately developed — so please allow me that degree of vanity necessary to refer to it from now on as the Abrams Automatic Profit-Taker. It is this tested concept that, when grasped, is capable of doubling your money in less than six months in good or bad markets.

Skeptical? That would be a natural reaction. But follow along, and be prepared to be stirred to greater monetary heights.

If the Abrams Automatic Profit-Taker is as profitable as you claim, is there not a high degree of risk?

A fallacious yet common belief exists that there is a direct relationship between risk and profit potential. That is, if you take small risks you must expect small profits. Conversely, if you take extravagant risks, then you must forfeit a large degree of security. Not true! The concept of the Abrams Automatic Profit-Taker will, I hope, destroy this myth. It will demonstrate plainly — and in non-technical language — how you can take a manifestly minimum risk and still achieve large profits. If doubling your investment in less than six months meets your standard of financial success, then you will be elated with this strategy. Random trades from my own records will illustrate this technique.

This method that allows you to take profits automatically from the relatively minor fluctuations of your stock is, to the best of my knowledge, unique. Over the past ten years I have thoroughly examined many investment systems, including some practiced by stockbrokers themselves and known to them as "convertible hedging." The Abrams Automatic Profit-Taker evolved from this day-to-day exploration and through actual investment. This immensely exciting technique is particularly lucrative for the small investor, indeed it is tailored for him.

13

Many authors of investment books promise profits, often very small, without having practiced their strategy. Anyone who has been stirred by the lure of stock market profits knows that what appears to be alluring in theory often proves to be impractical and barren when implemented. It is reprehensible, in my opinion, to recommend investment concepts without having applied them. Using the Abrams Automatic Profit-Taker, not only can you reasonably expect handsome profits, but you will immeasurably reduce the risks that would be inevitable if you were simply holding common stocks. Poppycock, you say, or worse? I challenge you to read on. You will be elated.

Like other strategies, does the Abrams method require me to predict in which direction the market will move?

The Abrams Automatic Profit-Taker requires no crystal ball. This strategy does not take hours of searching for patterns in graphs to foretell future movement. It does not require endless reading through annual reports to find a revealing statement that might influence the stock.

The crystal-ball gazer at best must become accustomed to seeing hazy outlooks, at worst he must be prepared to pawn his crystal ball.

Most investment strategies proposed by brokers

and investment advisers are profitable only if the stock happens to move in the one, foretold, direction. By using the Abrams Automatic Profit-Taker, you will not have to interpret market movements. The game of peeping into the future, even though cloaked in impressive financial jargon by the Wall Street and "newsletter" pundits, is as reliable as tea-cup reading. When Bernard Baruch, the often quoted financial adviser to presidents, was asked "What will the stock market do tomorrow?" he gave an astute and honest answer. "It will fluctuate," he said. This is the simple truth upon which the Abrams Automatic Profit-Taker is based. You will see how you can "lock in" and take profits by riding even the relatively minor fluctuations. No longer will you find you have overstayed the market.

Should I rely on my broker to explain and institute a strategy such as the Abrams Automatic Profit-Taker?

Emphatically, no! Do not lean on your broker to volunteer and explain the dynamics of such a strategy as the Abrams Automatic Profit-Taker. Your broker, who is likely on straight commission, simply does not have the time to explain such a "sophisticated" concept. If he has five to ten minutes a day to spare for you, you may consider yourself unusually lucky. How rapidly you can double your money — and how often — will depend mainly on your own relentless perseverance. So avoid an overdependence on your broker. Control your own account. Expect your broker only to provide first-hand price information and execute your orders efficiently, and a harmonious, businesslike partnership should follow.

In this book, technical and financial jargon will be used only where it is necessary to aid you in speaking to your broker while setting up your own Abrams Automatic Profit-Taker.

On a day-to-day basis, will this strategy demand a great deal of my time?

As you will see, once you have set up your plan for the Abrams Automatic Profit-Taker, very little time will be required daily.

Most of the money-making orders will be filled automatically.

Inevitably however, you will be so fascinated with this strategy that a phone call to your broker after the close of the market will become irresistible. It may well be the sweetest and most rewarding call of your day.

2. The Convertible Bond
The Beginning of a
Beautiful Relationship

For my purposes, what is the critical difference between common stock and bonds?

The holder of common stock is an owner of the corporation. The holder of a bond is a creditor of the corporation.

As a shareholder or part owner, you are entitled to your proportion of the earnings *after the prior claims of the corporation have been paid.* These profits may be paid to the shareholder in the form of a dividend.

However, one of the prior claims that must be satisfied before you receive any dividends is the interest to the bondholder.

The amount of interest, which is paid regularly to the bondholder, is usually fixed at the time the bond is first issued.

For our purposes, it is crucial to appreciate the salient fact that *the interest on the bond receives priority and must be paid before any dividends are paid to the shareholder.* In other words, the bond is the senior security. Similarly, in the case of bankruptcy, this senior status entitles the loan by the bond holder to be satisfied in full before any remaining cash from the sale of the assets is distributed to the shareholder.

What is so special about the convertible bond?

The convertible bond combines the characteristics of an ordinary bond with the privilege of exchanging the bond for a predetermined number of common shares.

The convertible bond, like an ordinary bond, has a fixed interest rate and a maturity date on which the principal amount (usually $1,000) must be repaid. The full amount of the principal must be paid on the maturity date by the issuing corporation regardless of what the price of the common stock might be at that time. This comforting assurance, combined with the knowledge that the convertible bond has the status of being a senior security, creates a situation that will work hard for you.

Why should I care that the convertible bond has senior status over the common stock?

The senior status of the convertible bond guarantees that your interest-carrying convertible bond will be paid before any dividend can be paid on the common stock.

This senior status assures you as well that in a case of dissolution your convertible bond, like the ordinary bond, must be paid in full before any asset of the company can be assigned to the common stockholder.

Is there any other advantage to the convertible bond?

Even allowing the above strengths, the best is yet to come.

The commission you pay your broker is usually much less than you would pay him to buy the equivalent amount of common stock. Often the commission on the convertible bond is only a third or even a quarter of the commission paid when buying the equivalent amount of preferred or common stock. (Margin accounts and brokers' commissions are more fully discussed in chapters 8 and 11.)

Furthermore, the privilege of being able to convert your bond into common stock is perhaps the most creative feature of all. Read on, and see how this feature, when grasped, can indeed double your money in less than six months when its full potential is realized by following logically through to the Abrams Automatic Profit-Taker technique.

When can the convertible bond be exchanged for common stock?

Normally, the convertible bond can be converted into common stock at any time up to the date this conversion privilege expires.

The expiration of this privilege is a fixed date, usually the same as that at which the bond matures.

What happens if the common stock into which the convertible bond is exchangeable moves up?

Let's assume you purchased a convertible bond on which you paid no premium. (A premium is an additional value that may accrue to the convertible bond holder depending on the bond's relationship to the price of the common stock for which it can be exchanged.) In our theoretical case, the amount you paid for the bond was exactly the same as the amount of the common stock into which the bond may be exchanged. (Value of bond = value of shares into which the bond is convertible.)

Now, if the common stock moves up, the value of the bond must move up in direct relationship.

Figures 1, 2 and 3 illustrate typical examples of this occurrence. I must stress that in the upside situation illustrated here (where the stock and the convertible bond are moving up), the bond is as volatile and exciting as the common stock.

Remember, you can convert the bond into common stock at any time up to the due date.

The price at which the convertible bond would sell if it did not have the privilege of being exchanged for a set number of stocks is known as the investment value. The generally prevailing interest rates and the considered quality of the bond are the chief factors in predicting this investment value. Both these factors are constantly changing in response to changing company and over-all market conditions. Estimates of these investment values are provided by financial services and it is also possible for you to judge the situation for yourself. Remember, however, that these arc only estimates and in a constantly varying market they are consequently subject to change. In any case, in order to implement the dynamic strategy that is now to unfold, it is not necessary for you to know the precise investment value of the convertible bond.

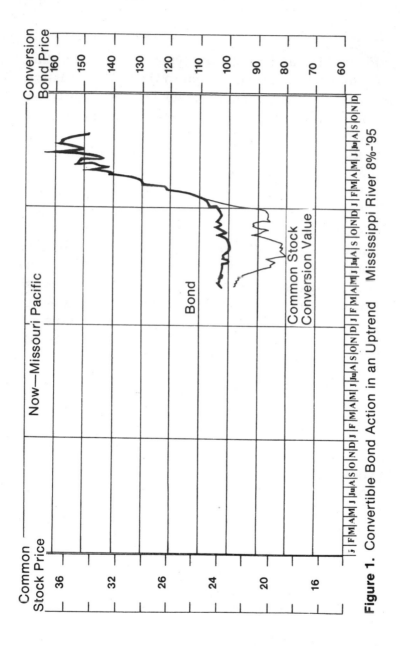

Figure 1. Convertible Bond Action in an Uptrend   Mississippi River 8%–'95

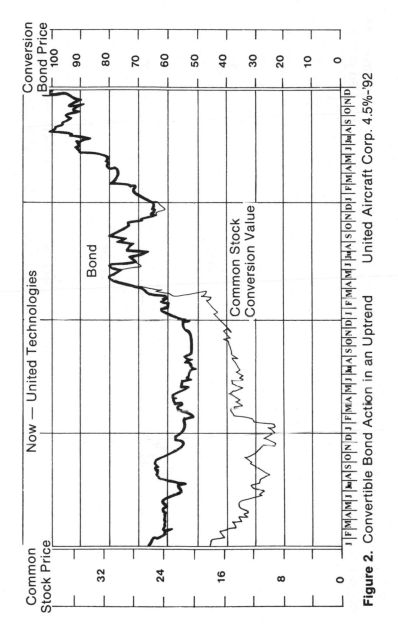

Figure 2. Convertible Bond Action in an Uptrend

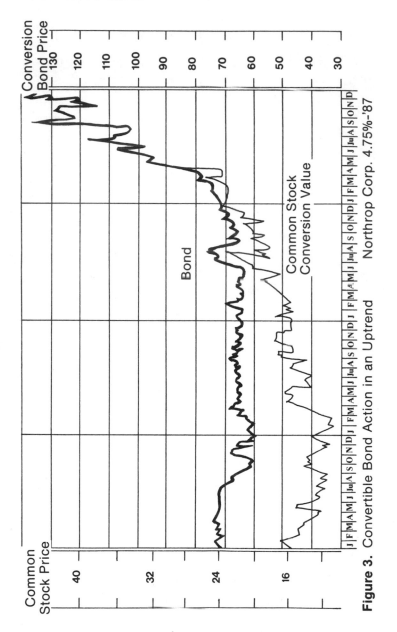

Figure 3. Convertible Bond Action in an Uptrend   Northrop Corp. 4.75%-'87

On the downtrend, won't the convertible bond also decrease in value directly with the common stock?

Typically the convertible bond provides formidable protection on the downtrend. This protection is provided largely by the senior rank of the convertible bond and the strength of a definitive interest rate.

In a downtrend market, the convertible bond will invariably take on the characteristics of an ordinary bond. Figures 4, 5 and 6 show what happens in a downtrend situation.

As you see, the convertible bond price typically slows down on the downtrend. Note the different value of the convertible bond (investment value) and the value of the common stock into which the convertible may be exchanged. I should explain here that the value of this common stock represented by the convertible bond is referred to as the conversion value. For example, if a bond is convertible into 30 shares and the common stock is selling at $20 a share, the bond's conversion value is $600 (30 shares x $20).

Buying a convertible bond is, in itself, a more astute investment than simply buying the common stock. But please don't stop here. Persist, for you will find that this protective advantage is merely the first step — although you are on your way — to the phenomenon of the Abrams Automatic Profit-Taker. In due course you will see how you can double your money in less than six months, while reducing your risk even further.

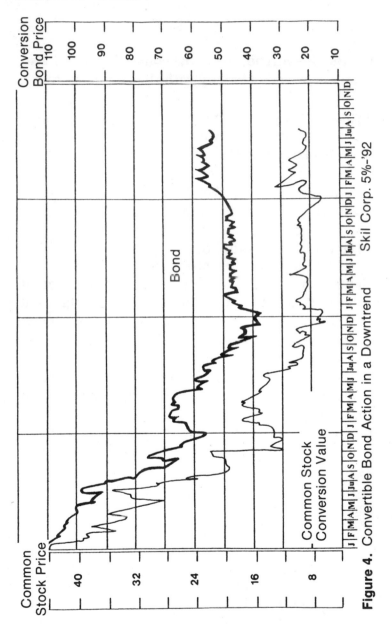

Figure 4. Convertible Bond Action in a Downtrend   Skil Corp. 5%-'92

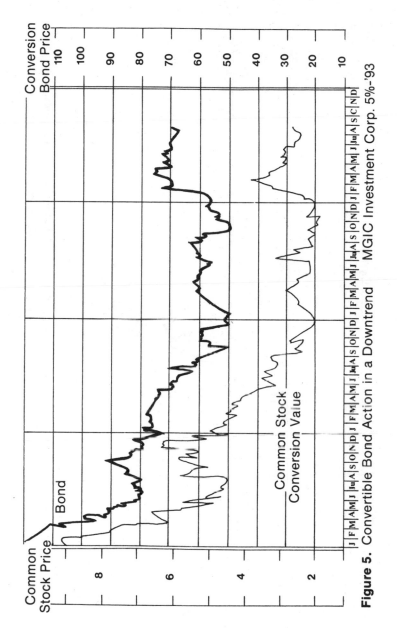

Figure 5. Convertible Bond Action in a Downtrend   MGIC Investment Corp. 5%–'93

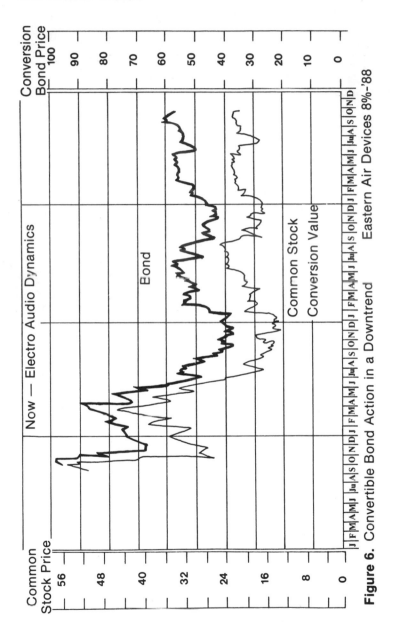

Figure 6. Convertible Bond Action in a Downtrend   Eastern Air Devices 8%-'88

3. The Short Sale
The Mighty Marriage of the Convertible Bond with the Short Sale

What is the short sale?

Few investors fully grasp the short sale. Follow the reasoning through here and you will understand its mystery. A short sale is an often misunderstood and seemingly complicated technique. It needn't be.

The short sale is simply, for our purposes, the opposite of buying a stock. The mechanics of carrying out your short sale order is the responsibility of your broker. As it is the opposite to buying a stock, the short sale involves simply selling a stock you do not own with the promise that you will pay for it later. Sound strange? Keep reading.

As it is the opposite to buying, any *decrease* in the stock price is your profit (less commissions).

Conversely, any *increase* in the stock price is your loss (including commissions). There is no time limit on how long a short sale may be held.

Suppose, for example, you believe stock A will fall in price. You advise your broker to "sell short" 100 shares of stock A, now selling on the market for $10 each. If your hunch is accurate and stock A falls to, say, $5, you can then advise your broker to "cover" or "buy in" stock A at its new price of $5. You would then make a profit of $5 on each share — the difference between the price when you decided to short-sell and the price when you actually "bought in." You can make a profit of up to 100 per cent on a short sale if the stock falls from its original price to no value — a decrease in price of 100 per cent.

The danger of the short sale is that the loss you can suffer is limitless. Stock A might rise to several times its original value and, in the short sale situation, any rise in price is your loss.

The Abrams Automatic Profit-Taker uses the short sale as part of its strategy; however, with the Abrams strategy the short sale is always made with stocks covered by the convertible bond and in conjunction with the other techniques implicit in the Abrams strategy, thereby practically eliminating any risk.

How can I sell something I don't own?

Let me use an example that is common to us all. When your favorite magazine publisher sells you a subscription, he is selling you a magazine he has not produced. You, on the other hand, accept this promise to deliver in good faith based on your belief that he is reliable.

Your broker does the same. Based on your credit standing and required down payment (margin), he will allow you to sell a stock you don't own.

Isn't the short sale terribly speculative?

The technique of short selling by itself can be an exceedingly speculative technique. Theoretically, when you buy a stock you can only lose the market price you paid. But with a short sale, you can lose more than you invested. Remember, your loss in a short sale is the amount the stock increases in value. Theoretically it can increase any amount in value — consequently your loss can be unlimited.

However, when the technique of short selling is married with the convertible bond of the same corporation, the combination tames the speculative nature of the short sale. This synergistic combination of the convertible bond with the short sale preserves a high profit potential and yet, remarkably, is almost risk-free.

The convertible bond, as you have explained, is normally more secure than common stock. Why hazard the setting up of two different techniques —particularly when one involves the selling short of common stock?

By combining the convertible bond with the speculative short sale of the common stock, paradoxically you reduce your risk as you will clearly see in the following chapters. By combining these two investment techniques, you will practically eliminate the risk of buying the convertible alone, at the same time avoiding the usual dangers of short selling.

When selecting this combination of the convertible bond and the short sale are there any criteria pertaining to the short sale that I should consider?

Perhaps the most important consideration concerning the short sale is that you must pay the dividend, if any, on the common stock.

Why must both I and the issuing corporation pay the dividend on the same stock?

Stock exchange regulations state that the equivalent stock you sold short must be held by your broker. He is permitted to hold this stock in the form of borrowed stock, that is, he can borrow from his clients who have margin accounts (similar to credit accounts) or, if not available there, from other brokers, who may, in turn, borrow from their customers' margin accounts. The rightful owner of this borrowed stock (remember you do not own it) is entitled to any dividends. Similarly, there is a real buyer of the stock you sold short on the stock exchange and he is also entitled to any dividends. Consequently, you must remember to compare the yield of the convertible bond (which you receive) against the annual dividend declared on the common stock (which you must pay on a short sale).

Don't be daunted by this revelation. Often the most appropriate and potentially profitable stock pay little or no dividends and you will, therefore, have no dividends to pay on the short sale.

Check with your broker whether or not the stock you wish to sell short is on the restricted list. This list reports those corporations for which the short sale is not immediately available or those which should be treated with caution. If a corporation is on the restricted list, proceed cautiously, investigating the reason for its being there.

How does my broker execute and maintain a short sale?

Figure 7 illustrates the steps in a short sale. (Note that to sell short, you must have a margin account.)

Step 1. You advise your broker to sell short a specific number of common stock. In order to fill your order to sell short, your broker must borrow the stock.

Step 2. Your broker (broker A) performs an inventory check to see if any of his own clients hold the stock required for your short sale. He is permitted to borrow this stock from his own clients who have margin accounts. (Note customers v, w, x, y and z in figure 7.) This permission by the client to loan his stock is regularly included in the initial margin agreement.

Step 3. If the stock is not in his own inventory, your broker may well borrow it from another broker (broker B). Broker B welcomes the chance to loan the requested stock because he receives in return interest-free cash to use.

Step 4. The short sale must be declared by the investor to his broker. The broker notifies the exchange after the borrowed stock has been acquired. This stock is then recorded by the exchange as stock sold which was not owned, hence

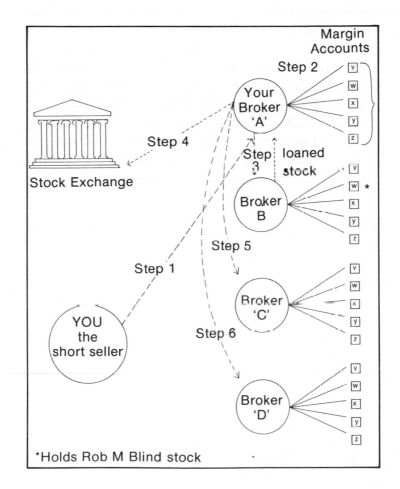

Figure 7. The Inner Operation of the Short Sale

the meaning of the phrase "sold short." Once the short sale is noted, the order to sell is transacted in the normal way.

Steps 5 and 6. If the original owner of the borrowed stock (in this case broker B, account w) decides to sell, your broker must then return the stock. Consequently, he must scurry around to other brokers (brokers C and D) to replace your borrowed stock. Usually you are completely unaware of all this action. However, if your broker cannot obtain a replacement, you are obliged to liquidate this short sale position. I have found this necessity to liquidate a short sale exceedingly rare.

4. The Full Hedge
The 99 44/100 per cent Safe Strategy

Would you demonstrate how a convertible bond combined with a short sale might react to an uptrend and a downtrend market?

As a cornerstone to understanding the Abrams Automatic Profit-Taker, you must fully grasp the reasons for combining the convertible bond with the short sale of the common stock of the same issuing corporation.

Consider first the combination of equal numbers of common stock into which the convertible bond is exchangeable and stocks sold short. (Number of common stock represented by convertible bonds = the number of short sales.)

This 100 per cent balance of common stock

(represented by the convertible bonds) with the short sale is perhaps the best illustration of a strategy with an almost risk-free profit potential. This particular combination is known by brokers as the "full hedge."

Let's say, for example, you have selected the Rob M Blind Convertible Bond. The situation is this:

- There is no premium on the convertible bond, that is, you have paid no more for the convertible bond than you would have paid for the common stock the bond represents.

- Each bond is exchangeable into 30 shares of Rob M Blind common stock.

- Rob M Blind convertible bond is now selling at $900 (stated as a percentage in the financial papers; in this example it would be stated as 90).

- Rob M Blind Corporation common stock is now available on the market at $30 a share.

- Commissions are not included in these examples.

Now you take action

- You buy 10 Rob M Blind convertible bonds at $900 each, a total of $9,000.

- You sell short the same number of stock that the convertible bonds would be exchangeable for. The 10 bonds are convertible into 300 shares, therefore

300 shares are sold short at \$30 each, a total of \$9,000. See figure 8.

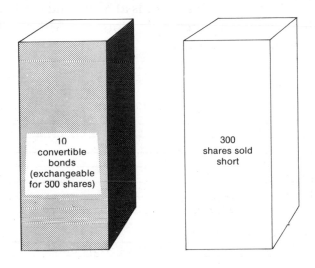

10
convertible
bonds
(exchangeable
for 300 shares)

300
shares sold
short

Figure 8. The Full Hedge

In summary, here's how it looks:
10 convertible bonds at \$900 each = \$9,000
(exchangeable for 300 shares)
300 shares sold short at \$30 each = \$9,000

What happens if the Rob M Blind stock falls drastically from the \$30 purchase price to \$15?

You are already aware that in a declining market the convertible bond is invariably more resistant to the downside than the common stock. Let us assume that the investment valuc of the Rob M Blind convertible in this case holds at $750, and the Rob M Blind common stock falls from the $30 purchase price to $15. See figure 9.

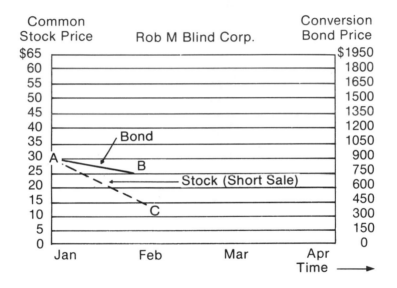

Figure 9. Downtrend Price Action of the Full Hedge

In this situation

- You would have *a gain* on your 300 shares sold short (300 shares sold short x $15 decline) of $4,500.

- You would have *a loss* on each convertible bond

(the decline of the $900 purchase price to $750) of $150, for a total loss (10 bonds x $150) of $1,500. Over-all, a gain ($4,500 – $1,500) of $3,000.

Thus the natural premium the bond develops on the downtrend generates a profit, with practically no risk.

At the end of a full hedge situation it is important to note that the number of shares for which the convertible bonds may be exchanged still equals the number of shares sold short.

What happens if the Rob M Blind stock doubles in price from $30 to $60?

The upward price action is shown in figure 10. If the common price doubles from $30 to $60, not including commissions, the situation in this full hedge would be this:

- You would have *a loss* on your 300 shares sold short (300 shares sold short x $30 advance) of $9,000.

- You would have *a gain* on each of your convertible bonds (30 shares x $30 advance) of $900.
  Therefore your 10 convertible bonds must show a gain (300 shares x $30 advance) of $9,000.
  In other words, you would have a $9,000 gain offset by a $9,000 loss. *No loss on the upside.*

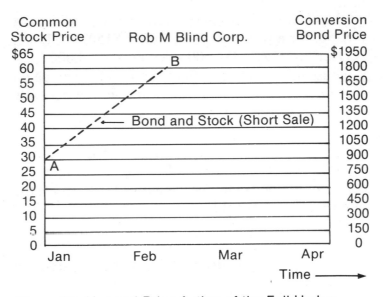

Figure 10. Uptrend Price Action of the Full Hedge

What then are the disadvantages of this strategy —the full hedge?

The premium on the convertible bond — which, of course, is your gain — can be discouragingly slow to form on the downside. On the upside the full hedge cannot produce a profit at all — it can only hold its own. There are absolutely no profits captured on the smaller swings that inevitably occur.

In my opinion, what prohibits the full hedge as a viable strategy is its almost boring approach to often tiny profits. But it is important that you understand this strategy. You will now be able to see and appreciate how the protective principles involved here can be employed yet the weaknesses overcome with the Abrams Automatic Profit-Taker. You will see how the Abrams Automatic Profit-Taker uses the cushion effect of the full hedge — but snags the profits on the invariable minor swings. This will prove to be true on both the upside and the downside.

5. The Half Hedge
Grooming the Convertible Bond for the Uptrend

How would a convertible bond combined with a short sale of, let's say, half the stocks represented by the convertible bond react in an uptrend or downtrend?

This combination is referred to by brokers as a "half hedge." Let's take an example. You have again selected the Rob M Blind Convertible Bond. The situation is the same. Let's review it.

- No premium on the convertible bond.
- Each bond is exchangeable into 30 shares of the Rob M Blind common stock.
- Rob M Blind convertible bond is now selling at $900.

- Rob M Blind common stock is now available at $30 a share.

Now you take action

- As previously stated in the full hedge example, you buy 10 Rob M Blind convertible bonds at $900 each, a total of $9,000.

- This time, however, you sell short only half the stock into which the 10 Rob M Blind convertible bonds are exchangeable (figure 11).

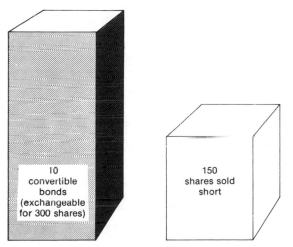

Figure 11. The Start of the Half Hedge

The 10 bonds are convertible into 300 shares. But this time sell short only half this amount, or 150 shares, a total of $4,500.

In summary, here is how it looks:

10 convertible bonds at $900 each = $9,000
(exchangeable for 300 shares)

150 shares sold short at $30 each = $4,500
(half the full number of shares represented by the convertible bond)

What if the Rob M Blind common stock now doubles in price from $30 to $60?

This price action is shown in figure 12.

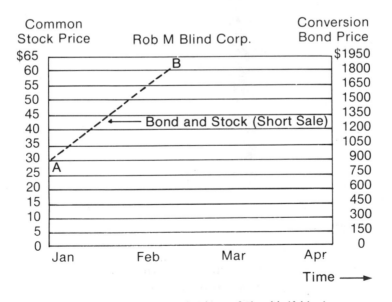

Figure 12. Uptrend Price Action of the Half Hedge

46

- The *loss* on our short sale of 150 shares (150 shares sold short x $30 advance) is $4,500.

- *But* each Rob M Blind convertible bond is now worth $1,800 (30 shares x $30 advance) or $900 profit.
  As we have 10 bonds we have a profit (10 bonds x $900) of $9,000.
  Over-all profit on the uptrend ($9,000 − $4,500) is $4,500.

What if the Rob M Blind common stock drops in price one-half from $30 to $15?

Figure 13 shows that the Rob M Blind convertible bond typically resists the downtrend (as has been demonstrated with the full hedge) at a reasonable $750.

- The *gain* on the 150 shares sold short (150 shares sold short x $15 decline) is $2,250.

- The Rob M Blind bonds have lost $150 each ($900 − $750), so the *loss* on the 10 convertible bonds (10 bonds x $150) is $1,500.
  The over-all profit on the downtrend is $750.

Great! A substantial profit on the uptrend and a smaller profit on the downside. But the best is yet to come. These two examples are given to advance the remarkable concept that the combination of the convertible bond with the speculative short sale can create an ultra-conservative, yet high-powered situation. The exact value at which the convertible bond will resist the downward pressure is unpredictable.

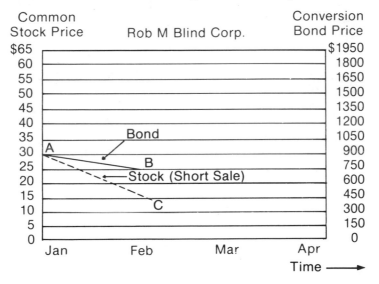

Figure 13. Downtrend Price Action of the Half Hedge

But the proposition that the typical convertible bond resists the downward trend as the common stock continues to slump is incisively clear. Irrefutably the short sale shelters you further on the downside — sometimes even producing a profit.

Is not doubling of the common stock a super-optimistic hope? Might I not become very bored waiting for this to happen?

The answer is categorically YES. This was my experience until I developed the Abrams Automatic Profit-Taker. Its fast-acting technique takes the boredom out of investing in longer-term hedge strategies. As you will see, the Abrams Automatic Profit-Taker applies the main thrust of the preceding enunciated hedge concepts, yet captures the rapid gains of often temperamental stock moves. These smaller but more frequent "locked-in" and realized gains will of course allow you to re-invest your profit at a much faster rate.

6. My Winning Discovery
The Abrams Automatic Profit-Taker

How could the Abrams Automatic Profit-Taker be more exciting than simply combining convertible bonds with a short sale?

Certainly the Abrams Automatic Profit-Taker takes advantage of the opportunities of the convertible hedges (the full and the half hedge) we have just examined, but I discovered it to be a far more rapid money-maker. My Profit-Taker technique makes the reasonable assumption that stocks will continue to fluctuate. An ultra-conservative assumption? Of course, stocks always have. Figure 14 illustrates the constant fluctuations, sometimes tumultuous, of the Dow Jones Industrial Index, perhaps the best known of the stock indices. If you call your broker and

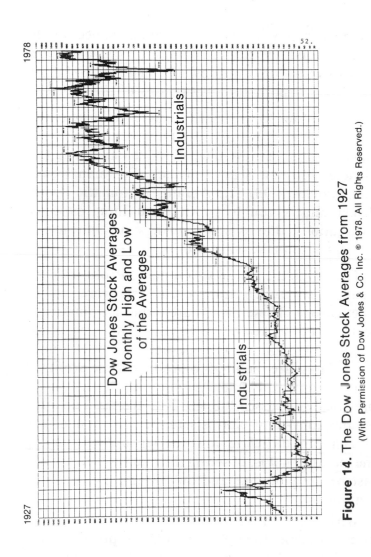

Figure 14. The Dow Jones Stock Averages from 1927

51

merely ask how the market is doing, chances are he will respond by stating whether the Dow Jones Industrial is "up" or "down." Walter Cronkite of CBS daily reports the fluctuations of this index.

Is the Dow Jones, then, an index of speculative stocks? On the contrary, the Dow Jones Industrial Index comprises 30 blue chip stocks, including General Motors, Sears Roebuck, Eastman Kodak and Standard Oil. The Abrams Automatic Profit-Taker allows you to profit from these expected fluctuations. Large stock swings are no longer necessary to make large profits.

The key to the Abrams Automatic Profit-Taker is that you profit from even relatively minor fluctuations. These profits are either automatically realized, or "locked in" to be taken later, regardless of the direction of the market. As only minor fluctuations are required to produce these profits, it is a far more rapid and dynamic technique than the previously discussed full and half hedges. The often tedious long-term plan is scrapped. No longer will you have the disheartening experience of overstaying the market, that is, of seeing the market turn around just before your one and only long-range profit is realized .

With the Profit-Taker technique it is a waste of your valuable time to attempt to prophesy the direction of the stock movement. It is simply not necessary. The thorough understanding and careful application of the Abrams Automatic Profit-Taker will place you in a consistently winning position.

How do I set up the Abrams Automatic Profit-Taker, which will self react, locking in and realizing profits?

This plan must be understood unequivocally. You must grasp the concept that distinguishes the Abrams Automatic Profit-Taker from the previously described combinations of convertible bonds and short sales (hedges).

Using our now familiar Rob M Blind convertible bond, here is the situation again:

- No premium on the convertible bond.

- Each bond is exchangeable into 30 shares of the Rob M Blind common stock.

- Rob M Blind convertible bond is now selling at $900.

- Rob M Blind common stock is now available at $30 per share.

Be prepared now to taste the excitement of the Abrams Automatic Profit-Taker.
As with the half hedge,

- Buy 10 Rob M Blind bonds at $900, a total of $9,000.

- Sell short only half the stock into which the 10
  Rob M Blind convertible bonds are exchangeable.
  The 10 bonds are convertible into 300 shares, so
  sell short 150 shares, a total of $4,500.
  See figure 15.

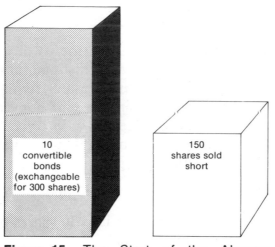

Figure 15. The Start of the Abrams
Automatic Profit-Taker

What are the steps for setting my goals on the uptrend and downtrend?

Your longer-term goal may well fall within a range of
45 to 100 per cent of the purchase price of the
underlying common stock sold short. Setting the
longer-term goals, on both the uptrend and the
downtrend, is a personal decision. Using the higher

percentage of the range to set the long-term goal makes a conservative strategy even more secure. Once you have established your longer-term goals and your short-term goals, as a general rule hold fast.

Step 1. After you have purchased your convertible bonds and established your short sale position, then set your longer-term goals (figure 16). When setting up your longer- and shorter-term goals, use the price of the common stock as your index, not the price of the bond. It may be wise to use a range of 60 to 100 per cent for the longer-term goals, at least until you feel completely comfortable with the techniques of the Abrams Automatic Profit-Taker. If there should be a premium on your bond, allow for it by adding it to your long goal on the upside only. For our example the longer-term goal on the uptrend is $60, a 100 per cent increase in price. The longer-term downtrend goal is also set at 100 per cent, or $0.

Step 2. Set your short-term goals as denoted. Simply divide your uptrend longer-term goal into three equal parts. Similarly divide the downtrend into three equal parts. This will give you two subgoals and one long-term goal on both the uptrend and the downtrend.

Place your "open" order (also called "good till cancelled") with your broker to sell short on the immediate upside subgoal, and to buy in on the immediate downside subgoal. This is simply an open

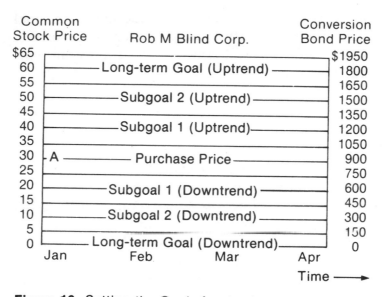

Figure 16. Setting the Goals for the Abrams Automatic
Profit-Taker

order that remains on your broker's records until the order is filled or you cancel it. The advantage of this is that orders placed at the same specific price receive priority according to the time of placement. This means that, other things being equal, your order would be filled ahead of someone who placed an order at the same price at a later time. Place your open orders immediately upon setting up your plan. Remember — we do not try to predict the direction of the stock. Place your open orders for both immediate short-term goals simultaneously, that is, on both the uptrend and on the downtrend.

7. Making Big Money
on Small Fluctuations

What if the most likely situation occurs, that is, the stock fluctuates?

This is by far the most likely situation. Why? Because stock practically always does fluctuate. It would be difficult to imagine a stock market graph extended over a reasonable period of time that didn't fluctuate. It is the way it uses these fluctuations that distinguishes the Abrams Automatic Profit-Taker as an uncommonly profitable, yet conservative, strategy. With this technique time is not wasted attempting to read the future. You do not have to predict whether your stock is going to go up or down. *You are in the enviable position of making money regardless of which direction your stock moves.*

How do I automatically "lock in" and later realize a profit from a relatively minor fluctuation using the Abrams Automatic Profit-Taker?

Read and re-read this answer until the vital precept is fully understood, that is, how profit-taking is triggered by the normal fluctuations of the common stock. When you have mastered this principle, congratulate yourself. You will be in possession of a lucrative yet conservative strategy.

Please examine figure 17 carefully as you follow this explanation. Our Rob M Blind stock rises in price from the purchase price of $30 (point A on the price graph in figure 17) to $40 (point B) and then falls again to $30 (point C) — a relatively minor fluctuation for a volatile stock. If your final goal had been set at $60, with no subgoals in between, you would have completely lost the profit involved in this fluctuation. Fortunately, we don't worry, we make money on these minor swings.

To explain fully, when the stock reached $40, our first subgoal, the situation was this:

- The 300 shares represented by the 10 convertible bonds each gained $10 in value for a total *gain* of $3,000.

- The 150 shares sold short each lost $10 in value for a total *loss* of $1,500.
  At point B on the price graph in figure 17 there has been an over-all gain in value of $1,500 .

When you apply the concept of the Abrams Automatic Profit-Taker, you insure or "lock in" one-third of your profit by selling short one-third of the outstanding shares represented by the ten convertible bonds.

As 150 shares were sold short at the start of the Abrams Automatic Profit-Taker action, this left 150 shares outstanding. Therefore, 50 further shares are now sold short (column B in figure 17). This guarantees you a $500 profit regardless of the direction in which your stock decides to move.

Even though the stock did not continue on, but returned to the original position of $30, we captured our profit of $500. Each time the stock seesaws between any two subgoals you either "lock in" or realize a profit. *This profit would have been lost using the conventional technique of longer-term goals only.*

What actions do I take when the stock triggers the short-term goal and then returns to the previous position?

Each time your stock moves sufficiently in any one direction to touch off a subgoal, regardless of the direction, place two new open orders with your broker. One open order for the immediate upside goal and another for the immediate downside goal. Impress on your mind *always to sell short on the upside and always "buy in" (cover) on the downside.*

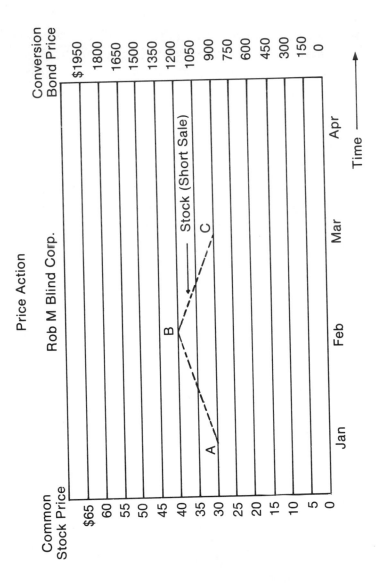

Price Action

Rob M Blind Corp.

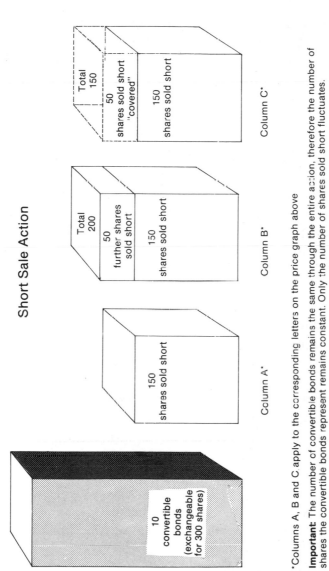

Figure 17. The Abrams Automatic Profit-Taker in Action Uptrend Fluctuations in Price

*Columns A, B and C apply to the corresponding letters on the price graph above

Important: The number of convertible bonds remains the same through the entire action, therefore the number of shares the convertible bonds represent remains constant. Only the number of shares sold short fluctuates.

Short Sale Action

Total 150 | 50 shares sold short "covered" | 150 shares sold short — Column C*

Total 200 | 50 further shares sold short | 150 shares sold short — Column B*

150 shares sold short — Column A*

10 convertible bonds (exchangeable for 300 shares)

Remember always to cancel the outstanding open order that results from a subgoal being filled. This keeps your plan up to date and less subject to an order you had forgotten about being filled. When your stock returns to the original position of $30 (point C on the price graph), then "buy" (cover) the 50 shares you previously sold short at $40 (column C in figure 17). True, you are back at your starting point, nevertheless you have locked in $500 by this relatively minor fluctuation, *a profit you would have lost under the conventional longer-term situation.* Many of these minor fluctuations may occur before the longer-term objectives are reached and you profit from each one as the fluctuation triggers your order. You will no longer be frustrated by watching your investment rise and then fall without capturing any of the gains. It is this realization of rapid profits based on minor swings combined with a small-scale risk that characterizes the Abrams Automatic Profit-Taker.

What happens if the stock fluctuates on the downside rather than the upside, and then returns to the original position? Do you mean this is also profitable?

Absolutely. The same principle applies here that applied in the previous example of the uptrend fluctuation — only in reverse.

Here's the situation when the Rob M Blind shares

slip from $30 to $20, illustrated in figure 18.

- The 150 shares sold short each gained $10 in value to you for a total *gain* of $1,500 .

- The 10 convertible bonds (representing 300 shares) characteristically resisted the downward trend to hold at $750 for a total *loss* (10 bonds x $150) of $1,500 .

At this position there has been no loss and no gain or, rather, the loss has been cancelled by the gain. Furthermore, remember the premium percentage of the convertible bond typically increases if the stock should decline further. Consequently, you are now secure in the knowledge that this holding and protective power of the bond, reinforced with the shares sold short, militates against loss.

Why not take advantage of this situation? Mercurial profits can now be realized because of, not in spite of, a downtrend. Use the same procedure to take profits on the downside, only in the opposite sequence. At the $20 position of the stock (point B on the price graph in figure 18), "buy in" (cover) 50 of your shares sold short (column B). This action secures $500 on your profitable short sale position (50 shares sold short x $10 decline), leaving 100 short sales to resist possible further declines.

However, when the stock bounces back to the original purchase position (point C on the price graph), you sell short 50 shares (column C). The

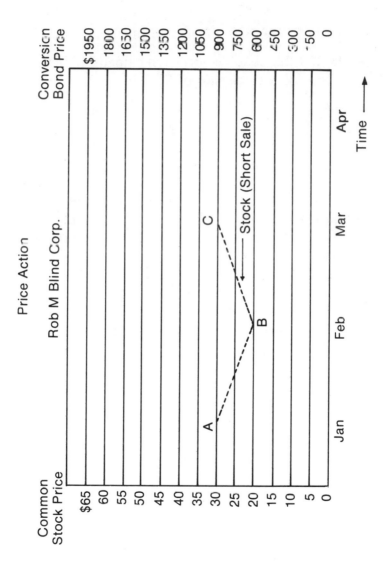

Price Action

Rob M Blind Corp.

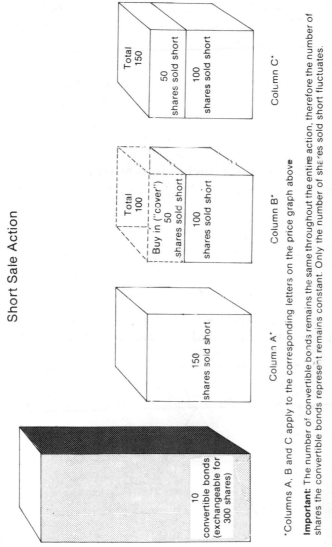

Short Sale Action

10 convertible bonds (exchangeable for 300 shares)

150 shares sold short

Column A*

Total 100

Buy in ("cover") 50 shares sold short

100 shares sold short

Column B*

Total 150

50 shares sold short

100 shares sold short

Column C*

*Columns A, B and C apply to the corresponding letters on the price graph above.

Important: The number of convertible bonds remains the same throughout the entire action, therefore the number of shares the convertible bonds represent remains constant. Only the number of shares sold short fluctuates.

Figure 18. The Abrams Automatic Profit-Taker in Action Downtrend Fluctuations in Price

situation then is exactly the same as when we started, that is, we own 10 bonds and we have 150 common shares sold short. But there is one categorical difference. The Abrams Automatic Profit-Taker allowed us to profit as a result of this minor change, even a change on the downside. *This profit would have been lost forever if we had waited for the usual longer-term objective.*

Can relatively minor fluctuations prove as profitable at any stage of the upside or downside trend?

Gains will be generated whenever the common stock bounces between any two of our subgoals, resulting in the filling of our previously placed open orders. Each time the stock fluctuates between our subgoals, it automatically scores a profit for us.

This is profitable when it seesaws between any two subgoals on an uptrend, for example, between $40 and $50:

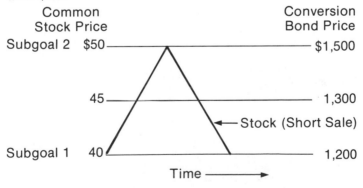

The fluctuations are correspondingly profitable when they bounce between two subgoals on a downtrend, for example, between $20 and $10:

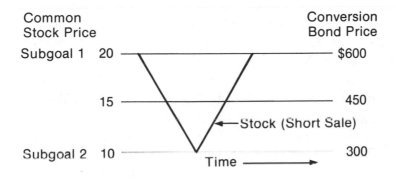

There is absolutely no limit to the times the fluctuations may shuttle between your subgoals, each time putting more money in your account — well before your long-term goals are met.

There is, of course, an almost unlimited number of combinations the movement of the common stock might form; however, the same profitable concept applies.

It is imperative that you select securities whose market prices are "lively" or volatile in nature, as the faster the common stock moves the larger your profits are likely to be — in less time. The standards for selecting such exciting and swiftly developing situations will be revealed later.

On the uptrend wouldn't it be simpler just to sell off a number of my convertible bonds at different price levels rather than accumulate short sales?

Theoretically, it might appear that it would be less expensive — as commissions on bonds are smaller —to sell the bonds rather than sell short the stock on the uptrend. Practically, once your strategy is set up, it is far more efficient to "lock in" profits or realize gains by the selling and "buying in" of short sales. It is this "hair trigger" efficiency in filling your short sale orders, as opposed to the slower and often sloppy execution of bond orders, that qualifies the short sale for this position of profiting by small fluctuations.

Remember that the premium the convertible bond inevitably develops can be somewhat elusive. Consequently the convertible security is not sufficiently sensitive to small stock price changes to make it appropriate to ride the fluctuations of the common stock. For this purpose, the short sale is particularly advantageous.

Opportunely, at the point of conversion (at which the shares represented by the convertible bond equal the short sales) absolutely no commissions are charged to liquidate the situation. It is at this point that you realize your profits.

Are there not some dangers in the Abrams Automatic Profit-Taker?

There is no unconditional guarantee that a premium must form at any predetermined price on the convertible security on the downside. It is possible, therefore, that the convertible security and the underlying short sale may slide a distance together before the premium forms. This is a possible disadvantage. It is also unlikely.

If little or no premium is formed when the longer-term objective is reached on the downtrend, this may well be a superb opportunity to turn a seeming setback into a profit and re-establish the Abrams Automatic Profit-Taker. Cherish the knowledge that you have the profits from the short sales and the fluctuations between the subgoals, as well as the normal protective premium on the downside. Consequently the much lower market price of the convertible security places you in an enviable situation to re-establish your position.

It is also possible, as previously explained, that a broker might find at some point that there is no stock to borrow to maintain the client's short position. Then the client may be obliged to cover or "buy-in." This situation is exceedingly rare. If it does happen, it certainly does not necessarily mean a loss. On the contrary it may well show a profit if, for example, there has been a significant rise in the common stock, resulting, of course, in a high market price for the convertible. Should this situation occur, always consider converting those bonds that are fully covered by the number of short sales held and that have little or no premium. Then simply sell the remaining bonds not covered by the stock sold short. *Remember, there are no commissions when converting.* On the downside a profit occurs if a substantial premium has formed on the convertible.

There is also, of course, the possibility, as with any investment, that nothing happens — the stock does not move. However, if you choose your stock carefully, by following the Abrams Automatic Profit-Taker checklist in chapter 10, you should not be faced with a situation in which the movement of the stock is sluggish. If you have properly applied the checklist, then be patient —the movement of a volatile stock can be quite erratic. It is more important that you focus your attention on the over-all movement over a reasonable period of time.

The chief danger in the Abrams Automatic Profit-Taker manifests itself early, largely in the form of overconfidence. The Abrams Automatic Profit-Taker possesses the rare advantage that it places you in the enviable position to capture profits during both uptrend and downtrend markets. As a result of this advantage, I have observed students of this strategy implement it exceedingly profitably — initially. The exhilarated beginner — armed with infallible hindsight information — calculates the extra gains he would have made had he not secured himself with the protection of the Abrams Automatic Profit-Taker. In other words, the new investor, overconfident with his newly found success, breaks the basic premise of our Profit-Taker concept by reverting to the practice of attempting to predict the direction of the market. It is this relapse in judgment that constitutes the chief danger of the Abrams Automatic Profit-Taker.

In summary, what are the steps in sequence to implement the Abrams Automatic Profit-Taker?

1. Set up a margin account with a broker who deals on the New York and American exchanges. It is preferable if your broker is familiar with such hedging concepts as the Abrams Automatic Profit-Taker.

2. Regardless of whether you use a U.S. discount broker to substantially reduce expenses as will be revealed in Chapter 11, or use a Canadian broker to take advantage of more liberal margin rules as will be unfolded in Chapter 8, request a U.S. margin account. The U.S. interest you are required to pay on your margin account is frequently substantially lower than the Canadian interest. You will also save the exchange rate each time a trade is made.

3. Pre-select the eligible convertible bonds and preferred shares from the current and relevant

sources of information. These sources of information are contained in chapter 11.

4. Apply the checklist of the Abrams Automatic Profit-Taker to extract the most volatile and potentially profitable situations. This checklist is explained in detail in chapter 10.

5. Next, obtain the up-to-the-moment prices from your broker on both your pre-selected convertible bonds or convertible preferred shares and the corresponding common stock. This latest information will refine and identify the most profitable situations.

6. Ask your broker to inquire about the availability of the short sales in advance of placing any orders. At times stock to be sold short is not available in board lots (regular trading lots), but is available in lesser or odd lots. Occasionally, when stock has not been available in board lots of 100 shares, I have obtained them in odd lots of 99. Do not depend on your broker to advise you on this point. Be in control of your account. Ask him.

7. Once you have selected the convertible situation, place your order for the convertible bond or preferred stock first. Place a limit order for one day only, that is, limit the price you wish to pay for the convertible bond within the confines of one business day. Your broker may then execute your order only at this price or at a better price in your favor.

8.   Once your order for the convertible bonds or preferred shares has been filled, without delay place a market order for the common stock to be sold short. A market order is simply an order to buy or sell a number of shares at the best possible price at the time. After the convertibles have been purchased, it is a needless risk to wait for better prices to develop on the stock before purchasing your short sale. When your short sale order has been filled, you have implemented the Abrams Automatic Profit-Taker.

9.   Set your longer-term goals. So far in our example we have established the longer-term goals at a conservative 100 per cent of the underlying common stock sold short. *Personally I apply a longer-term guide of only 50 per cent of the underlying common stock sold short.* For example, if the common stock sold short was $30, my longer-term objective on the uptrend would be $45, and on the downtrend, $15. This allows me more stock action between the shorter subgoals, in this instance 16.6 per cent apart.

10.   Set your short-term goals by simply dividing the longer-term goal into three equal parts. Generally speaking the longer-term goal objective should not be less than 45 per cent, which would result in the subgoals being about 15 per cent of the purchase price of the underlying stock sold short. Remember you want to realize, or lock in, a

significant profit each time the common stock activates a subgoal, after commissions are paid.

11.   Now that your Abrams Automatic Profit-Taker has been set up, simply place the two open orders for your subgoals — one order on the upside and one order on the downside. You now have the privilege and excitement of allowing your stock to decide which order will be filled first, with the comfort of knowing you can profit regardless of the direction the stock happens to take.

8. Margin Accounts
Advice Worth a Thousand Times the Value of this Book

How can I substantially increase the amount of my investment?

Use a margin account. A margin account is a type of brokerage account that permits you to buy securities on credit. Your broker loans you part of the purchase price. The word margin refers to the amount you must deposit, that is, the difference between the market value of the securities and the amount of the loan your broker will make against it.

The present margin needed to buy U.S. listed equities selling at $2 and over is 50 per cent of the market value.

Is it possible, using the Abrams Automatic Profit-Taker, to improve on the 50 per cent initial margin required?

Happily yes! Bear in mind that the Abrams Automatic Profit-Taker does not involve the direct purchase of common stock, but only stock represented by convertible bonds.

A Canadian margin account therefore allows you a substantial increase in money, borrowed from your broker, to invest. With a Canadian margin account you will be elated to find that the percentage you may borrow for the purchase of convertible bonds largely depends on your creativity.

Now hear this

In Canada the stock exchanges regulate the amount of credit that may be extended to you. The current minimum Canadian margin requirements for both United States and Canadian convertible bonds is 10 per cent on par ($1,000) and 10 per cent on the market value of the represented bond if selling at or below par. For example if a convertible bond now sells at $900 you would be required to post approximately 21 per cent.

10 per cent of par on $1,000   = $100
10 per cent of $900   =   90
Total margin requirement   =   190

If the convertible bond is selling at over $1,000, the

margin requirement is then 10 per cent on the par ($1,000) and 50 per cent on the excess over par. However, the convertible selling under par is the more usual situation when setting up a technique such as the Abrams Automatic Profit-Taker.

The above margin requirements are based on the Toronto Stock Margin Bylaw No. 16. 15. Canadian investment dealers normally require you to post from 22 to 30 per cent of the market value of the convertible bond, as opposed to the required initial minimum of 50 per cent by the United States Federal Reserve Board. This 22 to 30 per cent requirement to be posted on a convertible bond may, in certain situations, be reduced to no requirement at all. Incredible? Here is how I have done it.

When setting up a hedge situation in Canada such as the recommended Abrams Automatic Profit-Taker, the convertible bonds offset by short sales may require no margin money to be posted. However, one condition must exist: the market value of the stock into which the convertible bonds are exchangeable must be the same as the market value of the stock sold short. The only margin you are required to post in this offsetting situation is the difference between the market value of the convertible bond and the market value of the equivalent amount of associated stock sold short.

Let's take our example of the Rob M Blind convertible bonds.

- Each bond is exchangeable into 30 shares of Rob M Blind common stock.
- Rob M Blind convertible bonds are now selling at $900.
- Rob M Blind corporation common stock is now available at $30 per share.
  Therefore, 30 shares x $30 a share = $900.

In this case there is no premium on the bond exceeding the worth of the stock. Consequently, if you buy the bond and sell 100 per cent of the exchangeable stock short no margin is required, only the commissions. However, if the market value of the bond exceeds the market value of the exchangeable stock, that is, if a premium exists, naturally you must post this "risk" money.

This is the practice with a Canadian margin account. However, in the United States, even in this situation, you would still be required to post 50 per cent of the market value of the convertible bond.

Do I have to post additional margin money for the offsetting short sales?

NO. Did you hear? An extraordinary NO. Not a penny more margin money must be put up to support your short sale when combined with a convertible security. This is a sensible rule. In a technique such as the Profit-Taker, the short sale actually reduces the risk yet maintains a high profitability.

If your broker should not be familiar with this remarkable privilege, then refer him to the authority — the Federal Reserve Board's Regulation T, Section 220.3 (d) (3). It states in effect that no margin is required on a short sale of an associated stock of a convertible bond or convertible preferred stock. Incidentally, an initial margin of 50 per cent is currently required on a short sale when transacted without the benefit of the offsetting convertible bond. This rule is equally applicable in Canada.

Happily, no interest is charged by the broker on the short sale, increasing even more the attraction of the Abrams Automatic Profit-Taker.

How are the minimum initial margin requirements established?

The New York Stock Exchange sets its own margin rules, which are applicable to the other United States exchanges. The brokerage firms themselves set margin policies which may well exceed the minimum requirements. The New York Exchange requires a minimum $2,000 deposit to establish a margin account.

Naturally, the larger proportionate amount your broker will loan you, the more money you will have working for you. This increased leverage magnifies your potential profit. Ordinarily the borrowed funds might be considered risky, even foolhardy; however, these additional borrowed funds are no longer exceedingly speculative when the protective and conservative nature of the Abrams Automatic Profit-Taker is taken into account. The proportionate amount you can actually borrow varies from broker to broker. Do your comparative shopping before you establish your margin account.

What are the minimum requirements for a credit (margin) account that can be used with the Abrams Automatic Profit-Taker?

The initial margin requirement in the United States is currently 50 per cent on convertible bonds and listed stocks. (Margin requirements are set by the Federal Reserve Board in the United States.) This is how the 50 per cent margin rule would apply on $10,000. You would put up $5,000 plus commission. The broker would then loan you $5,000. However, the U.S. citizen or resident can be innovative and do immensely better than this. You will soon see how the Abrams Automatic Profit-Taker will allow you to further magnify the money loaned relative to the amount you in fact invest, giving you greater investment power.

How can an American reap the benefits of the more generous Canadian "little or no margin" situations?

The security authorities in Canada do not permit a salesman to sell securities outside his provincial jurisdiction or in American states where he is not registered. In Ontario this regulation is based on Section 67 of the Ontario Securities Act. Other provinces of Canada have similar legislation. However, if a Canadian salesman receives an unsolicited order from outside his jurisdiction he may act on that order in the same manner as if the order had been given within his jurisdiction.

For the purposes of setting up a Canadian account, including a margin account, a Canadian address must be obtained within the jurisdiction of your Canadian investment dealer, that is, a Canadian investment dealer whose parent company is in Canada. Your broker would then forward the confirmation of your orders to this Canadian address. There would be no problem, of course, placing the order by telephone from outside the provincial jurisdiction you select.

A Canadian address might be arranged by having an account at a Canadian trust company or bank, even perhaps through a friend located in Canada. This address is usually quite sufficient to satisfy Canadian margin regulations, which means you can then take advantage of the more abundant Canadian benefits. Let me again emphasize that United States convertible bonds and associated stock sold short may be financed by means of the far more generous rules of the Canadian margin regulations. Remember to use a Canadian investment firm whose parent company has headquarters in Canada.

9. Doubling Your Money in Less than Six Months
A Personal Demonstration of the Abrams Automatic Profit-Taker

To prove that this book is not mere theory, would you show me a random example from your own account to demonstrate the Abrams Automatic Profit-Taker?

Certainly. For purposes of clarity we have so far used practical but nevertheless theoretical examples. Now I will use an actual example from my own account to demonstrate irrefutably the principles of the Abrams Automatic Profit-Taker.

The Ehrenreich Photo-Optical 4¾ per cent of 1987 convertible bond is the example I will use. If you thoroughly follow this example you may be justifiably proud of yourself. You will have understood a technique which has the potential to double your money consistently in less than six months.

Here is the situation:

- The Abrams Automatic Profit-Taker plan was implemented and the subgoals and long-term goals set based on the pre-determined common share prices in figure 19. Although the common share prices are here given in decimals, the actual orders were recorded with the brokers to the nearest 1/8.

- Each Ehrenreich convertible bond is exchangeable for 65.23 shares of Ehrenreich common shares.

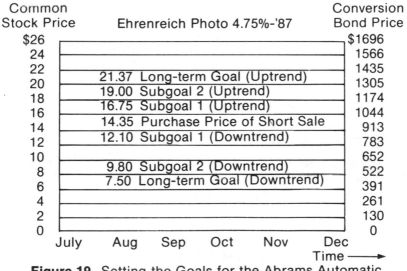

Figure 19. Setting the Goals for the Abrams Automatic Profit-Taker — A Personal Demonstration

- Four Ehrenreich convertible bonds were bought at $965 each. Each share the bond represented cost $14.79 ($965 ÷ 65.23 shares = $14.79).

- Half the shares into which the convertible bonds could be exchanged were "sold short" (there were 260 shares, so 130 were sold short) at approximately $14.35 for each share.

The following conditions existed at the point of initiating the plan.

Ehrenreich Convertible bond had a premium over the conversion value of the Ehrenreich common shares of 3.09 per cent after being implemented. This is calculated easily by the following formula:

$$\frac{\text{market price - conversion value* }}{\text{conversion value}} \times 100 \text{ per cent}$$

$$= \frac{\$965 - \$936.05}{\$936.05} \times 100 \text{ per cent}$$

$$= \frac{\$28.95}{\$936.05} \times 100 \text{ per cent}$$

$$= 3.09 \text{ per cent}$$

---

* The conversion value is simply determined by multiplying the conversion ratio by the price of the common stock. Here the conversion ratio is 65.23 shares per bond. Use the purchase price of the shares sold short as the price of the common stock to calculate a meaningful premium. In this instance it is $14.35 per share. Therefore, the conversion value in our example is:
65.23 shares x $14.35 = $936.05.

Ehrenreich Photo-Optical common shares compared very favorable with other volatile and "under 10 per cent premium" convertible bonds. (The importance of volatility and "under 10 per cent premium" will be discussed in chapter 10.) The dividend on the Ehrenreich Photo common shares was non-existent. Consequently, no dividend had to be paid on the short sales.

The action of Ehrenreich Photo-Optical produced 94 per cent profit in approximately four and a half months and is illustrated in figure 20. Each of the following situations (A,B,C etc.) refers to the corresponding letters on the price action graph in figure 20 and to the columns showing the short sale action.

Situation A. The Starting Point.
The convertible bonds were bought (4 bonds worth 260 common stock) and half the underlying stock sold short (130 stock sold short).

Situation B. The First Order Filled
The immediate action of Ehrenreich Photo-Optical common stock was downwards. The open order to cover one-third (43 shares) of the short sales (leaving 87 shares sold short outstanding) was set at $12.10 per share according to plan but the stock fell so sharply that it was executed at $11.12 per share. This automatically granted me a bonus, which sometimes happily happens. It is important to note here that when you place an open order, it must be filled at

your requested price or *better*. It cannot be filled to your detriment.

This extra profit allowed me to adjust the plan proportionately. As the bonus was almost a full point gain, the adjustment consisted of lowering the subgoals and final goal by one point. The gain on the downside was $3.23 per share ($14.35 – $11.12), always measured from the purchase price of the short sale, producing a total profit of $138.89 (43 shares sold short x 3.23 gain = $138.89 gain).

Situation C. The Second Order Filled
The next open order on the immediate upside on the adjusted plan was $13.35. It was filled at $13.50.

Now I have my initial inventory of 130 shares sold short. Even though the stock made a relatively small swing, I have automatically locked in my profit.

Situation D. The Third Order Filled
The Ehrenreich Photo stock continued upward and my open order to sell short 43 shares at the adjusted subgoal of $15.75 was filled. To stress a point, it is a fact that I have more shares represented by the convertible bonds (long side) than I have shares sold short (short side). This allows me to "lock in" profits on the uptrend.

Now I have 173 shares sold short.

Situation E. The Fourth Order Filled
Again the stock advanced and filled my open order to sell 43 shares short (making a total of 216 on the short side) at exactly the adjusted subgoal of $18.

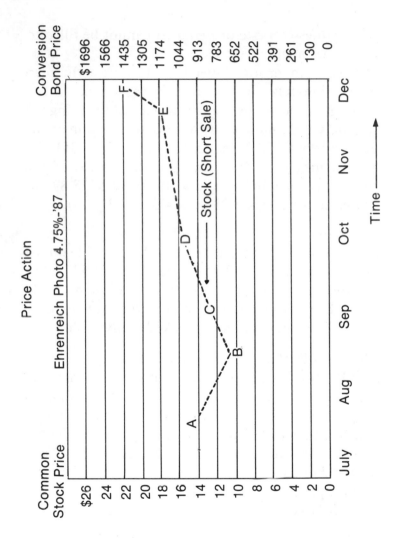

Price Action

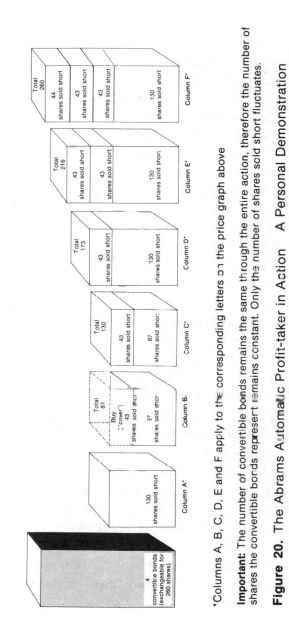

Short Sale Action

*Columns A, B, C, D, E and F apply to the corresponding letters on the price graph above

Important: The number of convertible bonds remains the same through the entire action, therefore the number of shares the convertible bonds represent remains constant. Only the number of shares sold short fluctuates.

Figure 20. The Abrams Automatic Profit-taker in Action — A Personal Demonstration

This automatically takes a profit from the long side of 43 shares included in the inventory of stock represented by the convertible bonds.

Situation F. The Fifth and Final Order Filled
The last surge upwards in my stock filled the last order, which stood at the adjusted goal of $20.37. The profits from the remaining 44 shares represented by the convertible bonds were now locked in by this final short sale of 44 shares.

When the number of stock sold short and the number of shares the convertible bonds represented were the same, I terminated the situation. This can be accomplished most advantageously by merely advising your broker to convert the convertible bonds and cover them with the equivalent number of stock sold short. There are absolutely no commission charges to you when you terminate this situation in the described manner.

When you convert your bonds, you do not receive any of the accrued interest. However, when you are in the position to convert your bonds — hesitate and consider the possible opportunity of holding this "full hedge" situation until the next installment of interest on your convertible bond is paid (normally interest is paid twice a year). After collecting your interest, then convert. Remember, you should not be required to maintain any margin on a full hedge situation, other than the premium on the convertible.

In summary, I gained 94 per cent profit on my investment in four and a half months. With comparable situations, it is possible to triple or better your initial investment in a year even disregarding the profit potential of reinvested profits.

Using the Ehrenreich Photo example, how do you determine the performance of an individual profit-taker strategy?

Here is a straightforward and effective procedure for determining the financial performance of each of your Profit-Taker strategies. Please note the two following salient rules.

- On your monthly statements, the sale of securities will be listed in the "credit" columns of your account — *and will include short sales.*
- In the "debit" columns will be listed the purchase of securities, such as the buying of convertible bonds — *and will include the "covering" or "buying-in" of short sales.*

With these two points impressed on your mind, simply proceed to:

1. Sort out the "debits" and "credits" into individual Profit-Taker situations.
2. Deduct the total of the "debit" column from the total of the "credit" column to find your gross profit.

Using this procedure, here is the picture in summary of Ehrenreich Photo:

	Debit	Credit
Situation A. The Starting Point		
(i) 4 Ehrenreich convertible bonds were bought at $965.00 each	$3,860.00	
(ii) 130 shares were sold short at $14.35		$1,865.50
Situation B. The First Order Filled		
43 shares were covered (bought in) at $11.12	478.16	
Situation C. The Second Order Filled.		
43 shares were sold short at $13.50		580.50
Situation D. The Third Order Filled.		
43 shares were sold short at $15.75.		677.25
Situation E. The Fourth Order Filled.		
43 shares were sold short at $18.00.		774.00

	Debit	*Credit*

Situation F. The Fifth and
Final Order Filled.
(i) 44 shares were sold
short at $20.37   896.28
(ii) The 260 shares now
sold short were covered by
the 4 convertible bonds
(exchangeable for 260
shares).

| TOTAL | $4,338.16 | $4,793.53 |

CREDITS	$4,793.53
Less DEBITS	4,338.16
TOTAL PROFIT	$ 455.37

Total cost of bonds (4 bonds x $965) = $3,860.00

Margin: 3.09 per cent of $1,930
(2 bonds)   = $59.63
(Premium only is required as
margin when underlying
shares sold short are balanced
by the convertible bonds, as
here.)

22 per cent of $1,930 (2 bonds) $424.60
(Minimum margin required
for bonds not balanced by underlying short sale.)

No margin whatsoever on the
short sale

Total margin   = $484.23

The profit here is 94 per cent, almost doubling your money in less than 4½ months. The magnitude of the profit potential is in your hands, based on your own astute application of the Profit-Taker checklist which is to follow.

For purposes of clearness, please note the examples do not include the usual expenses — such as commissions and interest on the margin account — which may vary. The usual extra gains — such as the interest accrued on the convertible bonds and the compounding of reinvested profits — have also not been included.

Confirmations of locked-in or realized profits (figure 21) will be a delight to receive as you proceed with your Profit-Taker technique.

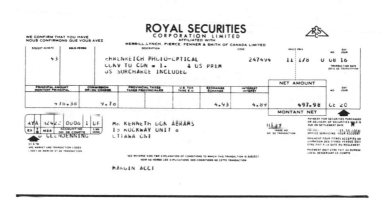

Figure 21. Typical Confirmations of Profits Resulting from the Abrams Automatic Profit-Taker

10. A Profit-Taker Checklist
to Ensure Your Success

Is there a checklist for the selection of the most likely situations to double my money in less than six months?

Yes. I have formulated and practiced with a checklist to assist me in evaluating various situations. This is based on years of experimentation with convertible bond strategies, culminating in the Abrams Automatic Profit-Taker plan. I wish to share this with you. You will notice in figure 22 that I have assigned different values to each point on the checklist. After you have practiced the Abrams Automatic Profit-Taker and understand what tremendous profits are involved, you may wish to reapportion the assigned values. These are only suggested ways to

Name of Security _____   Symbol_____

Rate and Maturity_____   Interest Date_____

Bond Purchased at_____   No. of shares (Short sale) _____

Date of Purchase _____   Price of stock share_____

No. of shares _____

	Suggested 100% Ideal	Actual Rating
1 ___ The premium of the bond under 10%.	10%	
2 ___ Of the situations being considered, how does the volatility of this common stock compare with the other candidates.	50%	
3 ___ Is the market price of the convertible bond under $1,000 (par value).	10%	
4 ___ Does the yield (%) paid by the bond less the common stock yield at least offset the interest paid to your broker for margin privileges?	5%	
5 ___ Does the company pay dividends on the stock?	10%	
6 ___ A record of convertible premiums.	5%	
7 ___ Does the company have assets in excess of the face value of the bonds?	5%	
8 ___ Is the company in an industry in which there is a possibility of growth?	5%	

Figure 22. Abrams Automatic Profit-Taker Checklist for Convertible Bonds

97

aid you initially in choosing the most lucrative selections. The checklist is based on a "100 per cent" ideal situation. Your task is then to select the situation which most closely approaches this ideal.

It is my genuine desire that you will have all the information necessary to duplicate or better the success proven here. Through relentless application of the checklist, you will become a predator of the most exciting and volatile profit-making situations.

√ 1. *Consider the convertible bonds with an "under 10 per cent" premium.*

What is an "under 10 per cent" premium?

An "under 10 per cent" premium convertible bond is one for which you pay less than 10 per cent over and above the total amount you would pay for the common stock into which the bond is exchangeable, or the conversion value. Let us say you pay $820 for a convertible bond. You know the bond can be exchanged for 20 shares of the same company. The current market price of these shares is $40, so your $820 bond can be exchanged for $800 (20 shares x $40 per share). The difference between the market price you paid for the convertible bond ($820) and the worth of the shares if you converted ($800) is the true premium ($20). So that you can easily compare these premiums, they are normally given in percentages, and are calculated as follows:

$$\frac{\$20 \text{ (market price of the bond } - \text{ conversion value)}}{\$800 \text{ (conversion value)}}$$

x 100 per cent

= 2.5 per cent

Sources of information listing these percentages for your comparison will be provided in chapter 11.

Why is the "under 10 per cent" premium so important?

Remember, you can convert the convertible bond at any time up to the due date. Consequently the lower the premium, the more immediate the profitability on the upside. This principle was described in chapter 2.

Please recall also that on that portion of convertible bonds offset by an equivalent number of stock sold short you are required to post only the premium as margin. That is, if the premium is 3 per cent you are required to post only 3 per cent of the conversion value. If there is no premium, no further margin is required other than, of course, the initial margin to open your account.

√ *2. Consider the degree of volatility of the common stock associated with the convertible bond.*

Why is this volatility so critical?

You have already considered the appropriate convertible bonds based on the "under 10 per cent" premium rule. Now evaluate your selection based on volatility of price, that is, the volatility of the common stock. This is simply a comparison of the price action of the common stock into which your convertible bond is exchangeable. This comparison of price action allows you to select the most likely active and alive stock and, consequently, the most likely convertible bond. This is most important. A high degree of volatility costs you no more with the Profit-Taker technique; this is not the case with other investment strategies such as stock options. This factor takes into account the critical time element. The comparison of volatility percentages may make the difference between a convertible situation that doubles your investment in two years and a situation that doubles your investment in less than six months.

The excitement and profit of the Abrams Automatic Profit-Taker technique flourishes on a volatile and fluctuating stock. As you have seen, the active fluctuations (both upward and downward) can add greatly to your profits, so look for active stocks. I have welcomed the most variable and unsettled stocks represented by the convertible bond.

A Profit-Taker strategy with an underlying common stock possessing a high degree of volatility will most certainly reap the benefits of this ongoing momentum, so search for volatility as if it were a jewel of great value.

On the checklist I have allotted a thumping value of 50 per cent to volatility. You will certainly appreciate the magnitude of the proportion assigned to volatility as you prosper with this strategy.

How do I calculate and compare volatility of price?

Very simply. Volatility of price is primarily useful when calculated as a percentage. You simply take a time span — anywhere from three months to one year — from your regular financial source. (I also compare the volatility of the previous month.)

Be certain that the length of time compared is the same for all the situations studied. You then calculate this percentage by subtracting the "low" price of the stock from the "high" price for the same period. This difference is then translated into a percentage of the low price. For example:

The "high" of Stock A	=	$60.00
The "low" of Stock A	=	40.00
Difference	=	$20.00

Volatility, $\dfrac{20}{40} \times 100 = 50$ per cent

If you follow the Profit-Taker Checklist, particularly with regard to the volatility factor, then you may reasonably assume that the sub-goals of your plan will be filled at a gratifying pace. There are no set time spans, of course, within which each sub-goal will be filled. Certainly, based on my experience, this time span between sub-goals can be quite erratic, taking from days to weeks.

No doubt, the acid test of true profitability of an individual Profit-Taker strategy must be at the natural time of completion. This is when the last sub-goal on the uptrend or on the downtrend has been filled.

√ 3. *Consider the market price of the bond.*

Why is it important that the market price of the convertible bond be close to $1,000 par value or lower?

This is important because the protective premium we have examined normally forms in this area. Generally speaking, the lower the market price of the convertible bond, the more advantageous it is to you.

Most convertible bonds also have a feature whereby the company can "call in" the bonds at a predetermined price. Usually the bonds are not called in until the market price is well above the call price, because the company really wants you to convert the convertible bonds into the higher price common stock rather than have you request the call price of the bond. This is simply common sense as the company does not then have to pay the outstanding debt. A superb situation for the corporation and a superb situation for you.

√ 4. *Consider the yield (%) paid by the bonds against the common stock dividends (%).*

How important is the bond yield? After all, with such a profitable technique why concern ourselves with a few percentage points?

It is often possible to select situations in which the yield of the convertible bond is sufficiently high to pay the broker's interest charge on your margin account. Profits can be made even here. This is good business and gives you a comfortable feeling.

As you see from the checklist, I do not give this high priority, nevertheless it is worthy of consideration.

√ *5. Consider the percentage of dividends paid on the associated common stock.*

Why is it important that the company pay little or no dividends?

Remember that when you hold short sales you must pay the dividends. These dividends are an expense to you. They must be borne in mind when you make your selection.

√ *6. Consider the record of premiums forming on the convertible bond.*

Why is a "record of premiums" included in the checklist? Does not this premium form automatically on the downside?

There is probably no accurate way to measure the exact resistance price of a convertible bond. Although many analysts attempt to determine the investment value, it is still largely speculative.

However, the previous history of the premium can give you a sense of assurance that deep discounts do materialize. For this purpose, you might use a graph designed to compare the convertible bond with its common stock. These graphs are available from sources listed in chapter 11.

I simply determine the conversion price of the common stock, that is, the market price of the shares the convertible bonds represent based on the low of a certain period — say a year. Deduct this conversion price of the common stock from the low of the convertible bond price based on the same period, and calculate the premium percentage.

Again in summary:

$$\frac{\text{market price of bond (low)} - \text{conversion value of common stock (low)}}{\text{conversion value of common stock (low)}}$$

x 100 per cent = premium percentage

√ *7. Consider the assets of the issuing corporation.*

Why is it important to evaluate the assets of a corporation?

This information is a "line of defense." Certainly it is worthy of consideration, but it is not as important as the others on the checklist. I have only allotted 5 per cent weight to it.

It is important to evaluate the corporation's assets to find out whether the company will substantially cover its debts (your convertible included) in case of liquidation. The information is certainly available from your broker, Standard and Poor's Services or Moody's.

√ 8. *Consider the growth potential of the related industry.*

Why is the "possibility of growth" important to our plan?

This is primarily meant to remind you that it is desirable for the corporation you choose to have strong possibilities of growth. This is an indication that the volatility, particularly upwards, may well continue. With our technique however, erratic fluctuation on the way can be very profitable and consequently welcome.

11. Popular Questions
about Information Sources and Brokerage Commissions

Is it better to buy United States or foreign convertible bonds for my purposes?

The best selection of convertible bonds and convertible preferred shares is found on the U.S. exchanges. As a result, this wide selection spawns more opportunities to apply money-making strategies. By all means periodically investigate the 20 to 30 Canadian convertible bonds for possible opportunities; however, there are some 850 to 900 U.S. convertible situations to be examined.

Where will I find the best sources of information required to initiate the Abrams Automatic Profit-Taker?

Check with your broker first. He should subscribe to at least one of the following sources. The business section of your local university or college library may carry a subscription.

1. *K. V. Convertible Fact Finder,* Kalb, Voorhis and Co., 27 William Street, New York, N.Y. 10005. This weekly print-out provides an excellent, comprehensive service on convertible bonds, convertible preferred shares and warrants. The computerized print-out presents most of the information necessary to satisfy our Abrams Automatic Profit-Taker checklist and enables you to select the most profitable situations. It is a superb starting point for your selections.

2. *R. H. M. Convertible Survey,* 220 Fifth Avenue, New York, N.Y. 10001. This service is similar to the Kalb and Voorhis *Fact Finder.*

3. *Standard and Poor's Bond Guide,* 345 Hudson Street, New York, N.Y. 10014. This guide includes the necessary data on most convertible bonds.

4. *Moody's Investors Service,* 99 Church Street, New York, N.Y. 10007. Moody's provides a wide range of services, including comprehensive articles on various aspects of investing.

5. *The New York Times* Sunday Edition (Business and Finance Section), 229 W. 43rd Street, New

York, N.Y. 10036. Particularly useful when making your final selection to apply the Profit-Taker plan, the *Times* contains most of the current market prices of convertible bonds and convertible preferred shares. It has very complete business and investment news coverage and because of its availability at the newsstands on Sundays, I have found it valuable for checking the closing Friday prices before the market opens Monday morning.

6. *Barron's National Business and Financial Weekly,* 200 Burnett Road, Chicopee, Mass. 01021. This useful weekly is put out by Dow Jones, which also publishes the *Wall Street Journal.* Recent market prices on convertible bonds and convertible preferred shares are contained in the statistical section.

7. *The Wall Street Journal,* 30 Broad Street, New York, N.Y. 10004. Like Barron's, the statistical section on convertibles is comprehensive. However, in many areas, you cannot get *The Wall Street Journal* as easily at the newsstands as you can *The New York Times.*

What about brokers' commissions? Can I save on commissions using the Abrams strategy?

Categorically yes! Here is how it works.

The commission must be paid in the normal way when setting up your Abrams Automatic Profit-Taker strategy. Commission is relatively small on the convertible bond — typically $5 a bond depending on the policy of your investment dealer. The equivalent number of shares for which your convertible bonds are exchangeable would likely cost you three or four times more in commissions. The commission on the short sales is generally the same as on corresponding stocks selling at equivalent prices on the long side.

When your stock sold short equals the shares represented by your convertible bonds, you have no doubt made an enviable profit and are prepared to convert. Little or no premium usually exists on your convertible bonds at this position of your Profit-Taker. Simply tell your broker to convert the bonds that are balanced (covered) by the short sales. Your situation is then liquidated at no cost to you. That is, *no commission is charged against you to liquidate your situation.*

You are then in a position to take your profits and select and set into motion new and exciting Profit-Taker selections.

It has been my experience that, regardless of the over-all type of existing market, new potentially money-making situations continually develop.

How can I further substantially reduce my commissions?

You now know how to control your own account with the Profit-Taker technique. Why then should you pay a full-service broker for services, counseling and "hand-holding" you don't use or need? Good news! At long last, the self-directed investor can get his or her commissions "wholesale" by engaging a discount broker. There is nothing mysterious about the business of discounting commissions. Spurred on by Congress, the New York Stock Exchange abolished fixed rates on small trades in May of 1975. To reduce commissions, the discount brokers have simply eliminated the research people and the traditional type of salesperson — the registered representative. They are "order-takers," never pushing stocks or soliciting business in other ways. Why shouldn't you reap the additional bonus of reduced commission for masterminding your own account? After all, your order will be filled as effectively by the discounter as by the "full commissioned" broker.

Remember that these savings on commissions allow you to lock in larger profits on each fluctuation between your sub-goals.

Discount brokers are not ragtag fugitive upstarts. Nearly all of them belong to the National Association of Security Dealers, and many are members of the New York and American Stock Exchanges. All offer individual account protection, usually in the range of $100,000 to $500,000.

The actual amounts of commission deductions offered by the discount brokers do vary somewhat from one to another.

There is no problem transacting even convertible bonds at reduced commission rates, which usually improve with the size of the order. Practically all the discounters now offer margin accounts, and consequently sell short at their reduced rates. In other words, the discounter offers all the essential services, even including open orders, required to set up your Profit-Taker strategy plus the ever appreciated reduction. If you have received good service from your full-service broker of long standing, but still object to paying heavy commissions, ask for a reduction of commissions. It is, after all, a reasonable request.

Who are these discount brokers?

As an introduction to the discount broker, I have surveyed for you a group of New York discount brokers. Also, I have included discount brokers located outside New York City. If you do not have a discount broker in your town, it is not a problem, as most have toll-free telephone numbers or will accept collect calls from customers.

New York City discount brokers include:

Company	Minimum Charge	Account Protection	Rates (In Brief)
Discount Brokerage Corp.	$30.	$100,000	70% off previous fixed rates
Marquette de Bary Co.	20.	500,000	Discount ranges from 0% to 75%; increases sharply with the size of trade.
Muriel Siebert & Co.	25.	300,000	50% off old fixed commissions.
Odd Lot Securities	25.	100,000	20% to 85% based on size of trade.
Quick & Reilly	30.	100,000	45% off on NYSE market orders before 9:45 A.M.; 40% off on other market orders; 35% off on limit orders.

Company	Minimum Charge	Account Protection	Rates (In Brief)
Shearman, Ralston	25.	500,000	First 100 shares, 40 cents each; next 100, 30 cents; next 100, 20 cents; remainder, 10 cents; or 30% off old rates, whichever is lower.
Source Securities	25.	500,000	Discounts up to 81% on large trades by active customers.

Discount brokers located outside New York City include:

Atlanta, Ga.	Quick & Reilly
Baltimore, Md.	Quick & Reilly
Boston, Mass.	Stock Cross
Chicago, Ill.	Burke, Christensen & Lewis Securities Inc.
Fort Lauderdale, Fla.	Quick & Reilly
Hartford, Conn.	Quick & Reilly
Indianapolis, Ind.	Springer Investment & Securities Co. Inc.

Memphis, Tenn.	Kahn & Co. Inc.
Miami, Fla.	Quick & Reilly
Minneapolis, Minn.	Thrift Trading Inc.
Newport Beach, Calif.	Letterman Transactions Services
Palm Beach, Fla.	Quick & Reilly
Philadelphia, Pa.	Quick & Reilly
Rochester, N.Y.	Odd Lot Securities; Quick & Reilly
St. Petersburg, Fla.	Quick & Reilly
San Francisco, Calif.	Charles Schwab & Co.
Springfield, Va.	Kulak, Voss & Co., Inc.
Tampa, Fla.	Odd Lot Securities
Washington, D.C.	Odd Lot Securities; Quick & Reilly

Does the Abrams Automatic Profit-Taker work equally well with convertible preferred shares?

The technique can be applied effectively with convertible preferred stock, although some caution is in order here. I have learned that situations in convertible preferred shares are usually not quite as suitable. The convertible preferred share is a superior security to the common share and consequently usually forms a premium. However, the convertible preferred share is a junior security to the convertible bond. I have found the premium on the convertible preferred share does not develop as dramatically on the downside as the premium that forms on the convertible bond.

Another point to consider is that the Canadian margin for convertible preferred shares is higher (currently 50 per cent) than the approximately 22 per cent margin of the convertible bond. This higher margin reduces your ability to invest larger amounts with a small amount of capital.

As in the case of the common stock, you pay much higher commission rates for convertible preferred shares.

Opportunities do arise, however, with convertible preferred shares and they should be searched carefully. Apply the Abrams Automatic Profit-Taker checklist to the convertible preferred shares in the same manner you do to the convertible bonds.

How much money do I need to set up a strategy based on the Abrams Automatic Profit-Taker?

Your broker will tell you the minimum amount required to open a margin account. This margin account allows you to immeasurably increase the size of your investments. Remember, the Abrams Automatic Profit-Taker not only has an impressive profit potential, but, as demonstrated, is a relatively conservative strategy. Typically it takes a minimum of $2,000 to open a margin account, but in Canada this is merely a house rule of the investment dealer.

Some brokers will open a margin account for much less. So if you have $400 or $500 with which to open a margin account — shop around. You will no doubt find a broker who will do business.

As more people learn about the Abrams Automatic Profit-Taker technique, won't the eligible profitable situations tend to disappear?

This question was a serious consideration of mine before I wrote this book. I craved to share the exciting experience of investing using the technique I have called the Abrams Automatic Profit-Taker with other investors. I naturally wondered if by sharing this concept the opportunities would dry up proportionate to the number of participants.

After careful investigation, I am now convinced that as more small investors become familiar with and profit from this technique the opportunities may well increase rather than decrease. The main reason for this conclusion is that increased participation in convertible bonds may well encourage corporations to issue more convertible bonds, thereby increasing the opportunities for the investor.

Corporations also have a great deal going for them when they issue convertible bonds. A little encouragement goes a long way to produce more favourable situations for you. One very tempting incentive for the corporation to issue a convertible bond, when popular with investors, is that should the common stock rise to or above the call price, the corporation may call in the bond. This practice usually encourages the investor to convert the common stock, thus eliminating the corporation's debt. Good for the corporation — good for you!

Should I have more than one Profit-Taker situation working for me at a time?

Once you feel comfortable and fully understand the money-making capacity of the Abrams Automatic Profit-Taker technique, I strongly urge you to capitalize on your gains by setting up new Profit-Taker strategies.

Naturally, as stock prices change, the opportunities to apply the Profit-Taker also change. Consequently, as you pyramid your profits, re-examine all the convertible bonds and to a lesser degree the convertible preferred shares for possible new opportunities which may have materialized. Use my checklist as an aid to select the best candidates. Personally, I often have several separate Profit-Taker plans working at the same time.

12. Your Own Investment Strategies
Planning and Co-ordinating

Using such profitable strategies as the Abrams Automatic Profit-Taker may be very exciting, but oh how lonely! How can I, a small investor, discuss and exchange views on investment strategies with others besides my broker?

The zealous investor is irresistibly drawn to share and exchange his personal views on investment strategies with other investors. It is not sufficient to talk with your broker for a few minutes each day. With the broker's phone ringing constantly (with calls from his other 50 to 150 customers) he simply cannot linger to discuss important details of your strategy.

The loneliness of being a small investor led me to search for a group of other investors like myself, but without success. Instead, I initiated an investment strategies course at a college in my area.

The course was based on my own lectures and those of guest speakers, mostly prominent local brokers. For me, this was truly a labor of love. My guests have been most co-operative, the students most receptive and enthusiastic.

You can encourage your local university, community college, high school or perhaps YM-YWCA, to set up a similar course. If enough people show interest in a particular subject, educational institutions are usually only too willing to find the right person to lead or tutor the class. I assure you that it can be a very gratifying experience to organize or belong to a group that shares the common interest of exploring investment strategies such as the one we have discussed.

I have long searched for a concept that is at once highly profitable and highly protective of my initial investment. I have found it in the Abrams Automatic Profit-Taker.

Naturally I constantly apply it for the further profits it brings me. But I am equally impelled, as a teacher of investment strategies, to share this technique with others — as I have shared it with you in this book.

It is my genuine hope that you in turn will share

your success in the application of the Abrams Automatic Profit-Taker with others.

If you are interested in organizing or belonging to an investment strategies course, I will be pleased to send you a course outline, recommendations and suggestions for publicizing the course in your community.

How do I keep a record of my plan and open orders for the Abrams Automatic Profit-Taker?

The most important thing to consider in keeping your records is how meaningful they are to you. You will no doubt eventually develop your own method of keeping the records of your plan and open orders. One of the many desirable features of the Abrams Automatic Profit-Taker is that once you have established your plan, few records need to be maintained. For instance, it is not necessary to spend valuable time recording or graphing daily stock movements. Your goals have already been strategically set, to be touched off automatically to your financial advantage.

For your assistance, I have included the records I keep during the life of each investment based on the Abrams Automatic Profit-Taker technique.

You now have the tools of extraordinary financial success. From now on, it is up to you to take action.

Abrams Automatic Profit-Taker Action Worksheet

Convertible Security _____

Interest Rate and Maturity Date _____

Number of Convertibles Purchased _____

Number of Shares (for which the
convertibles may be exchanged) _____

Interest/Dividend Rates _____

Number of Shares Sold Short _____

Price of Shares Sold Short _____

Premium Paid on Convertible _____

Date of Implementation _____

Plan of My Goals

Common Stock Price	Name of Convertible Security
	Long-term Goal (Uptrend)
	Subgoal 2 (Uptrend)
	Subgoal 1 (Uptrend)
	Purchase Price
	Subgoal 1 (Downtrend)
	Subgoal 2 (Downtrend)
	Long-term Goal (Downtrend)

OPEN ORDERS

Date of Order	Name, Quantity of Stock Sold Short (Uptrend)	Name, Quantity of Stock Covered (Downtrend)	Date Filled	Date Cancelled

DEFENDER
IN CHIEF

DONALD TRUMP'S
FIGHT FOR
PRESIDENTIAL
POWER

JOHN YOO

ALL POINTS BOOKS  NEW YORK

First published in the United States by All Points Books, an imprint of St. Martin's Publishing Group

DEFENDER IN CHIEF. Copyright © 2020 by John Yoo. All rights reserved. Printed in the United States of America. For information, address St. Martin's Publishing Group, 120 Broadway, New York, NY 10271.

www.allpointsbooks.com

Library of Congress Cataloging-in-Publication Data

Names: Yoo, John, author.

Title: Defender in chief : Donald Trump's fight for presidential power / John Yoo.

Other titles: Donald Trump's fight for presidential power

Description: First edition. | New York : All Points Books, 2020. | Includes bibliographical references and index.

Identifiers: LCCN 2020010723 | ISBN 9781250269577 (hardcover) | ISBN 9781250269614 (ebook)

Subjects: LCSH: Trump, Donald, 1946- | United States––Politics and government—2017- | Constitutional law—United States.

Classification: LCC E912 .Y66 2020 | DDC 973.933092—dc23

LC record available at https://lccn.loc.gov/2020010723

Our books may be purchased in bulk for promotional, educational, or business use. Please contact your local bookseller or the Macmillan Corporate and Premium Sales Department at 1-800-221-7945, extension 5442, or by email at MacmillanSpecialMarkets@macmillan.com.

First Edition: 2020

10   9   8   7   6   5   4   3   2   1

Dedicated to my mother, Sook Hee Yoo, M.D.

CONTENTS

DEFENDER
IN CHIEF

INTRODUCTION

T he Constitution has become the sword for Democrats who want
Donald Trump removed from office. In her December 5, 2019,
speech formally calling for articles of impeachment, House Speaker
Nancy Pelosi declared, "The president's actions have seriously violated the
constitution, especially when he says and acts upon the belief 'Article 2 says
I can do whatever I want.' No." She portrayed Trump's actions as a fundamental threat. "His wrongdoing strikes at the very heart of our constitution. A separation of powers, three co-equal branches, each a check and
balance on the other. A republic, if we can keep it, said Benjamin Franklin."[1] Senate Minority Leader Chuck Schumer agreed: "If we don't reckon
with President Trump's persistent transgressions, the very foundation of
this great republic is at risk. The president kept pushing and pushing and
pushing the constitutional envelope. Finally, the president's conduct made
an impeachment inquiry unavoidable."[2]

Democratic critics have made violations of the Constitution a regular
part of their litany attacking the Trump presidency for breaking the law.
Hillary Clinton took to the airwaves in September 2019 to dismiss President Trump as an "illegitimate president" and a "corrupt human tornado,"
and to declare that "he knows" he stole the 2016 election."[3] Her 2016 vice
presidential candidate shared the view of Trump's unconstitutional conduct. "President Trump's decision to launch airstrikes against Syria without
Congress's approval is illegal and—absent a broader strategy—it's reckless," Senator Tim Kaine said in 2018 after U.S. missile strikes against the
Assad regime.[4] Liberal Harvard Law professor Laurence Tribe, perhaps
the most distinguished constitutional law scholar of his generation, barely

1

gave Trump time to adjust his desk chair before declaring the Constitution violated. "I wouldn't say he's bumping into the Constitution, he's crashing through it," Tribe said on January 31, 2017. Tribe, who joined a lawsuit against Trump over, of all things, the Emoluments Clause, declared, "I've never seen anything like this in my lifetime."[5]

This book will explain why Trump has not become the Constitution's destroyer, but instead its most unlikely defender. Rather than a sword, the Constitution has become Trump's shield. Even though he had not had any previous government or military office or public policy experience, Trump has defended the constitutional text, structure, and design for an independent, vigorous executive. Trump has fought off the efforts of progressives who have wanted to revolutionize our constitutional order by vesting ever more power in a permanent bureaucracy of virtually limitless authority and to undermine institutions designed to channel and balance pure majority rule. Whether consciously or by following his own political incentives (which the Constitution itself creates, as we will see), Trump has become a far more stout defender of our original governing document than his critics have. Should he win a second term, Trump's exercise of presidential power to protect the nation's security, slim the federal government, and appoint originalist judges may engineer a radical return of our constitutional system to its founding roots.

If friends had told me on January 21, 2017, that I would write a book on Donald Trump as a defender of the Constitution, I would have questioned their sanity. I had not voted for Trump in the 2016 primary or general elections. His many personal and professional flaws, including his bankruptcies, sexual scandals, crude and cruel language, repelled me. I saw him as a populist, even a demagogue, who had not prepared for the heavy responsibilities of the presidency. My study of the separation of powers, and my time in the three branches of government, led me to worry that Trump would test, evade, or even violate the Constitution. And let us just say that the University of California at Berkeley, my place of work for nearly three decades, did not foster an environment for Trump supporters.

Boy was I wrong. Trump campaigns like a populist but governs like a constitutional conservative. Throughout American history, presidents who believe they represent a popular movement have sought to overturn established constitutional practices. Thomas Jefferson, Andrew Jackson, Abraham Lincoln, Franklin Roosevelt, and Ronald Reagan did not just win the presidency with broad support; they sparked revolutions in constitutional understandings. They aggressively wielded presidential power to advance their political agendas against a resistant establishment.[6] But these greatest American presidents succeeded because their circumstances demanded the vigorous exercise of executive power. I worried that Trump would draw upon the great reservoir of presidential power during times that did not need it.

After Trump won the Republican primaries, he gave traditional Republicans a lot to like. Tax cuts and deregulation would jump-start the economy, which had recovered listlessly after the Great Recession. Appointing conservative judges would end the cultural wars in the courts and return social questions to the democratic, federal, political process. Recognizing the rising threat of China, he would rebuild a military hollowed out by years of "sequesters" and spending caps, one that had played defense on the new battlefields of cyber, drones, and space. But he also broke with Republican orthodoxies on generous immigration and international trade, where union-led Democrats had the longer record of hostility toward the free movement of people, goods, and capital. While I never signed the Never Trumper letters that freely circulated among former Bush national security officials, I could not bring myself to support the nominee of my party because I felt that his rashness could lead to a foreign policy disaster, even if he were to appoint a conservative Supreme Court or cut taxes.

In the first few months of the Trump presidency, I even wrote an op-ed in the *New York Times* to warn about "executive power run amok."[7] I have consistently defended the presidential power, such as the right to wage war unilaterally, of George W. Bush, in whose administration I served, but of Barack Obama and Bill Clinton too. But President Trump's first moves gave even me pause. During the campaign, he had displayed little knowledge of the Constitution—recall that he thought the Constitution had 11 or 12 articles. It only has 7. He claimed the unilateral right to build a wall along the Mexican border without congressional funding or authorization. His first executive order banning travel from Muslim nations violated the Religion Clauses of the First Amendment. He threatened to terminate the North American Free Trade Agreement, which takes the form of a law passed by Congress rather than a treaty. "Even Alexander Hamilton, our nation's most ardent proponent of executive power, would be worried by now," I suggested.

Trump is disrupting the political system, perhaps for good. He has transformed presidential speeches, for example, from formal addresses into stream-of-consciousness rallies. He speaks directly to the American people through social media, randomly calls in to Fox News shows, and engages the press in off-the-cuff, spontaneous arguments. Trump's direct talk to the American people has banished the formal Oval Office address and press conference to the dustbin of history—thankfully. Trump has brought the combative politics that he brandished on the campaign trail into the Oval Office. He boasted about the size of his inauguration crowds, refused to release his tax returns, attacked "so-called" federal judges who ruled against him, and labeled a range of news stories and media organizations as "FAKE NEWS." He attacked opponents with a variety of nicknames, such as "Pocahontas" for Senator Elizabeth Warren, "Crooked Hillary" for Clinton, and "Shifty Schiff" for Representative Adam Schiff of California. He threatened to inflict "fire and fury" on "Little Rocket Man" North Korean leader Kim Jong Un. Trump seemed to delight in violating the rules of political correctness whenever he could.

We could explain much of Trump's political brashness and destructiveness by referring to the American people's desire to disrupt the country's ossified political system, which he called "the Swamp." No doubt he had the good fortune in 2016 to run against Hillary Clinton. Despite her sterling résumé as first lady, senator, and secretary of state, Clinton campaigned terribly and made elemental mistakes, such as taking the Midwestern states of Pennsylvania, Michigan, and Wisconsin for granted. If Trump had a past dogged by scandal, ethical controversies, and shady business deals, he could have found no better opponent to run against than Hillary Clinton.

But Trump represented more than an anyone-but-Clinton impulse. Any of the establishment Republicans on the 2016 primary debate stage could have filled that role nicely. Wisconsin governor Scott Walker or Texas senator Ted Cruz would have ably carried the Republican flag into battle against Clinton. But as Victor Davis Hanson has argued, the American people wanted more. They wanted a president whose speech, mannerisms, and policies came from so far outside the political system that he might even bring down the existing political order. Trump echoes no one less than Andrew Jackson. Jackson had fought duels, owned slaves, killed Native Americans, hanged spies, and carried a lifelong hatred of both the British (because of his service as a boy soldier during the Revolutionary War) and the east coast cultural elite. He had no famous, learned, or wealthy ancestors, did not attend college, and raised himself up by the bootstraps to become the nation's savior at the Battle of New Orleans and the first president who could claim to head a popular movement. Like Jackson, Trump promised to attack the governing elites of both parties with a no-holds-barred style rather than polite debate. Populists like these usually strain at the Constitution's limits to fulfill their electoral mandates.

But a funny thing happened—or didn't happen—during the Trump storm. The new president did not brandish any novel assaults on the Constitution. His opponents did. Democratic presidential candidates, such as Senators Elizabeth Warren and Kamala Harris and South Bend, Indiana, mayor Pete Buttigieg, among others, called for expanding the size of the Supreme Court from 9 to 15 justices so that the next Democratic president could pack it with liberals. They have threatened to impeach Justice Brett Kavanaugh for sexual harassment claims that the Senate fully aired before voting to confirm him in 2018. In spring 2019, Democratic senators Brian Schatz, Dick Durbin, Dianne Feinstein, and Kirsten Gillibrand introduced a constitutional amendment to abolish the Electoral College. Democratic representative Alexandria Ocasio-Cortez explained that the Electoral College is "a shadow of slavery's power on America today that undermines our nation as a democratic republic."[8] Progressive intellectual leaders and retiring representative John Dingell, the longest-serving member of the House, want to abolish the Senate too.[9]

Democrats would do even more damage to the constitutional order if they were to win the 2020 elections. They plan to implement proposals for a Medicare-for-all healthcare system that would abolish private insurance, impose federal wealth or sales taxes that violate the income tax amendment, and nationalize areas of state competence ranging from criminal justice to consumer contracts to property. Trump protected the Constitution merely by winning the 2016 election through the Electoral College, governing with the Senate, and stopping Democratic efforts to bestow vast new powers on a permanent, unaccountable bureaucracy in Washington, D.C.

But Trump's defense of the constitutional order went beyond simply stopping bad ideas. His battle for the Constitution took three basic forms. First, he fought Robert Mueller's special counsel investigation and the Ukraine impeachment, which challenged the president's authority to govern the executive branch and to fulfill his constitutional duty to "take care that the laws be faithfully executed." By prevailing, Trump obeyed the Constitution's command for an energetic unitary executive who would participate in a separation of powers where each branch remains independent of the other. Second, he stood up for traditional executive leadership in foreign affairs and war. While Congress may seek to advance different policies through spending or legislation, the Constitution designed the executive branch to have the advantages of unity, speed, and decision, specifically so that it could protect the national security and pursue our interests abroad. Third, Trump appointed a Supreme Court that could return the Constitution to its original understanding on questions ranging from governmental power to individual liberties.

This book will explain how Trump's political battles have become part of a larger struggle to defend the original Constitution from progressives who would transform it. Chapter 1 argues that Trump's election fulfilled the Framers' purposes behind the Electoral College and rejects accusations that the Constitution's method of presidential selection is racist. Chapter 2 presents the heart of this book's theory by describing the nature of executive power and the Founders' design of the presidency. Chapter 3 reveals the special counsel and impeachment investigations to be challenges to the presidency's independence and energy by the permanent law enforcement and national security bureaucracies. Chapter 4 shows how Trump has used his executive power to replace the Obama administration's efforts to expand the federal government with a deregulatory agenda that has sparked the economy.

To defend Trump's constitutional positions is not to agree with his policy views. In particular, I do not share Trump's restrictionist approach to immigration or his suspicion of free trade and the American-led postwar order. Nevertheless, as president he has the legal right to devise and carry out most of those policies. Chapter 5 addresses his immigration policies, in particular his border wall, the travel ban, and birthright citizenship. Chapters 6 and 7 argue that Trump can draw upon the executive powers over foreign affairs and war to introduce a new doctrine that reorders America's grand strategy abroad. If the Trump presidency ends up pulling back America's global commitments, I would regret the moves and question whether they serve our national interests, but they would represent another Trump campaign promise kept.

Trump's exercise of executive power may not even represent his greatest impact on the Constitution. Chapter 8 discusses the battle over his Supreme Court nominees, Neil Gorsuch and Kavanaugh, and the broader effort to place conservatives on the lower courts. Trump may exceed all other presidents not just in the youth and number but also in the ideological commitment of his judicial picks, who will interpret the Constitution for decades after he leaves office. Chapter 9 takes up impeachment. As we will see, the Framers designed impeachment to be a rare tool for extraordinary circumstances that go beyond partisan fighting. By vigorously contesting the process of his impeachment, Trump has defended the Constitution's design of a presidency against any Congress all too willing to convert impeachment into a tool of everyday political combat.

At the end of this book, I consider the larger lessons of the Trump presidency. He is a contradiction that scrambles many of the traditional assumptions of the presidency. Even though he did not represent the choice of the majority of the population, he has governed as a populist who rejects moderation and accommodation. He has acted as a political "bad boy," in Hanson's terms, who has sought to overturn the established political order. Yet, Trump has not followed in the constitutional footsteps of past populists. While he has broken political norms, he did not seek to break constitutional understandings. In part, Trump did not need to seize new powers because the presidency already provides them. We have already delegated great authority to our chief executives as our world has become more complex and the challenges abroad have become more dire. But Trump could also achieve his political agenda because he has returned to the Framers' original vision of the presidency as an office of unity, vigor, and independence. In securing the benefits of an energetic executive for his successors, Trump may have done the nation his greatest service.

CHAPTER 1

"YOU'RE HIRED!": TRUMP AND
THE ELECTORAL COLLEGE

For a populist, Donald Trump ironically owes his presidency to a Constitution that limits democracy.

On Election Day, 65,853,514 Americans voted for the Hillary Clinton/Tim Kaine ticket. Only 62,984,828 chose Donald Trump and Mike Pence.

But thanks to the Constitution, Trump won. The Founders rejected the direct popular election of the president. Instead, they required in the Constitution that voters choose electors, who meet to select a president and vice president. Each state receives electoral votes equal to their representation in the House and the Senate. Because it grants each state two extra votes for their senators, the Constitution gives an advantage to smaller states. The smallest state in the Union by population, Wyoming (563,626 residents in 2010), receives three electoral votes, while the largest, California (37,253,956 residents), receives 55.[1]

Trump won the vote of the electors 304–227. While Clinton won the popular vote by 48 to 46 percent, Trump won by a comfortable 57 percent of the electors.[2] Even though Trump did not fulfill the Framers' original purpose behind the Electoral College, he won fair and square under the rules.

Critics immediately attacked Trump's legitimacy. The *New York Times* declared the Constitution's system for selecting the president "antiquated" and called for replacing it with a direct national vote.[3] The Electoral College, it argued, "is more than just a vestige of the founding era; it is a living symbol of America's original sin" because it originally advantaged slave states in the electoral count. Hillary Clinton agreed that the Electoral

College "needs to be eliminated," and 2000 presidential candidate Al Gore argued that adopting a popular vote for president "will stimulate public participation in the democratic process like nothing else we could possibly do." Senator Barbara Boxer filed a lawsuit to overturn the results of the electoral vote and declared, "[t]he Electoral College is an outdated, undemocratic system that does not reflect our modern society, and it needs to change immediately."[4]

These critics could appeal to an unlikely ally: the winner of the 2016 contest. Four years earlier, Trump had declared that the Electoral College "was a disaster for democracy."[5] Shortly after his 2016 victory, he even conceded that he "would rather see it where you went with simple votes. You know, you get 100 million votes, and somebody else gets 90 million votes, and you win."[6] He recognized that winning a direct popular election would require a different strategy. As he said in April 2018, "I would rather have a popular election, but it's a totally different campaign. If you're a runner, you're practicing for the hundred-yard dash as opposed to the mile."[7]

Attacks on the Electoral College after the 2016 elections echoed the controversy surrounding the 2000 contest. While Democratic candidate Al Gore barely won the popular vote, 50,999,897 to 50,456,002, George W. Bush won the Electoral College vote 271 to 266. Only a monthlong dispute, and the intervention of the U.S. Supreme Court in *Bush v. Gore*, awarded Florida (by a 537-vote margin)—and the Electoral College majority—to Bush. Critics then argued that Bush too lacked legitimacy because he had lost the popular vote. But while the 2000 election ended up in a virtual dead heat, the 2016 election decisively awarded the popular vote to Hillary Clinton. Trump became only the fifth president—along with John Quincy Adams (1824), Rutherford Hayes (1876), Benjamin Harrison (1888), and George W. Bush (2000)—to lose the popular vote.

Trump's victory prompted critics to attribute an even more nefarious purpose to the Electoral College than simply moderating democracy. In addition to Ocasio-Cortez and the *New York Times*, serious legal scholars made similar charges that tied the Electoral College to slavery. Of Trump's victory, law professor Akhil Amar declared, "[s]tandard civics-class accounts of the Electoral College rarely mention the real demon dooming direct national election in 1787 and 1803: slavery."[8]

Accusations of racism follow Trump wherever he goes, but they miss the mark here. Instead of a white supremacy device, the Electoral College imperfectly balances nationalism with federalism and leavens democracy's passions with deliberation. It may seem ramshackle today, but the Electoral College advances the people's voice over the centrifugal forces of states and local interests.

I.

The Electoral College remains vulnerable to attack because it can select presidents who lack majority support. A number of candidates have done exactly that. This includes not just presidents who lost the majority vote, such as Donald Trump and George W. Bush, but also those who only won a plurality, such as Clinton, Nixon, Kennedy, and Truman. Abraham Lincoln in 1860 and Woodrow Wilson in 1912 did not win a majority of the vote. Pure democracy does not always produce the best outcomes.

The system gives candidates an incentive to ignore large parts of the country and focus their efforts on states where elections are close. States choose to award all of their electoral votes to the winner, rather than dividing them proportionally. Therefore, candidates rationally will not campaign in states where they have little chance to prevail. Trump did not challenge Clinton in California, where Democrats had majorities in the millions, while Clinton did not contest Texas. Most campaigns will invest their energies on competitive states with rich elector hauls. These battleground states may have little similarity or importance to the nation as a whole, while states with large populations can go uncontested.

The winner-take-all rule in almost all states creates the possibility of a president who wins the most electoral votes while simultaneously losing the national popular vote. A strategic candidate could win bare popular majorities in enough states to carry the Electoral College, even while losing the most populous states by large margins. While about half of America lives in California, Texas, Florida, New York, Pennsylvania, Illinois, Ohio, and Georgia, those eight states have only 226 out of the 270 electoral votes needed to win. A candidate could assemble the electoral votes of the smallest states, essentially concede the largest states, and still prevail. Whether by intention or luck, Trump won with this strategy. Though he took Texas and Florida, Trump did not compete for California, New York, or Illinois. The Constitution's allocation of electors, with its extra two votes per state, allowed him to win the election while losing the popular vote.

The Constitution's protections for federalism explain this feature of the Electoral College. Article II establishes: "Each State shall appoint, in such Manner as the Legislature thereof may direct, a Number of Electors." In the earliest American elections, states used a variety of methods for choosing electors. While the South Carolina legislature would continue to choose electors until the Civil War, most states soon adopted the popular vote. But the states also adopted a rule that reinforced the federalist nature of the electoral system. Most states follow a winner-take-all rule that awards all of a state's electoral votes to the winner of the statewide popular vote. Win a plurality of the popular vote within enough states that hold 270 electoral votes, and a candidate wins the election, even without a national majority.

States could prevent Donald Trump from winning reelection. They need only to allocate their electoral votes proportionally. If Trump were to win Pennsylvania by a margin of 60 to 40 percent, the state would award 12 votes to him and 8 to his challenger. Only Maine and Nebraska, however, divide their votes. States realize that under the current system, candidates will concentrate their time and resources in states where they have a chance to win all of the electoral votes. It is the states (both big and small), rather than the Constitution, that allow a candidate to win without a majority of the popular vote.

The Constitution pays more solicitude toward the states. If no candidate gains a majority of the Electoral College, the Constitution throws the election to the House of Representatives. There, each state delegation has one vote—giving Delaware the same weight as California. If a third-party candidate can block an Electoral College majority, the selection of the president does not just fall to the states, it also becomes subject to legislative deal-making. In 1824, Andrew Jackson won the most electoral votes, but he fell short of a majority. When the election went to the House, it chose John Quincy Adams instead, with Henry Clay allegedly exchanging his support for appointment as secretary of state.

In the wake of the 2000 and 2016 elections, a new criticism has arisen: racism. "The records of the Convention show that in fact the connection between slavery and the college was deliberate, and very much on the minds of many delegates, including James Madison," argues professor Paul Finkelman.[9] Because the Electoral College awards electors chiefly on the number of House representatives, Amar notes, it originally incorporated the Constitution's count of slaves as three-fifths of a person for allocating House seats among the states. This gave the slaveholding states a crucial advantage in the selection of both the House of Representatives and the president. By 1800, Pennsylvania had 10 percent more free people than Virginia, but it had 20 percent fewer electoral votes.[10] Finkelman observes that John Adams would have won the 1800 election over Thomas Jefferson if the Constitution had only counted free citizens for Electoral College purposes.[11] "Jefferson metaphorically rode into the executive mansion on the backs of slaves," writes Amar.[12]

This new claim attacks not only Trump, but also the system we have used to choose presidents for more than two centuries. It adds to efforts to replace the Electoral College with a direct national election of the president. But, as the next section will show, race had little to do with the adoption of the Electoral College. While a stray comment in the Constitutional Convention may have pointed out its benefits to the southern states, this argument did not come to public attention during the ratification debate. Any benefit disappeared with the erasure of the Constitution's protection for slavery during the Civil War and Reconstruction.

II.

The Electoral College provoked little debate during the Constitution's ratification by the states. "The mode of appointment of the Chief Executive," Alexander Hamilton observed in *Federalist No. 68*, "is almost the only part of the system, of any consequence, which has escaped without severe censure, or which has received the slightest mark of approbation from its opponents."[13] He even declared, "I venture somewhat further, and hesitate not to affirm that if the manner of it be not perfect, it is at least excellent."

Hamilton may have accurately described the discussion in the state conventions that approved the Constitution. Opponents there—the Anti-Federalists—devoted most of their energies to attacking the expansion of federal power, the Senate's strange mixture of roles, and the lack of a Bill of Rights. If the Electoral College held a racist purpose to defend slavery, it did not appear obvious to those who ratified the Constitution.

But Hamilton's words could not fairly describe the Constitutional Convention, which first drafted our founding document. It invented the Electoral

College to balance the same competing values that determined the Constitution's overall design: big states versus little states, nationalism versus federalism, North versus South, free states versus slave states.[14] The first draft of the Constitution, the Virginia Plan, proposed an executive "chosen by the National Legislature."[15] When debate opened on June 1, 1787, Pennsylvanian James Wilson argued that "in theory he was for an election by the people."[16] The experience in Massachusetts and New York showed "that an election of the first magistrate by the people at large, was both a convenient and successful mode." Roger Sherman of Connecticut took immediate exception. He "was for the appointment by the Legislature, and for making him absolutely dependent on that body."[17]

If the Virginia Plan had prevailed, our chief executive would look similar to that of a European democracy. In these parliamentary systems, the majority party of the legislature chooses a prime minister to lead the executive branch. No true separation of powers exists between the two branches. Many Framers, however, believed that legislative control in the revolutionary states had produced unstable and unfair laws, government favoritism and partisanship, and flagrant abuse of property and contract rights.[18] To reduce congressional influence over the president, Wilson persuaded the Convention to limit the executive to a single seven-year term, without possibility of reelection.[19] But he could not persuade the delegates to discard legislative selection of the president.[20]

Small states had even greater objections to the Virginia Plan. Their alternate draft, the New Jersey Plan, gave each state equal representation in Congress regardless of population. The conflict between large and small states paralyzed the Constitutional Convention. It ended in the Great Compromise, which divided Congress into the popularly elected House and the state-representing Senate. The Senate became the central institution in the legislature: legislation could not pass without its cooperation; presidents could not make treaties or appoint judges or cabinet officers without its advice and consent; constitutional amendments could not go to the states without its agreement; it acted as the judge and jury in impeachment trials. With legislative selection still in the draft, the states held an effective veto over the president.

Large states reacted by fighting to shift authority from the Senate to the president and to break presidential dependence on Congress.[21] Reopening debate over presidential selection on July 17, Gouverneur Morris demanded that the president "ought to be elected by the people at large, by the free-holders of the Country," who would "never fail to prefer some man of distinguished character, or services, some man, if he might so speak, of continental reputation."[22] If Congress selected him, on the other hand, "he will be the mere creature of the Legisl[ature]," and the choice would be "the work of intrigue, of cabal, and of faction." Wilson proposed that only deadlocks in the election would go to Congress.

Supporters of congressional selection stressed concerns that have returned in the Trump years. Sherman argued that the people would "never be sufficiently informed" and would tend to choose candidates from their own states, which would give larger states the advantage. Charles Pinckney of South Carolina feared "a few active & designing men" would manipulate the people, or that "the most populous States by combining in favor of the same individual will be able to carry their points."[23] Even though he was from a large state, Virginian George Mason agreed that "the extent of the Country" made it nearly impossible for the people "to have the requisite capacity" to judge the candidates.[24] "It would be as unnatural to refer the choice of a proper character for a Chief Magistrate to the people," Mason declared, "as it would, to refer a trial of colours to a blind man." Mason's statement often supplies the evidence for those who believe that the Electoral College advanced an anti-democratic agenda. While Mason may well have held such views, he arguably did not influence the Constitution, as he refused to sign the final product and became one of its leading opponents during the ratification.[25]

It was only at this point that race first arose. Hugh Williamson of North Carolina compared popular election to legislative choice as the difference between "app[ointment] by lot, and by choice."[26] But "this will not be Virg[ini]a however. Her slaves will have no suffrage," Williamson then said.[27] He was pointing out a loss of power for the slave states under direct election of the president. Infamously, the Constitution included three-fifths of slaves in a state's population for allocating seats in the House, even though the South did not allow them to vote. If the Constitution replaced legislative choice with direct election by the people, the southern states would lose their advantage. After Williamson spoke, the Convention rejected direct election.

The delegates soon backtracked. In late July, the Convention made the choices that led to the Electoral College. Nationalists first succeeded in

lifting the single-term limit on the president. They then argued that a president eligible for reelection would become too dependent on Congress.
Reopening the battle he had just lost, Morris again moved for the direct
popular election. "If he is to be the Guardian of the people, let him be appointed by the people."[28] Like many of the delegates, Morris believed that
unrestrained legislatures posed the greater threat to the people's liberties.
"The Executive Magistrate should be the guardian of the people, even of
the lower classes, a[gainst] Legislative tyranny." With the president eligible for reelection, a majority of the delegates agreed that Congress should
no longer hold the power to choose the executive. "A dependence of
the Executive on the Legislature would render it the Executive as well as
the maker of laws," Madison observed. "[T]hen according to the observation of Montesquieu, tyrannical laws may be made that they may be
executed in a tyrannical manner."[29]

Madison joined Wilson in successfully replacing Congress with a vote
by the people. But in so doing he also brought race back to the surface. Because legislative selection would introduce "intrigues and contentions" that
would produce "an improper connection between the two departments,"
Madison concluded that "the people at large" were "as likely as any that
could be devised to produce an Executive Magistrate of distinguished
Character."[30] But popular election created an important "difficulty." The
northern states had granted the right to vote more broadly than the southern states, "and the latter could have no influence in the election on the
score of the Negroes." To maintain the South's advantage under the three-
fifths rule, Madison declared that "the substitution of electors obviated this
difficulty and seemed on the whole to be liable to the fewest objections." By
a 6–3 vote on July 19, 1787, the Convention approved a motion to adopt
the Electoral College system.[31]

Critics believe that this vote revealed a desire to protect slavery and
introduced racism into the Constitution. This conclusion, however, does
not comport with the vote in the Convention. In the July 19 vote adopting
the Electoral College, the states did not vote along slavery lines. William
Paterson, who first proposed the system, was a New Jersey abolitionist. The
Articles of Confederation "had been ashamed to use the term 'Slaves' & had
substituted a description," he told the Convention.[32] Connecticut, Delaware,
Maryland, New Jersey, Pennsylvania, and Virginia approved the elector

system. Georgia, North Carolina, and South Carolina voted against it. The free states voted unanimously for the electoral system, but so did Virginia, the leading slave state. Only three states—all slave—voted against an Electoral College.

Several twists and turns, often overlooked by scholars, followed this vote. Soon after, the Convention reversed course again to restore congressional election of the president,[33] and even reconsidered a single-term limit and a period in office of anywhere from 6 to 20 years. Debate began to roam all over the map, with one delegate proposing a three-person presidency, another suggesting that a subcommittee of Congress pick the president, and yet another giving the choice to state governors.[34]

During these wanderings, Madison again urged the use of electors but without mentioning the consequences for the slave states. He continued his opposition to congressional elections, which he worried could "agitate and divide the legislature," lead to "intrigue" between the president and the congressional majority, or provide an opening for interference from abroad.[35] Madison stressed that electors "would [provide] very little opportunity for cabal, or corruption." If the Convention rejected an electoral college, Madison believed that the only alternative was direct popular election. "With all its imperfections he liked this best." Madison conceded that the northern population would grow faster and eventually outweigh the South, but as a southerner, "he was willing to make the sacrifice."[36]

Madison's defense of popular election did not win any converts. Support instead continued to build for electors because of concern about executive independence. "The two great evils to be avoided are cabal at home, & influence from abroad," Pierce Butler of South Carolina declared. "It will be difficult to avoid either if the Election be made by the Natl Legislature."[37] Furthermore, "the Govt. should not be made so complex & unwieldy as to disgust the States," Butler warned. "This would be the case, if the election shd. be referred to the people."[38] The best way to accommodate state interests was election by electors, he concluded. Morris again attacked "the undue influence of the Legislature." He "considered an election by the people as the best, by the Legislature as the worst, mode." Morris supported electors as a compromise.

When the Committee of Detail reported its draft of the Constitution to the full Convention, the delegates at first debated the congressional process for choosing the president. At the end of their deliberations, on August 31, Morris suddenly moved to strike out the draft's authorization for Congress to choose the president. He prevailed by the extraordinary vote of 9–1. The debates contain no explanation why, but as historian Jack Rakove has argued, "a growing reaction against the Senate worked in favor of the presidency, encouraging those framers who opposed legislative election and favored re-eligibility to renew their efforts."[39] As the delegates realized that the body representing the states would have a veto over most powers of the federal government, the nationalists sought to free the president.

On September 4, a second committee returned a final draft. It contained today's Electoral College, though with the Senate serving as the backup method should no candidate win a majority. The delegates agreed that the final system would grant the president full independence from Congress without disrupting the Great Compromise between large and small states. While conceding that the Electoral College represented a compromise itself, Morris explained that the new system would address "the danger of intrigue & faction if the appt should be made by the Legislature" and "the indispensable necessity of making the Executive independent of the Legislature."[40] The Convention rejected every proposal to restore the choice to the legislature, but also voted 10–1 to give the House the power to choose the president should the Electoral College fail to agree.

When the Constitution went to the states for approval, the issue that had so bedeviled the Philadelphia delegates did not trigger widespread concern. Most Anti-Federalist objections to the presidency focused on its substantive powers or the possibility of collusion between the executive branch and the Senate to seize power. Mason's *Objections to the Constitution*, a leading Anti-Federalist critique, does not even mention the Electoral College. To the extent that they attacked it, Anti-Federalists worried more about the chances for foreign bribery of the electors or the president himself rather than racism or state advantages.[41]

Hamilton responded that democracy remained the guiding principle for the Electoral College. "It was desirable, that the sense of the people should operate in the choice of the person to whom so important a trust was to be confided," he wrote in *Federalist No. 68*. But in order to foster deliberation and access the broadest knowledge, the Constitution placed the choice in the hands of electors who "will be most likely to possess the information and discernment requisite to so complicated an investigation."[42] Mediating the choice through the electors, Hamilton predicted, would also "afford as little opportunity as possible to tumult and disorder."

Hamilton also described the defects of legislative selection. He predicted that "cabal, intrigue, and corruption" would arise if Congress were to choose. Congress would become the seat of such conspiracies, Hamilton observed, and hence the presidency should be made independent of it. The Philadelphia delegates "have not made the appointment of the president to depend on preexisting bodies of men, who might be tampered with beforehand to prostitute their votes," but instead vested the power into a group of electors chosen "for the temporary and sole purpose" of selecting the president. Choice by electors would also support the president's continuing independence from Congress, rather than "sacrifice his duty to his complaisance for those whose favour was necessary" for his continuance in office.[43] The Electoral College advanced the fundamental principle that "the executive should be independent for his continuance in office, on all but the people themselves."

The Federalists, however, failed in their predictions that this system would produce presidents of the highest caliber. "The process of election affords a moral certainty," Hamilton promised, "that the office of president will seldom fall to the lot of any man who is not in an eminent degree endowed with the requisite qualifications."[44] Hamilton's praise for the Constitution here certainly went too far. The Federalists could not clearly explain why the Electoral College would produce "characters preeminent for ability and virtue." They may have relied on the widespread understanding that George Washington would be the first president. They may have further assumed that only the truly outstanding leaders would enjoy the continent-wide reputation to win an Electoral College majority.

But the Framers did not anticipate that the Electoral College would establish a framework that created room for other purposes. It was of a piece with other mechanisms, most notably the Senate and the judiciary, designed to decentralize and diffuse power over domestic issues within the federal government. But others, such as Jefferson, Martin Van Buren, and most especially Woodrow Wilson, would use party government to modify the Framers' design. It is their innovations that have given us a quasi-plebiscitary process in which political parties cooperate to choose a candidate and advance a political platform in presidential elections.

III.

Rather than a racist institution, the Electoral College advanced a more democratic voice in the selection of the president. The Framers reached a compromise in the Electoral College that balanced nationalism with federalism. But unlike the Great Compromise over the makeup of Congress, the nationalists prevailed in centering the selection of the president in popular choice, but mediated through the states. "Thus the essential spirit of the Electoral College, like that of the Constitution in general, was fundamentally democratic from the outset," observed political scientist Martin Diamond.[45]

Criticism that the Framers intentionally designed the Electoral College to "advantage Southern white male propertied slave owners in the antebellum era," as Amar says, seems off the mark. The Founders believed that their unusual system would organize democracy through the states. If we should discard the Electoral College as an obstacle to the majority, critics should explain why the American people should retain the Constitution's other limits on pure majoritarian democracy. The separation of powers, for example, handicaps Washington, D.C.'s ability to govern. Why not replace it with a British-style parliament that controls both the legislative branch and the executive agencies? Federalism further restricts national powers. Why not follow European models and replace the states with administrative districts subordinated to the national government? Judicial review and the Bill of Rights also pose limits on the majority. We could again follow modern Britain and leave the creation and definition of individual liberties to the legislature.

The same charges that critics bring against the Electoral College apply to Congress as well. The claim that the Electoral College rests on racist foundations has force only because the same three-fifths rule that applied to the allocation of House seats applied to the assignment of electoral votes too. But the Civil War and the Reconstruction Amendments ended slavery, the three-fifths rule, and the advantage of the slave states in the Electoral College. A century would pass until a southerner would win the presidency— Lyndon Johnson in 1964. Like the Constitution as a whole, the Electoral College may still protect federalism, but it no longer benefits the former slave states.

If critics dislike the magnified power of the states, they have more to worry about than the Electoral College. The Constitution channels and limits majority rule throughout its basic structure. The Electoral College may have allowed the states to choose Trump despite the small difference in the popular vote. But the states enjoy an even greater advantage in the Senate, where state equality gives the same number of votes to Wyoming as to California. The Framers routed all of Congress's important powers through the Senate and hence gave the states a veto over most major federal policies.[46] Congress cannot pass laws, raise taxes, or spend money without approval by the representatives of the states. The president cannot appoint any judges, cabinet members, or principal government officers or make any treaties without the Senate. The Constitution established these supermajority and nondemocratic procedures to promote more reason and less passion in government, and to rest public policies on a broader consensus in society.[47]

Even the Constitution's most democratic element, the House of Representatives, gives states an advantage. While the number of House seats depends on the population, the Constitution grants them to the states by districts. Only an allocation of seats by national party performance, where a Democratic nationwide victory of 60 percent would receive exactly 261 of the 435 Representatives, would follow majoritarianism perfectly. Otherwise, the diversity of people, interests, and geography will produce uneven results across districts. Imbalances in party performance in different districts, for example, could easily produce legislative majorities that do not reflect the popular will.[48] The Constitution vests the power to draw House districts in the state legislatures, subject to federal regulation, which recognizes state sovereign interests in the House.[49]

Even in Britain's parliamentary system, use of geographic districts has yielded governments that won a majority of the seats without a majority of the population. Such a result is even more likely with more than two political parties. Thanks to Ross Perot's two runs for president, Bill Clinton handily won the Electoral College even though he won only 43 percent of the national vote in 1992 and 49 percent in 1996. Eighty years earlier, the third-party effort by former president Theodore Roosevelt swung the victory to Woodrow Wilson, who ran up 435 of the electors but only 41.8 percent of the popular vote.

A state-based district system provides other benefits. Dispersing the power to choose the president to 50 states, with winner-take-all rules, tends to undermine the formation of large interest groups that can dictate the outcome. Of course, such groups could form, and one might even argue that the two political parties are great "factions." But coordinating their campaigns across the states necessary to win 270 electoral votes presents greater costs and challenges than assembling a popular majority in the largest cities. In close elections, the Electoral College will give minorities an exaggerated influence in comparison to their national size. These tendencies also give the candidates the incentive to bring together a broad, nationwide coalition that can compete in different regions. A direct popular election would instead encourage the candidates to only campaign in the major cities of the east and west coasts. Regional candidates could still prevail, as Lincoln demonstrated in 1860, but many (if not most) who have appealed solely to sectional interests have lost.

Other arguments in favor of the Electoral College, however, do not persuade as once they might have. Some have observed that the system magnifies the political legitimacy of the president, because the winner-take-all rule transforms state pluralities into electoral vote majorities.[50] Bill Clinton might win just 43 percent of the national vote, but his large Electoral College majority gave him a political legitimacy he might have lacked otherwise. It seems unclear, however, whether presidents with large electoral majorities should have a false sense of confidence in their political support, or whether the other branches should grant these chief executives the same political respect they would grant a large popular majority. Presidents elected by pluralities or slim majorities might pursue a course of cooperation with Congress rather than pressing an agenda born out of a false electoral mandate.

Another defense of the Electoral College makes much of certainty. Supporters once claimed that the Constitution's system provided a clear winner by the end of election night, due again to the winner-take-all rule. Once a candidate reached enough states to get to 270 electoral votes, it no longer mattered to get the nationwide popular vote count precisely right. Under a direct popular election, however, a close election might require the exact vote count, which could lead to long delays or open the door to cheating and fraud. Very close elections might place the country in a state of uncertainty that it cannot suffer for very long, given the central role of the president for national security and law enforcement.

The general democratic criticism ultimately asks the wrong question.

Simple majoritarianism is not in itself an end of government; rather, we should ask whether the Electoral College advances other values in our republican system. The Framers originally set out to block factional or regional candidates by creating a system in which only candidates with a continent-wide reputation could succeed. They worried that faction would pose a dire threat to the new government. Structures such as the separation of powers responded to the threat of instability and oppression from simple majority rule.[51] The Electoral College's decentralization would shunt aside candidates who catered to a specific faction or region.

Donald Trump's victory demonstrated not the realization of these hopes, but its failures. Early days had borne out Hamilton's promise in *The Federalist* that our chief executives would be the leading political figures of their day: Washington won the nation's independence; Adams led the political fight for independence; Jefferson drafted the Declaration of Independence; Madison drafted the Constitution and led the fight for its ratification. But the United States has also had its runs of mediocre presidents, especially just before the Civil War and after Reconstruction. The years 1850–61 included Millard Fillmore, Franklin Pierce, and James Buchanan, while 1877–96 had Rutherford Hayes, James Garfield, Chester Arthur, Grover Cleveland, and Benjamin Harrison. Average to poor performance in office, however, may owe more to circumstances than to ability. We see no great presidents in these eras because the nation did not need greatness in its presidents.

Trump's election, however, proved Hamilton wrong in his claim that the Electoral College would weed out poor candidates. Because they had such faith in the people, the Framers attributed such problems to unreflective majority rule unconstrained by "a more perfect structure." The Constitution would prevent the people from making rash decisions by hemming in the legislature with the executive and judicial branches. But the presidency also raised the possibility of demagogues, who could use their powers of persuasion to further mislead the people. Hamilton argued that such figures could not deceive the Electoral College, which represented the great breadth of the nation. "Talents for low intrigue, and the little arts of popularity, may alone suffice to elevate a man to the first honours of a single state," Hamilton wrote in *The Federalist*. "But it will require other talents, and a different kind of merit, to establish him in the esteem and confidence of the whole union, or of so considerable a portion of it, as would be necessary to make him a successful candidate for the distinguished office of President of the United States."[52] Hamilton's words could not have anticipated Donald Trump's public life in more accurate terms.

The Federalist assumed that a demagogue could not successfully appeal to the people in all of the states, separated as they were by the slowness of communication, the differences in political culture, and the lack of knowledge of national affairs. But the Framers could not predict the changes in technology and media that have accelerated the spread of information, the emergence of a common political culture, and the nationalization of politics. They believed that the states would stand athwart populism rather than elevate a populist candidate such as Trump.

The Electoral College's failure to filter out such a candidate, however, does not demonstrate the need for radical change. Political theorists once thought that direct democracy might make demagogues more likely—after all, the word refers to someone who is speaking to the people, the *demos*, for their support. A direct election would make the demagogue's path to power easier, by allowing him to win the presidency by appealing only to the inhabitants of the nation's largest cities. Political practices have also grown up around the Electoral College to increase the legitimacy of the winner. As political scientist James W. Ceaser argues, succeeding generations have built upon the Framers' design to pursue different theories of presidential selection.[53] Jefferson replaced the Framers' original vision with the idea that the presidential election would present a choice between policy programs. Martin Van Buren developed national political parties to present consistent platforms in each state. Woodrow Wilson saw the selection of a president as a plebiscite that would give him the legitimacy to lead sweeping reforms. Wilson's views have prevailed: it was his idea that the people, rather than the parties, should control the nominating process; that the president should draw legitimacy for his agenda from his nationwide selection; and that the political party instead should help the president in enacting his program.[54]

This is not to argue that direct national election of the president would not have the same features. It certainly would, and probably in greater degree than the Electoral College. But the Electoral College system can promote these purposes too. Perhaps the Electoral College does so without running as high a risk of demagogues or of majority oppression as direct popular election. The Electoral College fits in with other aspects of the original constitutional design—the separation of powers, the Senate, and federalism—designed to limit government powers and to render political change difficult.

CONCLUSIONS

Critics claim that Trump's election shows the bias and racism of the Electoral College. They would respond to Trump's 2016 victory by replacing all elements of federalism, including the means of selecting the president. But doing so would make the rise of a future demagogue far more likely. Under pure majority vote, a future populist need only appeal to urban majorities to win the presidency. Our constitutional system relies upon the state structure to dissipate and ultimately defuse rash popular movements. It is no different when it comes to choosing a president. Overreaction to Trump could do far more long-term harm to the Constitution than Trump could ever do.

CHAPTER 2

"THE END OF MY PRESIDENCY": TRUMP AND ENFORCING THE LAW

On May 9, 2017, Donald Trump started a war that almost rendered his presidency stillborn. On that day, he fired FBI director James Comey and sparked a two-year war between the White House and the federal law enforcement and intelligence bureaucracies.

Trump had to fight Comey, the special counsel who followed, their FBI and Justice Department (DOJ) allies, and even the CIA and the NSA. Personal ambition and political self-preservation no doubt drove him to wage all-out constitutional war. But Trump had to prevail in order to preserve the office of the presidency. Article II vests "the executive power" of the United States solely in the president, and it gives him alone the duty to "take care that the laws be faithfully executed." These clauses give the president the right to fire the FBI director, and any other subordinate executive officer, to ensure that they enforce the law consistent with his views. As a reality show persona, Trump made "you're fired" his signature line. In this case, television previewed Trump's greatest power as president. Without an executive power to remove—and the control of law enforcement that it guarantees—Congress could come to dominate the government and transform the separation of powers into a regime resembling European parliaments.

I.

Trump removed an FBI director who believed himself above regular Justice Department procedures and who took the unprecedented step of publicizing—three times—FBI investigations that affected the course of the 2016 presidential elections. Judge Laurence Silberman wrote that Comey's "performance was so inappropriate for an FBI director that [he] doubt[s] the bureau will ever completely recover." Deputy attorneys general for Bush and Clinton observed that Comey had "chosen personally to restrike the balance between transparency and fairness, departing from the department's traditions," and had violated his obligation to "preserve, protect and defend" the Justice Department and the FBI.[1]

Democrats, however, portrayed Comey's removal as a Nixonian effort to interfere with the investigation into Russian meddling in the 2016 elections. Representative Adam Schiff compared Comey's firing "to a similarly tainted decision by President Nixon."[2] Senate Minority Leader Chuck Schumer warned that if the Justice Department (DOJ) did not "appoint an independent special prosecutor, every American will rightly suspect that the decision to fire Director Comey was part of a cover-up."[3]

But firing Comey failed to restore presidential control over DOJ. Instead, the FBI director had laid a trap for the president that escalated the assault on executive power. As a DOJ inspector general report later established, Comey had written memos recording seven one-on-one conversations with Trump between the transition and April 2017.[4] In the most important of those moments, Comey had informed the president-elect of salacious information allegedly held about him by the Russian government, but at the same time told Trump that he was not a target of the investigation. According to Comey, Trump said that he hoped Comey could "see [his] way clear . . . to letting [Michael] Flynn go"—Flynn, the former national security advisor, was under FBI investigation. When Trump fired Comey, the FBI director had a friend leak the memos to a reporter for the *New York Times*. "I thought it might prompt the appointment of a special counsel," Comey told a congressional hearing.[5]

Comey's insurance policy paid off. In response to the firing, acting FBI director Andrew McCabe (himself soon to be removed from office) opened a criminal investigation into Trump for obstruction of justice. Panicked by claims of a cover-up, Deputy Attorney General Rod Rosenstein soon appointed a special counsel.[6] Rosenstein charged Robert Mueller "to investigate Russian interference with the 2016 presidential election and related matters."[7] The raids for evidence, arrests of campaign officials, and plea bargains and trials that followed struck at the very heart of the White

House. When he learned of Mueller's appointment, Trump blurted out, "Oh my God. This is terrible. This is the end of my Presidency."[8]

Mueller's investigation quickly claimed its first high-profile scalp, Flynn, for lying to FBI agents about whether he discussed sanctions with Russia. It soon swept others into its net, such as Paul Manafort, for concealing millions in lobbying for Ukrainians and tax cheating. It caught low-level campaign aide George Papadopoulos for lying to the FBI. It expanded to pursue more sordid matters, such as whether Trump had paid off women to keep silent about affairs.

The probe opened a floodgate of Trumpian tweets swearing innocence, accusing Mueller of partisan bias, and even attacking his own hand-chosen attorney general and deputy attorney general. On the anniversary of Mueller's appointment, Trump declared, "Congratulations America, we are now into the second year of the greatest Witch Hunt in American History . . . and there is still No Collusion and no Obstruction." Information soon came to light of the Justice Department's aggressive investigation into the Trump campaign. As another DOJ IG report would confirm, these extraordinary methods included the use of the "Steele dossier," a file of raw intelligence assembled by political opponents, to justify wiretaps on Trump aides, and even undercover sources to question campaign staff.

Trump's attacks culminated in the president's claim that he had the right to fire the special counsel "directly." His White House resembles a merry-go-round, with three chiefs of staff and four national security advisors in just three years. He seems to delight in firing his own cabinet members, such as the attorney general or Homeland Security secretary. But Trump never took the fateful step of firing the special counsel. According to the Mueller report, White House counsel Donald McGahn refused to do so.[9] Trump had also ordered Corey Lewandowski, his former campaign manager, to fire Attorney General Jeff Sessions.[10] Like McGahn, Lewandowski never carried out Trump's wishes. But Trump still relies on his removal power to control the government like no president before him.

Toying with firing the special counsel raised comparisons with Nixon's efforts to defeat the Watergate investigation more than four decades earlier. In the "Saturday Night Massacre," Nixon fired the attorney general and the deputy attorney general until the number-three DOJ official, Solicitor General Robert Bork, removed special counsel Archibald Cox. Trump would have had to trigger the same series of events to fire Mueller, as Sessions

had recused himself and Rosenstein had declared that he would protect the special counsel. Members of Congress attempted to shield Mueller too. The Senate Judiciary Committee passed a bill to prohibit Mueller's removal except "for cause"—which requires a crime, violation of the law, or abuse of power.[11] "Firing Mueller would cause a firestorm and bring the administration agenda to a halt," Senator Orrin Hatch warned. "It could even result in impeachment."[12] Senator Ben Sasse said it would be "politically suicidal for the president."[13]

While firing Mueller would have been a grave mistake, resurrecting an independent prosecutor would have inflicted a cure worse than the disease. As a special counsel, Mueller held the same formal status as any other prosecutor. Only DOJ regulations granted him the independence and budget to investigate Russian collusion. But Congress wanted to transform Mueller into a different creature, an independent prosecutor—an office created by legislation, rather than the DOJ regulations that establish the special counsel. Rather than the president or the AG, post-Watergate reforms gave the appointment to a special panel of judges. The prosecutor has full independence with a virtually unlimited call upon DOJ budget and personnel. The independent prosecutor cannot be removed except for cause.

Protecting Mueller might have served the short-term political cause of constraining Trump. But allowing Congress to isolate parts of the executive branch from presidential control would wreak long-term damage on the constitutional system. Creating executive officers who operate independently would fragment the executive branch and give Congress power over law enforcement. As Montesquieu observed, combining the power of legislation and executive is "the very definition of tyranny." Protecting executive officers from removal might even create agencies free from any political accountability. Either result would injure the separation of powers, which separates the executive and legislative to make both more effective and responsible.

In considering the removal of the special counsel, Trump may have had self-interest at heart. Or he may have had more worthy goals, such as ending a wasteful investigation. But firing Mueller, like firing Comey, would have reinforced a crucial element of the constitutional structure: presidential control over the executive branch. Democratic willingness to create a new independent prosecutor shows how far they were willing to undermine constitutional principle to harm Trump. By fighting for his right to

fire Mueller and Comey, Trump defended the removal power for all future presidents.

An FBI search of Michael Cohen's offices only continued the controversy over the executive's power of removal. The FBI sought evidence of hush money payments that allegedly violated federal campaign finance laws. In a meeting with military leaders, Trump called the search "disgraceful" and "a total witch hunt."[14] Trump had legitimate grounds for complaint. Critics such as the *New York Times* argued that these transfers constituted an illegal campaign contribution, but they had no precedents in their favor. A federal jury acquitted 2004 vice-presidential candidate John Edwards of a similar charge. It is true that Cohen eventually pled guilty to federal charges of "knowingly and willfully" seeking to evade campaign finance laws for arranging the payments to two women who had accused Trump of extramarital affairs. Federal law imposes limits on "contributions" and "expenditures" to campaigns and defines those as anything "for the purpose of influencing an election." But the law also sensibly recognizes that spending that would have taken place regardless of the campaign cannot count as an expenditure. Otherwise, as former federal elections commissioner Bradley Smith observes, "almost anything a candidate does can be interpreted as intended to influence an election."[15]

With hush money, Stormy Daniels, and Michael Cohen on offer, many might overlook the fundamental constitutional issue at stake: whether the president has the authority to fire any law enforcement officer for any reason. Digging into Trump's personal life, no matter how distasteful, and his efforts to conceal parts of his life, no matter how sordid, have no connection to Russian meddling in the 2016 election. Mueller's most concrete progress came with the convictions of Paul Manafort, the Trump campaign chairman during the convention, and his deputy, Rick Gates. These charges, however, involved Manafort's work for the Ukrainian government and his efforts to hide the proceeds.[16] Manafort's conviction had little to do with Russian efforts to interfere with the 2016 election. Though he pursued a number of detours and efforts to win cooperating witnesses, Mueller found no evidence of a conspiracy between the Trump campaign and the Russian government.

Nevertheless, Mueller's far-ranging investigation directly raises the question of whether the president could fire the special counsel. It is no sheer coincidence that this question arose from the activities of a special counsel appointed because of the president's earlier firing of yet another DOJ official. But this conflict is not one of Trump's own making—its roots stretch back to the Constitution's earliest years. Presidents have long claimed the authority to remove subordinate officials. The constitutional text, however, only grants the power to create offices and the appointment of their occupants. It remains silent on how to remove them.

Nevertheless, Trump could fire Mueller for ignoring the limits on his original mandate. Because the Constitution charges the president with the duty to "take care that the laws are faithfully executed," Trump is the top federal law enforcement officer. If the president disapproves of his subordinates' conduct, he can fire them. Ever since the Founding, all three branches have recognized the president's removal power. As Madison observed in 1789, "Is the power of displacing an executive power? I conceive that if any power whatsoever is in its nature executive, it is the power of appointing, overseeing, and controlling those who execute the laws." In *Myers v. U.S.* (1926), the Supreme Court held that "it was natural, therefore, for those who framed our Constitution to regard the words 'executive power' as including" the power to remove executive officers.[17] Even when the Court upheld the independent prosecutor in *Morrison v. Olson* (1988), it stressed that "there are some 'purely executive' officials who must be removable by the President at will if he is to be able to accomplish his constitutional role."[18]

In his lonely dissent in *Morrison*, Justice Antonin Scalia foresaw that independent prosecutors would become Inspector Javerts who obsessively pursue their targets, waste time and resources, and upset the separation of powers. "Frequently an issue of this sort will come before the Court clad, so to speak, in sheep's clothing," Scalia wrote. "But this wolf comes as a wolf."[19] But led by Chief Justice William Rehnquist, the Court found that the Ethics in Government Act contained enough limits on the prosecutors, such as making them subordinate to the attorney general and removable for misconduct, to justify the independence needed to investigate high-ranking executive branch officials. Limiting removal does not "sufficiently [deprive] the President of control over the independent counsel to interfere impermissibly with his constitutional obligation to ensure the faithful execution of the laws."[20]

The following decade proved Scalia right and Rehnquist wrong. Kenneth Starr's Whitewater probe wasted political resources, focused both branches on scandal rather than policy, and resulted in impeachment by the House but acquittal by the Senate. The Iran-Contra investigation used the criminal law to wage a foreign policy dispute between Reagan and Congress. By 2000, the political parties finally learned Justice Scalia's lesson and let the independent prosecutor law die. In asserting the right to fire Mueller, Trump defended his power and those of his successors to carry out their constitutional responsibilities with officials responsible to them. Without such control, presidents could not exercise the energy and vigor for which the Constitution calls and the public expects.

Trump's approach struck a balance between defending the constitutional order and investigating scandal. Trump hated the probe; anyone under investigation would. He asserted his right to fire Mueller. White House allies questioned Mueller for hiring Democrats to serve on his team and claimed he had conflicts of interest.[21] Trump could have fired Mueller because he knew that he had not conspired with Russia. Or he could have fired Mueller for no reason at all.

But Trump wisely did not fire Mueller. Trump criticized the investigation for its hardball tactics but still did not issue any orders to restrain Mueller. Instead, he ordered all executive officials to cooperate, turned over millions of pages of documents, and declined to invoke attorney-client or executive privilege. Principal White House officers freely recounted their private conversations with Trump. Yes, Flynn pled guilty to lying to investigators about discussing sanctions with the Russian ambassador. George Papadopoulos may have pled guilty to lying to the FBI about meetings he had with suspected intermediaries for Russia. A jury convicted Manafort of evading federal tax and lobbying-disclosure laws. But Mueller uncovered no evidence of a conspiracy with Russia to win the 2016 elections. Whether Trump realized it or not, a prosecutor of Mueller's reputation and integrity could do far more to clear his name than any congressional report or campaign ads. By allowing DOJ to complete the probe without interference, the White House cleared itself of Russian collusion.

II. LAW ENFORCEMENT

This part explains why Trump had the right to fire Comey and Mueller or to end their investigations. Trump's power did not rely on wild tweets or abrupt claims. Instead, it drew upon the constitutional text and structure and two centuries of government practice. The president alone bears the constitutional duty to execute federal law. That responsibility requires presidential control over all federal officers who assist him in carrying out the law. Condemning presidential interference in law enforcement is akin to criticizing justices for interfering in Supreme Court cases. Like presidents before him, Trump's control over DOJ gave him the right to remove any executive officer, including the special counsel or the FBI director.

A. CONSTITUTIONAL TEXT

Presidential control of law enforcement springs directly from the constitutional text. Article II vests the president with "the Executive Power" of the United States. Unlike Article I's vesting of the legislative power in Congress, which is limited to those authorities "herein granted," Article II's Vesting Clause contains no textual limit or definition of the executive power. Article II "does not mean *some of* the executive power, but *all of* the executive power" is vested in the president, as Justice Scalia observed in *Morrison*.[22]

At the time of the Framing, Americans would have understood the executive power to centrally involve enforcement of the law. As Hamilton argued in *Federalist No. 75*, "[t]he execution of the laws and the employment of the common strength either for this purpose or for the common defense, seem to comprise all the functions of the executive magistrate."[23] Article II, Section 3 further underscores the executive's responsibility to enforce the law. It declares that the president "shall take Care that the Laws be faithfully executed." Both the Executive Power and Take Care Clauses restrict and empower the president.[24] While they declare that the president cannot suspend the law of the land, they also give the president authority to enforce the law and to interpret it. Enforcing the law gives the president the right to compel the obedience of private individuals, and even states, to federal law. To carry out the laws, the president must also determine their meaning. Sometimes those laws will be clear, as when the Constitution sets the minimum age for a president, but often the laws are ambiguous or delegate decisions to the executive.

While the Constitution provides for the appointment of subordinates, it places the duty to execute the laws on the president alone. The president cannot execute all the laws himself. Washington could not personally collect customs in both Charleston and Boston. It would be an "impossibility," he wrote in May 1789, "that one man should be able to perform all the great business of the State," which explains the creation of "the great Departments, and appointing officers therein, to assist the supreme Magistrate in discharging the duties of his trust."[25] As the Supreme Court recognized in *Myers*, Article II "grants to the President the executive power of the government—i.e., the general administrative control of those executing the laws, including the power of appointment and removal of executive officers."[26]

Scholars argue that the Take Care Clause's reference to "the laws" requires the president to obey congressional directives, including their decisions on agency structure. The president, however, has no duty to enforce statutory law or treaty provisions that he reasonably and in good faith considers to be unconstitutional.[27] As the Supreme Court recognized in *Marbury v. Madison*, all government officers obey the Constitution first, and then only those laws that are consistent with it.[28] The president can also execute federal law according to his interpretation of ambiguous terms, set enforcement priorities to husband limited resources, and command inferior officers to follow his policies.

Critics of presidential power respond that the White House cannot investigate itself. Presidents, however, have long directed law enforcement and prosecution, and they and their cabinets have also fallen subject to criminal investigations. In 1875, President Ulysses S. Grant appointed a special counsel to investigate the so-called Whiskey Ring, in which distillers bribed federal Treasury officials to evade liquor taxes. The trail led to Grant's own private secretary, whom Grant tried to protect by firing the special counsel. In 1924, President Calvin Coolidge appointed special counsels to prosecute the Teapot Dome scandal, in which a cabinet secretary had accepted bribes in exchange for favorable leases of public lands. When claims arose that Richard Nixon's reelection campaign had broken into the Democratic Party headquarters in the Watergate Hotel, DOJ launched a special counsel investigation. After surviving the firing of the first counsel, the investigation brought the resignation of the president and the conviction of his closest advisors.

After Watergate, Congress sought to contain the executive with extraordinary mechanisms to prevent such meddling. Jimmy Carter even proposed an independent DOJ with an attorney general protected from firing.[29] Once in office, Carter realized that freeing DOJ from control by the elected branches would violate the Constitution, if not make for bad policy. In 1978, Congress established an independent prosecutor to investigate claims of lawbreaking by cabinet-level officers.[30] The Ethics in Government Act required the attorney general to request an independent counsel upon credible allegations of violations of federal law, but vested the counsel's appointment in the federal appellate court in Washington, D.C., and prevented his or her removal except for cause. It launched the probes that came close to sinking the Reagan and Clinton presidencies.

Supporters of the independent prosecutor have challenged the idea that the president can and should control all federal law enforcement. In *Morrison v. Olson*, all of the justices agreed that prosecution remained fundamentally an executive power. "There is no real dispute that functions performed by the independent counsel are 'executive' in the sense that they are law enforcement functions that typically have been undertaken by officials within the Executive Branch," Chief Justice Rehnquist wrote.[31] Congress could still shield the independent prosecutor from direct removal because the president could supervise the counsel to ensure obedience to the law and DOJ policy. "We simply do not see how the President's need to control the exercise of [the counsel's] discretion is so central to the functioning of the Executive Branch as to require as a matter of constitutional law that the counsel be terminable at will by the President," Rehnquist found.[32] Nor did the independent counsel disrupt the separation of powers. Congress had not sought to transfer authority from the executive to the legislature. Instead, Congress was advancing an important public purpose: to solve the conflict of interest when the executive branch investigated itself.

Most liberal scholars praise *Morrison*. Some even claim that prosecution is not a core executive function.[33] They argue that the Constitution's vesting of "the executive power" in the president serves only ornamental purposes, and that Congress can control enforcement through its creation of federal agencies under the Necessary and Proper Clause.[34] Lawrence Lessig and Cass Sunstein, for example, maintain that the Vesting Clause only establishes that the chief executive is a single person whose formal title is the president.[35] Liberal scholars argue that the Constitution only grants the president the explicit authorities listed in the rest of Article II: commander in chief, the Take Care Clause, and the pardon. Most other significant executive powers require the president to share power with Congress or the Senate: the qualified veto over legislation, the appointment of executive officers, and the treaty power. Without Article II's listing of these authorities, these scholars argue, the president would have no other inherent executive power. By contrast, Article I's broad Necessary and Proper Clause gives Congress the right to "determine the means for specifying *how* powers—and again, *all powers*—in the federal government are to be exercised."[36] If these scholars are correct, then Congress could well insulate a special counsel from the control of the attorney general or the president, as many have proposed with the Mueller investigation.

This theory, however, misreads the constitutional text. The Vesting Clause grants the president all the executive power available to the federal government in the Constitution.[37] Article II's subsequent clauses only narrowly condition or divide aspects of that general executive power. Hamilton made this argument in defense of President Washington's right to issue the 1793 Neutrality Proclamation. Article II's enumeration of powers was intended "to specify and regulate the principal articles implied in the definition of Executive Power; leaving the rest to flow from the general grant," he wrote. "The general doctrine then of our constitution is, that the *Executive Power* of the Nation is vested in the President," he concluded, "subject only to the *exceptions and qualifications* which are expressed in the instrument."[38]

Following Hamilton, we first ask whether the understanding at the time of the founding would classify a function as executive, legislative, or judicial. If executive, Article II's Vesting Clause grants it to the president, unless the Constitution elsewhere modifies it. Consider the treaty power. Under eighteenth-century British constitutional practice, the Crown exercised the exclusive power to make treaties and conduct foreign affairs. Article II, Section 1 would vest the treaty power in the president, but Section 2 subsequently carves out the advice and consent power for the Senate. The president still retains everything not explicitly given away, such as the right to negotiate and complete treaties.[39] A similar structure governs appointments. In the eighteenth century, the British Crown enjoyed the exclusive right to judges and executive officers. Article II's default rule gives this authority to the president too, subject to the narrow exception of Senate advice and consent.

Hamilton's approach supports the president's exclusive control of law enforcement. Prosecution rests within the core of the executive power; Article II's Vesting Clause grants it fully to the president. No other constitutional clause dilutes that power. Congress's legislative powers "herein granted" do not explicitly include any role in enforcing the law. Only the Take Care Clause addresses enforcement; it rejects any inference that the president might have a right to suspend legislative acts.[40] While subordinate government officials may assist the president in the execution of this duty, they do not have any independent constitutional authority. The only figure given the constitutional authority to exercise the executive power is the president.

Reversing appointments—the power to fire—plays a vital role in the operation of executive power. While the Constitution grants the power to enforce the law to the president, it does not address his or her right to command subordinate officers. Suppose the president believes the public interest is best served by reducing the enforcement of minor drug possession. He believes those resources will produce better results for the prosecution of financial crimes. But he cannot fulfill his constitutional duty to enforce the law unless the attorney general, the director of the FBI, and other inferior officers follow his orders. If those officials refuse to follow the new policy, the only way that the president can compel compliance is through removal.

Critics of presidential power argue that Congress can set the standard for removal when it creates an office in the first place. Granting Congress such discretion, however, would significantly upset the separation of powers. Congress could prevent the firing of all cabinet officers except for cause, which would make them independent of presidential control. Executive branch officers would look more to Congress for accountability, and our government would begin to resemble a parliamentary system.

Article II's Vesting Clause answers this problem. If the executive power includes the power to appoint and to remove executive officers, then the Vesting Clause grants that power to the president. While the Appointments Clause makes an exception to the process of naming someone to office, it does not address the process of firing. Therefore, the removal power still resides in the presidency, and congressional efforts to transfer or restrict it violate the Constitution. The Framers would more easily recognize Trump's right to fire in their constitutional text than the strained proposals for independent prosecutors and decentralized agencies.

B. CONSTITUTIONAL STRUCTURE

Even if the Executive Vesting and Take Care Clauses did not exist, placing prosecution in the executive branch would best fit with the constitutional structure. Our Constitution injects elements of checks and balances into a deeper structure of separation of powers. In this system, the three branches can use their unique authorities to contest for primacy or to forge a consensus. Depriving the executive of its central power over law enforcement would throw this system out of joint.

The Constitution structures each branch differently. Article I grants Congress only legislative powers, which it carefully enumerates to prevent the implication of any broader authorities. It divides the legislative power between two houses, which must concur before Congress can enact any laws. Congress cannot regulate the other branches or private citizens other than by a law that survives bicameralism (approval by both houses) and presentment (presidential signature). As the Supreme Court ruled in *Immigration and Nationalization Service v. Chadha*, Congress cannot give a single house of Congress, or a committee, the power to reverse presidential execution of a law, in that case the attorney general's choice not to deport an alien. "The bicameral requirement, the Presentment Clauses, the President's veto, and Congress's power to override a veto were intended to erect enduring checks on each Branch," the Court found, "and to protect the people from the improvident exercise of power by mandating certain prescribed steps."[41]

The Framers gave Congress this structure because of the nature of legislation. As the Court observed in *Chadha*, statutes have "the purpose and effect of altering the legal rights, duties, and relations of persons" outside the legislature and in the greater society. Because of the general nature of the laws, Congress can better gather information, discuss, and reach consensus through a large, multi-member body. Madison defended the dual-house structure of the Constitution because it would deliberate slowly and act only after the public welfare became clear.

By contrast, the Constitution concentrates the executive power in the president to take advantage of the decisiveness of a single person. Constitutions have always faced the challenge of creating an executive strong enough to promote the common good, but not so strong as to risk despotism. Our Constitution errs on the side of executive energy. During the ratification, Hamilton famously declared that "energy in the executive is a leading character in the definition of good government."[42] Most obviously, the Constitution centralizes leadership of the executive branch in a single official, the president. "Unity" in office would bring "[d]ecision, activity, secrecy, and dispatch," Hamilton wrote.[43] In the Pennsylvania ratifying convention, Wilson observed that "we well know what numerous executives are. We know there is neither vigor, decision, nor responsibility in them."[44] The Constitution placed executive power in a "single magistrate" so as to bring "strength, vigor, energy, and responsibility."[45]

No advisory council dilutes the president's authority or responsibility. To diffuse executive power among multiple parties or to require the approval of a council of state would endanger virtues needed for good government. A plural executive would "conceal faults and destroy responsibility," Hamilton observed, allowing the blame for failure to shift elsewhere. A "cabal" within a council would "enervate the whole system of administration" and produce "habitual feebleness and dilatoriness." Under a republican government, the buck should stop with the chief executive, who is not hampered by divided responsibility or free to deflect blame onto a committee. "A council to a magistrate, who is himself responsible for what he does, are generally nothing better than a clog upon his good intentions, are often the instruments and accomplices of his bad and are almost always a cloak to his faults."[46]

A second pillar of executive power is duration in office. In all but two of the revolutionary states, executives were chosen annually. "Where annual elections end, tyranny begins," went the revolutionary slogan. Most states placed term limits on their executives to prevent "the danger of establishing an inconvenient aristocracy," in the words of the Pennsylvania constitution. The Constitution rejected term limits because short terms contributed to instability, leading to rule by the whim of the majority. In *Federalist No. 71*, Hamilton explained that a longer term would promote stability as well as "the personal firmness of the executive magistrate, in the employment of his constitutional powers."[47] A longer term with the opportunity for reelection gave a president the time to "plan and undertake the most extensive and arduous enterprises for the public benefit." If his term were too short, popular opinion would sit foremost in the president's mind, and short-term political gain and hopes for reelection would come before the public interest. Longer terms create fewer shifts in policy, as new presidents take office less often. A "change in men" would create "a mutability of measures." The two-term tradition started with Washington but only entered the constitutional text after Franklin Roosevelt's unprecedented four victories. For the Federalists, the prospect of reelection would encourage the chief executive to pursue policies in the broader public interest.

A third structural pillar was "adequate provision for its support." Here, the Framers meant support in the sense of salary, which Congress could not reduce during a president's term. The Framers wanted a president independent of Congress and the courts but accountable to the people. "The Legislature," Hamilton warned, "with a discretionary power over the salary and emoluments of the Chief Magistrate, could render him as obsequious to their will, as they might think proper to make him."[48] Independence from Congress's power of the purse reinforced the structural freedom created by shifting the selection of the chief executive from the legislature to the Electoral College. The Constitution gives the president the incentive to compete with Congress for popular approval, rather than set him in a subordinate position to the legislature.

The fourth pillar of the presidency was "competent powers." In *Federalist No. 72*, Hamilton observed that the "administration of government" falls "peculiarly within the province of the executive department." Chief among the president's enumerated powers was law enforcement. "The execution of the laws and the employment of the common strength, either for this purpose or for the common defense, seem to comprise all the functions of the executive magistrate,"[49] Hamilton observed. As we will see in later chapters, Hamilton's competent powers include control over war and peace, foreign affairs, executive personnel, and regulation-making, as well as law enforcement.

Rather than guarding against an imperial executive, the constitutional structure treats the legislature as the main threat to liberty. Congress has the power of the purse and the right to subject private citizens to public rules of conduct. Hamilton regarded the gravest threat to the separation of powers to be the "legislature's propensity to intrude upon the rights and to absorb the powers of the other departments."[50] Skeptical of "a mere parchment delineation of the boundaries," Federalists believed instead that each branch needed "constitutional arms for its own defence." For the executive, that weapon is the veto. Today, presidents often veto bills on policy grounds, needing the support of only 34 senators to prevail. Constitutional objections are left to the courts. This reverses the Framers' expectations. In

Federalist No. 73, Hamilton explained that the veto would allow the president to deflect "an immediate attack upon the constitutional rights of the executive." Blocking an act of Congress would have been regarded at the time as aggressive for courts, but not presidents. Between 1789 and 1861, presidents vetoed roughly two dozen bills for constitutional reasons; the Supreme Court struck down only two.[51] Jefferson even doubted whether he could veto a law for anything but constitutional reasons. Under this view, if a bill only made bad policy, a president had no choice but to sign it. Hamilton thought a president could veto on both grounds. The veto would not just serve as a "shield to the executive" but would "furnish[] an additional security against the enaction of improper laws." For him, the president could veto laws because they were too partisan, too hasty, or "unfriendly to the public good."[52]

Indeed, the constitutional structure implies that the president could use his power to enforce the laws to check Congress. Some have argued that the Take Care Clause requires a president to carry out a law faithfully, even if he believes it to be unconstitutional.[53] Textually, however, this argument ignores the fact that the Constitution is the highest law of the land. The obligation to faithfully execute the laws requires the president to obey the Constitution first above any statute to the contrary.[54] To require the president to carry out unconstitutional laws would defeat the larger purpose behind the veto. James Wilson anticipated that the president, like the courts, might have to restrain unconstitutional Acts of Congress: "[T]he legislature may be restrained and kept within its prescribed bounds by the interposition of the judicial department. In the same manner the President of the United States could shield himself and refuse to carry into effect an act that violates the Constitution."[55]

Another aspect of the Take Care Clause is the prosecutorial discretion to enforce some laws more vigorously than others. Presidents may decide to devote few investigatory resources to laws with which they disagree while transferring more to priorities on their agenda. The pardon power enhances this discretion. A pardon is not subject to review by any other branch; President Jefferson used the pardon to free persons convicted of violating criminal laws that he regarded as unconstitutional. The pardon power was reinstated after several state constitutions had removed it from the executive during the revolutionary period. However, as Hamilton predicted and President Gerald Ford's pardon of President Nixon proved, the main check on abuse is public opinion.[56]

The Supreme Court has long accepted the logic of this constitutional text and structure. In finding that Congress could not insulate post office officials from removal by the president, Chief Justice William Howard Taft explicitly linked the removal power to the president's broader responsibility to enforce the law. "Made responsible under the Constitution for the effective enforcement of the law, the President needs as an indispensable aid to meet it the disciplinary influence upon those who act under him of a reserve power of removal," he wrote in *Myers*. Taft rejected the argument that cabinet officers and those below had a higher duty to follow statutory law that superseded presidential orders.[57] The national government would fail unless the president could call upon cabinet officers and assistants to aid in the performance of his office. "The discretion to be exercised is that of the President in determining the national public interest and in directing the action to be taken by his executive subordinates to protect it. In this field his cabinet officers must do his will." If, however, the president "loses confidence in the intelligence, ability, judgment, or loyalty of any one of them, he must have the power to remove him without delay."[58]

The Supreme Court has answered the question of the "commandeering" of state officials with similar principles. In *Printz v. United States*, the justices examined a law that authorized state officers, rather than federal officials, to conduct record checks on the purchase of handguns.[59] The Supreme Court struck down the law primarily on federalism grounds because the Constitution forbids the federal government from commandeering state officials to carry out federal laws. But in a secondary holding, the Court also observed that allowing Congress to transfer law enforcement responsibilities to state officials violated the separation of powers. The law violated the Constitution, Justice Scalia concluded, because it "left [to state law enforcement] to implement the program without meaningful Presidential control (if indeed meaningful Presidential control is possible without the power to appoint and remove)."[60]

Congress has no authority to enforce the laws. Article I makes clear that the legislature's primary duty is to make laws instead. It details the procedures for elections and passage of bills, and it sets out the subjects over which Congress can legislate. In contrast to the Articles of Confederation,

Congress can regulate individuals directly without relying upon the cooperation of the states.[61] Reasonable observers at the time of the ratification
would not have thought of the Constitution as merging executive authorities into the legislature. Instead, the Constitution's reform came in giving
Congress, for the first time, its own spending and taxing ability and the
power to directly regulate citizens.

To be sure, the Constitution does not enforce a complete separation of
powers in which each branch exercises only its own inherent functions.
It also imposes some checks and balances before the federal government
can exercise certain powers. The Constitution dilutes the unitary nature
of the executive branch when it requires the consent of the Senate in treatymaking and appointments. But this compromise does not transfer appointments to Congress. Instead, the Constitution grants those powers
in Article II, with the rest of the executive power, and then specifically
includes the Senate. When the Constitution includes Congress in the exercise of an executive power, it clearly says so. Allowing Congress to have
a hand in the enforcement of the laws would run against the Constitution's
structural limits on the legislature.

C. CONSTITUTIONAL HISTORY

This reading of Article II, sometimes referred to as the "unitary executive
theory," finds significant support from history. The Framers well understood
that public executives should control law enforcement; in fact, they often
defined the executive power as the power to execute the law. They would
have formed this understanding from the seventeenth- and eighteenth-
century political philosophers who created the background to the Framing
period. To them, the essence of the executive power was to act quickly,
decisively, and with energy in response to unforeseen events or serious
dangers to the nation's security.

Machiavelli, who first liberated theories of government from natural law,
religion, and social class, identified decisiveness as the reason to vest law
enforcement in the executive. Princes were "quick" to execute the law and
could act "at a stroke," unlike fractious legislatures.[62] Acting "uno solo," the
successful executive's ambition will either cause him to pursue the common good or provide accountability to the public for his failures.

Political thinkers followed by seeking to accommodate the executive
within a formal constitutional order. John Locke divided the executive and

legislative power and argued that a constitution should vest them in different institutions. While legislatures possessed the "Supream Power" to set the rules of private conduct, society requires "a Power always in being, which should see to the Execution of the Laws."[63] Legislatures could not constantly stay in session to attend to execution. Laws "need a perpetual Execution or an attendance thereunto," he wrote. Dividing the power to make laws from executing them, Locke argued, was necessary to prevent government officials from benefiting themselves—they would otherwise be able to "suit the Law, both in its making and execution, to their own private advantage." Unanticipated threats and emergencies demanded the talents of the executive, because legislatures could not sit continuously, anticipate every contingency, or take immediate action. "Many things there are which the law can by no means provide for," Locke wrote. "Those must necessarily be left to the discretion of him that has the executive power in his hands."

Montesquieu expanded on Locke. As one of the most influential thinkers in the American colonies, he famously declared in his *Spirit of the Laws*: "[W]hen the legislative and executive powers are united in the same person, or in the same body of magistrates, there can be no liberty."[64] Montesquieu defined the legislative power as control over domestic policy, taxing and spending, and private rules of conduct. "The executive power of the state," according to Montesquieu, is the power by which the magistrate "punishes criminals." Thus, the prince "is established for the execution of the laws," and he "prosecutes" those who violate the laws. Following Locke, he viewed the executive power as enforcing the laws and conducting foreign relations. Apart from inventing the independent judiciary, Montesquieu did not fundamentally alter Locke's approach. But the French philosopher placed more emphasis on the idea that maintaining a sharp separation of the powers would protect individual liberty.[65]

William Blackstone transformed these theories into something resembling constitutional law. Widely read in the colonies, Blackstone retained Locke and Montesquieu's distinction between lawmaking and execution. The "making of the laws is entirely the work of a distinct part, the legislative branch, of the sovereign power."[66] He defined the executive's primary job as prosecution of the laws, and he praised the British constitution's concentration of executive authority in a "sole magistrate of the nation" because it produced "unanimity, strength, and dispatch."[67] Blackstone criticized the idea of dispersing the executive power. "Were it placed in many hands, it would be subject to many wills: many wills, if disunited and drawing different ways, create weakness in government." For that reason, the British constitution made the king of England "not only the chief, but properly the sole magistrate of the nation; all others acting by commission from, and in due subordination to him."

Early practice confirms that the Framers understood the executive branch to control law enforcement. During the colonial period, governors regularly began and ended prosecutions and directed attorneys general on their conduct.[68] Upon revolution, the newly independent states rejected the British Crown by dividing the executive power between councils and governors selected by the legislature. But they still kept the power to enforce the law within their executive branches.[69] Even at the height of hostility toward the executive, the revolutionaries did not give legislatures a direct hand in law enforcement. Rather, they sought to make the governors institutionally dependent on the legislature, as recommended by John Adams.[70]

Those who drafted and adopted the new Constitution held the same understanding. Delegates to the federal and state conventions commonly referred to law enforcement as one of the executive's core powers. The Virginia Plan established that "besides a general authority to execute the National laws," the executive "ought to enjoy the Executive rights vested in Congress by the Confederation."[71] The New Jersey Plan also recognized that the executive would enjoy a "general authority to execute the federal acts."[72] While Wilson initially rejected the British king as a model for the United States, he began debate in the Constitutional Convention with the remark that "the only powers he conceived strictly Executive were those of executing the laws, and appointing officers."[73] He supported vesting the executive power in a single person to ensure "the most energy, dispatch, and responsibility" in carrying out these duties. Madison agreed that "certain powers were in their nature Executive"; he proposed that the national executive should have the "power to carry into effect the national laws."[74] As Sai Prakash has shown, the Convention generally approved vesting the executive power and the duty to execute the laws in a single person through the Vesting and Take Care Clauses that we have today.[75]

Leading nationalists at the Convention were more concerned about containing Congress than restraining the president. "Experience had proved a tendency in our governments to throw all power into the legislative vortex," Madison declared. "The Executives of the States are in general little more than cyphers; the legislatures omnipotent."[76] Madison argued that the president must remain independent of Congress, or Congress would become "the Executor as well as the maker of laws; & then according to the observation of Montesquieu, tyrannical laws may be made that they may be executed in a tyrannical manner."[77] The delegates gave the presidency a unitary structure, with separate election and financial support, precisely so the president could enforce the laws independently of Congress.

The Constitution's ratification confirms this understanding. Anti-Federalists attacked the Constitution for blending the three powers of government, such as the president's veto power over legislation or the Senate's role in appointments and treaties. Federalists defended their handiwork by emphasizing the clear separation between the making and enforcing of laws. Should Congress seek to concentrate power in its hands, Madison argued in *Federalist No. 44*, "the success of the usurpation will depend on the executive and judiciary departments, which are to expound and give effect to the legislative acts."[78] Even though "representatives or senators could make corrupt laws," Federalist William Davie said in North Carolina, "they can neither execute them themselves, nor appoint the executive."[79] Hamilton repeated this view in *Federalist No. 70*, where he famously defended "energy in the executive" because "it is essential to the protection of the community against foreign attacks; it is not less essential to the steady administration of the laws."[80] Hamilton further observed that "the execution of the laws and the employment of the common strength, either for this purpose or for the common defense, seem to comprise all the functions of the executive magistrate."[81] Neither Federalists nor Anti-Federalists believed that the responsibility to enforce the laws should rest anywhere other than with the president.

Washington set the precedents that would govern the executive branch ever after. He rejected any notions that Congress would share in administration or that cabinet members, as in a parliamentary system, would enjoy significant independence. Instead, Washington immediately modeled the executive branch along the lines of his military command. He would bear the ultimate responsibilities for all important decisions. Cabinet secretaries would counsel the president, assist him in the execution of his duties, and supervise the inferior officers. Throughout his two terms in office, Washington made clear that all important decisions were his to make and that executive officials served as assistants rather than independent power centers.[82]

Removal was critical to Washington's vision of a hierarchical, unified executive branch. In the Decision of 1789, Congress rejected proposals to require legislative consent to the removal of cabinet officers. When Congress enacted legislation creating the first great departments of government—War, Foreign Affairs, and Treasury—some members argued that they could include a provision on removal of officers. Madison responded by defending the president's prerogative. "Now if the heads of the executive department are subjected to removal by the President alone, we have security for the good behavior of the officer," Madison argued. "If he does not conform to the judgment of the President in doing the executive duties of his office, he can be displaced." Madison concluded: "[T]his makes him responsible to the great executive power, and makes the President responsible to the public."[83] After much debate and several close votes, Congress rejected proposals to limit the president's removal power and thereby established its own interpretation of the Constitution.

This history supports Trump's authority over law enforcement and executive personnel. The Founders understood that they were creating a powerful executive. Although they had rebelled against King George III, they soon understood that the weak national and state executives of the revolutionary period led to oppression, anarchy, and ineffectiveness. The Constitution recognizes not only the return of traditional executive powers to the president but also his personal control of the executive branch. It concentrates all of the executive power in one person: the president. All other officials are subordinates who exist only to assist the president in carrying out his constitutional responsibilities. As the Supreme Court declared in *Myers*, "it was natural, therefore, for those who framed our Constitution to regard the words 'executive power' as including" the power to remove executive officers. A president, therefore, has the right to direct all executive agency officials on the performance of their duties and, if they refuse, to remove them from office.

III.

This spartan approach to the separation of powers made clear who would win any fight between Trump and Mueller. The Constitution makes the president head of the executive branch. No special counsel, prosecutor, or even cabinet member can operate independent of the president's oversight. If subordinate executive officers refuse to follow presidential policy, they are preventing him from carrying out his duty to execute the law. If they refuse to obey the president, no matter what a statute or regulation may say, President Trump may fire them immediately. Whether such a move is politically wise, the Constitution cannot say.

Critics, however, believe the greater threat to the constitutional order still comes from a powerful president. White House control over law enforcement could create opportunities for corruption. It could allow a president to cover up the abuse of power or even the criminal acts of executive officials. After Watergate, Congress displayed a lack of faith in the normal constitutional checks and balances by introducing an independent prosecutor. Leading liberal scholars defended this disruption of the executive branch on the ground that the Constitution did not create a unitary executive.[84] They argued that Congress not only could pass the laws but also design the agencies that are to administer them—they theorized that the president may have the executive power, but he does not control the power of "administration."[85] Others claimed that the Constitution creates only a loose system of checks and balances that gives Congress room to create new institutional designs to govern the administrative state and limit the growth of the presidency.

These arguments contain two flaws. First, they do not comport with the Framers' original understanding of the Constitution. During the ratification, delegates did not distinguish between a power to enforce the laws and a power of administration. Instead, they referred simply to the execution of the laws. No Framer appears to have thought that this responsibility should rest anywhere but in the executive branch. They had experienced state constitutions with subservient governors, executive boards, and dominant legislatures. Rejecting these experiments, the Framers restored the marriage of a unitary executive branch with traditional executive powers over law enforcement and national security. As we have seen, the first Congress gave the president ultimate control over the first cabinet agencies. While the Framers might have permitted a variety of agency designs, they would not have understood law enforcement to rest outside presidential control.

Second, these critics discount the Constitution's existing restraints on executive power. Defenders of the special counsel worry that the White

House will abuse its power to protect a president and his or her allies. In their minds, transferring prosecutorial power beyond the president's control is the only remedy. As formidable as the presidency has become, however, the Constitution already establishes several mechanisms to limit executive power. It creates a single executive elected by the people; gives Congress control over the size, organization, and authorities of the executive branch; and, ultimately, vests solely in Congress the power of the purse. The Framers created a single chief executive because, as Alexander Hamilton argued, a triumvirate or executive council would "tend to conceal faults and destroy responsibility."

The Framers expected that presidential electors could humble a corrupt president by denying him reelection. This constraint weakened when the American people amended the Constitution to limit presidents to two terms; presidents have much less to lose during their second and final term. A modern substitute—public opinion—may prove equal to the task. As Lincoln observed, "Public sentiment is everything. With it, nothing can fail; against it, nothing can succeed."[86] Trump could ease policy toward Russia or repeal environmental regulations wholesale, but public opinion would deter him from taking unpopular steps.

Congress can always check the president. Only Congress can create and fund executive agencies. Only Congress can enact the laws that authorize prosecutions, investigations, and regulations. Trump cannot appoint judges, confirm executive officers, or make treaties on his own. The funding power creates a perfect check on executive authority. Not only can Congress defund specific programs or offices, it can put the president on the defensive simply by doing nothing. If Congress believes that Trump is abusing his powers, it can simply sit by and not pass any funding bills. Impeachment is the capstone of these constraints. Even though it requires two-thirds of senators to convict, the mere threat of removal will influence presidents. Impeachment may well cause a president to moderate his policies, as he needs to maintain the support of a majority in the House and at least one-third of the Senate to prevent removal.

Rather than accept anomalous structures, the Trump White House has sought to return—intentionally or not—to the original version of the separation of powers. Just as the Constitution requires that the president control the executive branch, it also recognizes that each branch operates independently in the performance of its unique constitutional roles. Neither the president nor Congress can dictate to the judiciary how to decide cases or controversies. Neither the president nor the Supreme Court can seize from Congress the power of legislation. As Hamilton argued, when the Constitution creates exceptions to the tripartite system of government, it does so explicitly. Otherwise, the president exercises the executive power alone.

Progressives have long criticized this formalist approach. They believe the separation of powers allows new forms of government to handle a society and economy unforeseeable in 1789. They praise the structure of agencies such as the Federal Reserve Bank, which seeks to shield interest rates from political interference by making the board independent, or the Securities and Exchange Commission, whose members are also independent. The New Deal and the Great Society created hundreds of alphabet agencies, ranging from the Federal Communications Commission to the National Labor Relations Board, which regulate the economy and society without having to obey the president or observe the Constitution's process for enacting laws.

But the Trump White House may have sparked a counterrevolution to this free-and-easy attitude toward the separation of powers. It has sought to fight the notion of independent law enforcement. It has launched a second front to restore the separation of powers with its focus on judicial nominations. Trump's justices, Neil Gorsuch and Brett Kavanaugh, may provide enough votes on the Supreme Court to overturn deviations from the Framers' design. The separation of powers is far more than an obsolete theory of government or a protection against tyrannical executives. Its most fundamental and important purpose is often overlooked. As Justice Scalia loved to say, "every tinhorn dictator" has a beautiful bill of rights, but it's the separation of powers that protects liberty.

The original Constitution included very few individual rights, but not because the Founders did not seek to protect liberty. Far from it. Rather, they understood that tyranny spreads when power is concentrated, and that freedom flourishes when power is diffused. If the executive subsumes the judicial power, for instance, courts cannot protect individual liberty against executive incursions. If any single branch can make, enforce, and interpret the law, the temptation might become too great to wield the powers of a philosopher king. Only by pitting ambition against ambition, branch against branch, and giving them their own spheres of power did the Framers hope to preserve liberty. Thus, power is parsed out: the president (and his subordinates) exercises the executive power, Congress exercises the legislative power, and the Supreme Court and "inferior" federal courts exercise the judicial power. Each branch can use its own powers to try to frustrate the designs of the others.

There are reasons why we have wandered from the protective barrier of the separation of powers. The Supreme Court's unwillingness to challenge the president and Congress's collusion in creating the administrative state is one. The political incentives of the elected branches are another. Congress often passes legislation without determining its constitutionality, instead leaving it up to the courts to decide. The president signs bills that he doubts are constitutional, content instead to outsource his constitutional judgment to the judiciary. And the judiciary will sometimes (though not often) bend over backward to defer to the work of the bureaucracy.

The separation of powers does not just seek to limit government for its own sake. It has the broader goal to protect religious liberty, free speech, due process, and every other constitutional liberty. By design, the Constitution pits the president against Congress for control of law enforcement—we see that fight in the twenty-first century in Trump's struggle for control over the special counsel investigation. A modern president cannot fulfill his duty to execute the laws without control over the bureaucracy, which he can only exercise through the removal power and the Take Care Clause. By fighting to preserve presidential control over the executive branch, Trump—whether consciously or not—advances the separation of powers and its benefits for liberty.

CHAPTER 3

"I NEED LOYALTY!": TRUMP AND THE REVOLT OF THE BUREAUCRACY

I n fall 2019, Trump faced the most direct challenge to his control over the executive branch. Members of the Foreign Service and the National Security Council (NSC) testified in public hearings that Trump had made a phone call to the Ukrainian president that justified impeachment. According to these career staff, Trump had dangled the prospect of a White House visit, and later a resumption of foreign aid, in exchange for a Ukrainian investigation into Joe Biden and his son, Hunter. House Democrats, led by Intelligence Committee chair Adam Schiff and Judiciary Committee chair Jerry Nadler, argued that this "quid pro quo" amounted to "treason, bribery or other high crimes and misdemeanors."[1]

While we will examine impeachment in chapter 9, the revolt of the Foreign Service illustrates the battle for control at the heart of the Trump presidency. Armed with "the executive power" and the sole right to enforce federal law, Trump has the formal constitutional authority to execute policy and direct those who assist him. But the Ukraine impeachment controversy unveiled a "resistance" built into the very fabric of the government. The bureaucracy refused to take direction from a president who held a far less favorable view of Ukraine than that of the national security establishment. The civil service went to Congress when it believed that Trump had made an inappropriate request of the leader of a modest nation, though one that had become a battleground between Russia and NATO. Career diplomats believed that their views should prevail over those of a president whose policies struck them as irrational, ill-considered, and dangerously self-interested.

The revolt of the diplomats represented the final round of a longer struggle between President Trump and the permanent government. Even before Trump had entered office, the FBI and the Obama Justice Department launched counterintelligence operations against members of his campaign staff. "The Obama administration, abetted by Washington's politically progressive order, exploited its control of law-enforcement and intelligence agencies to help Clinton and undermine Trump," former federal prosecutor and *National Review* columnist Andrew McCarthy charges in *Ball of Collusion*.[2] Even after Trump won the November election, leaders of the law enforcement and national security agencies continued their hostility toward Trump. The bureaucracy not only sought to undermine the elected leader of the executive branch, it sought to investigate him for crimes, culminating in the appointment of Mueller as special counsel. Nevertheless, President Trump wisely chose not to interfere with the investigation, and Mueller kept to his professional standards and cleared the president of conspiring with the Russians. But it would take the appointment of a new attorney general, William Barr, on his second tour of duty in the job, to put the revolt of the Justice Department and the FBI to rest.

The end of the Mueller probe and the revolt of the Foreign Service, however, should not distract from the direct threat that they posed to the presidency. Prominent members of both the national security and foreign policy bureaucracies believed that Trump posed a threat to the Republic. They sought to use the machinery of government to restrain or even prematurely end his presidency. If Trump had not fought back by removing these officials from office and keeping his foreign policy on course, he would have allowed the permanent bureaucracy to dictate policy to those elected by the American people. This would have run directly counter to the Framers' design, which subjects the president to popular election so that the nation can hold him responsible for the conduct of policy. Allowing the bureaucracy—no matter how expert, educated, or well meaning—to prevail in its test of wills with Trump would have undermined one of the Constitution's primary conduits for democratic accountability. Regardless of Trump's motives, his struggle with the national security and diplomatic establishment defended the original Constitution.

I. THE REVOLT OF THE FOREIGN SERVICE

In late September 2019, accusations flew that President Trump had abused his power over diplomacy to target his political opponents. A confidential whistleblower charged that Trump had pressured a foreign leader to investigate a political rival, former vice president Joseph R. Biden and his son, Hunter Biden. Trump characteristically poured gasoline on the fire. He acknowledged that he had discussed Biden in a July 25 phone call with the new Ukrainian president, Volodymyr Zelensky, but that the call was "perfect." Meanwhile, the White House had held up nearly $400 million in foreign and military aid appropriated by Congress. While Ukraine never announced an investigation, the White House released the aid on September 11, 2019. In the end, the Trump administration had supported Ukraine far more than had the Obama administration, which allowed only humanitarian aid and defensive, nonlethal equipment.

Nevertheless, the House opened an impeachment investigation only a month after the public disclosure of the whistleblower complaint. The workings of a resisting bureaucracy set off the escalation. In an August 12, 2019, letter to the chairs of the Senate and House Intelligence Committees, a career CIA officer alleged that "the President of the United States is using the power of his office to solicit interference from a foreign country in the 2020 elections." The letter disclaimed any direct knowledge of the events described, but instead it summarized the accounts of "more than a half dozen U.S. officials." Nevertheless, the whistleblower charged that Trump's "actions pose risks to U.S. national security and undermine the U.S. government's efforts to deter and counter foreign interference in U.S. elections."[3]

What, exactly, did the whistleblower claim that posed such a serious threat to the United States? First, he alleged that in the July 25 phone call, Trump had "pressured" Zelensky to launch an investigation into the Bidens and any Ukrainian interference in the 2016 elections. Second, he charged that the White House had moved the call transcript onto a classified computer system not normally used to store such communications. Third, he objected to subsequent meetings between Gordon Sondland, the ambassador to the European Union, Kurt Volker, the U.S. special representative on Ukraine, and Rudy Giuliani, Trump's personal attorney, with Zelensky and high-ranking members of the Ukrainian government. Fourth, the whistleblower raised concerns that Giuliani had engaged in "circumvention of national security decisionmaking processes to engage with Ukrainian officials and relay messages back and forth" with the president. Giuliani allegedly supported a former Ukrainian prosecutor who had been prevented from investigating Burisma Holdings, the company on whose board Hunter Biden had served.

The whistleblower complaint expressed the bureaucracy's hostility toward the elected leader of the executive branch. Take, for example, the whistleblower's claim that he could make a complaint at all. Federal law allows employees to report matters of "urgent concern" to the inspector general of the intelligence community. This statute generally applies only to members of the intelligence community; employees have no right to complain about actions taken by anyone and everyone in government. Nevertheless, the whistleblower believed that the president should fall subject to the rules that govern the intelligence community bureaucracy. The inspector general naturally agreed. Both sought to expand the power of the career civil service over the president—to make him a regular employee, as it were.

But Congress cannot subject the president to the supervision, control, or review of a subordinate officer. As the previous chapter established, all executive branch officials—and no one argues that members of the intelligence agency are anything but executive—exist to assist the president in the performance of *his* constitutional duties. An intelligence officer cannot file a whistleblower complaint against Trump, because Trump is not a member of the intelligence community, and his phone calls with foreign leaders do not qualify as intelligence operations. The intelligence community works for the president, not the other way around.[4] For that reason, the Supreme Court has traditionally refused to apply congressional enactments to the president, unless the text specifically says so, in order to avoid any constitutional conflicts between the branches.

The whistleblower complaint advanced an even more serious misunderstanding of the Constitution, one fully on display during the impeachment hearings. The whistleblower complaint assumed that Congress, and even inferior executive officials acting pursuant to the law, could regulate the president in the exercise of his core constitutional authorities. In their quest to oppose Trump, House leaders ignored the constitutional dangers of interfering with the president's conduct of foreign policy. The

Framers learned all too well the failures brought by legislative control over foreign policy. Article II sought to cure the disease by vesting "the executive power" in the president, which (as the next chapter will explain) includes the power over national security and foreign affairs. "Of all the cares or concerns of government, the direction of war most peculiarly demands those qualities which distinguish the exercise of power by a single hand," Hamilton wrote in *Federalist No. 74*. "The direction of war implies the direction of the common strength," he continued, "and the power of directing and employing the common strength forms a usual and essential part in the definition of the executive authority." The Framers concentrated these powers in the president alone so that the nation could act effectively in a dangerous world. "That unity is conducive to energy, will not be disputed," Hamilton observed in *Federalist No. 70*. "Decision, activity, secrecy, and despatch, will generally characterize the proceedings of one man."

Allowing Congress to interfere with presidential conversations with foreign leaders would violate Article II's vesting of these powers in a single person. Under the Constitution and long practice, the president *alone* conducts foreign relations. As the Supreme Court made clear in *United States v. Curtiss-Wright Export Corp.* (1936), the "President is the sole organ of the nation in its external relations, and its sole representative with foreign nations." Writing for the majority, Justice George Sutherland observed that the president's Hamiltonian speed and unity, combined with the high stakes in national security affairs, justified a broad executive power over foreign affairs. "In this vast external realm, with its important, complicated, delicate and manifold problems, the President alone has the power to speak or listen as a representative of the nation." Beginning with George Washington's 1796 refusal to provide the House with treaty negotiating records, presidents have claimed the right not just to communicate with foreign leaders but also to keep national security information secret.

Good constitutional structure matches good policy. If Congress could interfere with communications with foreign leaders, presidents would stop making the calls or would speak less candidly. Other nations would no longer trust American leaders to keep their talks confidential. U.S. foreign policy—approved by the American people at each election—would become more difficult to carry out. We have seen the harm when Congress seizes a dominant role in foreign affairs, from the Neutrality Acts that barred U.S. assistance to the Allies before Pearl Harbor to the setbacks of the 1970s.

Watergate crippled the ability of Presidents Gerald Ford and Jimmy Carter to successfully respond to the Soviet military buildup, communist expansion in Latin America and Africa, the fall of Vietnam, and the Iranian revolution. Only with Ronald Reagan's restoration of executive power could the United States execute the strategy that ultimately won the Cold War. Democrats may regret handicapping the presidency when Trump's successors grapple with the rise of China, Russia's revanchism, Iran's quest for regional hegemony, and North Korea's nuclear proliferation.

Even if the allegations against Trump were true, and he delayed $400 million in aid until Ukraine launched an investigation against the Bidens, the matter would best be settled by election. The Framers openly worried about a president who might use his foreign affairs powers for personal or political gain. But, as we will see in the last chapter, the Founders also believed that impeachment should only come as a last resort. Nevertheless, critics disappointed in the outcome of the Mueller investigation saw a second chance to remove Trump even before a probe could start in earnest. "If the president is essentially withholding military aid at the same time he is trying to browbeat a foreign leader into doing something illicit, providing dirt on his opponent during a presidential campaign, then [impeachment] may be the only remedy that is coequal to the evil," Adam B. Schiff, chairman of the House Intelligence Committee, said. House Speaker Nancy Pelosi told her Democratic majority that if the Trump administration continues to stonewall, it "will be entering a grave new chapter of lawlessness which will take us into a whole new stage of investigation."

On September 25, 2019, Trump attempted to head off the constitutional confrontation by releasing a transcript of the July 25 phone call. After exchanging pleasantries and claiming that "the United States has been very very good to Ukraine," Trump blurted out: "I would like you to do us a favor."[5] In a rambling series of allusions to conspiracy theories, he said, "I would like you to find out what happened with this whole situation with Ukraine, they say Crowdstrike . . . I guess you have one of your wealthy people . . . The server, they say Ukraine has it." Here, Trump referred to the discredited rumor that Ukraine, rather than Russia, had stolen Hillary Clinton's email server during the 2016 presidential campaign, as well as to a report that a cybersecurity firm had wiped those servers for Clinton and hidden them somewhere in Ukraine (the two conspiracy theories about Ukraine seem to contradict each other).

Then came the part of the call that triggered impeachment. It was Ukraine's president, rather than Trump, who first raised the issue of investigations. After noting that his staff had met with Rudy Giuliani, Zelensky declared, "I guarantee as the President of Ukraine that all the investigations will be done openly and candidly. That I can assure you." But Zelensky did not mention any specific prosecutions. Trump filled the gap. "There's a lot of talk about Biden's son, that Biden stopped the prosecution and a lot of people want to find out about that," Trump said. "So whatever you can do with the Attorney General would be great. Biden went around bragging that he stopped the prosecution so if you can look into it . . . It sounds horrible to me." Based on this transcript, Trump did not demand a quid pro quo—in fact, neither president mentioned U.S. military or financial aid. Trump's mention of the Bidens took place as part of a rambling discussion about why the previous Ukrainian administration had fired a prosecutor looking into corruption.

Nevertheless, the House Intelligence Committee began an impeachment investigation the same day that Trump released the transcript of the July 25 call. A long line of career diplomats and national security officials soon testified behind closed doors. State Department career officers included George Kent, the deputy assistant secretary of state for Europe; William Taylor, acting ambassador to Ukraine; Marie Yovanovitch, the past ambassador to Ukraine; as well as political appointees Gordon Sondland, ambassador to the EU, and Kurt Volker, special representative to Ukraine. National Security Council officials included Lieutenant Colonel Alexander Vindman, the director for European affairs; Tim Morrison, senior director for Europe and Russia; and Fiona Hill, a senior advisor on Russia. Even though employed by the State Department or the executive branch, these officials ignored White House orders against testifying. Senior political appointees, such as acting White House Chief of Staff Mick Mulvaney, former national security advisor John Bolton, and Secretary of State Mike Pompeo, generally refused to cooperate. Bolton's deputy, Charles Kupperman, even sued the House in federal court for a ruling on whether to appear.

This testimony signaled the career bureaucracy's second rejection of the president's authority to manage the executive branch. Presidents have long claimed privilege to protect information in the national interest, to preserve the independence of the executive branch, and to maintain control over their subordinates. Beginning with Washington, presidents have sought secrecy in foreign policy to protect the candid communications and negotiations needed for successful foreign policy. With domestic affairs, confidentiality will encourage candid advice and debate among advisors and reduces the outside political pressure on government decisions. The Framers conducted the Constitutional Convention itself in secret.

Executive privilege has only taken on the taint of cover-up since the Watergate and Whitewater investigations. In response to Senator Joseph McCarthy's investigations into communist infiltration of the government, for example, President Dwight Eisenhower refused to allow any Defense Department officials to testify or provide information that was confidential or related to national security. As he explained to top Republican lawmakers, "any man who testifies as to the advice he gave me won't be working for me that night."[6] Without confidentiality in its deliberations, the executive branch could not function—just as members of Congress and their staff or Supreme Court justices and their clerks depend on privacy in their own internal deliberations.

Watergate, of course, put executive secrecy in a bad light. President Nixon notoriously prohibited administration officials from cooperating with Congress and a special counsel, and he invoked executive privilege to keep the Watergate tapes secret. In *United States v. Nixon*, the Supreme Court rejected Nixon's blanket claim of privilege to prevent any internal executive branch discussions from disclosure. Chief Justice Warren Burger wrote for a unanimous Court that the Constitution recognized some form of executive privilege. "A President and those who assist him must be free to explore alternatives in the process of shaping policies and making decisions," he found, "and to do so in a way many would be unwilling to express except privately." Executive privilege derives from the separation of powers itself because the right to keep internal deliberations confidential is part of the "supremacy of each branch within its own assigned area of constitutional duties." It would hold almost absolute with diplomatic and military information, but a president's "undifferentiated claim of public interest" in confidentiality might give way before the constitutional need for the information by the other branches. In *Nixon*, the judicial system's need for the Watergate tapes in order to conduct a fair trial outweighed the president's right to speak privately with his aides.[7]

While Watergate made executive privilege more difficult to claim politically, it still set it on more secure legal foundations. *Nixon* affirmed the existence of the privilege and rooted it in the president's supremacy over the constitutional activities of the executive branch. For the first time, the Supreme Court ratified the claims of presidents ever since Washington that effective control of the executive branch required confidentiality. If Congress could force subordinate executive branch officials to disclose any discussions it wished, it could interfere with advice to presidents and the execution of their policies.

By testifying in defiance of White House orders, the Foreign Service sought to free itself of direct presidential control. Presidents have long failed to exercise the same control over the Foreign Service that they have over other agencies. As Judge Laurence Silberman argued in his classic 1979 *Foreign Affairs* article "Toward Presidential Control of the State Department," friction has erupted between the Foreign Service and presidents since at least the 1920s because of the desire of career officers to control top diplomatic appointments.[8] Unlike the other cabinet agencies, the State Department fills many of its top leadership positions with Foreign Service officers rather than White House appointments. Not just many ambassadors but many of the assistant secretaries and some of the undersecretaries who develop American foreign policy are career Foreign Service officers. These officials have an interest in claiming that foreign policy represents the product of knowledge and expertise rather than ideology because otherwise a president would have a better democratic claim for filling State Department posts.

One could hear this struggle between the Foreign Service's expertise and a president's popular accountability in the Ukraine controversy. Foreign Service officers testified that they believed a group of political outsiders had attacked, undermined, and competed against a policy consensus within the national security bureaucracy. In describing Giuliani's activities, for example, NSC official Vindman told the House Intelligence Committee, "In the spring of 2019, I became aware of outside influences promoting a false narrative of Ukraine inconsistent with the consensus views of the entire interagency. This narrative was harmful to U.S. Government policy."[9] Ambassador Taylor held similar worries. "I became increasingly concerned that our relationship with Ukraine was being fundamentally undermined by an irregular, informal channel of U.S. policymaking and by the withholding of vital security assistance for domestic political reasons."[10] After he listened in on the July 25 Trump-Zelensky call, Vindman reported it to NSC lawyers because "I did not think it was proper to demand that a foreign government investigate a U.S. citizen," but just as importantly, "I was worried about the implications to the U.S. government's support for Ukraine."[11]

Both Taylor and Vindman believe that "U.S. government" policy holds a superior claim to President Trump's views. Even though the latter come from the nationally elected officer constitutionally charged with pursuing foreign policy, the bureaucracy sees it as irregular, politically motivated interference with a harmonious interagency process. Ambassador Yovanovitch similarly viewed President Trump's reliance on figures outside the usual State Department channels as representing an illegitimate form of diplomacy. She described Giuliani's campaign to have her removed as a case where "private interests circumvent professional diplomats for their own gain, not for the public good." This would create a broader "harm [that] will come when bad actors and countries beyond Ukraine see how easy it is to use fiction and innuendo to manipulate our system."[12] In other words, Trump's exercise of his constitutional authority over foreign policy violated an interagency U.S. government policy. In the minds of the Foreign Service, the latter should prevail.

Trump defends the Constitution's separation of powers by demanding that his views prevail over the Foreign Service and NSC establishment. Presidents do not have to trust their decisions to the Foreign Service. Indeed, Washington asked John Jay, who was then serving as chief justice of the Supreme Court, to journey to London in 1794 to negotiate a treaty with Great Britain. Woodrow Wilson relied upon Edward House, who held no government position, as an envoy in World War I. FDR used secret emissaries, including friends from his New York social circle, to carry out missions in Europe. After the Foreign Service's revolt against Trump, we can expect presidents to call upon private emissaries even more often. The bureaucracy's vision of itself as representing a non-ideological national interest will inevitably conflict with the agenda of elected presidents, regardless of party.

Both Republicans and Democrats should oppose this resistance to the nation's elected leadership, regardless of their views toward Ukraine. I agree with the foreign policy pursued by President George H. W. Bush and his successors to slowly integrate Eastern Europe into NATO and the European Union. I think that the United States should support Ukraine to fend off Russian aggression. Trump has made the right moves in providing lethal weapons to Ukraine even as his political dealings with investigations and foreign aid have disrupted our foreign policy there. But that policy should come from the president, not simply a committee of career civil servants. It is a constitutional contradiction for the president of the United States to conduct a foreign policy at odds with the United States government. When the president decides to favor or disfavor another nation, *that* is the foreign policy of the United States government.

We will return to the question of impeachment in the last chapter. But regardless of the House's rushed investigation and the Senate's acquittal, Trump had to fight the revolt of the Foreign Service. A president must have the right to decide the foreign policy of the United States and who shall carry it out. Like other bureaucracies, the Foreign Service resists political control with a claim to technical expertise and non-ideological principles. But that position pretends that the bureaucracy can drain policy questions of all ideological choice. While some decisions may indeed have technical or scientific answers, many great questions of state require trade-offs between different values. We can have higher fuel efficiency requirements for cars and reduce carbon emissions, but their lighter weight will produce more harm in accidents. These difficult questions do not depend on science as much as on what the American people prefer, which makes the decisions best resolved by an elected president and his appointed officials.

Foreign policy questions will involve trade-offs even less subject to scientific knowledge. Take policy toward Ukraine. Bringing Ukraine into the Western orbit could advance the national interest by containing Putin's revanchist designs in Eastern Europe. But it is difficult to prove definitively that this policy is obviously superior to the alternative that Ukrainian aid does not justify the costs that NATO and the EU risk by expanding to the borders of Russia. A strategist might even argue that the United States should ally with Russia against the greater threat posed by China, just as Nixon went to China in 1972 to balance against Moscow. Friendlier relations with Putin might call for returning to the Obama policy of providing only humanitarian aid to Ukraine. But making that decision will involve more than just experts' scientific calculation. "[T]he very nature of executive decision as to foreign policy is political," Justice Robert Jackson observed in rejecting judicial review of a presidential foreign policy decision. "They are delicate, complex, and involve large amounts of prophecy."[13]

Democratic theory requires that the elected officials of government make such decisions. "They are and should be undertaken only by those directly responsible to the people whose welfare they advance or imperil."

I am not arguing that political ideology should spark swings in foreign policy to the same extent that it does domestically. The United States has permanent political and economic interests upon which both Democrats and Republicans can agree, such as defense of the continental United States or maintaining U.S. hegemony in the Western Hemisphere. Today, both parties may well agree on taking a tougher line on China. But beyond these core goals, the political parties will have different ideological approaches to both means (such as whether to participate in international organizations) and ends (whether to promote a Middle East peace that favors Israel). In fact, it would be surprising if Republicans and Democrats did not differ on these questions. And in this case, the Constitution establishes that the president sets the policy and commands the executive branch in carrying it out.

II. THE REVOLT OF THE FBI

The revolt of the Foreign Service followed an even more serious challenge to Trump's constitutional position atop the executive branch. In what might be called "the revolt of the FBI," Director James Comey and his inner circle orchestrated an investigation into Trump based on the specious idea that he had conspired with Russia to win the 2016 elections. The charge turned out to be so frivolous that special counsel Robert Mueller, the gold standard among federal prosecutors (he had served as FBI director, head of DOJ's criminal division, and as U.S. attorney in San Francisco), found no evidence at all of such a conspiracy. After an expensive, damaging, two-year probe, Mueller did Trump a great favor by definitively clearing him, his campaign, and his administration of conspiring with Russia to break federal law. Mueller's investigation found significant Russian efforts to influence the elections and to harm Hillary Clinton's candidacy, but it found no cooperation with the obvious beneficiary, the Trump campaign.

Nevertheless, efforts by the FBI to gin up such an investigation amounted to the first great effort by the permanent bureaucracy to resist a constitutionally elected president. As the previous chapter explained, the Constitution vests the president alone with the responsibility to ensure that the laws are faithfully executed. Even though he delegates most of the cases to the attorney general, the president formally remains responsible for all federal investigations and prosecutions. He retains the constitutional authority to overrule his subordinates at the FBI or DOJ and order them to open or drop cases.

Comey, however, believed that the FBI could target not just the Trump campaign but Trump himself without notifying the president and seeking his approval. Resistance to the president's constitutional authority escalated when Trump properly removed Comey from office. The FBI responded by opening a criminal obstruction of justice case against Trump, and DOJ responded by appointing a special counsel. In yet another constitutional contradiction, the DOJ/FBI bureaucracy attempted to enforce the criminal law against a president who bears the final duty to execute that law. Using law enforcement to investigate a major party's presidential candidate, within months of the election itself, violated the basic norms of the American political system. Watergate began with President Nixon's use of the CIA and FBI to harass and surveil his potential rivals in the 1972 elections. It would be as if John Adams, our second president and head of the Federalist Party, used federal officials to investigate Thomas Jefferson during the 1800 election over his well-known French sympathies.

The FBI's resistance began even before Trump won in November 2016. In an extraordinary move, the FBI decided to open the "Crossfire Hurricane" investigation into Russia and the Trump campaign four months earlier. As Andrew McCarthy argues, the FBI really started investigating Trump as early as the spring of 2016, when Carter Page, George Papadopoulos, and other bit players joined the campaign's nascent foreign policy advisory committee.[14] The FBI already had Page in its sights because of Russian efforts to recruit the pro-Russian energy businessman (and former navy officer) as an intelligence asset—except that Page had helped the FBI identify the Russian spies. Even though conspiracy theorists believed that Page had traveled to Moscow in July 2016 to meet with Kremlin officials, the Mueller report found that he had not worked with the Russians to interfere in the elections.[15]

When Page turned up a dead end, the FBI pursued 28-year-old Papadopoulos, who had almost no serious foreign policy background at all—he was still listing Model United Nations on his résumé. In the spring and summer of 2016, Papadopoulos met with Joseph Mifsud, a Maltese professor based in London and a possible spy (though for whom remains unclear). Allegedly Mifsud told Papadopoulos that the Russians had obtained "dirt" on Hillary Clinton by stealing her emails, which Papadopoulos repeated to Trump campaign officials and a foreign diplomat. But again, the Mueller report found no evidence that the Trump officials actually knew of the Russian hack of the Clinton emails or conspired to disseminate them.[16]

With these unproven Russian contacts with peripheral campaign staff, the FBI believed it had enough grounds to launch Crossfire Hurricane. As the Mueller report has shown, Russian intelligence clearly sought to interfere with the 2016 elections.[17] Its agents hacked into Democratic Party computer networks, stole emails, and transferred the materials to WikiLeaks for release. It used social media to spread false information about the candidates and the election. But there was no serious evidence of any conspiracy between Russia and the Trump campaign. It is for this reason that the FBI may have relied on the gossip and rumor supplied in July 2016 by former British intelligence agent Christopher Steele. In a series of memos written for Fusion GPS, a D.C. private intelligence firm working for the Clinton campaign, Steele made a number of outlandish charges that the Russians had obtained compromising material on Trump and had conspired with his campaign to win the 2016 election. The Mueller report did not rely upon, or even try to verify, any of the Steele dossier's claims. The DOJ inspector general continues to investigate the improper use of the dossier to justify enhanced surveillance of the Trump campaign, while the federal court that granted those warrants has opened its own investigation into DOJ abuse of power.

The willingness of the nation's intelligence agencies to take the Steele dossier seriously shows the bureaucracy's deep anti-Trump bias. Counterintelligence against foreign spies and terrorists involves predicting and stopping future harmful actions rather than punishing criminals for their past bad acts.[18] These operations might depend upon rumor, gossip, and unproven innuendo that would never survive in an American courtroom. Nevertheless, I am astounded by the flimsiness of the evidence that opened the FBI investigation of a presidential candidate for one of the two major political parties. As a Justice Department official in the wake of the 9/11 attacks, I reviewed the facts of cases that triggered major counterintelligence investigations. I cannot see how the Steele dossier's groundless suspicions could have supported the legitimate opening of a counterintelligence investigation of a presidential campaign, which ultimately led to a special counsel probe.

While DOJ's inspector general did not find any *partisan* political bias that would have motivated Crossfire Hurricane, ideology beyond Republican-Democratic rivalry could be at work. Instead of favoring one political party, the bureaucrats could easily have favored the very ideal of an establishment candidate, Hillary Clinton, over the outsider Donald Trump. Clinton had already served as first lady, senator, and secretary of state—plus, she looked like she was cruising to a landslide victory. Trump challenged the liberal international order, American foreign policy, and our national security policies. The hostility of the Obama administration's top intelligence and law enforcement toward Trump became only more apparent as he took office. Andrew McCabe, the FBI deputy director under Obama, told CNN in February 2019 that it was possible that Trump was "a Russian asset," a view that James Clapper, the Obama director of national intelligence, agreed with "completely." Obama CIA director John Brennan called Trump's performance at the 2018 U.S.-Russia summit "nothing short of treasonous."[19] These Obama officials made these accusations even though they must have known, as the Mueller report showed, that no evidence existed of any Russia–Trump conspiracy. FBI officials didn't need the kind of bias revealed in the texts between counterintelligence director Peter Strzok and his girlfriend, FBI counsel Lisa Page (Page: "[Trump's] not ever going to become president, right? Right?!"; Strzok: "No. No he won't. We'll stop it.") to launch the unfounded "Russian collusion investigation." They had already decided that Trump posed a threat to their agencies and American national security, and the lack of evidence would not delay their quest.

Bureaucratic hostility toward Trump came to the fore not just in the opening of Crossfire Hurricane but also in its methods. The FBI not only used regular techniques on the Trump campaign but also unleashed its most powerful tool, the 1978 Foreign Intelligence Surveillance Act (FISA). FISA allows the government to intercept the emails, phone calls, texts, and other communications of Trump campaign officials without having to meet the standards for regular searches. Perhaps the most important constitutional issue raised by FISA is that the search warrant isn't based on the Fourth Amendment's standard for a criminal warrant. Under the Fourth Amendment, as it has been interpreted by the courts, a judge can issue a search warrant if there is "probable cause" to believe that the target has been or is involved in criminal activity. The government cannot engage in a search just because it imagines that someone has committed a crime. It must have some proof—not beyond a reasonable doubt, not even more likely than not—but *some* proof that an individual is involved in a crime. FISA, however, permits search warrants based on a lower standard—probable cause that the individual is an agent of a terrorist organization. For agents of a foreign power who are either citizens or permanent resident aliens, FISA also requires that they "knowingly" engage in "clandestine intelligence gathering activities," a standard somewhat closer to that of a normal warrant. Under a FISA warrant, the FBI could read through the communications of not just a Page or a Papadopoulos but more important figures, such as campaign manager Paul Manafort, without the Fourth Amendment's requirement of probable cause of a crime.

FISA's very purpose was to prevent the kind of FBI surveillance conducted in the summer and fall of 2016. Congress enacted FISA to prevent a repeat of Watergate. Before 1978, presidents had conducted national security surveillance under their sole authority because signals intelligence constituted part of military and national security operations, not those of the criminal justice system. FISA replaced presidentially ordered monitoring of national security threats with a system similar to law enforcement monitoring of criminal suspects. FISA requires the government to show probable cause that a target is "an agent of a foreign power," which includes terrorist groups.[20] A special court of federal district judges, the Foreign Intelligence Surveillance Court (FISC), examines classified information in a secret hearing before issuing the warrant.

FISA strikes a compromise between the wartime and criminal approaches to surveillance. It establishes a system that bears strong resemblances to the criminal justice system, such as the requirement of an individual target, probable cause, and a search warrant. On the other hand, in a nod to counterintelligence's unique character, it does not require a showing of probable cause of criminal activity by the target. Instead, FISA only demands that the government show probable cause that the target is linked to a foreign power or terrorist group. As a Justice Department official during the September 11, 2001, attacks, I took part in the Patriot Act overhaul of FISA. I worked on fixing FISA's most important defect: the legal "wall" that had separated foreign intelligence agencies and domestic law enforcement from sharing information about terrorists and spies. In order to force the agencies to cooperate, we lowered the standard so that a FISA search could have "a" purpose to collect foreign intelligence, but one that also allowed for its use domestically. We understood that this would allow FISA surveillance of targets (and their communications) that did not remain abroad but might cross into the United States.

But these post-9/11 changes never sought to reverse FISA's fundamental purpose: to prevent the government from using national security surveillance to interfere with domestic politics. That, after all, was the lesson learned from Watergate. The Obama administration's intelligence agencies crossed that red line. As Victor Davis Hanson has explained in *The Case for Trump*, Hillary Clinton lost the 2016 elections for many reasons: dismissal of a middle class ravaged by globalization, failure to campaign with an eye to the Electoral College, neglect of the Midwestern states, and overconfidence.[21] The specific misuse of spying powers would not have come before the public, but a broader sense of the Obama administration's self-interested abuse of law enforcement power did.[22] A majority of the American people may have had enough of the FBI's games after James Comey's July 5, 2016, press conference in which he cleared Clinton of any crimes for routing her government emails through a vulnerable, unsecured private server. Voters might have seen Comey's arrogation of the power of DOJ prosecutors to make the charging decisions—the FBI's job is to collect the facts; the Justice Department decides whether to prosecute—as another example of the Obama administration's faithless execution of the laws. Clinton's loss could have represented a desire to clean up the law enforcement bureaucracy that had grown so powerful it could decide the fate of elections.

After November 8, 2016, Comey and the FBI leadership could have recognized the constitutional authority of the new president. They could have informed Trump of the investigations into his campaign and asked him whether they should continue. If they believed that Trump had interfered with a valid investigation out of his own self-interest, they could have resigned and taken their concerns of a cover-up to Congress. Instead, they redoubled their efforts, treated the new president himself as a target, and then dared Trump to stop them, even though control over the FBI falls under the executive's constitutional authority.

We can see this in Comey's dealings with Trump. From January 6 to

April 1, 2017, Comey memorialized every one-on-one conversation he had with the president and then hid the memos at home. When asked about this extraordinary practice in Senate hearings, Comey claimed that it was necessary because he didn't trust the president to tell the truth. While that may be partially true, a DOJ inspector general report on Comey's memos reveals a more serious motive. Comey had his first meeting with Trump on January 7, 2017, to brief the president-elect on the intelligence community's assessment of Russian interference with the 2016 elections.[23] But Comey's real punch would come in the second half of their meeting, when he would spring on Trump the "salacious and unverified" rumors in the Steele dossier. Even though Comey's staff claimed they did not want to hold the information over Trump in a "Hoover-esque type of plot," they also hoped that the disclosure would cause Trump to "make statements about, or provide information of value to, the pending Russian interference investigation." Immediately after his meeting with Trump, where the president-elect denied the Steele dossier claims, Comey rushed to a waiting FBI vehicle where he started recording his recollections on a secure laptop. After arriving at FBI New York City offices, he briefed the top FBI leadership and "supervisors of the FBI's Crossfire Hurricane investigative team." As McCarthy observes, "Comey was the investigator" who was hoping to get the suspect, Trump, to "blurt out either an implicit admission of guilt or a false exculpatory statement."[24] Even though Comey would tell Trump that he was not the target of the investigation, the FBI director was only playing semantics—the FBI was investigating his campaign, in which Trump was the major figure, even if the FBI never named Trump himself as the main suspect in any documents.

Comey and the FBI leadership misrepresented the truth about their investigations in order to shield themselves from presidential control. The bureaucracy decided that it knew better than the elected leader of the executive branch how best to exercise the power to enforce the laws. It then went further to inform Congress and the public that it continued to investigate Trump even after the elections. On March 20, 2017, Comey testified before the House Intelligence Committee on the Russia investigation. In his opening statement, he declared that "the FBI, as part of our counterintelligence mission, is investigating the Russian government's efforts to interfere in the 2016 presidential election."[25] This violated standard DOJ procedure, which is not to confirm or deny any ongoing investigation. He further confirmed that the operation "includes investigating the nature of any links between individuals associated with the Trump campaign and the Russia government and whether there was any coordination between the campaign and Russia's efforts." Ominously, this would "also include an assessment of whether any crimes were committed." No one could doubt that Comey had announced to the world that the FBI had placed Trump under investigation.

Trump asked the FBI director several times to make clear that the FBI was not investigating him. Comey never did. Trump finally lost his patience and fired him on May 9, 2017. Only then did Trump finally exercise his constitutional authority to rein in a resistant FBI bureaucracy. Even then, Comey had set a trap. Comey had written in a memo about a February 14, 2017, meeting that Trump believed Michael Flynn "had done nothing wrong." The FBI had quickly investigated and arrested the national security advisor and former U.S. Army general at the start of the administration for failing to tell the truth about a phone conversation with Russian officials on sanctions. Trump "hoped" that Comey could "see his way clear to letting this go, to letting Flynn go." After his firing, Comey sent the memo of this conversation to a friend to forward to the *New York Times*. Asked by the inspector general to explain his breach of FBI rules on securing law enforcement information, Comey responded: "[I]f I put out into the public square that encounter, that will force DOJ, likely to appoint a Special Counsel."[26]

In the ultimate sign of DOJ opposition to Trump, the Justice Department's second in command, Rod Rosenstein, fulfilled Comey's wish. Rosenstein could have come out of central casting to play the role of the career bureaucrat. He had served in DOJ positions in both the George H. W. Bush and Clinton administrations, joined Ken Starr's Whitewater probe, worked as a deputy assistant attorney general in the George W. Bush Justice Department, and then took over as U.S. attorney for Maryland. He became the only Bush-appointed U.S. attorney who remained throughout the entirety of the Obama administration—a fact often mentioned to prove Rosenstein's political neutrality. Trump appointed him deputy attorney general, and, because Jeff Sessions had recused himself from the Russia investigation, Rosenstein headed DOJ for that matter.

At first, Rosenstein supported Comey's removal. He sent a memo to the president reciting the criticism, from former DOJ leaders of both parties, of Comey's July 2016 public declination to prosecute Clinton. According to

Rosenstein, Comey had "usurp[ed] the Attorney General's authority" and had broken DOJ policy by "releas[ing] derogatory information" about Clinton, who went uncharged. But Rosenstein soon changed his tune. After a meeting with the Russian foreign minister the day after Comey's removal, Trump said, "I just fired the head of the FBI. He was crazy, a real nut job. I faced great pressure because of Russia. That's taken off." In a TV interview Trump said that as he decided to fire Comey, he thought to himself, "[y]ou know, this Russia thing with Trump and Russia is a made-up story, it's an excuse by the Democrats for having lost an election that they should have won." Rosenstein took these opportunities to appoint Robert Mueller, perhaps the greatest living federal prosecutor, as special counsel. The permanent bureaucracy could not have launched any greater retaliatory strike against a president.

Under the Take Care Clause, Trump could have countermanded Rosenstein's order. He could have fired Sessions (as he ultimately did), Rosenstein, and Mueller. He could have ended the special counsel investigation. But he chose not to exercise his constitutional authority and wisely allowed the probe to proceed. He ordered his staff to cooperate with the special counsel—it is the very interviews with White House officials such as counsel Donald McGahn, chief of staff Reince Priebus, and counselor Stephen Bannon that provided the grounds for claims that Trump had committed obstruction of justice. He also waived executive privilege and allowed the special counsel access to virtually all relevant documents held by the White House. Once Mueller cleared Trump and his campaign of any conspiracy with Russia, the special counsel's very independence made his findings unassailable.

Comey, the FBI, and the special counsel, however, compounded their constitutional errors by investigating Trump for obstructing their own groundless probe. Critics chimed in by comparing Trump's decision to fire Comey to Nixon's removal of Special Prosecutor Archibald Cox during the Watergate investigation. CNN legal analyst Jeffrey Toobin claimed that the United States was undergoing "the kind of thing that goes on in nondemocracies." He sagely opined that "they will put in a stooge who will shut down this investigation." Trump's critics are the captives of their overwrought imaginations. The Watergate analogy was misplaced; Comey had to go for the nation's best interests. Indeed, Trump's biggest mistake was one of timing—he should have told Comey to pack his bags on January 21,

2017, rather than waiting until the White House had become embroiled in controversy over Russia.

Contrary to critics, Trump could not have committed obstruction of justice by exercising his constitutional authority to fire Comey. As explained in the last chapter, Article II gives the president the right to remove subordinate executive officers, for any reason or no reason, because they assist him in executing federal law. Independent counsels also have the convenient effect of relieving Congress of its own constitutional duty to constrain an abusive president. If Trump had truly impeded a valid investigation, Congress initially could have blocked Trump's legislative agenda and funding for White House priorities. If these responses failed, Congress could have turned to impeachment, which allows for the removal of a president for "high Crimes and Misdemeanors." Contrary to common wisdom, as chapter 9 will discuss, impeachment does not require the president to commit a crime but instead refers to significant political mistakes or offenses.

To forestall this awful result for his presidency and, more importantly, the nation, Trump may have studied the history of the last transformative chief executive, Ronald Reagan. The Iran-Contra controversy nearly destroyed Reagan's presidency and could have led to his impeachment. After revelations that his NSC staff had traded arms for hostages held by Iran and then transferred funds to support the Nicaraguan Contras, Reagan sent credible signals that he would change his ways. He removed the NSC advisors responsible and replaced his chief of staff with former Senate minority leader Howard Baker. Reagan appointed Texas senator John Tower to lead a presidential commission with a full mandate to lay out all the facts in public. He agreed to reforms of the process for approving covert action. Reagan ended his presidency on the high notes of a booming economy and a subsiding Cold War.

Trump followed the Reagan example by cleaning house. He fired Priebus and Bannon, as well as all the others who brought the chaos of the presidential campaign into the White House. He replaced them with more experienced government hands, much as he replaced Flynn with General H. R. McMaster. Trump conserved his political capital by deferring to the Republican Congress on domestic policy and focusing more on his national security and foreign policy duties, rather than trying to act as a prime minister. Trump's victory over the special counsel investigation struck a blow not just for himself, though it surely did, but more importantly for the presidency. It served as a clear reminder of the president's constitutional authority to direct law enforcement, and it beat back the bureaucracy's first attempt to resist his election. Unfortunately, it came at the cost of the first two years of his presidency.

CHAPTER 4

DRAINING THE SWAMP: THE PRESIDENT'S POWER TO REVERSE

President Trump has fulfilled his most compelling campaign promise by boosting the economy. By early 2020, the Trump economy had added more than 7 million new jobs. Unemployment reached the lowest level ever recorded at 3.5 percent, with joblessness for African Americans, Hispanics, and Asian Americans hitting the lowest levels ever measured. Annual economic growth beat predictions by hitting 3 percent in 2017 and 2018, though it began to slow in the second half of 2019.[1] Job openings exceeded the number of unemployed for the first time ever. This performance represented a sharp break from the Obama administration, when annual growth sputtered along at 1.5 percent in 2016, and set the United States apart from the economic stagnation in much of the developed world. If the American people reelect Donald Trump, this sterling economic performance will have much—if not all—to do with it.

Trump could not have achieved his economic success without his constitutional powers. The administration itself attributes the new economic growth to two major factors. First, the Tax Cut and Jobs Act, signed by the president on December 22, 2017, reduced personal tax rates on the margins, capped deductions for the wealthy, and engineered a large cut in the corporate tax (from 35 to 21 percent) to attract capital back to the United States. While the White House played an important role, through its veto over legislation and its leadership of the Republican Party, constitutional credit for the tax cut rested primarily with Congress, which holds the powers over taxing and spending.

But the second contributor to the nation's economic success depended wholly on Trump's exercise of presidential power. Regulation under

President Obama had gone so into overdrive as to burden the economy. Trump entered office with a mission to deregulate. "During my first year in office, we began by building a foundation of pro-growth policies. We initiated sweeping regulatory reform—issuing 22 deregulatory actions for every new one added—and signed into law the Tax Cuts and Jobs Act, the biggest package of tax cuts and tax reform in our country's history," Trump wrote in the foreword to the *Economic Report of the President 2019.* "Consumer and business confidence skyrocketed as we reversed incentives that had driven away businesses, investment, and jobs for many years."[2] Instead of increasing new regulatory measures, as had every administration since Reagan, the Trump White House instituted a new deregulatory program. By executive order, Trump set unprecedented cost caps that called for any new regulations to *reduce* the overall costs on the economy and required that an agency repeal two regulations for every new one.[3]

Trump's deregulatory agenda may have had an impact as great as the tax cuts in jump-starting the U.S. economy. According to a 2019 report by the White House Council of Economic Advisors, chaired by the Hoover Institution's Kevin Hassett, deregulation will increase GDP by 1.0 to 2.2 percent within a decade. More tangibly, deregulation is lifting average household income by $3,100 per year.[4] Trump's repeal of 20 burdensome regulations alone had the effect of saving the economy $220 billion per year in costs.

These economic gains required Trump to exercise a constitutional power not provided specifically in the text. Rather than use Article II's executive power to issue new regulations, Trump exercised the power of *reversal.* He claimed a constitutional power to undo the actions of past presidents. Critics, however, argue that President Trump lacks any such legal authority unless Congress has explicitly granted it to him. This view, advanced by scholars and anti-administration lawsuits, seriously misunderstands the nature of executive power and the constitutional system. Each branch always has the power to repeal its own decisions—this right of reversal imposes one of the most important checks on presidential power. To read the Constitution otherwise would create a one-way ratchet that would encourage presidents to over-exercise their powers to prevent their successors from undoing their work—rendering the government unworkable.

This chapter explains this power through the most controversial episode in Trump's deregulatory agenda: the reversal of President Obama's immigration policies. The president's power to reverse his predecessor's enforcement levels for federal laws supports Trump's broader deregulatory agenda. This chapter then takes up a second example of presidential reversal: the pardon power. It confirms that the pardon power grants the president the right to undo actions by his own branch, in this case the power to execute the laws. The pardon power most directly came up in the context of the Mueller investigation, in which some commentators urged Trump to pardon figures such as Michael Flynn and Paul Manafort, among others. Trump has even tweeted that he could pardon himself. While a right to self-pardon initially seems to violate rule of law norms, a careful examination of the sources shows that the Framers imposed no such limit on executive authority. Rather, the broad extent of the pardon power even to include a self-pardon of the president illustrates the reach of the president's general power of reversal.

I. THE POWER OF REVERSAL

A background principle of American law is that the authority to execute a power usually includes the power to revoke it, unless the original grant says otherwise. The Constitution provides several important examples of this principle, which reinforces the right of a new president under the Executive Vesting Clause to modify or even revoke the regulations of his predecessors.

There are scores of congressional statutes authorizing the executive branch to issue regulations to protect the environment, workers, consumer products, highways, air traffic, consumer finances, food and drugs, and many others. These laws confer vast discretion on the federal agencies because of their vague terms and broad subjects. In the Clean Air Act, for example, Congress transferred its legislative power to the Environmental Protection Agency to set air quality standards that "protect the public health" with "an adequate margin of safety." Under this power, the EPA sets all air pollution, auto and truck fuel efficiency, and energy plant standards in the nation.[5] When using delegated power from Congress, executive branch agencies must follow the Administrative Procedure Act (APA), which requires public notice of proposed rules and the opportunity for public comments. When Congress gives an agency the authority to issue regulations, we presume that the agency also has the authority to repeal those regulations.[6] The agency need only follow the APA in modifying or repealing a regulation if it used the APA in the first place.

Presidents regularly revise or revoke hundreds of executive orders and administrative regulations throughout the administrative state. Many scholars, however, have argued that Trump lacks that authority. Hundreds of environmental law professors, for example, argued that Trump could not reverse Obama's last-minute designation of millions of acres of land as national monuments.[7] Interest groups have gone to court to block Trump's imposition of cost caps on regulation and the requirement that agencies repeal two regulations for every new one issued. If their arguments were correct, most administrative regulations would operate as one-way ratchets, not subject to repeal or modification by future presidents. Under this logic, many Trump executive orders have permanent and binding effect on future presidents. Suppose Trump were to designate all of his hotels and resorts as national monuments. Surely environmental scholars would argue after he left office that the next president could repeal those designations.

A basic principle of the Constitution is that any branch of government can reverse its earlier actions using the same process. Thus, Article I, Section 7 describes the only process for enacting a federal law. A statute must pass through both bicameralism (approval by both houses of Congress) and presentment (presidential approval). But the Constitution describes no process for repealing a statute. Our governmental practice simply has assumed that Congress may eliminate an existing statute by enacting a repealing measure through bicameralism and presentment.

Under the logic of the opponents of a presidential reversal power, however, Congress could not repeal previous statutes because of the Constitution's silence. While passage of an earlier law may make its repeal politically difficult, due to the need to assemble majorities in both Houses and the requirement of presidential signature, no Congress can bind future Congresses in the use of the legislative power.[8] This point seemed so obvious at the time of the Framing that it merited only passing mention. In addressing the Constitution's allocation of the treaty power, for example, John Jay observed, "They who make laws may, without doubt, amend or repeal them."[9]

This principle applies to all three branches of the federal government. The Supreme Court can repeal past opinions simply by overruling the

earlier case, though the Constitution does not expressly provide for such reversals. *Brown v. Board of Education*[10] famously overruled *Plessy v. Ferguson*'s rule of "separate but equal."[11] While the Court may choose to follow past precedent out of *stare decisis*, it employs the same procedure to reverse past cases, as Congress does to reverse earlier statutes. Both a precedent and its subsequent overruling decision require only a simple majority of the justices. No Supreme Court can bind future Supreme Courts.

This rule also applies to the Constitution as a whole. In Article V, the Constitution creates an additional process for amending its own text, which requires two-thirds approval by the House and the Senate and then the agreement of three-quarters of the states. Without Article V, the Constitution would require the same or a very similar process for its amendment as for its enactment (which would have impractically required a new constitutional convention). The Framers decided to set out explicit mechanisms for repealing part of the original constitutional text when they wanted to provide a means that did not mirror the original process.

The same principle applies to the constitutional amendments themselves. The Constitution contains no provision for undoing a constitutional amendment. Instead, we use constitutional amendments to repeal previous constitutional amendments. The Twenty-First Amendment repealed the Eighteenth Amendment, which had imposed Prohibition. When the Constitution is silent about a method for repeal, it is assumed that it permits the same process as that of enactment.

The executive branch operates under the same rule. The Framers created an executive that could act unilaterally and with dispatch because its constitutional and statutory responsibilities demanded swift action. They wanted the electorate to hold each president fully accountable without the diffusion of responsibility of an advisory council. The same reasons that counsel for unitary executive action in the first instance support unilateral reversal. The Framers' careful protection against arbitrary government would be turned on its head if one president could insulate his policies against reversal by a subsequent president—for then the constitutional difficulty of enacting a statutory override would further entrench executive policy against electoral or statutory change.

Besides the U.S. Constitution itself, the only relatively permanent domestic policies in America are in statutory text. This is by design. The Framers made statutory enactment difficult to better protect individual

liberty against arbitrary government. Passage requires simultaneous agreement between two houses of Congress and the president (or a supermajority in both houses of Congress after a presidential veto). As the Supreme Court observed in *INS v. Chadha*, "[t]he bicameral requirement, the Presentment Clauses, the President's veto, and Congress's power to override a veto were intended to erect enduring checks on each Branch and to protect the people from the improvident exercise of power."[12] Laws require consensus and compromise between constitutional actors with three different constituencies and electoral time horizons. Since it takes the same, if not greater, political effort and consensus to repeal a statute, they tend to endure. America retains many of the statutory policies enacted by the First Congress in 1789, such as the design of the federal court system in the Judiciary Act of 1789 and the establishment of the four great agencies: War, State, Treasury, and the Attorney General.

By contrast, unilateral executive actions are, and necessarily must be, easy to reverse by a subsequent president. There is no exception to this background principle for regulations or executive orders. Those who seek permanent federal law immune from presidential change must go to Congress and be prepared to compromise. According to this constitutional principle, no president can bind future presidents in the use of their constitutional authorities. Presidents commonly issue executive orders reversing, modifying, or even extending the executive orders of past presidents. No court has ever questioned that authority, even when it is used to carry out powers delegated by Congress. Good examples include the successive executive orders of Presidents Ford, Carter, Reagan, Clinton, Bush, and Obama requiring agencies to submit proposed regulations to cost-benefit review by the White House.[13] It would be anomalous for any executive order or presidential proclamation to become immune to repeal or amendment by later presidents.

Presidents can always reverse their predecessors' exercise of executive power under the Constitution too. Presidents regularly add or remove executive branch officers appointed to White House committees or even the cabinet. They have created and eliminated whole offices in the Executive Office of the President. They have increased or reduced the use of cost-benefit analysis in regulatory decisions.

Critics of presidential power have attempted to distinguish these examples. Congress must have the power to repeal its own statutes; otherwise

no one else could. The same applies to the Supreme Court and its opinions. By contrast, they argue, Congress can overrule regulations, so the president need not have that power. Courts, however, have recognized unilateral executive revocations or reversals even when Congress could potentially do the same. The clearest example is the president's removal power. Under Article II, Section 2, the president nominates and, with the Senate's advice and consent, appoints high executive branch officers, judges, and ambassadors. The Constitution, however, does not explicitly address removing an officer. As chapter 2 shows, Congress accepted that the president has the constitutional authority to remove the chiefs of the first great departments. The Framing generation understood the Constitution's silence to allow the president to reverse the appointment process, even without congressional consent. The Supreme Court firmly recognized this principle in *Myers v. United States*.[14] In revoking an official's commission that was issued after Senate confirmation, the president is clearly negating a specific, deliberative, and official Senate act. Indeed, the Court has recognized that a removal process that mirrored the appointment process—requiring the Senate's advice and consent—would effectively transform an executive branch official into a legislative official, one who could not assume law enforcement functions.[15] While *Humphrey's Executor v. United States* and *Morrison v. Olson* permit Congress to limit the president's discretion with a "for cause" requirement, both cases still recognize the basic principle that the president can remove subordinate officers without the Senate's advice and consent.[16]

A similar dynamic applies to treaties. Under Article II, Section 2, the president makes treaties subject to the advice and consent of the Senate. As with appointments, the Constitution deviated from British constitutional practice at the time, which placed treaty-making under the sole control of the Crown.[17] Again, the Constitution does not explicitly set out the procedure for terminating a treaty. According to the logic of opponents of a presidential reversal power, however, once the federal government enters into a treaty, the United States cannot withdraw. They interpret constitutional silence as a decision to withhold a withdrawal power from the president, the president and the Senate, and Congress as a whole. A more reasonable but still erroneous position is that constitutional silence requires the federal government to use the exact same process for undoing a treaty as for making one. In *Federalist No. 64*, John Jay suggested exactly this process.[18]

American practice, however, has never followed this formalist approach to the repeal of treaties. As with firing officers, Article II's silence on the termination of treaties has been understood to vest that power in the president alone. Congress terminated the 1778 alliance with France when it authorized the Quasi-War in 1798. While President Adams signed the legislation, the process did not mirror the treaty process, as it included the House, did not require a supermajority of the Senate, and certainly did not seek France's approval.[19] Presidents have long terminated treaties too, most recently Bush's 2002 withdrawal from the Anti-Ballistic Missile (ABM) Treaty with the Soviet Union and Trump's termination of the Intermediate Nuclear Forces Treaty.[20] In *Goldwater v. Carter*, a four-justice plurality of the Supreme Court agreed that the president retains the traditional executive authority to terminate treaties.[21] Presidents and Senates cannot bind future presidents to treaties, just as they cannot prevent future presidents from removing executive branch officials.

This is not to argue that presidents should repeal all regulations, even though they place a heavy burden on the economy. When their benefits outweigh their costs, rules can protect the health and safety of consumers and workers and advance the economy as a whole. President Reagan acknowledged this by requiring that all regulatory rules that had a major effect on the economy undergo a White House cost-benefit review. But different presidents, chosen by the electorate in part because of their domestic agendas, can give more weight to some regulatory values over others. The American people elected Donald Trump to turn the economy around, and his use of constitutional authority launched a deregulatory campaign that has boosted economic growth in his first term.

II. PROSECUTORIAL DISCRETION: DACA AND DAPA

Once Republicans won one of the houses of Congress, President Obama responded with unilateral action rather than legislative compromise. "I've got a pen and I've got a phone," he famously said in 2014. "And I can use that pen to sign executive orders and take executive actions and administrative actions that move the ball forward." One thing he would not do? "We're not just going to be waiting for legislation."[22] Using a combination of powers delegated by Congress and his own constitutional authority,

Obama redoubled his efforts at regulation in his last two years. His administration issued new rules on everything from emissions standards to antidiscrimination to college sexual harassment.[23] But, as the discussion in section I suggested, Obama's strategy suffered from a deadly vulnerability. Without Congress, Obama had to use executive orders and regulations that his successor could easily repeal. If presidents cannot work with Congress to cement their policies into legislation, they leave those policies open to change by their successors.

Nowhere was this more true than with immigration, perhaps the most volatile and divisive issue facing our nation today (and the full subject of the next chapter). In 2012, the Obama administration announced the Deferred Action for Childhood Arrivals (DACA) program, a nonenforcement policy that halted the deportation of illegal aliens brought to the United States as children.[24] In November 2014, the administration followed up with the Deferred Action for Parents of Americans (DAPA) program, which blocked the removal of illegal aliens whose children were either U.S. citizens or green card holders.[25] According to estimates, these two policies combined allowed at least five million aliens—about half of the entire illegal alien population—to remain in the United States in violation of federal immigration laws. Congress had failed throughout the 2000s to enact legislation that would have granted either class of aliens a legal status within the United States.

President Obama chose to exercise prosecutorial discretion: the president's right to allocate law enforcement resources among different cases. But that left his policy vulnerable to attack. The lower courts enjoined the programs, and the Supreme Court could not muster a majority to revive the case (due to the untimely death of Justice Scalia).[26] Once in office, Trump issued orders reversing DACA and DAPA on the ground that they violated the Constitution. Trump stood on strong constitutional ground. As Robert Delahunty and I argued at the time of DACA's announcement, the president's prosecutorial discretion did not allow him to reduce enforcement of a law to zero cases.[27] While President Obama could refuse to enforce an unconstitutional law (and even that remains a controversial claim among legal scholars), no one plausibly argued, not even the White House, that the immigration laws violate the Constitution. A president has no authority otherwise to refuse to enforce a law simply because he disagrees with Congress's policy choices. While the Take Care Clause empowers presidents to

supervise all federal law enforcement, it also acts as a restraint to prevent presidents from canceling a law through nonenforcement.

Nevertheless, the resistance to the Trump administration devised a new version of the argument used against deregulation. It claimed that President Trump could not simply repeal DACA and DAPA by executive order, but instead that he had to use the APA. The legal resistance to Trump's anti-DACA and -DAPA orders found welcome fora before federal district judges in San Francisco, New York, and Washington, D.C. These courts, and eventually the federal appeals court in the Ninth Circuit (which governs the west coast states), agreed that the administration had not followed the APA and, in any event, that its justification that DACA and DAPA violated the law did not satisfy the arbitrary and capricious standard.[28]

The Supreme Court has agreed to review these decisions and will issue its ruling in the summer of 2020. Two reasons should lead the Supreme Court to uphold Trump's reversal of DACA and DAPA. First, Trump need not follow the APA because Obama did not follow the APA when he issued DACA and DAPA. Obama characterized his refusal to execute the immigration laws as an exercise of prosecutorial discretion. Trump used that same constitutional power to increase the level of immigration enforcement. The Supreme Court has forbidden courts from reviewing an executive's exercise of prosecutorial discretion, except when it becomes complete nonenforcement of a law.[29] Second, even if the Trump administration had to provide a reasoned explanation to the courts for its resumption of immigration law enforcement, ending the unconstitutional DACA and DAPA programs should meet the requirement. It cannot be the case that the courts can force a president to continue to enforce a policy that he believes to be—and in fact is—unconstitutional.

This section will explain both the basis of prosecutorial discretion and why DACA and DAPA went beyond the limits of executive power under the Constitution. In fact, if DACA and DAPA rely on an illegal exercise of prosecutorial discretion, the Constitution compelled Trump to repeal the policies and return to the regular enforcement of immigration law. Doing so would rest on grounds similar to those invoked by Jefferson, who pardoned those convicted under the Sedition Act, which had made criticism of the government a crime, and ordered all pending prosecutions dropped. "On coming into office," Jefferson explained, "I released these individuals by the power of pardon committed to executive discretion, which could

never be more properly exercised than where citizens were suffering without the authority of law, or, which was equivalent, under a law unauthorized by the constitution, and therefore null."[30] Even though the courts and Congress had found the Sedition Act to be constitutional, Jefferson correctly concluded that the law violated the right to free speech. He used his prosecutorial discretion to prevent its execution. If presidents can decline to enforce unconstitutional laws, the Take Care Clause makes inescapable the reverse—that presidents have no choice but to enforce constitutional laws. The Constitution required Trump to make his own judgment about whether a president could refuse to enforce immigration law so completely as Obama had done, and if not, to reinstate its execution.

A. DACA AND DAPA

In creating DACA and DAPA, the Obama administration created exceptions that swallowed the rule. Illegal aliens present in the United States are of two kinds: those who have entered the country illegally and those who, having entered legally (such as with a tourist or student visa), are nonetheless now present illegally (visa "overstayers"). The Immigration and Naturalization Act (INA) provides for the removal (or, in older language, deportation) of aliens not lawfully present in the United States. Aliens may be removed if they were "inadmissible" at the time of entry, have been convicted of certain crimes, or meet other criteria set by federal law.[31] Immigration and Customs Enforcement (ICE), an agency within the Department of Homeland Security (DHS), has the responsibility of removing illegal immigrants from the United States. Realistically, ICE cannot remove much of the illegal immigrant population unless Congress increases its funding by a factor of 10. With current resources, ICE removed 256,086 illegal aliens in fiscal year 2018, out of a population estimated at 10–12 million.[32]

Due to its massive caseload and limited funding, ICE must develop enforcement priorities. These may vary from one administration to the next. But under DACA and DAPA, the Obama administration designated about five million illegal aliens a low priority for enforcement. Throughout the first two decades of this century, Congress refused to amend the immigration laws to grant such an exception. It failed several times, for example, to pass the DREAM Act, which would have allowed aliens illegally brought to the United States as children to remain if they had lived there for five years, were of good moral character, had graduated from high school, and were attending college or serving in the military.[33] On June 15, 2012, DHS secretary Janet Napolitano instructed subordinate officials to "defer action" against "certain young people who were brought to this country as children and know only this country as home."[34]

There are good reasons to support broad discretion in immigration enforcement. The president's ability to moderate legislative purposes through enforcement is a necessary and desirable consequence of a constitutional system that seeks to protect individual liberties by separating the power to legislate from the power to enforce. This separation creates a space in which liberty can be protected by executive discretion to reduce enforcement of laws that are oppressive or harsh. As liberal legal scholar and former Obama White House official Cass Sunstein has written, in our constitutional scheme, the "class of legitimate official revisions" of statutory law by executive officials "is large."[35]

This seems particularly obvious in the area of criminal law enforcement. Even if sufficient resources had been available to enforce obsolete laws against, say, the sale of contraceptives, many would argue that the executive could choose to leave those laws unenforced. Likewise, the executive can recognize changing social attitudes toward illegal drugs by choosing not to prosecute dying cancer patients who purchase marijuana. And given that no federal prosecution has been brought under the Logan Act in the more than 200 years of its existence, are United States attorneys at fault if they decline to bring cases under that act—even though Congress has resisted efforts to repeal it?

Even the enforcement of civil law needs discretion. The many responsibilities of the modern administrative state dictate nothing less. The courts have acknowledged implicitly that judicial review of executive nonenforcement decisions in the civil context is, for most practical purposes, nonexistent. The Supreme Court has affirmed that judicial review does not extend to agency nonenforcement decisions under the APA.[36] In *Arizona v. United States*, the Court emphasized that the executive branch enjoyed broad discretion in the enforcement of immigration. "A principal feature of the removal system is the broad discretion exercised by immigration officials," the Court observed. "Federal officials, as an initial matter, must decide whether it makes sense to pursue removal at all."[37]

But on the other hand, the Constitution assumes that the executive will enforce the laws in a nonarbitrary manner. It imposes on the president a duty to enforce existing statutes, regardless of any policy differences with the Congresses that enacted them or the presidents who signed them. President Washington first declared that "it is the particular duty of the Executive 'to take care that the laws be faithfully executed.'"[38] Unlimited discretion in enforcement policy can become a greater threat to personal liberty and security than the mechanical enforcement of the law. Even while rejecting judicial oversight over the executive's nonenforcement decisions, the Supreme Court warned that review might still be available in "a situation where it could justifiably be found that the agency has 'consciously and expressly adopted a general policy'" so extreme as to amount to an abdication of its statutory responsibilities.[39]

There are many reasons for a robust understanding of the executive's duty to enforce the law. The passage of legislation is ordinarily an arduous and slow-moving process, requiring proponents of a new law to assemble majorities on repeated occasions to overcome Congress's built-in inertia. The Framers designed multiple veto points such as bicameralism and presentment to impede the passage of all but well-considered legislation. With its own internal procedures (including the filibuster) and complex committee structure, Congress itself has substantially added to the bias in favor of inaction. For legislation of any real significance to be enacted, many interested players representing many different perspectives, interests, and constituencies must agree. This complicated process encourages legislation that reflects what Madison called in *Federalist No. 63* "the cool and deliberate sense of the community."[40] The difficulty of achieving a consensus in favor of the legislation should give the president little discretion to set Congress's policies aside.

If carried to an extreme, prosecutorial discretion can distort the lawmaking process. First, Congress might overregulate in certain areas, with the expectation that the executive will correct for it with remissive enforcement policies. Second, the threat of nonenforcement gives the president improper leverage over Congress by providing a second, post-enactment veto. Much like the line-item veto held unconstitutional by the Supreme Court, a second veto gives him a bargaining edge in negotiating with Congress for which the Constitution did not provide.[41] Third, the possibility of class-wide nonenforcement creates an incentive for members of Congress to bypass each other in fashioning legislation and to deal directly with the executive instead. By inviting the president to unilaterally enforce the laws along the DREAM Act's terms, some senators short-circuited the legislative process. Rather than redoubling their bargaining efforts with their fellow senators, they opened bargaining with the executive instead. Finally, legislators will be less likely to resist poor legislation if they can make favorable deals with the White House to exempt their favored constituencies.

All of this goes to confirm Hamilton's claim in *Federalist No. 70*, that "a government ill executed, whatever it may be in theory, must be in practice a bad government."[42] Our scheme of separated powers, even the very conception of "executive" power itself, supports a stringent view of the president's duty to enforce an act of Congress. The constitutional text also speaks emphatically in several places—notably, in the Take Care Clause—in favor of that view and against a more permissive understanding of "prosecutorial discretion." If the idea of executive power can seem to imply an authority, in proper cases, to deviate from the law, the idea of constitutional government requires that the executive power remain subordinate to the law.

B. THE DUTY TO ENFORCE THE LAW

The president's constitutional duty to enforce the law stands as the main textual obstacle to claims of a broad power of prosecutorial discretion. The Take Care Clause naturally reads as a command to the president to put the laws into effect, or at least to see that they are put into effect "without failure" and "exactly." It would be implausible and unnatural to read the clause as creating a power in the president to deviate from the strict enforcement of the laws. The president's responsibility is supervisory: he is not charged with executing the laws himself. Not only would this obviously have been impossible (how could the president collect customs in both Charleston and Boston at once?), but it is reflected in the phrasing of the clause. It does not say that the president "shall take Care to execute the laws faithfully," but rather that he take care that they "be faithfully executed." Others will "execute" the laws; the president's role is to see to it that they do so "faithfully."

Article II's vesting of the "executive power" of the federal government solely in the president makes clear that the Take Care Clause prescribes a duty. The Vesting Clause is a broad grant of power, comparable to those for Congress and the judiciary. But if the Vesting Clause confers the entirety of the "executive power" on the president, what additional power would the Take Care Clause confer? It seems likely that the Vesting Clause

confers a power that could, at least initially, include a power to decline to execute the laws, but that the Take Care Clause rejects that implication.

Finally, what does the Take Care Clause mean by "the laws"? The president has an obligation to enforce all the laws, including the Constitution itself. In the event of a conflict between the Constitution and an act of Congress or a treaty, he may or must refuse to enforce the latter. As the Supreme Court recognized in *Marbury v. Madison*, judicial review flows from the principle that a court cannot enforce a law that conflicts with the Constitution.[43] To require the president to carry out unconstitutional laws would violate his duty to obey the higher law of the Constitution. James Wilson, for one, anticipated that Congress might seek to grab executive power: "[T]he legislature may be restrained, and kept within its prescribed bounds, by the interposition of the judicial department . . . In the same manner, the President of the United States could shield himself, and refuse to carry into effect an act that violates the Constitution."[44]

The Take Care Clause's history at the Constitutional Convention supports the natural reading that the text imposes a duty and a constraint. In regard to the president, Wilson proposed: "It shall be his duty to provide for the due & faithful exec—of the laws."[45] The Committee of Detail altered this draft to read, "[H]e shall take care that the laws of the United States be duly and faithfully executed."[46] The Committee on Style simplified that version, drafting the final form of the clause: "[H]e shall take care that the laws be faithfully executed."[47] Years after the Convention, Wilson explained that the clause meant that the president has "authority, not to make, or alter, or dispense with the laws, but to execute and act the laws, which [are] established."[48]

Unlike some state constitutions, the federal Constitution contains no express provision precluding the president from suspending the laws. There is apparently no evidence explicitly linking the Take Care Clause to the elimination of those powers.[49] Nonetheless, the Take Care Clause is closely related to the 1689 English Bill of Rights, which formed an essential part of the great constitutional settlement after the Glorious Revolution and included in its first two sections prohibitions on suspending or dispensing with the law.[50] The Framers would not have vested a federal executive modeled on the governor of New York with a power that had long since been denied to the English king.

English monarchs had long claimed an extraordinary power to "dispense

with" the law, along with a related but less significant power to "suspend" the law. Kings could hold that a law did not apply to a specific person, or they could relieve someone of punishment. There were some limits to the dispensing power. James II and, occasionally, his predecessors landed in serious trouble when they used the dispensing power to accomplish policy objectives of their own that cut against the clear preferences of Parliament.[51] His broad use of the dispensing power was a major cause of the Glorious Revolution. The Glorious Revolution led to fundamental constitutional changes in English law, some of which entered into our own constitutional history. In 1689, Parliament formally abolished the royal dispensing power altogether. English law acknowledges no dispensing power unless specifically provided for by Act of Parliament. Thoroughly versed in England's constitutional history, the Framers were surely aware that by 1787, dispensation formed no part of the executive power, a principle underscored by the Take Care Clause.

C. THE PREROGATIVE

If the Take Care Clause shows that Obama could not decline to enforce the immigration laws, the Constitution did not just permit, but required Trump to reverse DACA and DAPA. At times of crisis in our history, however, a prerogative has emerged that could authorize deviation from, or even outright violation of the law on the grounds of compelling public necessity. If the Constitution contained an unenumerated prerogative power, it could have provided Obama with some general power not to execute the law. But a careful examination of constitutional history shows that the Constitution contains no such prerogative, at least over domestic affairs.

The prerogative made its first appearance in the writings of John Locke. Locke gave birth to the modern separation of powers by dividing the executive from the legislative power. Because legislatures could not always remain in session, society requires "a power always in being which should see to the execution of the laws that are made and remain in force," which he termed the executive.[52] Locke also vested the executive with the "federative" power over "war and peace, leagues and alliances, and all the transactions with all persons and communities without the commonwealth."[53] Though the federative and executive were "really distinct in themselves," Locke observed that "they are always almost united" because the former "is much less capable to be directed by antecedent, standing positive laws."[54]

Locke proposed the prerogative to deal with unforeseen events. In an emergency, the prerogative allows the executive "to act according to discretion for the public good, without the prescription of the law, and sometimes even against it."[55] Like the federative power, the prerogative operated in a zone that general, antecedent laws could not address. "Many things there are which the law can by no means provide for, and those must necessarily be left to the discretion of him that has the executive power in his hands." The legislature was "too slow for the dispatch requisite to execution." Unlike the royal prerogative, the executive's authority had to be exercised in the public interest and for the common good. The existence of such power still raised the "old question" of how to resolve conflicts between emergency power and the standing laws. To Locke, there were no preexisting answers to this problem, and there was "no judge on earth" who could resolve it.

Scholars have long debated whether the Framers included the prerogative in their conception of the executive power. There are also two types of prerogative: the first simply to act in the absence of any laws, and the second to actually violate the law during an emergency. Filling in the gaps in the laws seems well recognized in American constitutional practice. Violating the law, however, has been highly controversial. Locke argues that "a strict and rigid observation of the laws may do harm—as not to pull down an innocent man's house to stop the fire when the next to it is burning."[56]

Even if the prerogative existed, however, it would not include DACA and DAPA. First, any presidential prerogative should only extend to national security and foreign affairs. Legislatures have institutional difficulty in anticipating and responding to unforeseen events. The executive is the only branch designed to respond swiftly and decisively to an emergency. The challenge is investing the executive with sufficient discretion to handle a crisis without veering into dictatorship. American constitutional practice shows that the executive possesses adequate powers under the Constitution to cope with extreme national emergencies. Ever since Abraham Lincoln's presidency, the nation's emergency powers have rested within Article II, not outside it.

The controversy over the placement of the prerogative can be illustrated through the differences between Jefferson and Lincoln. Jefferson believed that presidents could refuse to enforce laws that they believed to

be unconstitutional (even when the courts had found otherwise).[57] Jefferson also believed that presidents could act outside the Constitution altogether if circumstances demanded it. His 1803 Louisiana Purchase avoided war with France and Spain and doubled the size of the nation. But Jefferson believed that the Constitution did not permit the acquisition of new territory that would become states (his view strangely ignored Congress's constitutional power to govern the territories and admit new states).[58]

Despite his constitutional views, Jefferson bought Louisiana from Napoleon. His believed his only authority was the prerogative. "The Executive in seizing the fugitive occurrence which so much advances the good of the country, have done an act beyond the Constitution," Jefferson wrote. It was up to Congress to support the unconstitutional act. "The Legislature in casting behind them metaphysical subtleties, and risking themselves like faithful servants, must ratify & pay for it, and throw themselves on their country for doing for them unauthorized what we know they would have done for themselves had they been in a situation to do it." Jefferson believed it was best to admit openly the violation of the Constitution and seek popular support. "We shall not be disavowed by the nation," he predicted, "and their act of indemnity will confirm and not weaken the Constitution, by more strongly marking out its lines."[59]

Jefferson claimed that unforeseen circumstances, produced either by necessity or by opportunity, required him to exceed his legal powers to protect the greater good. In an 1810 letter he wrote, "A strict observance of the written laws is doubtless *one* of the high duties of a good citizen, but it is not *the highest*. The laws of necessity, of self-preservation, of saving our country when in danger, are of higher obligation."[60] Obeying the higher law of protecting the nation could only be called upon during genuine moments of crisis, not when "consequences are trifling, and time allowed for a legal course."

Jefferson's prerogative has no clear legal source. One possibility is that an emergency power is inherent in the executive. Another is that the power rests outside the Constitution entirely. The former approach locates broad formal powers in the presidency and might require the president to seek approval after the fact from Congress, but for political rather than constitutional reasons. On the other hand, viewing the prerogative as resting outside the Constitution relieves the executive of stretching the law so drastically to permit more freedom of action. Jefferson's appeal to the

prerogative allowed him to keep to his generally strict construction of the Constitution overall.[61]

Lincoln resolved this question by firmly planting emergency powers within the Constitution. Some leading scholars have argued that Lincoln exercised unconstitutional powers in order to save the Union. Arthur M. Schlesinger Jr. viewed Lincoln as a "despot," while both Edward Corwin and Clinton Rossiter judged Lincoln's presidency a "dictatorship."[62] These views echo arguments made during the Civil War itself, even by Republicans who believed that the Constitution could not address such an unprecedented conflict. Lincoln surely entertained the idea that he could draw on an extraconstitutional power to preserve the nation. He wrote in 1864, "Was it possible to lose the nation, and yet preserve the Constitution?" To Lincoln, common sense supplied the answer: "By general law life and limb must be protected; yet often a limb must be amputated to save a life; but a life is never wisely given to save a limb." Necessity might justify unconstitutional acts. "I felt that measures, otherwise unconstitutional, might become lawful, by becoming indispensable to the preservation of the constitution, through the preservation of the nation."[63]

Lincoln, however, was no dictator. While he used his powers more broadly than any previous president had, he was responding to a crisis that threatened the very life of the nation. He relied on his power as commander in chief to give him control over decisions ranging from tactics and strategy to reconstruction policy. Like his predecessors, Lincoln interpreted his constitutional duty to execute the laws, his role as chief executive, and his presidential oath as grants of power to use force, if necessary, against those who opposed national authority. Rather than claim a greater power outside the Constitution to protect the nation, Lincoln found it in Article II. The Vesting Clause gave Lincoln the authority to respond to secession with military force and a wide range of corollary measures: raising an army, invasion and blockade of the South, military government of captured territory, and the suspension of habeas corpus. Lincoln consistently maintained that the Constitution gave him sufficient war powers to respond to the threat to the nation's security. Lincoln claimed that he had moved forcefully with the support of public opinion. "These measures, whether strictly legal or not, were ventured upon, under what appeared to be a popular demand, and a public necessity; trusting, then as now, that Congress would readily ratify them."[64]

The president's duty to enforce federal law became one of Lincoln's central powers to stop secession. Resistance to federal law and institutions was the work not of the states themselves but a conspiracy of rebels who were illegally obstructing the national government. The Constitution called upon Lincoln to use force, if necessary, against these rebels in order to see "that the laws of the Union be faithfully executed in all the States." Lincoln had no choice; the Constitution required him to put down the rebellion. "You have no oath registered in Heaven to destroy the government," Lincoln told the South, "while I shall have the most solemn one to 'preserve, protect and defend' it."[65] Lincoln's political rhetoric invoked Jefferson, but his constitutional logic followed Hamilton.

Regardless of whether the prerogative rests within the Constitution or outside of it, American constitutional practice shows that it has been reserved to national security and foreign affairs. If broad executive powers were to exist anywhere, they would exist in foreign affairs, where the limitations of republican government are most pronounced. It is here where the Constitution is most vague, giving the president the opportunity to act with the most discretion. In contrast, the domestic powers of the government are strictly defined and limited. Article I makes clear that it limits the power of Congress to the powers "herein" enumerated, the most prominent of which are the Commerce Clause and the Taxing and Spending powers. Unlike the "invitation to struggle" that is foreign affairs,[66] the process for enacting legislation is strict and defined. Both houses of Congress must approve legislation, which must then be signed by the president as required by Article I, Section 7 of the Constitution.

Domestic affairs permit a constitution designed to slow down, rather than speed up, federal action. Challenges at home do not tend toward the unforeseen and unprecedented. Domestic issues involve systemic social and economic problems rather than the unexpected actions of international competitors. Sometimes the most difficult problems, such as balancing the federal budget or fixing entitlement programs, can build for decades before they reach a point of crisis. Even sporadic events, such as natural disasters and economic fluctuations, might be predicted and provided for, just as with private insurance.

Domestic and foreign affairs differ in their costs of inaction. With the latter, passivity may allow a sudden attack or a serious foreign setback to occur. With the former, however, passivity may allow for better policy. In-

action provides for more time to collect information, consider alternatives, and deliberate on the best policy. As the analysis of rules versus standards suggests, errors decrease under a more flexible approach that considers the totality of the circumstances. The trade-off is that gathering more information and considering more alternatives drives decision costs up. Domestic matters can tolerate longer decision processes and higher costs because the government has more time to act. Foreign affairs, however, impose greater costs on slower decisions because of the harms that can occur to the nation from a sudden attack or foreign setback.

In addition, the Constitution can treat presidential prerogative differently in foreign affairs than in domestic affairs because of federalism. In foreign affairs, the president is the only branch that can respond to a looming threat or emergency. If the executive fails to act, the United States has failed to act. There is no backup system. In fact, Article I, Section 10 of the Constitution does its best to prohibit states from acting in national security affairs. Even when Section 10 permits states to respond where the federal government cannot, such as in cases of imminent danger, the forces available to decentralized states may well prove inadequate to a nation state–level threat.

Domestic affairs give rise to opposite demands. The Constitution's structure recognizes that states provide the default system for addressing social and economic problems. State common law establishes a universal, background level of regulation in the absence of any federal action. The Constitution's enumeration of Congress's powers in Article I, Section 8 means that federal intervention is interstitial, specialized, and limited, while state common law is general and universal. Unlike foreign affairs, if the president fails to act to solve a domestic problem, the states can act instead. The states are not constitutionally disabled; rather, the Constitution is biased in favor of state initiative. And the decentralized nature of the states may in fact lead to superior policy outcomes when facing the type of systemic, persistent problems that characterize domestic affairs.

A prerogative in domestic affairs would raise the risk of the kind of authoritarianism that worried the Framers. Domestic challenges tend toward persistent, society-wide problems that do not have set beginnings or endings nor come at the hand of a single opponent. Poverty and crime have been permanent features of the human condition; no single person or institution is responsible for their existence. Invoking a prerogative to combat

such decentralized problems would produce an extraordinary executive power of long duration. It seems impossible to believe that the Framers, Jefferson, or Lincoln would have thought that any presidential prerogative to act in emergencies would extend to the right to suspend laws on immigration.

D. THE PROBLEM OF RESOURCES

Faced with the absence of any right to ignore the immigration laws, President Obama claimed that the agency simply lacked sufficient resources—funding, staffing, or leadership—to discharge its enforcement duty in full. In such cases, the agency is pleading an excuse: it admits to having failed in its duty but argues that the responsibility is really that of Congress. There is no doubt that ICE, like its predecessor the INS, has faced acute resource constraints. The agency has long sought to cope with these limitations by establishing enforcement priorities. During the Obama administration, ICE focused its enforcement efforts on removing illegal immigrants who had committed felonies while in the United States. Correspondingly, the agency dedicated fewer resources to other categories, such as workplace enforcement or the prosecution of visa overstayers. Given the budgetary constraints on the agency, few if any would argue that these priorities were unreasonable, let alone unconstitutional.

The unreasonableness as opposed to the unconstitutionality of a nonenforcement decision, though related, are distinct questions. A decision to seek the deportation only of visa overstayers would be an unreasonable and inefficient use of ICE's resources, but arguably not an unconstitutional one, even if it meant that illegal immigrants who had committed serious crimes while in the United States remained here. On the other hand, whether or not judicial review of the action is possible, an enforcement decision to seek the removal only of Haitians, as distinct from members of any other national origins category, would be unconstitutional. So would a decision to remove deportable aliens because they had not contributed to the president's reelection campaign.

A categorical refusal to enforce the removal statutes against any deportable alien—effectively, the adoption of an "open borders" policy—would also be unconstitutional. Even if enforcement resources were constrained, it would be an obvious refusal to perform the constitutional

duty of faithful execution of the laws. Yet the logic of the DACA and DAPA nonenforcement policies would lead inexorably to the conclusion that the president may adopt exactly such a policy. If the president may constitutionally permit 50 percent of the illegal immigrant population to remain in the United States without fear of removal, why may he not do the same for the other 50 percent? True, as long as some funding was available to ICE for enforcement, the president could not claim that an appropriations shortfall justified the total end to deportation activities. Still, the president could deliberately allocate ICE's resources in such a way as to achieve essentially that result. But if the president can constitutionally implement an open borders policy on his own initiative and without authorization from Congress, what remains of the immigration law? DACA and DAPA thus lead to absurdity. The failure of an agency to perform its ordinary enforcement duties may be so unreasonable as to be considered unconstitutional, notwithstanding limitations on its resources.

Even though the question whether resource constraints excuse an agency's nonenforcement decisions is almost always one for Congress, large-scale nonenforcement (such as exists here) nonetheless calls for a reasoned public explanation and defense. One has first to consider whether the excuse is factually true or not. If it is not true, the excuse should likely be rejected. But even if the circumstances were as the party offering the excuse claimed, the excuse may still be rejected as flimsy or insufficient. DACA and DAPA purported to be based on budgetary constraints. The president himself defended the decision by arguing that, "in the absence of any action from Congress to fix our broken immigration system, what [DHS] has taken steps to do is focus immigration enforcement resources in the right places."[67] But there are obvious reasons to question the truth of this assertion.

First of all, the Obama administration provided no evidence to substantiate its claim of inadequate resources. It gave no estimates of what the cost savings from its initiative would be. It did nothing to show that the savings from this additional nonenforcement measure would be significant. It did not explain how the resources freed up by the nonenforcement decision would be used to improve ICE's enforcement efforts in other areas. It did not (and probably could not) show why the grant of work authorization to the DREAMers would result in cost savings for ICE rather than in extra

costs. Indeed, DHS's own immigration policy advisors and strategists had found that a "deferred action" program for the DREAMers would "likely be controversial, not to mention expensive."[68]

Justice Scalia, for one, did not credit the administration's rationalization for its nonenforcement decision. "The husbanding of scarce enforcement resources," he wrote in *Arizona v. United States*, "can hardly be the justification for this [policy], since the considerable administrative cost of conducting as many as 1.4 million background checks, and ruling on the biennial requests for dispensation that the nonenforcement program envisions, will necessarily be *deducted* from immigration enforcement."[69] Justice Scalia is quickly being proven right. ICE would have to hire hundreds of full-time workers, in addition to contract labor, to handle DACA and DAPA applications.

Furthermore, cost savings alone cannot possibly explain the fact that the contours of the nonenforcement decision dovetailed so neatly with those of the DREAM Act. That could hardly have been a pure coincidence; rather, it was proof that the administration's true purpose was not that of economizing or prioritizing. There is no reason to think that the administration or ICE considered alternative nonenforcement measures that would not have been so overtly antagonistic to Congress's choice to reject the DREAM Act, or even a nonenforcement measure that would not have applied to DREAMers who were already subject to removal orders.

But did President Obama nonetheless have the authority to close down enforcement against the DREAMers simply because he considered those enforcement costs to be money wasted? The answer is no. The executive is still duty bound to bring those cases for removal. That duty grows directly out of the original meaning of the Take Care Clause. Congress has identified the activity that it expects to be prosecuted and has provided sufficient resources. Congress's judgments, both as to the nature of the proscribed activity and as to the provision of the means to prosecute it, trump the executive's judgment. In *Tennessee Valley Authority v. Hill*, the Supreme Court confirmed the principle here. The Court upheld an injunction against the completion of a federal dam because its operation would endanger a protected species, the snail darter.[70] Plausibly, the survival of the snail darter was simply "not worth" the cost of enjoining the dam, which might have brought substantial benefits to electricity consumers and on whose construction considerable sums had already been expended. But

Congress's judgment that the survival of the snail darter took priority was definitive. If Congress directs that a particular type of civil enforcement action should occur and provides the means, the president may not override that judgment by concluding that the expenditure is wasteful.

The next chapter will more directly address the many controversies that have arisen over Trump and immigration, but this section has taken up the example of DACA and DAPA to address the separate constitutional question of presidential reversal. Trump reversed DACA and DAPA, despite his expressed policy preference to find a solution to the problem of Dreamers, because he believed Obama had no constitutional authority to impose the two policies. Obama claimed that he could implement DACA and DAPA as a matter of prosecutorial discretion. If that were true, Trump could simply restore the preexisting enforcement levels as a matter of his own exercise of prosecutorial discretion. Each new president's right to reverse the exercises of executive power by his predecessors means that no level of enforcement can bind any future administrations. If Obama were indeed free to set immigration removal levels to 50 percent of past cases, or even zero, Trump had the constitutional right to restore removals to those that prevailed before.

Lower courts nevertheless have blocked Trump's reversal of DACA and DAPA because they say he provided an insufficient justification. As this section has shown, Trump's rationale was correct: the Obama administration had no constitutional authority to refuse to enforce the immigration laws against whole classes of aliens, amounting to 50 percent of the possible removal cases. Indeed, in DACA and DAPA, Obama failed to live up to his constitutional responsibility to take care that the laws were faithfully executed. In such a situation, the Constitution compelled Trump to restore immigration enforcement to pre-DACA and -DAPA levels. Even should the Supreme Court disagree, Trump on this point has proven a strong defender not just of presidential power but also of constitutional restraint.

III. THE POWER TO PARDON

Even if a legion of permanent government employees still refused to obey the president, and a bevy of federal judges blocked his every move, the Constitution still gives him one last tool of reversal. Suppose the president's removal power does not prevent the bureaucracy from pursuing its

own agenda. The Framers reinforced the president's plenary control over law enforcement and executive policy with one last provision: the pardon power. Article II declares that the president "shall have Power to grant Reprieves and Pardons for Offences against the United States, except in cases of Impeachment." In granting the executive this unreviewable authority, the Framers sought to vest the president with an important tool to display mercy, soften harsh laws, or to break up conspiracies. But they also gave the president an important check on a bureaucracy that might pursue cases beyond his agenda.

To be sure, President Trump immediately pushed the power to its limits. In June 2018, he tweeted that he had the right to pardon himself from possible crimes related to Russian meddling into the 2016 elections. "I have the absolute right to PARDON myself," Trump wrote. He then quickly assured us that he wouldn't use that power. "But why would I do that when I have done nothing wrong?" He further accused the special counsel investigation brought by Robert Mueller of being "UNCONSTITUTIONAL."

Trump's comments followed those of his private legal counsel, Rudy Giuliani. Giuliani declared that the Constitution allowed the president to pardon himself. "He has no intention of pardoning himself," Giuliani told ABC News. "It would be an open question. I think it would probably get answered by gosh, that's what the Constitution says, and if you want to change it, change it. But yes."

A group of prominent lawyers, including Professor Laurence Tribe and former White House ethics czar Norm Eisen, immediately fired back. "The Office of the President is not a get out of jail free card for lawless behavior," they wrote in a group letter. "Our Founders would not have created—and did not create—a Constitution that would permit the President to use his powers to violate the laws for corrupt and self-interested reasons."[71]

Trump has the better of his critics. In the words of the Supreme Court, the Constitution grants the president a virtually "unlimited" power to issue pardons, subject to two important limitations: state crimes and impeachment.[72] He can even pardon himself. While such a result may seem to violate the idea that no one can be a judge in his own case, the constitutional text itself contains no such principle. In fact, the Framers considered exactly such a possibility and chose not to exempt a presidential self-pardon. But in their quest to stop Trump, critics would read into the Constitution a

provision that simply does not appear and therefore prevent the fulfillment of the Framers' purposes.

A.

Pardons had become an angle of attack on President Trump from the early months of his term. In part, Trump prompted criticism by not limiting pardons to deserving, but obscure, convicts, such as those who may have served unjust sentences or had contributed to the community in a remarkable fashion. Instead, Trump granted reprieves to high-profile, controversial figures. Critics claimed that these cases reeked of partisan favoritism or that Trump was using the pardons to encourage figures caught up in the Mueller investigation not to cooperate. For example, Representative Jerry Nadler claimed that Trump wields the pardon power as "a favor to bestow on the well-connected . . . when a celebrity friend . . . has lobbied on their behalf" or to "signal[] the promise of a pardon to those with potentially damaging information about him, to encourage them not to cooperate with investigators."[73] Senator Chris Coons also voiced his concerns that Trump might "misuse his pardon power . . . to challenge or push back on the whole Mueller investigation."[74]

In April 2018, for example, Trump granted a pardon to Lewis "Scooter" Libby. Special counsel Patrick Fitzgerald had indicted Libby for false statements, perjury, and obstruction as part of his probe into whether Bush administration officials had leaked classified information in the run-up to the Iraq War. After a jury convicted Libby and he began serving prison time, President George W. Bush commuted the sentence to time served but left the conviction in place. Trump went further and issued a full pardon, which had the effect of eliminating the conviction and restoring Libby's full rights.

Critics claimed that Trump pardoned Libby in order to interfere with the Mueller investigation. They argued that by pardoning Libby, Trump was dangling the hope of a pardon to those swept up in the probe. Adam Schiff characterized the Libby pardon as "sending a message to those implicated in the Russia investigation: You have my back and I'll have yours."[75] Of course, the parallels were not lost on observers. Libby had fallen prey to a special counsel created under the same regulations as those that led to the Mueller appointment. Fitzgerald had already known that Libby had

not leaked the classified identity of CIA agent Valerie Plame but instead prosecuted him for lying to FBI agents—much as Mueller appears to have decided early on that no evidence showed collusion between the Trump campaign and Russians and instead pursued obstruction of justice charges. From these parallels, targets such as Michael Flynn, Paul Manafort, and even Michael Cohen allegedly would refuse to cooperate in the hope of receiving a presidential pardon.

Mueller even directly investigated whether Trump had offered pardons in order to obstruct justice. On June 15, 2018, before a court hearing in the Paul Manafort prosecution, President Trump declared that Manfort's prosecution was "unfair."[76] While he said that "I don't want to talk about that" when asked about pardons, Rudy Giuliani made matters worse by speculating that "when the whole thing is over, things might get cleaned up with some presidential pardons." After a Virginia jury found Manafort guilty on August 21, 2018, on eight felony counts, Trump responded to a question about pardons by saying, "I have great respect for what he's done, in terms of what he's gone through."[77] Giuliani continued to dig the grave deeper by telling the *Washington Post* that Trump had asked his lawyers for advice about pardoning Manafort and other aides under prosecution by the special counsel. In his final report, Mueller listed this episode as an example of possible obstruction of justice, which he could not pursue because of the Justice Department's opinion that prosecutors cannot indict a sitting president.

A straightforward reading of the constitutional text makes clear that President Trump could have pardoned anyone indicted in the Mueller investigation, including himself. Article II shows that the Framers made only three exceptions to the pardon power. First, the president can only issue pardons for federal crimes, not state crimes. Second, the clause's limitation to federal crimes suggests that pardons do not reach civil actions under federal law. Third, the president cannot grant pardons for impeachment. The constitutional text contains no other limitations on the presidential pardon power, and the Supreme Court has never attempted to impose one.

Observers have described the breadth of the pardon power as plenary, unfettered, unqualified, and not subject to checks and balances from the other branches. Presidents have used it to pardon targets before prosecutors have charged them, while trials have been ongoing, or even long after conviction and sentencing. They have granted pardons to hundreds of

thousands simultaneously, as with President Andrew Johnson's December 25, 1868, grant of amnesty to members of the Confederacy from the crime of treason, or President Jimmy Carter's blanket pardon to all Vietnam War draft evaders. While no president has ever pardoned himself, Presidents Nixon and George H. W. Bush considered the possibility.[78] But in light of the text of the pardon power and its breadth of use, the Constitution does not appear to prohibit presidents from pardoning their co-conspirators or even themselves.

B.

Historical evidence from the Constitution's framing cannot overcome the plain meaning of the constitutional text—if anything, it supports this textual reading. As with other elements of the executive power, the American revolutionaries initially sought to restrict the pardon power. States restricted the authority once held by the royal governors by transferring the power to the legislature, restricting the crimes eligible for pardons, and by excluding impeachments.[79] It should come as little surprise that early drafts of the Constitution, the Virginia and New Jersey Plans, did not provide for pardons. But Hamilton, among others, led an effort to include a pardon power that mirrored the British practice, with its location in the executive, but with an exception for impeachments. Delegates proceeded to reject limits on the president's power, such as proposals requiring Senate consent or allowing pardons only for actual convictions.[80]

An important exchange in the Constitutional Convention previewed our arguments today over the idea of a presidential self-pardon. Edmund Randolph moved to amend the pardon clause to exclude treason as well as impeachment because the current text involved "too great a trust." Randolph worried that a president could use pardons to advance his own treasonous plots. "The President may himself be guilty," Randolph worried. "The traitors may be his own instruments."[81] Rising to defend the traditional grant of the pardon power in the executive, James Wilson rejected the idea that a British episode where a king pardoned a treasonous minister could occur under the constitution. "If the President be himself a party to the guilt he can be impeached and prosecuted."[82] Rufus King of Massachusetts criticized vesting the power in Congress as "inconsistent with the Constitutional separation of the Executive and Legislative powers." King argued that "a legislative body is utterly unfit for the purpose" because "they are

governed too much by the passions of the moment." Unusually, Madison supported anti-executive sentiment and declared his preference for "an association of the Senate as a Council of advice, with the President."[83] Wilson and King, however, carried the day. The delegates rejected Randolph's amendment by an 8–2 vote. When they had the chance to explicitly prevent presidential self-pardon (by excluding treason), the delegates clearly rejected the opportunity. Wilson's grounds, however, seemed to mistakenly assume that a pardon would not apply to the prosecution of a president after impeachment. But the Convention clearly understood that the president's pardon power would extend even to co-conspirators in an alleged treason plot.

During the ratification debates, Anti-Federalists repeated Randolph's argument that a president could abuse pardons to protect his fellow co-conspirators in a plot to overthrow the government. "The President of the United States has the unrestrained power of granting pardons for treason," George Mason argued in his widely disseminated *Objections to the Constitution*, "which may be sometimes exercised to screen from punishment those whom he had secretly instigated to commit the crime, and thereby prevent a discovery of his own guilt."[84] During the Virginia ratifying convention, Mason repeated his charge. "[T]he President ought not to have the power of pardoning, because he may frequently pardon crimes which were advised by himself," Mason alleged. "If he has the power of granting pardons before indictment, or conviction, may he not stop inquiry and prevent detection?"[85]

In *Federalist No. 74*, Hamilton responded to Mason and other Anti-Federalists with two reasons for pardons. The Constitution creates a pardon power "out of humanity and good policy" to allow for "mitigation from the rigour of the law."[86] As a result, it should be "as little as possible fettered or embarrassed." Recalling the original purposes of the pardon in British history, mercy propels most of the pardons in our history. Hamilton provided a second, broader defense of pardons that bears directly on today's Trump controversy. According to Hamilton, the Anti-Federalists argued that "the connivance of the chief magistrate ought not to be entirely excluded" in cases of treason. In such cases, critics demanded, the Constitution should give only Congress the right to pardon. Hamilton, however, defended an unlimited pardon power, even in cases of treason, and even when the president himself was one of the conspirators. He explained that

the pardon power must remain unfettered so it could help end public disorder or civil war. "In seasons of insurrection or rebellion, there are often critical moments, when a well-timed offer of pardon to the insurgents or rebels may restore the tranquility of the commonwealth," he wrote. Only the president could act vigorously in times of crisis and use pardons.

Hamilton speaks almost directly to today's controversy. Critics claim that Trump could pardon his co-conspirators from the Mueller investigation or later prosecutions. Nancy Pelosi voiced her concern that Libby's pardon sent a "troubling signal to the president's allies that obstructing justice will be rewarded."[87] Federalists could have added treason as a third exception to the pardon clause, or they could have required Senate consent to a pardon. Instead, they stood their ground and defended the sweeping scope of the power on the ground that the president might need to act quickly in times of rebellion and even civil war. Federalists did not contest that the president could pardon conspirators or even himself; they answered that such a possibility was the price of the broader benefits of the unfettered power.

Hamilton's argument on the pardon power built on the Constitution's structure, which concentrates the executive power in a single person, the president, so that the nation can act with decision, speed, and energy. The pardon power would bring benefits not just by moderating the harshness of the criminal law but in advancing the nation's security. Pardons did not just come about from executive grace; rather, they served the instrumental purpose of benefiting the public welfare. Hamilton's wisdom undoubtedly served the nation well during the Civil War, when President Lincoln used not only the executive power to respond energetically to the existential threat of secession but also the pardon power to begin the process of national healing. The benefits of such a power, Hamilton believed, outweighed the possibilities that a future president might use pardons to corruptly benefit himself.

It is this use of the pardon power that is potentially most sweeping and controversial. An early example came with the Whiskey Rebellion, where none other than George Washington pardoned several leaders of the insurrection in 1795. At the end of the Civil War, President Lincoln pardoned "all persons who have, directly or by implication, participated in the existing rebellion." It is estimated that Lincoln and his successor, Andrew Johnson, ultimately pardoned 200,000 former members of the Confederacy.

Faced with this text and constitutional history, presidential opponents appeal to two abstract principles. First, they argue that a presidential self-pardon would violate ancient Anglo-American rules against conflicts of interest. "The arguments against self-pardons begin with generally recognized principles of justice in the United States," argues professor James P. Pfiffner.[88] "No man is allowed to be a judge in his own cause," in the words of James Madison in *Federalist No. 10*, "because his interest would certainly bias his judgment, and, not improbably, corrupt his integrity."[89] Pfiffner concludes that a president pardoning himself "clearly violates this principle." Jed Shugerman and Ethan J. Leib similarly argue that "[t]he framers imported the well-known fiduciary duty of loyalty from the common law precisely to constrain the exercise of the president's powers under the Constitution . . . Those duties prohibit self-dealing and acting under a conflict of interest. Therefore, 'self-pardoning' . . . should not pass legal muster, because it violates the fiduciary law of public office."[90] DOJ's Office of Legal Counsel (OLC) declared in a legal opinion that Nixon could not pardon himself "under the fundamental rule that no one may be a judge in his own case."[91]

Though this principle appears early in the common law and finds expression during the Framing in Blackstone as well, it does not appear in the constitutional text or structure. When the Constitution prohibits self-dealing, it does so clearly, such as the constitutional amendment prohibiting Congress from raising its own pay in between elections, or impeachment's replacement of the vice president with the chief justice as the presiding judge when the president is in the dock. We can understand the Bill of Rights as an effort to prevent the government from suppressing certain political rights in an effort to stay in power.[92]

But other than these clear examples, the Constitution does not weave an anti-self-judging principle throughout its structure. If anything, important features of modern government have long discarded this idea. Take, for example, constitutional interpretation on key questions involving the separation of powers or federalism. The Constitution itself does not declare that any branch has a unique or final say on resolving constitutional questions. Nevertheless, the Supreme Court has both declared that its interpretation of the Constitution enjoys the same status as the Constitution itself, and that the other branches of government cannot seek to change it.[93] Or consider questions on the scope of federal power against the states. In such questions, the federal government has the final say on interpreting the extent of its own powers.[94]

The Constitution does not create a true checks-and-balances system, in which all three branches take part in every significant act of government. That mechanism might have described the classic English constitution that required approval by Crown, Commons, and Lords, but not the U.S. Constitution, which commits some acts wholly to the discretion of a specific branch. A president's choice not to prosecute remains unreviewable; Supreme Court justices decide for themselves when they must recuse themselves from a case; Congress alone sets its own procedural rules and whether to expel a member. The Constitution simply does not contain a government-wide principle against self-judging; if it had, it would surely have stated so in the text.

Critics of self-pardons also appeal to a second abstract idea: the rule of law. It is customary, for example, to hear attacks on executive power begin with the claim that ours is "a government of laws, and not of men," as Chief Justice John Marshall famously wrote in *Marbury v. Madison*. David Gray Adler criticizes the broad scope of pardons: "[A]n illimitable, unchecked power is alien to a nation committed to the rule of law and to a Constitution that was designed to corral all governmental authority and to prevent the exercise of arbitrary power."[95] As Brian Kalt argues, the rule of law means that no official or no one can be exempt from the law.[96] James Pfiffner and Justin Florence similarly argue that "such a pardon—for example, one that blocks an investigation—would place the president or his allies above the law by allowing them to break the law with impunity (without 'inquiry' or 'detection')."[97]

But "rule of law" can be a rhetorical phrase without real specifics. Appealing to an abstract concept cannot prevent the Constitution itself from excluding certain subjects from its reach. In *Marbury v. Madison*, for example, Marshall himself ultimately found that even if William Marbury had a legal right to his federal commission, the Supreme Court would not order Secretary of State Madison to hand it over. Governmental sovereignty, to take another example, makes the federal and state governments and their officials immune from many damages lawsuits. The pardon power similarly can exempt individuals from the criminal law, not because it violates the rule of law but because the rule of law requires us to follow the words of the Constitution.

Attempts to read a principle against self-dealing into the pardon power where none appears in the text amounts to the type of judicial activism that

has undermined the legitimacy of the Supreme Court and does violence to the process for democratic self-government written into the Constitution. There may be cases where the Constitution leaves gaps that we choose to fill in rather than follow the principle of *expressio unius*. For example, the great case of *McCulloch v. Maryland* upheld the creation of a federal bank under the Necessary and Proper Clause even though the Constitution contains no specific provision for such institutions. The Supreme Court read the Equal Protection Clause to prohibit racial segregation in the public schools in Washington, D.C., even though the clause appears in the Fourteenth Amendment, which applies only to the states. But unlike these cases, here we have a provision designed carefully by the Founders to incorporate British constitutional practice, which placed no limits on the king's pardon power. Anti-Federalists further attacked the clause for exactly the same reasons debated today—that it could allow a president to pardon an anti-government conspiracy of his advisors—but the Federalists flatly rejected their concerns. Silence in the text here does not extend an invitation to import new limitations on the pardon power but instead reflects the Federalists' considered choice to leave the authority unfettered.

The broad scope of the pardon power allows President Trump, therefore, to constrain efforts by the bureaucracy, or Congress, to encourage subordinates to pursue an agenda at odds with his own. Suppose that a "deep state" had indeed cooked up a Trump-Russia collusion story, as some Republicans have argued. Suppose further that the bureaucracy advanced this narrative by abusing its powers under FISA to conduct surveillance of Trump campaign officials and, ultimately, opened an investigation and prosecution of members of the Trump team. Mueller critics viewed the special counsel investigation in this light. If Trump believes the investigation spurious, he can pardon Flynn, Manafort, Stone, Papadopoulos, and the others caught up in Mueller's net. Trump may yet issue the reprieves, but so far he has not because the defendants proved guilty of crimes not associated with Russian collusion. Manafort evaded taxes and engaged in money laundering for payments received before he chaired the Trump campaign, while Stone and Papadopoulos lied to Congress or federal investigators. President Trump has learned to accept the verdict of federal prosecutors and juries.

The pardon power gives Trump the ultimate control over law enforcement. It may not expand an executive's ability to begin investigations or

prosecutions. The president already has that authority due to his executive power and the Take Care Clause. But he may face a recalcitrant bureaucracy and subordinates who hold more loyalty to their own notions of justice and fair government than to the constitutional chain of command. In that case, Trump can use the pardon power to overturn law enforcement decisions made in resistance to his policies. Like other constitutional powers, pardons can only be used by the president to block others rather than to engage in action. In the chapters on foreign affairs and war, we will see areas where the president has far more constitutional authority to carry forward an affirmative agenda even in the face of a hostile bureaucracy or Congress.

CHAPTER 5

"WE HAVE TO HAVE BORDERS": TRUMP AND IMMIGRATION

Immigration has dominated the Trump presidency like nothing else. Trump's obsessive focus on illegal aliens can find its origins in the very beginnings of his political rise. Trump announced his candidacy in June 2015 by striding down the Trump Tower escalator to proclaim his dislike of Mexican immigrants. He declared that "[w]hen Mexico sends its people . . . they're bringing crime."[1] Once in office, Trump sought to keep his promises by blocking the entry of Muslims into the United States, speeding up the removal of aliens in the nation illegally, and tightening enforcement at the border. He even declared the flood of immigrants crossing from Mexico a national emergency and transferred billions of dollars from military projects to border wall construction.

Trump might even owe his election to his aggressive stance on the issue. He broke out of the Republican primary pack after the December 2015 San Bernardino terrorist attacks, which killed 14 and injured 22. After police identified the killers as recent immigrants of Pakistani descent, Trump called for "a total and complete shutdown of Muslims entering the United States until our country's representatives can figure out what the hell is going on."[2] Trump immediately surged to a 20 percent lead in Republican polls—a lead that dipped, but never disappeared.[3] He continued the call for a ban on Muslim immigration and criticized Muslims themselves throughout the 2016 election season.[4] He promised a wall on the U.S.-Mexico border and proposed the "extreme vetting" of aliens. "A Trump administration will stop illegal immigration, deport all criminal aliens, and save American lives," he promised just before the election.[5]

Within days of taking the oath of office, Trump followed through. He

111

issued an executive order banning the entry to the United States of aliens from specific Muslim countries—the so-called travel ban.[6] He reversed the Obama administration's DACA program for aliens brought to the United States as children and their parents.[7] He sought $20 billion for a wall along the Mexican border and cut funds to "sanctuary" cities and states that refused to cooperate with federal immigration enforcement.[8] As the 2018 midterm elections approached, Trump sent troops to secure the southern border against a "caravan" of Central Americans threatening to cross from Mexico. He even proposed an end to automatic citizenship for all children born on U.S. territory.[9]

Trump's policies raise difficult questions of presidential power. The travel ban raised the issue of whether the executive has the authority to block immigration from specific countries. It provoked lower courts into searching a president's state of mind for signs of racist or religious motives. Declaration of a national emergency prompted accusations that the president had seized the power to spend money unilaterally in violation of the Constitution. Pelosi and Schumer, for example, released a joint statement that Trump's border wall "clearly violate[s] the Congress's exclusive power of the purse."[10] Trump's decision to intensify immigration enforcement provoked conflict between the federal government and independent state and local officials. His attack on birthright citizenship raised fundamental questions over the president's right to interpret the Constitution and the meaning of the Fourteenth Amendment's Citizenship Clause.

For critics, Trump's sudden changes to U.S. immigration policy further revealed his disrespect for the Constitution. After Trump fired the secretary of the Department of Homeland Security in April 2019 for not stopping the flow of immigrants across the southern border, once-conservative columnist Max Boot went on the attack. "The real national emergency isn't at the border. It's in Washington," Boot wrote. "Trump is trashing the rule of law to stay in power—and the very same Republicans who excoriated President Barack Obama for his supposed misuse of executive power are meekly going along."[11] California and New York even went to federal court to challenge the administration's immigration policies.

But these critics go too far. Trump can claim support in the Constitution for his immigration policies. I say this despite disagreement with some of his choices. I believe he has the Constitution's fundamental approach to citizenship wrong. As a policy matter, I do not believe that our nation

should deport illegal aliens brought here as children, especially those who contribute to our society as adults. And at the time of the first travel ban order, I argued that banning Muslim immigrants violated the Constitution by discriminating on the basis of religion.[12] I think the United States should increase legal immigration from about one million aliens a year to two or even three million.

The Trump White House paused, stepped back, and brought its policies within the Constitution's ambit. Later versions of the travel ban, for example, cured its legal difficulties. Attacks on the travel ban risked greater harm to the constitutional order by calling on courts to speculate about the president's state of mind. In their haste to paint Trump as a dictator, critics deliberately ignored Supreme Court precedent and congressional recognition of presidential emergency powers that justify his border wall. Cities and states can refuse to cooperate with federal authorities, but the Supremacy Clause forbids them from interfering with federal officers. Despite protests and litigation by San Francisco and New York, the Constitution allows the federal government to cut off federal funding to coerce state governments that refuse to cooperate.

Trump's critics urge a cure that is worse than the disease. They would impose a double standard on presidential powers when they happen to be exercised by a conservative instead of a liberal. In order to stop his immigration policies, they would hamstring the ability of future presidents to respond to unforeseen emergencies and crises. They would have the Supreme Court play presidential psychiatrist by overruling decisions where they suspect the president harbors ulterior motives. Rather than create an office whose powers fluctuate based on whether the president meets a test for progressiveness or political correctness, critics should seek to change policy at the ballot box, as the Constitution requires.

When Trump took office, the nation remained paralyzed on immigration policy. Congress could neither increase nor reduce the level of legal immigration, could not reform antiquated categories of aliens that make little sense in a time of cheap travel and worldwide labor markets, nor could it even handle the narrow issue of the "Dreamers." Rather than wade gingerly into these waters, Trump charged right in. He summoned forth all of the elements of presidential power and ran headlong into unprecedented resistance. Critics in Congress, the media, and the academy accused the president of shredding the Constitution, breaking the law, and

violating basic norms of human decency. Opponents launched a bevy of lawsuits. They found federal trial judges all too willing to impose nation-wide injunctions against Trump's immigration policy. In their rush to tear down Trump, however, they advanced unprecedented theories of presi-dential limits that discarded constitutional text, history, and decades of practice. The resistance eventually failed. But if it had succeeded, it would have placed a straitjacket on executive power that would have made future presidential success all but impossible.

I. A SHORT HISTORY OF AMERICAN IMMIGRATION

Before tackling Trump's immigration policies, and their conflicts with the Constitution, we should better understand the immigration landscape. In the early twenty-first century, we are a nation of 325 million people span-ning a continent. Immigrants comprise a significant part of that popula-tion. In 2016, foreign-born residents reached a record 43.7 million, or about 13.5 percent of the U.S. population. About 33.8 million reside in the United States legally—three-quarters are naturalized citizens, and one-quarter are permanent or temporary resident aliens. About 1 million permanent res-ident aliens apply for citizenship every year.[13] According to recent figures, though there are varying accounts, the remaining 11 to 12 million remain in the United States illegally.[14] Children born on American territory to illegal aliens, thus becoming citizens, numbered about 250,000 in 2016.[15]

For much of the nation's early history, the federal government exercised no serious border control—Congress did not pass the first law restricting immigration until 1875—and states encouraged emigration from Europe to help settle the frontier and build the economy.[16] Although the United States had relatively open borders for its first century, the sharp rise in immigration during the 1890–1920 period sparked a backlash. In 1921 and 1924, Congress enacted immigration laws that used national origins quotas to maintain the ethno-racial composition of the country as it had existed in the 1890s. A 1952 law—which favored Western Europe—maintained the quotas for certain nations but created today's preferences for immigrants with economic skills or with relatives in the United States.[17]

All of that changed with the 1965 Immigration and Nationality Act, which replaced quotas based on nationality or race with ceilings for each

country.[18] It significantly raised the number allowed to come to the United States, and it created the structure that would allow even more in the future. Before the passage of the act, about two-thirds of those migrating to the United States legally came from Europe and Canada. By 1991, 51.8 percent of immigrants came solely from Mexico. Asia, which had sent virtually no one to the United States in the decades before, accounted for 19.6 percent of all immigrants.[19] After the Great Recession of 2008, Mexican immigration began to fall precipitously. Between 2009 and 2014, the United States witnessed a net decline in overall migration from Mexico.[20] Today, India is the number-one source of immigrants (126,000), followed closely by Mexico (124,000), then by China (121,000).[21]

Even as immigration patterns have radically changed, immigration law and policy have become steadily more chaotic. The Supreme Court has long recognized that the Constitution vests Congress with control over immigration, both because of its explicit power over naturalization and its implicit control over the borders.[22] Congress has passed very detailed rules about the lawful entry of aliens and the limited grounds on which they may remain.[23] Illegal aliens are those who enter or are present in the United States in violation of those rules. Immigration law provides for their removal (in older language, deportation) if they were "inadmissible" at the time of entry, have been convicted of certain crimes, or meet other criteria set by federal law. These rules make the tax code look like a model of clarity. Congress has made matters even worse by enacting very specific rules to control immigration but then delegating vast amounts of its authority to the executive branch.[24]

Presidents therefore exert great influence over immigration policy. The Supreme Court has suggested that the president has his own constitutional authority over immigration due to his control over foreign relations.[25] But the White House has an even greater role due to the executive's prosecutorial discretion to set priorities on enforcement, which essentially gives the executive branch the power to decide which classes of aliens to remove.[26] Statutes may prohibit restrictions on immigrants based on national origin, for example, but they also delegate to the president the right to "suspend the entry of all aliens or any class of aliens" whenever he "finds" that their entry "would be detrimental to the interests of the United States."[27] As we will see, resistance to presidential discretion to control immigration policy has failed due to his authority over law enforcement.

II. THE WALL

A clear example comes from one of Trump's most controversial immigration decisions. Due to a large migration of Central American aliens, Trump declared a national emergency and then transferred money from military construction to build a border wall. While dispute continues about conditions at the border, the data show that the rate of illegal border crossings shot up in Trump's first years in office. In the last year of the Obama administration, the Border Patrol apprehended 46,118 illegal aliens at the southwest border. In 2017, the Trump administration's anti-immigration rhetoric seemed to drive that number down to 16,794. But in the next two years, "caravans" of families from Central America approached the border to take advantage of asylum laws that protect those persecuted for their political or religious beliefs. Apprehensions of aliens shot up: 50,347 in 2018 and 103,492 in 2019—an increase of six times in just two years. In just the first three months of 2019, the number of unaccompanied children and families attempting to cross the border illegally doubled.[28]

The Trump administration responded by both blocking crossings and discouraging others from following suit. Media accounts focused on the terrible conditions for detained illegal aliens and the policy of separating families caught crossing the border, which the administration quickly dropped after public outcry. But Trump's policy centered primarily on the construction of a border wall that could prevent aliens from crossing except at guarded points of entry. In 1996 and 2006, Congress had passed laws that authorized at least 700 miles of "reinforced fencing," but not a physical wall, along the 2,000-mile border.[29] In one of his first acts in office, Trump issued an executive order to "immediately plan, design, and construct a physical wall along the southern border . . . to most effectively achieve complete operational control" there.[30] But without money, the White House cannot even build a rock garden. The 2017–19 Republican Congress declined the administration's request for $20 billion for the construction of a border wall. During the 2018–19 budget standoff, the new Democratic House majority rejected administration requests for $5.7 billion for a border wall.

Right after Congress passed a February 2019 budget ending a government shutdown, the White House swiftly went to work on the wall. Trump proclaimed a national emergency due to the entry of "criminals, gang

members, and illicit narcotics" and the "large-scale unlawful migration" through the southern border. He also justified the emergency on "the sharp increase in the number of family units entering" and the lack of detention space, which allows their release into the United States.[31] Trump tweeted: "We're going to be signing today and registering a National Emergency . . . We have an invasion of drugs, invasion of gangs, invasion of people—and it's unacceptable." The president then announced the transfer of $8 billion from military construction projects to fund the wall.

Critics immediately blasted the declaration of emergency. They argued that the president has no authority to build a wall after Congress had specifically rejected his $5.7 billion request. "This is plainly a power grab by a disappointed president, who has gone outside the bounds of the law to try to get what he failed to achieve in the constitutional legislative process," Speaker Pelosi and Senator Schumer said.[32] But fire rained down from conservatives too. *National Review*'s David French judged Trump's plan "a lawless abuse of power." A dozen Republican senators joined an effort to override the national emergency declaration, which Trump promptly vetoed.[33] "Never before has a president asked for funding, Congress has not provided it, and the president then has used the National Emergencies Act of 1976 to spend the money anyway," said Republican senator Lamar Alexander. "Our nation's founders gave to Congress the power to approve all spending so that the president would not have too much power. This check on the executive is a crucial source of our freedom."

These criticisms, however, discard traditional understandings of the Constitution simply out of disagreement with Trump's political goals. In order to win passing political battles with their hated target, they would willingly sacrifice the advantages of the American presidency and thereby handicap the nation's ability to respond to emergencies in the future. Most fundamentally, opponents ignored the very purposes behind the American presidency. Our Founders wisely chose not to try to limit beforehand the government's ability to rise and meet unforeseen crises and emergencies. Because the "circumstances that endanger the safety of nations are infinite," Hamilton warned in *Federalist No. 23*, "no constitutional shackles can wisely be imposed on the power."[34] Under the Articles of Confederation, the young republic had suffered from a Congress that could not effectively respond to foreign threats or internal disturbances.

The Founders chose to solve the problem of executive action with democratic responsibility by creating an independent, elected executive. They vested that power in a single person, rather than multiple officials as under the Roman Republic, so that the government could act swiftly and decisively in time of crisis and emergency. "Good government," Hamilton explained in *Federalist No. 70*, requires "energy in the executive," which is "essential to the protection of the community from foreign attacks" and "the steady administration of the laws." Hence, the Constitution creates a single president, elected independently, with its own powers to act with "decision, activity, secrecy, and dispatch."[35]

During critical times in American history, our elected leaders have understood the Constitution's grant of "the executive power" to the president to include a power to declare a national emergency. Jefferson effectively did so in response to Aaron Burr's effort to raise a rebellion in the Louisiana Territory. Lincoln declared an emergency, with far greater reason, at the start of the Civil War. With American entry into World War I approaching, Woodrow Wilson issued the first official "emergency" proclamation in February 1917 to expand the size of the maritime fleet to carry goods abroad. FDR, with far less justification, declared an emergency to handle the Great Depression, but he did so again with far more right to prepare the nation for World War II. Harry Truman properly declared one at the start of the Korean War, the first time that the communist nations would directly attack an American ally.

While presidents might misjudge a situation in hindsight, the branches of government understood that the Constitution erred on the side of safety by allowing for swift action. After the firing on Fort Sumter in April 1861, Lincoln called forth an army and sent it into battle, imposed a blockade on the southern states, and withdrew money from the Treasury to pay for it—all without congressional approval. Congress would bless his actions only three months later, on July 4, 1861. In *The Prize Cases*, the Supreme Court agreed that the president had to act first to respond to unprecedented threats to the nation. "If a war be made by invasion of a foreign nation, the President is not only authorized but bound to resist force by force. He does not initiate the war, but is bound to accept the challenge without waiting for any special legislative authority."[36] The Court expressly declared that the scope and nature of the military response rested within the hands of the executive.

Rather than fight this constitutional hardwiring, Congress has only followed it. In the wake of Watergate, critics of presidential power sought to place some restraints on emergencies. In the 1976 National Emergencies Act (NEA), however, Congress only set out a procedure for their announcement. It refused to define an emergency, though it also provided a method for Congress to override the president's finding.[37] Congress has never used this power; until President Trump's 2019 declaration on the border wall, it had never really tried. Nor has the Supreme Court ever overturned a finding of a national emergency, even in cases less dire than the crisis on the southern border. Barack Obama declared an emergency out of fear of the swine flu; Ronald Reagan used the law to maintain export controls when the authorizing law expired. Every president has used the NEA to declare a national emergency, several under circumstances far less immediate than this one.

Conditions at the U.S.-Mexico border could provide the grounds for an emergency declaration. At various times during their presidencies, both Bush and Obama deployed the National Guard to support border control agents struggling to handle surges of illegal aliens. In late 2018 and early 2019, the large number of aliens from Central America began to overwhelm facilities that process and detain illegal aliens, leading to poor conditions while they await court hearings. The main question is not whether the average observer would conclude these surges amount to an emergency, but whether the president can. Given his access to sources of intelligence and information both about migration and the government's resources, and given the jump in the number of aliens crossing the border, Trump had the discretion to declare the situation an emergency.

Critics of the Trump administration, however, seek to paint the emergency declaration as a shocking abuse of presidential power. They compare it to the last great constitutional confrontation over the emergency power, which occurred during the Korean War. David French and liberal law professor (and dean of my law school) Erwin Chemerinsky, for example, compare the Trump declaration to President Truman's seizure of the nation's steel mills, without congressional authorization, to keep steel and arms flowing to the battlefront. In *Youngstown Sheet & Tube Co. v. Sawyer*, a 6–3 majority of the Supreme Court concluded that Truman had violated the Constitution.[38] In the majority opinion, Justice Hugo Black found that taking possession of private property was a legislative function of government vested in Congress, not the president. Since Congress had just rejected amendments to the federal labor laws to grant Truman this power, Black concluded, the president was without constitutional or statutory authority to seize the mills. "This is a job for the Nation's lawmakers, not for its military authorities," Justice Black wrote.[39] In a famous concurrence, Justice Robert Jackson argued that when the president acted in the face of such congressional rejection, his power rested at its "lowest ebb" and would usually not survive judicial scrutiny.

According to these critics, Trump's border emergency was similarly illegal. Even sensible conservative thinkers, such as Ramesh Ponnuru and Yuval Levin, charge that "the emergency declaration is in fact highly objectionable and surely does fly in the face of our constitutional order."[40] Relying on *Youngstown*, however, badly misses the mark. Trump does not claim that he has an inherent power to declare an emergency and build a wall. If he did, *Youngstown* might govern. Trump instead claims authority under the Emergencies Act. He is not claiming a constitutional power to move money around during emergency (as Jefferson, Lincoln, and other presidents before him did). Instead, Trump is acting under a congressional delegation of authority to the executive branch. His claim is no different than the exercise of such authority by administrative agencies—from giving out Education Department grants to funding roads and bridges—that takes place every day.

Critics almost willfully ignore a more directly relevant Supreme Court case that strongly supports Trump's emergency. Unlike *Youngstown*, moreover, this case came after Congress's passage of the 1976 Emergencies Act and clearly addresses the delegated powers triggered by an emergency. In *Dames & Moore v. Regan* (1981), the Supreme Court reviewed the Carter and Reagan administrations' actions to settle the Iranian hostage crisis.[41] Under the deal reached with Tehran, the United States had to suspend claims against Iran in U.S. courts, nullify any attachments of Iranian assets pursuant to court order, and transfer all Iranian funds to a new international tribunal in the Netherlands. Carter triggered emergency powers under the International Emergency Economic Powers Act of 1977, which allowed him to suspend the claims and to transfer bank funds—but, importantly, did not allow him to lift court orders freezing assets.

The Court, however, upheld Carter's order *in toto* anyway. His action was "supported by the strongest of presumptions and the widest latitude of judicial interpretation," Justice William Rehnquist wrote at the time,

"and the burden of persuasion would rest heavily upon any who might attack it."[42] The Supreme Court upheld Carter's order because he declared an emergency and then unlocked broad powers delegated by Congress itself. Congress could not predict every emergency in the future; emergencies by their nature require vesting the executive with discretion to meet the necessity of circumstance. In such conditions, the Court will not read congressional silence to be a rejection of presidential power. "Congress cannot anticipate and legislate with regard to every possible action the President may find it necessary to take or every possible situation in which he might act," Rehnquist wrote. "Such failure of Congress specifically to delegate authority does not, 'especially . . . in the areas of foreign policy and national security,' imply 'congressional disapproval' of action taken by the Executive."[43]

Trump's border declaration falls within the scope of *Dames & Moore* rather than *Youngstown*. *Dames & Moore* refuses to second-guess the president's finding that the circumstances justify a national emergency or his decision to access powers delegated by Congress. *Youngstown*, by contrast, is a case decided twenty years before the Emergencies Act, where the Court found that Congress had refused to grant the president any emergency powers. While in Trump's case Congress declined to fund the $5.7 billion border wall request, it also did not forbid the use of emergency funds for the wall.

Claiming that *Youngstown* governs rather than *Dames & Moore* shows a willingness to impose a double standard on the Trump presidency. But even if *Youngstown* controlled, Trump would still win because Congress has passed at least two laws that give the president the power to transfer funds to a construction project in an emergency. The first states that when a national emergency "requires use of the armed forces," the president can order the Defense Department to transfer money from existing "military construction" funds to undertake new construction projects "necessary to support such use of the armed forces."[44] Trump's wall falls squarely within the terms of this law. Like Obama and Bush, Trump ordered troops to the border to assist in the apprehension of illegal migrants and to intercept drug smuggling. As commander in chief, the president could reasonably conclude that a wall would support those troops.

Critics respond, however, that the immigration emergency does not require "use of the armed forces" and that a wall is not "necessary to support"

them. They claim that border control falls under the jurisdiction of civilian authorities, namely, the Immigration and Customs Enforcement agency within the Department of Homeland Security, so that stopping aliens is a law enforcement function. They also rely on statistics that show no increase in illegal migration across the southern border, so no objective facts support deployment of troops or construction of a wall.

Putting aside the Supreme Court's repeated emphasis on the president's right to determine whether real-world conditions amount to an emergency, the publicly available facts support Trump. Trump has ordered at least 3,000 troops to defend the border. Border control is not simply a law enforcement exercise akin to chasing wire fraud or insider trading. This recalls the U.S. Army to its roots—safeguarding the frontier. For much of American history, the primary purpose of the armed forces was border defense. Congress cannot unilaterally transform a historic military mission—safeguarding the nation's territorial integrity—into a civilian law enforcement mission. That would effectively allow Congress to reduce the Constitution's grant of the commander in chief and executive powers to the president. This case is even stronger if, as appears to be the case, the military is not enforcing the immigration laws but providing protection of the border and supporting civilian agencies. The U.S. Army is not sending illegal aliens to the immigration courts. That remains ICE's job.

A second, similar law allows the president, in the event of an emergency, to transfer funds from Army Corps of Engineers projects. Under that law, the secretary of defense can reallocate funds from military civil works programs to "authorized civil works, military construction, and civil defense projects that are essential to the national defense." This statute appears even more generous than the first.[45] It does not demand that the national emergency require the use of the armed forces; it allows that it could be an emergency that "requires or may require" their use. It also does not require that the construction be necessary to support the armed forces.

Critics could argue that a wall would not be "essential to the national defense." But the federal courts are reluctant to judge what construction projects are essential or not to the national defense. This is especially so where, as here, the phrase is repeated but not defined in the U.S. Code. A quick spin through various federal laws and regulations indicates that the phrase arises primarily with regard to the president's authority to designate commodities, workers, and even industries as essential to the national

defense, or to the president's right to protect classified information. There does not appear to be any definition of what construction projects are essential to the national defense. As *Dames & Moore* indicates, the Supreme Court would give the president the broadest deference to decide whether any construction project, even a border wall, would satisfy this statutory language.

This makes perfect sense. It would be difficult, if not impossible, to define by antecedent law what makes for a military necessity. Would the courts review whether the president's decision to build a particular base, road, waterway, airport, fortification, defense structure, storage facility, arsenal, or even a bunker is "essential" to the national defense? Such a decision would depend on the circumstances and the nature of the threat. Indeed, the Framers created the federal government and the presidency exactly because they knew that it was impossible to define beforehand the nature of emergencies and crises, and that the better course was to create a body of government with the authority to act in the circumstances. Because the "circumstances that endanger the safety of nations are infinite," Hamilton warned in *Federalist No. 23*, "no constitutional shackles can wisely be imposed on the power."[46] In this case, the web of congressional authorizations and emergency powers does not contradict the constitutional scheme but instead amplifies it. Not only do presidents still have some reservoir of constitutional authority to respond to emergencies, but Congress has also seen fit to enhance it with the right to reallocate spending to support a president's decision to use the military. Despite the pleas of administration critics, the Supreme Court should agree.

III. THE TRAVEL BAN

While the fight over the border consumed the second half of Trump's term, the first half focused on the "travel ban." In the wake of the Boston Marathon bombing and the San Bernardino shooting, candidate Trump demanded a halt to all Muslim immigration. Upon taking office, the president ordered a ban on travel from several majority-Muslim nations. Claims of unconstitutionality immediately greeted the order, along with widespread judicial resistance.

At the time, I argued that a group of inexperienced campaign aides had written the order, outside the normal routines of the executive branch,

and as a result had violated the freedom of religion. Many critics also argued that the White House had exceeded the constitutional powers of the presidency. Trump's political opponents went farther. In their minds, the travel ban could not advance the nation's security. Nor could it serve as the opening salvo in a renewed debate with Congress over overhauling the immigration laws. Instead, Trump's critics accused the president of harboring a racist agenda.[47]

Trump, however, did the unexpected. Rather than charge headlong into the fray, he stepped back and allowed the normal wheels of government to turn. The Departments of Homeland Security and Justice corrected the initial errors. Experienced advisors rooted the order more firmly in the president's delegated powers. They removed provisions that appeared to favor Christians over Muslims. As with the border wall, Trump's travel ban ultimately fell within federal law, previous government practice, and the Constitution.

In the face of the new, more reasonable Trump, judicial opponents had to resort to extreme angles of attack. Instead of looking to the legal text, they overturned the travel ban because they believed the president held forbidden racial motives for it. They applied standards to Trump that courts had never applied to past presidents. Indeed, they had rarely applied such searching and critical review to any branch of the federal government, including themselves. If applied to future presidents, searching for executive motive would cause the government to grind to a halt. Trump had to fight for his travel ban not only to advance his immigration agenda but also to defend the ability of his successors to fulfill their constitutional responsibilities. In the face of widespread political and legal resistance, the administration would have to go to the Supreme Court three times to prevail.

The story begins in Trump's first weeks in office. On February 1, 2017, the president ordered the Departments of Homeland Security and State to conduct a review of foreign governments' screening of travelers leaving for the United States. While this review proceeded, the order barred anyone from Iraq, Iran, Libya, Somalia, Sudan, Syria, and Yemen from entering for 90 days. It allowed religious minorities in those countries to appeal for a waiver. It also suspended all refugee admissions for 120 days and further required that refugee policy prioritize admission for religious minorities. Trump declared the suspension necessary because these nations had be-

come hotbeds of terrorism. His order would allow the United States to remain "vigilant during the visa-issuance process to ensure that those approved for admission do not intend to harm Americans and that they have no ties to terrorism."[48]

Trump's order seemed aimed at Islam. Not only were the nations all majority Muslim but the exception for minorities seemed to apply primarily, if not exclusively, to Christians and Jews. At the Pentagon signing ceremony, Trump declared that the purpose of the order was to prevent "radical Islamic terrorists" from entering the nation.[49] He criticized previous restrictions, which had provided no priority entry for Christians. "If you were a Muslim you could come in, but if you were a Christian, it was almost impossible," Trump said.[50] The next day, Rudy Giuliani declared on television that "when Donald Trump first announced it, he said 'Muslim ban.' He called me up. He said 'Put a commission together. Show me the right way to do it legally.'"[51]

A federal district court in the State of Washington quickly enjoined the order, and the U.S. Court of Appeals for the Ninth Circuit refused to intervene on the grounds that Trump gave no reasons for the restrictions other than religious or racial bias.[52] Although the Trump administration modified the order with a new one that explained that each nation chosen was a state sponsor of terrorism, significantly compromised by terrorist organizations, or contained an active conflict zone, several courts enjoined that one as well.[53] The Supreme Court, however, blocked the lower court opinions and allowed the 90-day review to proceed.

Federal trial judges matched the sloppiness of the executive order with their own mistakes. The first federal court to stay the travel ban completely ignored the statutory basis for the president's authority. Judge James Robart in Washington state spent a few paragraphs describing the procedures involved but did not identify any provision of the Constitution or statutory law violated by the president's order, and then issued a nationwide injunction forbidding its enforcement.[54] Though his opinion contained no real analysis or legal reasoning, Judge Robart evidently thought that Trump had seized the authority to control the borders from the other branches of government.

This was far from the truth. The Constitution neither explicitly creates an immigration power nor assigns it to any branch of government. The Framers came closest in Article I, Section 8, which gives Congress

the power of naturalization. Naturalization creates the process by which immigrants become citizens, but it does not control the borders. In upholding the Chinese Exclusion Act of 1882 (a law that lived up to its name), however, the Supreme Court assumed that Congress possessed the immigration power because national sovereignty over the borders had to reside somewhere in the federal government. "That the government of the United States, through the action of the legislative department, can exclude aliens from its territory is a proposition which we do not think open to controversy," Justice Stephen Field wrote for the Court. "Jurisdiction over its own territory to that extent is an incident of every independent nation. It is a part of its independence. If it could not exclude aliens it would be to that extent subject to the control of another power."[55]

But claims that Trump had seized power from Congress badly missed the target. In fact, the parallels with the border wall issue are striking. Critics assert that the president had no independent power to build a border wall or restrict entry into the country. But neither the border wall nor the travel ban called upon any inherent presidential power. In both cases, President Trump could rely on Congress's vast delegations of authority to the executive branch. Congress has transferred even broader powers to the executive branch over travel into the United States than over military construction. In the Immigration and Naturalization Act, Congress authorized the president to block aliens from entering the United States for national security reasons. In Section 1182(f) of the immigration code, Congress used the most sweeping terms. "Whenever the President finds that the entry of any aliens or class of aliens into the United States would be detrimental to the interests of the United States," Congress declared, he may "suspend the entry of all aliens or any class of aliens."[56]

Congress could not have provided the president any more power with any fewer strings attached. The law allows the president to block not just individuals but whole classes of aliens, for as long as he "shall deem necessary." It makes clear that the decision is up to the executive's discretion—it is "whenever the President finds," not when Congress or the judiciary finds. The president must only make the judgment that the aliens' entry "would be detrimental to the interests of the United States." Congress did not provide examples of what would qualify under this standard, nor did it define the national interest. But presidents had used the power before without

question. In 1981, for example, President Reagan invoked Section 1182(f) to block the large number of Haitians sailing to Florida by barring entry to *all* aliens entering the United States from the high seas.[57]

Trump could have gone even further. The president arguably has the constitutional authority to seal the borders in the event of an emergency. Preventing an enemy or a sudden threat to the national security from crossing the frontiers should fall within any reasonable definition of the "executive" power. The Constitution's grant of the executive power to the president also includes the power to exercise the nation's sovereign power in foreign affairs (the subject of later chapters), which would have included the right to bar aliens from entering. The Supreme Court has recognized that the power to bar aliens from entering the nation could be a presidential as well as legislative power. "The exclusion of aliens is a fundamental act of sovereignty," the Court held in a 1950 case. "The right to do so stems not alone from legislative power but is inherent in the executive power to control the foreign affairs of the nation."[58] If the president bears the most serious constitutional responsibility to protect the nation's security from foreign threat, he ought to have a power to protect the border.

Instead, Trump grounded his order on Congress's delegation of authority in the immigration laws. The travel ban order took the form of another routine exercise of delegated authority, in which the executive branch acts within broad parameters set out by Congress. Had the president been anyone other than Donald Trump, no court would have ever dared override the executive's decision to impose a travel restriction on aliens under the immigration laws. On the other hand, had the president been anyone other than Donald Trump, the order likely would not have taken on the color of his harsh campaign statements about immigrants. Faced with the shoddy opinion by the Washington federal court, upheld on similarly light reasoning by the U.S. Court of Appeals for the Ninth Circuit in San Francisco, the White House prudently revised its order to correct its mistakes. In travel ban version 2.0, the Trump administration removed Iraq from the list of prohibited nations, and it now found that the remaining nations were either "state sponsor[s] of terrorism," "significantly compromised by terrorist organizations," or contained "active conflict zones."[59] Version 2.0 made clear that the order did not apply to green card holders and refugees already admitted to the country, and it gave embassy officials the right to issue

waivers to allow individual aliens from those countries a visa. It responded to accusations of religious animus by removing the exception for religious minorities, which had seemed designed to favor Christians living in Muslim nations.

Federal courts again enjoined the order on even more extraordinary grounds. In May 2017, the U.S. Court of Appeals for the Fourth Circuit enjoined version 2.0 not because it violated any law on its face but because it found that President Trump held an anti-Muslim motive.[60] It quoted Trump's demand on the campaign trail for a "total and complete shutdown of Muslims entering the United States" and his declaration that "Islam hates us" and that the United States was "having problems with Muslims coming into the country." It found that the government had not shown that any aliens were connected to terrorist organizations or that their entry would otherwise be detrimental to the national interest, as required by statute. It also found that the order violated a separate provision of the 1965 immigration act, which forbids discrimination in the issuance of a visa based on race, sex, nationality, birthplace, or residence. Chief Judge Roger Gregory claimed that the travel ban "drips with religious intolerance, animus, and discrimination."[61]

In an unprecedented move, the lower courts argued that they could strike down the order because of the president's hatred of Muslims. Version 2.0, however, no longer contained any hint of religious intolerance on its face and instead focused on the security threat posed by unstable nations. So instead, the court speculated on Trump's state of mind based on his pre–election campaign statements. In a March 2016 CNN interview, Trump said "I think Islam hates us," and professed that "we can't allow people coming into this country who have this hatred." Judge Gregory quoted Giuliani's interview on coming up with "a Muslim ban." Based on these comments, the court found that version 2.0's "stated national security interest was provided in bad faith, as a pretext for its religious purpose."[62] Stripped of its legalese, the court found Trump to be a liar and a bigot.

This was too much even for the Supreme Court. It blocked the lower courts and allowed version 2.0's temporary 90-day suspension of travel to come to its natural end. On September 24, 2017, the Trump White House issued its permanent order. Version 3.0 changed the list of banned nations: Iran, Libya, Somalia, Syria, and Yemen remained on the list, joined by the non-Muslim nations of Chad, North Korea, and Venezuela.[63] The

government stated that it had selected these nations because they posed national security threats and had inadequate information systems to collect background information on travelers. The order made no exception for religious minorities (indeed, it made no mention of religion), it recognized the right of green card holders to enter, and it allowed embassy officials to grant waivers case by case. Federal courts in Hawaii and Maryland still struck down version 3.0, with the approval of the appeals courts, on the same ground of presidential bias.

In June 2018, the Supreme Court finally put an end to the judicial resistance. It began by invoking the broad discretion granted to the president.[64] Writing for a 5–4 majority, Chief Justice John Roberts observed that Section 1182(f) "exudes deference to the President in every clause" and that version 3.0 "falls well within this comprehensive delegation."[65] The justices rejected the second-guessing of the president as "inconsistent with the broad statutory text and the deference traditionally accorded the President in this sphere." Roberts also quickly dismissed the lower courts' conclusion that other parts of the immigration laws limited the executive. Congress must have given the executive the power to "suspend entry from particular foreign states in response to an epidemic confined to a single region, or a verified terrorist threat involving nationals of a specific foreign nation, or even if the United States were on the brink of war," Justice Roberts wrote.[66]

Roberts made no great legal strides here. The federal courts have long deferred to the executive branch when it exercises powers delegated by Congress. Judges realize that they do not have the expertise or the democratic legitimacy, unlike a president elected every four years, to make policy decisions. Congress can always conduct oversight on the administration, withhold funding, or even amend or repeal the law. Lower court judges displayed their own biases in a rush to overturn decades of judicial deference to presidential management of delegated congressional powers, especially in the area of national security and foreign affairs.

The Court also rejected what has become the anti-Trump dog whistle: bigotry. It immediately dismissed the claim of the lower courts, amplified by Trump's political and legal critics, that the travel ban expressed Trump's personal animus against Muslims. Courts were not to search for hidden presidential motives for "immigration policies, diplomatic sanctions, and military actions."[67] At issue, the Court correctly observed, was "not only the statements of a particular President, but also the authority of

the Presidency itself." As long as the president had a rational basis for the travel ban, which appeared readily apparent from the face of the executive order, the Court would not intervene in an area of national security. "Any rule of constitutional law that would inhibit the flexibility of the President to respond to changing world conditions should be adopted only with the greatest caution," the Court declared.

Normally, this should have ended the matter. "The admission and exclusion of foreign nationals is a fundamental sovereign attribute exercised by the Government's political departments largely immune from judicial control," the Court made clear. The judiciary should limit its role "to whether the Executive gave a 'facially legitimate and bona fide' reason." But even the Court could not help itself. It too wanted to peer into the recesses of Trump's mind. Yet, it upheld the policy because "there is persuasive evidence that the entry suspension has a legitimate grounding in national security concerns, quite apart from any religious hostility."

In a concurring opinion, Justice Clarence Thomas set forth a better view. Rather than stumble around inside the president's brain, he would have stopped the analysis once the president issued version 1.0 of the travel ban. Justice Thomas argued that Congress "had not set forth any judicially enforceable limits that constrain the President" in restricting travel into the United States, and therefore courts would have to accept any presidential travel ban. He would have found that Congress could not impose any conditions on the delegated power because the president already "has *inherent* authority to exclude aliens from the country."[68] If the judiciary had the right to examine a president's motives, judges would know no bounds. Courts could review every executive order on the claim that the president harbored a secret animus against some group. Every administration would grind to a halt under the weight of such intrusive scrutiny.

The government's ability to protect the national security and advance America's national interests would suffer as a result. Suppose President Trump were to launch missile strikes on Iran. If *Trump v. Hawaii* had gone the other way, opponents could claim that Trump secretly harbored anti-Muslim bias for the attack and go to court to seek an injunction. In *Hawaii* itself, the lower courts issued a nationwide injunction of a national security order designed to prevent terrorists from entering the nation. Emboldened federal judges might claim a similar right to review overseas military ac-

tion. A president would have to plan for judicial sand in the gears when he most depends on "decision, activity, secrecy, dispatch," as Hamilton said in *Federalist No. 70*.[69]

Allowing courts to rummage around in a president's mind would not just have damaged Trump. It would have permanently crippled the presidency and its ability to carry out the laws by giving virtually any group the right to challenge any government action. In rejecting similar efforts in the past, the Supreme Court cautioned against making the courts "continuing monitors of the wisdom and soundness of Executive action." Such an approach would prevent the president from fulfilling his constitutional duty to execute the laws and replace it with a judiciary that "assume[s] a position of authority over the governmental acts of another and co-equal department."[70] Judicial examination of presidential motive would not only slow every government decision down to the walking pace of a lawsuit but also elevate the judiciary into a third house of the legislature or an executive council with veto power over the president.

This radical approach did not just emerge from the fevered dreams of a few anti-Trumpers. Four dissenting justices in *Trump v. Hawaii* embraced it. Justice Sonia Sotomayor claimed that the Trump administration had come up with a "Muslim ban" that "now masquerades behind a façade of national-security concerns." She accused the majority of "ignoring the facts, misconstruing our legal precedent, and turning a blind eye to the pain and suffering the Proclamation inflicts upon countless families and individuals, many of them American citizens."[71] According to her, "the words of the President and his advisers create the strong perception that the Proclamation is contaminated by impermissible discriminatory animus against Islam and its followers."[72] Sotomayor all but called the president a racist.

That Supreme Court justices would employ this inflamed rhetoric reveals two things. First, the judicial resistance to Trump overthrows legislative delegation, presidential execution, and judicial deference—the basic workings of the federal government for the last century. Opponents must justify drastic measures on the ground that Trump is an accidental president at best and a malign force at worst. These judges and lawyers may or may not believe that Trump stole the 2016 election, but they think that Trump's bad nature allows them to suspend the regular constitutional order of government.

Second, the resistance to Trump risks the permanent disfigurement of the presidency. Even though opponents may want to make their attacks on executive power a ticket good for one trip only, constitutional law resists such exceptions. The rules designed to stop one president will stop all future presidents. Trump had to win the travel ban case, not just to promote his own immigration policies but also to allow future presidents to fully exercise the discretion granted by Congress. By prevailing in the courts, Trump forestalled permanent damage to the presidency and preserved its ability to preempt future threats.

IV. BIRTHRIGHT CITIZENSHIP

Trump's most radical proposal to curb illegal immigration cuts right to the heart of citizenship. In October 2018, he threatened to end birthright citizenship—the right of anyone born in the United States to be a citizen. "It was always told to me that you needed a constitutional amendment. Guess what? You don't," he said.[73]

Birthright citizenship today recognizes that anyone born in the United States automatically becomes a citizen, regardless of the immigration status of the parents. But Trump shares the concern that aliens, both legal and illegal, visit the United States solely to bear children who become American citizens at birth. The parents could then claim that their responsibilities to raise the child justify their own legal status.

Conservative critics argue that reversing this rule will help stem the tide of illegal immigration. Leading groups, such as the Heritage Foundation and the Claremont Institute, have urged the repeal of the law that recognizes birthright citizenship, while members of Congress have introduced legislation following suit.[74] Prominent legal scholars, such as Richard Posner and Peter Schuck, have also questioned birthright citizenship.[75] Polls show that a near majority of Americans believe that the United States should not grant citizenship to the children of illegal aliens.[76]

Trump's comments followed news that his administration was studying whether to reject birthright. The White House had established a task force to denaturalize aliens who had gained citizenship through improper or questionable means. Administration officials vocally called for a stop to birthright citizenship entirely. "The notion that simply being born within the geographical limits of the United States automatically confers U.S. cit-

izenship is an absurdity," former National Security Council official Michael Anton wrote in a prominent *Washington Post* opinion piece.[77]

This nativist siren song rejects one of the Republican Party's greatest achievements: the Fourteenth Amendment. According to the best reading of its text, structure, and history, anyone born on American territory, no matter their national origin, ethnicity, or station in life, is an American citizen. Washington may need a program to deter illegal immigration, but seeking a difficult, controversial change to the Constitution is not worth stopping the small numbers who travel here for "birth tourism."

While the original Constitution required citizenship for federal office, it never defined it. The Fourteenth Amendment sought to correct that oversight. It provides that "[a]ll persons born or naturalized in the United States, and subject to the jurisdiction thereof, are citizens of the United States and of the State wherein they reside." Congress did not draft this language to alter the concept of citizenship but to affirm American practice dating from the Revolution. With the exception of a few years before the Civil War, the United States followed the British rule of *jus soli* (citizenship defined by birthplace) rather than the European rule of *jus sanguinis* (citizenship defined by the parents' origins).

The Fourteenth Amendment merely codified this ancient principle. As the eighteenth-century English jurist William Blackstone explained, "[t]he children of aliens, born here in England, are generally speaking, natural-born subjects, and entitled to all the privileges of such." When the colonies became independent, they retained the British rule. Justice Joseph Story's comment in an 1830 Supreme Court case summarized the traditional view: "Nothing is better settled at common law" than *jus soli*.[78]

That traditional rule, however, fell prey to the efforts of the slaveholding South to deny blacks any rights. In the infamous *Dred Scott v. Sanford*, Chief Justice Roger Taney held that a slave did not become free by crossing the Missouri Compromise line into a free state.[79] According to Taney, the slave could not even sue because the Constitution did not recognize African Americans as persons. Though born in the United States, slaves could never become citizens.[80]

Northern Republicans drafted the Fourteenth Amendment to correct slavery's grave distortions of the law. The Fourteenth Amendment directly overruled *Dred Scott* by declaring that all born in the United States, irrespective of race, were citizens. It also removed from the political process,

even from the hands of the Supreme Court, the ability to abridge the citizenship of children born to members of disfavored ethnic, religious, or political minorities.

The only way to avoid this straightforward understanding is to misread the Fourteenth Amendment's text. Next to the language extending citizenship to "all persons born or naturalized in the United States" sits the phrase "subject to the jurisdiction thereof." Some originalist scholars, such as Professors John Eastman and Edward Erler, argue that this language must exclude aliens, because they owe their allegiance to another nation and are therefore not "subject to the jurisdiction" of the United States.[81]

But this exception swallows the rule. The Fourteenth Amendment's reference to "[a]ll persons born or naturalized in the United States, and subject to the jurisdiction thereof" refers to children who are born in U.S. territory *and* are subject to American law at birth. Almost everyone present in the United States, even aliens, comes within its jurisdiction. If the rule were otherwise, aliens on our territory could violate the law with impunity because they would claim they were not subject to our jurisdiction.

Critics respond that this reading would make "subject to the jurisdiction thereof" redundant with being born in U.S. territory. But at the time of the Fourteenth Amendment's ratification, discrete categories of persons could be in U.S. territory but not subject to our laws, such as diplomats and enemy soldiers during war. International law grants both groups protected status when present on foreign soil. A third group at this time also was not subject to U.S. jurisdiction. Native Americans residing on tribal lands were not subject to U.S. law because the tribes exercised self-governance. In the late nineteenth century, the federal government began to regulate Indian life, substantially diminishing tribal sovereignty, and in 1924 extended birthright citizenship to them.

The Fourteenth Amendment's drafting history supports this reading. The Civil Rights Act of 1866, which inspired the amendment, extended birthright citizenship to those born in the United States except those "subject to any foreign power" and "Indians not taxed."[82] Here, "subject to any foreign power" meant those not within the power of another government, such as those in occupied territory. If the Fourteenth Amendment's drafters had wanted "jurisdiction" to exclude children of aliens, they easily could have required citizenship only for those with no "allegiance to a foreign power." It would have made no sense for Congress to approve a constitu-

tional amendment that rendered part of the Civil Rights Act unconstitutional, and no one understood it to do so.

Critics of the amendment recognized the broad sweep of the birthright citizenship language. Senator Edgar Cowan, a leading opponent, challenged the 1866 act because it would "have the effect of naturalizing the children of Chinese and Gypsies born in this country." "Undoubtedly," Senator Lyman Trumbull answered, "the child of an Asiatic is just as much a citizen as the child of a European."[83] When the Fourteenth Amendment itself came up for debate, Senator Cowan again asked: "Is the child of the Chinese immigrant in California a citizen? Is the child born of a Gypsy born in Pennsylvania a citizen?"[84] California senator John Conness answered yes. "We are entirely ready to accept the provision proposed in this constitutional amendment," he responded, "that the children born of Mongolian parents shall be declared by the Constitution of the United States to be entitled to civil rights and to equal protection before the law with others."[85] Conness later lost his seat due to anti-Chinese sentiment in California.

The Supreme Court has consistently followed this understanding. *United States v. Wong Kim Ark* (1898) upheld the American citizenship of a child born in San Francisco to Chinese parents, who themselves could never naturalize because of the Chinese Exclusion Acts.[86] The Court held that "the Fourteenth Amendment affirms the ancient and fundamental rule of citizenship by birth within the territory, in the allegiance and protection of the country, including all children here born of resident aliens." It also explicitly rejected the argument that aliens, because they owed allegiance to a foreign nation, were not within "the jurisdiction" of the United States. Critics of birthright citizenship respond that *Ark* did not involve illegal aliens and therefore doesn't apply to children of undocumented migrants. But in 1898, federal law did not define legal or illegal aliens, so the Court's opinion could not turn on the legal status of Ark's parents. The more recent *Plyler v. Doe* in 1982 reaffirmed *Ark*.[87]

Critics of birthright citizenship do not appreciate the consequences of opening this Pandora's box. *Jus sanguinis* could call into question the loyalty of millions of foreign-born aliens; the government would have to make open-ended, person-specific determinations of the ancestry of parents to decide whether their children qualify for citizenship. Washington, D.C., and the states would have to pour even more resources into an already

dysfunctional immigration bureaucracy. Reading allegiance into the Fourteenth Amendment would defeat the intent of its drafters, who wanted to prevent politicians from denying citizenship to those they considered insufficiently American. The Fourteenth Amendment settled the question of birthright citizenship. Conservatives should not be the ones seeking a new law or even a constitutional amendment to reverse centuries of American tradition.

CONCLUSIONS

Immigration law raises difficult questions of sovereignty, national identity, and minority rights. It is also an area where Congress has delegated much of its authority to the president. For good or ill, the nation elected Trump in part because of his promise to take a restrictionist approach to immigration and to stiffen control of the nation's borders. He has carried out his promises by imposing a travel ban on migrants from several nations around the world and transferred money from the Pentagon to the construction of a wall on the southern border. Trump has implemented his policies by taking advantage of the basic system of congressional delegation, executive discretion, and judicial deference that characterizes much of the modern administrative state.

I, for one, disagree with Trump's policies on immigration. Critics have every right to urge Congress to provide for more generous immigration laws or to even completely overhaul how the nation decides whom to allow across its borders. They can make immigration a central issue for the 2020 elections by supporting candidates both for the presidency and Congress who disagree with Trump's policies. But opponents instead resorted to extreme attacks on executive power that disregarded the constitutional text, history, and practice and would have hamstrung the ability of future presidents to implement their agendas. Because the resistance to Trump sought to sweep away constitutional norms, it made Trump's defense of his own policies a defense of the institution of the presidency as well.

CHAPTER 6

AMERICA FIRST: TRUMP AND FOREIGN POLICY

I n his first year in office, Donald Trump turned U.S. foreign policy upside down. On December 6, 2017, the White House announced it would formally recognize Jerusalem as the capital of Israel. Trump made the decision concrete—literally—by ordering the U.S. embassy to move there from Tel Aviv. "While previous presidents have made this a major campaign promise, they failed to deliver," Trump declared. "Today, I am delivering."[1]

For more than 20 years, Congress had demanded the transfer of the embassy. But presidents of both parties refused. They feared that recognizing formal Israeli control over Jerusalem would enflame the Palestinians and ruin the chances for a Middle East peace.[2] "Jerusalem's political standing has long been, and remains, one of the most sensitive issues in American foreign policy," Justice Anthony M. Kennedy wrote in a 2015 Supreme Court case, *Zivotofsky v. Kerry*. "Indeed it is one of the most delicate issues in current international affairs."

Those delicacies fell away like so many old spider webs before Trump. In one stroke, Trump tried to cut through the diplomatic knots that had paralyzed the Middle East by moving the U.S. embassy to Jerusalem. He continued by closing the Palestine Liberation Organization office in Washington, cutting U.S. aid to the Palestinian Authority, and recognizing Israeli sovereignty over the Golan Heights, a critical high ground between Syria and Israel.[3] Presidents had long refused to recognize Tel Aviv's annexation of the territory, which could jeopardize any final Arab-Israeli peace settlement. Trump's son-in-law and advisor Jared Kushner followed up with a 2020 peace plan that adopted a two-state solution that allowed Israel to

keep territory beyond its original borders. It offered economic development for the Palestinians in exchange for a political settlement.

Trump's support of Israel sparked outrage on the part of Democrats and State Department alumni. Democratic presidential nominee representative Tulsi Gabbard criticized Trump for "throwing out four decades of U.S. policy" when the Trump administration released their statements on the West Bank.[4] Senator Amy Klobuchar stated, "Once again Donald Trump is playing politics and taking us further away from a path to a two-state solution."[5] Senator Bernie Sanders stated that "Trump is isolating the United States and undermining diplomacy by pandering to his extremist base."[6]

Breaking agreements became a favorite tool of the new Trump Doctrine. On the campaign trail, Trump had attacked free trade as a poor deal that had sent American manufacturing jobs abroad. Upon entering office, he immediately withdrew from the Trans-Pacific Partnership Agreement, a free trade pact between the United States and leading Asian economies designed to exclude China. Trump then moved on to central pillars of Obama's foreign policy. Under the Joint Comprehensive Plan of Action (JCPOA), Obama had lifted economic sanctions on Iran in exchange for Tehran's promise to halt nuclear weapons research. Trump pulled the United States out of the JCPOA in 2017 despite overwhelming criticism from Obama administration alumni, European leaders, and experts.[7] Sanders labeled the withdrawal as "one of the most reckless moves of [the Trump] presidency."[8]

More criticism greeted Trump's reversal of U.S. international environmental policy. In June 2017, Trump pulled the United States out of the Paris Agreement, the ambitious global accord to reduce carbon emissions. While Obama had signed the pact, the Senate never agreed because of concerns over costs, lack of enforcement, and the fact that India and China did not bear their share of the burden. Trump cut through the debate over global warming by simply withdrawing the United States' involvement. Environmentalists greeted Trump's move with outrage. Al Gore stated that Trump's decision was "reckless and indefensible" and "undermines America's standing in the world."[9]

But the question remains whether Trump's decisions add up to anything more than knee-jerk opposition to all things Obama. *Washington Post* columnist Max Boot, for example, argues that Trump does not pursue

a coherent foreign policy so much as he seeks a series of photo ops, preferably with authoritarian dictators. Boot called Trump's meeting with North Korean dictator Kim Jong Un "symbolism utterly devoid of substance" and "a great reality show but lousy diplomacy."[10] Eliot Cohen labeled Trump's foreign policy as "deeply misguided" and "indifferent, if not downright hostile, to the liberal international order that the United States has sustained for nearly eight decades."[11] Walter Russell Mead, a foreign policy scholar and *Wall Street Journal* columnist, speculates that Trump has no principled policy aside from an allergy to foreign entanglements and an interest in quid pro quo transactions.

These observers may stare so long at specific problems that they miss the central principle of the Trump Doctrine: sovereignty. Upon issuing his 2017 National Security Strategy (NSS), Trump declared: "We are prioritizing the interests of our citizens and protecting our sovereign rights as a nation. America is leading again on the world stage."[12] While perhaps not given to easy definition, sovereignty asserts the absolute control of a nation over its territory and population. A sovereignty-based foreign policy would aim at securing control over national territory, which would include border security, immigration control, and internal law enforcement. It would view other great powers, rather than global problems, as the main threats to security. It would turn a skeptical eye toward international institutions and law, especially efforts that restrict American freedom of action or subordinate its interests to global norms. As the Trump NSS declared, "I promised that my Administration would put the safety, interests, and well-being of our citizens first. I pledged that we would revitalize the American economy, rebuild our military, defend our borders, protect our sovereignty, and advance our values."

Sovereignty lies at the heart of Trump's skepticism of international agreements. Trump did not just pull out of the Paris Agreement or the Iran nuclear deal; he withdrew from a series of international accords ranging from the major (nuclear weapon limits) to the minor (diplomatic relations). He threatened even more, such as terminating NAFTA, pulling out of NATO, and ending security treaties with Japan and Korea. But throughout it all, the Trump Doctrine advanced a self-interested foreign policy that looks to nation-states and their rational interests rather than international bodies and global norms as the motivating forces in world

affairs. The United States downplayed worldwide problems and focused instead on threats from its principal global competitor, China, and regional challengers such as Russia, Iran, and North Korea.

Trump could have no Trump Doctrine—nor could Obama have had an Obama Doctrine—without the constitutional powers of the presidency. The text of the Constitution does not assign foreign policy to any branch. It gives Congress a large set of authorities, such as the powers to declare war, raise the army and navy, regulate foreign commerce, and define international law. The Senate also enjoys a significant role in consenting to treaties and confirming ambassadors. Article II gives the president fewer explicit powers over foreign affairs, such as the role of commander in chief and the power to appoint and receive ambassadors. This has led some critics of presidential power, such as former Obama State Department official Harold Koh and Yale law professor Bruce Ackerman, to argue that Congress should hold the upper hand over foreign policy.

These arguments, however, misread the constitutional text and structure. This chapter shows that Trump could carry out his doctrine because the Founders understood the executive power to include the conduct of foreign policy. When Article II vests the executive power in the president, it grants him the authority over foreign affairs, subject to any specific exceptions (such as the Senate's advice and consent role with treaties) elsewhere in the document. Even though many scholars argue that the Constitution contains far more ambiguity, the practice of the elected branches has followed this understanding from the very beginnings of the Republic. Vesting the foreign affairs power in Congress would have created an utterly impractical governing structure out of character for the pragmatic men who adopted the Constitution.

In fighting for dominance in foreign affairs, Trump ends up fighting not just for himself but also for his future successors. That may not be Trump's immediate objective. In demanding that Ukraine launch an investigation into Hunter Biden's payday on the board of the Burisma natural gas company, Trump may have had in mind his own political self-interest rather than any broader foreign policy goals in Eastern Europe. Nevertheless, when Trump takes the lead in setting policy toward Ukraine and then seeks to keep secret his talks with foreign governments and his advice from aides, he is protecting the right of future presidents to develop and carry out an effective foreign policy.

I.

Trump has launched earth-shattering changes to our foreign relations. Consider the world as it was in 2016. The United States remained embroiled in the Middle East. It remained at war in Afghanistan. U.S. forces continued to fight in Iraq—though it had left in 2011, the United States returned to fight ISIS. Obama sent U.S. troops to fight ISIS in Syria, where they risked conflict with Russian, Turkish, and Iranian forces. Obama expanded American drone strikes against terrorist leaders in Afghanistan, Pakistan, Iraq, and other countries in the region. On the diplomatic front, the Obama administration sought to make peace with its primary rival in the Middle East. In concert with the European powers, the United States lifted sanctions on Iran and sent billions of dollars in exchange for a freeze of Tehran's nuclear weapons programs.

In much of the rest of the world, however, the Obama administration sat passively by as the American-created world order eroded. In Europe, it stuck by the declining Atlantic alliance that had won the Cold War. But a revanchist Moscow began to challenge the postwar peace. Obama had entered office with hopes of easing relations with Russia, and he went so far as to cancel the deployment of missile defense systems in Eastern Europe promised by the Bush administration. Moscow nevertheless followed up its 2008 attack on Georgia with the 2014 invasion and annexation of the Crimean Peninsula. It continued to support a breakaway eastern region that waged a civil war against the recognized Ukrainian government. Neither the United States nor its NATO allies responded with significant increases in defense spending or military deployments. Washington continued to shoulder the burden of providing for European security, even as most NATO countries refused to spend a promised 2 percent of GDP on defense. Germany, which may receive the greatest benefit from NATO, spends only 1 percent of its GDP on defense, while the United States spends more than three times that.[13]

In Asia, the United States maintained its traditional security alliances with a collection of nations, ranging from Japan to Korea to Australia. But challenges steadily arose to American hegemony. Both Republican and Democratic administrations midwifed China's emergence into the world's second largest economy. When combined with a newly nationalistic regime in Beijing, China's rapid economic growth suddenly gave birth to

America's clear strategic rival for the twenty-first century. China's military rise and North Korea's nuclear program threatened a peace built on American control of the air and seas, great power restraint, and a regional focus on economic development. The Obama administration found no solution to the threat of North Korea's nuclear weapons and ballistic missiles other than to pursue "strategic patience"—translation: doing nothing. When it came to the strategic challenge posed by a newly aggressive China, the United States fell into the same passivity. It had no counter to Beijing's militarization of several islands in the South China Sea, through which passes 20 percent of all world trade.[14]

American leaders instead placed their faith in international governance. Obama joined the Paris Agreement, which set long-range targets for reductions in carbon emissions by both industrial and developing nations. In the emerging cyber world, the United States did not respond to attacks on its government and corporate networks in the hopes that it could encourage Russia, China, and smaller nations to exercise mutual restraint. In space, the United States supported European efforts to establish a code of conduct designed to stop the spread of military activity. On Iran and North Korea, the United States joined multilateral efforts that used sanctions and the offer of normalization to stop nuclear weapons programs.

Along with U.S. alliances, free trade laid the foundation for the postwar order. Obama continued the free trade policies that had allowed Western Europe, the Asian tigers, and other allies to develop within a system of predictable rules. NAFTA welded North America into an integrated market that made Canada and Mexico the United States' largest trading partners. By making possible the movement of 500 million Chinese into the middle class, the World Trade Organization (WTO) helped lift the greatest number of people out of poverty in the shortest time in recorded history. The Obama administration sought to capitalize on the rise of Asia with a dramatic new free trade area, the Trans-Pacific Partnership (TPP). By excluding China, the TPP became the Obama administration's most prominent effort to contain Beijing.

These policies sought to maintain the liberal international order. Established at the outset of the Cold War, this system contained the Soviet Union by rebuilding Western Europe and Asia within a system of capitalism, free trade, and democracy. The United States led the free world

because of its good fortune: its large and dynamic economy, its growing population, its outstanding universities, its bounty of natural resources, its strategic location in the Western Hemisphere, and its large and effective military. It created international institutions that would provide certainty in foreign affairs, reduce the frictions that could lead to conflict, and organize collective action to address widespread problems. The United States underwrote this world order with a dominant military that deterred the Soviet Union while discouraging regional rivalries, and a financial system that provided secure trading, deep capital markets, and a reliable currency. It ended the great power wars that had killed millions and instead created the conditions for economic prosperity for itself and the world.[15]

After the collapse of the Soviet Union, the United States sought to spread the liberal order beyond Western Europe and East Asia to former Warsaw Pact members, Southeast Asia, and ultimately the Middle East. After the 9/11 attacks, the United States fielded a larger and more effective military than the rest of the world combined. Despite legal and political controversy at home and abroad, Washington could lead international coalitions to wage war in Afghanistan and Iraq. But those conflicts may have marked the limits of American power, with the losses in blood and treasure failing to transform those nations into anything resembling market democracies. Even as radical Islamic terrorism began to recede, China and Russia took advantage of America's shift in attention. Not only did Beijing and Moscow refuse to liberalize in response to liberal trade, they began to openly challenge a weakening liberal order. Russia invaded Ukraine and used the Syrian civil war to engineer its return to the Middle East. China sought to stitch together a network of dependencies with its Belt and Road Initiative and to seize control of the South China Sea. Both challenged U.S. dominance of the global commons in the sea, air, outer space, and cyberspace.

Obama responded, however, not by returning to the tough realities of great power politics. Instead, he advanced a postmodern agenda that reduced national sovereignty in favor of global governance as a solution to international problems. "We've bound our power to international laws and institutions," he told the United Nations in 2016. "I am convinced that in the long run, giving up freedom of action—not our ability to protect ourselves but binding ourselves to international rules over the long term—enhances our security."[16] Hence, the Obama administration sought to tame

global warming through the Paris Agreement; it addressed the Iranian nuclear threat through a multilateral agreement; and it hoped to draw China and Russia into a regime of self-restraint with cyber and space weapons.

I I.

In his 2016 campaign, Trump questioned the U.S.-led world order and yet also challenged the idea of relative U.S. decline. In a 2016 debate, Trump stated that the invasion of Iraq "may have been the worst decision" in presidential history. During his campaign, Trump lamented that the United States was spending "billions" of dollars "to support other countries that are, in theory, wealthier than we are."[17]

In rejecting Obama's faith in global governance, critics might say, Trump did not truly have a new foreign policy. But if there is a doctrine that draws Trump's impulsive acts together, it is sovereignty. In a 2017 U.N. speech, Trump made his approach clear. "In foreign affairs we are renewing the principle of sovereignty." By restoring their independence of action, he argued, nations could meaningfully cooperate. "Our success depends upon a coalition of strong and independent nations that embrace their sovereignty to promote security, prosperity, and peace." Sovereignty, not global governance, would bring economic stability and freedom: "[S]overeign and independent nations are the only vehicles where freedom has ever survived and democracy has ever endured," he told the United Nations in 2018. "We reject the ideology of globalism, and we embrace the doctrine of patriotism."[18]

Secretary of State Mike Pompeo further explained the link between sovereignty and a strengthened international system. Because of "multilateralism," he argued in a December 2018 speech in Brussels, the international order "has failed us and it failed you." He characterized the faith of Europeans in global governance: "Multilateralism has become viewed as an end unto itself. The more treaties we sign, the safer we supposedly are. The more bureaucrats we have, the better the job gets done."[19] Rejecting this view, the Trump administration would instead restore sovereignty in order to reform institutions and save the liberal order. In a May 11, 2019, speech at the Claremont Institute, Pompeo went even further in attacking multilateralism: "The institutions we built to defend the free world against the Soviet menace had drifted from their original mission set. Indeed, some of them had become directly antagonistic to our interests, while we kept

silent." The United States would respond by reasserting sovereignty and returning to the tough world of great power politics. "We had too much confidence in the international system and not enough confidence in our own nation. And we had too little courage to confront regimes squarely opposed to our interests and to our values."[20]

Great power competition became the focus of the Trump White House's new "America First National Security Strategy." Rather than global challenges, such as terrorism, economic development, or climate change, the administration identified other great powers as the primary threats to U.S. national security. "China and Russia challenge American power, influence, and interests, attempting to erode American security and prosperity."[21] It identified Iran and North Korea as regional threats while placing "jihadist terrorists" and "transnational criminal organizations" as third in importance. Trump rejected the guiding principle of the last 30 years that "engagement with rivals and their inclusion in international institutions and global commerce would turn them into benign actors and trustworthy partners." Put bluntly, the White House declared, "this premise turned out to be false." Instead, great power competitors were closing the gap in military capabilities, building WMD and cyber weapons, and bringing sophisticated challenges using low-intensity means of conflict. Trump effectively declared that the unnatural period of American hegemony in the world had come to an end.

In response, the administration identified four pillars of a new strategy. First, the United States would make its "fundamental responsibility" the protection of the homeland, which, in a first, included border control and immigration reform. Second, the White House identified "fair and reciprocal economic relationship to address trade imbalances," as well as maintaining U.S. leads in technology and energy development. Third, the administration called for renewed spending on the military and an expansion of operations in new domains, such as cyber and space. Fourth, the White House would seek to expand American influence through softer means, such as diplomacy and espousal of American values. At its root, the Trump Doctrine turned to the more hard-hearted realist view that military and economic power, derived from national sovereignty, would secure the United States and advance its interests abroad.

This strategy had an obvious focus on China and, to a lesser extent, Russia. The NSS identified "the revisionist powers of China and Russia" as

the preeminent threats to American security. They "compete across political, economic, and military arenas, and use technology and information to accelerate these contests" so as to gain dominance in their regions. Altering the approach toward China became necessary, the White House concluded, because a growing China did not liberalize but instead "expanded its power at the expense of the sovereignty of others." China poses a threat not just because of its capabilities, which include a growing nuclear arsenal and "the most capable and well-funded military in the world" after the United States. It also raises the specter of competition because of its intent to "expand the reaches of its state-driven economic model" and "spread features of its authoritarian system, including corruption and the use of surveillance," while it gains dominance of Asia.[22]

In this new world, Russia plays more of the role of spoiler than a global competitor like China. According to the Trump White House, Russia's main goal is "to weaken U.S. influence in the world and divide us from our allies and partners" due to its suspicion of NATO and the European Union. While possessing the only major nuclear arsenal that poses an existential threat to the United States, Russia has embarked on a military modernization program and used cyber weapons to destabilize other nations. Despite its intentions, however, Russia's capabilities are not those of the Soviet Union at the height of the Cold War. Moscow's greatest threat, the Trump administration worries, is the possibility of a conflict in Europe due to miscalculation.[23] While the Trump Doctrine did not call for tougher moves against Moscow, the Putin regime's invasion of Ukraine and its interference in elections in the United States prompted the White House and Congress to agree on increased economic sanctions against Russia. During Trump's first two years, Congress enacted two tougher sanctions bills to respond to Russia's Ukraine invasion, election meddling, and assassinations in Europe, while the White House expanded the individuals under sanction to include not just leading government officials but Russian oligarchs as well.[24]

A return to great power politics produced a corresponding, perhaps inevitable, reduction in concern about other nations' internal affairs. Trump's relative lack of concern about the internal affairs of other countries can lead to head-snapping changes of policy. North Korea, for example, operates the most repressive regime on Earth and has tested nuclear missiles capable of reaching the continental United States. Trump turned on a dime

from isolation and confrontation of the Kim regime to a charm offensive that made him the first American president to meet with a North Korean leader and even to cross the Demilitarized Zone (DMZ). Saudi Arabia's de facto leader, Mohammed bin Salman, likely ordered the assassination of *Washington Post* journalist Jamal Khashoggi and has conducted a brutal war against Iranian-backed rebels in Yemen. Nonetheless, Trump vetoed congressional bills to sanction Riyadh and instead increased arms sales to the desert kingdom. Critics charged that Trump seemed to treat authoritarian dictators with more deference than the leaders of democratic allies. CNN's Anderson Cooper stated that Trump was "happier talking to tyrants than democratic heads of state like himself." Cooper said these dictators made Trump "giddy," yet "for Theresa May, Angela Merkel, Shinzo Abe, well, they aren't accused killers, and it seems in the president's eyes, that means they don't have the right stuff."[25]

Even as he made public overtures to dictators in North Korea and Russia, Trump appeared far less generous toward America's longtime allies. In 2017, for example, he placed the Atlantic alliance in doubt by refusing to confirm that the United States would honor Article 5 of the NATO pact, which commits signatories to come to the defense of any member nation under attack. Instead, Trump described the agreement as "obsolete" and accused most NATO nations of failing to pay their fair share—a minimum of 2 percent of GDP for defense.[26] In 2018, Trump wrote to several European leaders that because of their refusal to increase defense spending, the U.S. commitment "is no longer sustainable," and he threatened at the NATO summit that year that the United States "would have to look to go its own way."[27] Trump expressed his bottom-line approach to alliance politics in a March 2017 tweet: Germany owes "vast sums of money to NATO & the United States must be paid more for the powerful, and very expensive, defense it provides to Germany!"[28]

Unhappiness over burden sharing also shaped Trump's view of Asia. In 2017, President Trump demanded that South Korea and Japan contribute more to the cost of American military deployments. South Korea steadily increased its cash payments to the United States to $925 million by 2020, more than half of the cost of the 28,500 U.S. troops stationed there.[29] Even though Japan paid about $1.8 billion a year to support large American navy and air bases, Trump privately has floated the idea of withdrawing from the U.S.-Japan security treaty and publicly complained about its unfairness. In

a June 2019 television interview, he said, "If Japan is attacked, we will fight World War Three . . . with our lives and with our treasure." But, he added, "[i]f we're attacked, Japan doesn't have to help us at all."[30] Trump continued to unsettle alliance relations by slapping trade sanctions on Canadian and Mexican products, imposing tariffs on European steel and aluminum imports, and threatening further restrictions on auto imports from various countries.

III. THE FOREIGN AFFAIRS POWER

Critics can question the wisdom of such sharp turnabouts in our foreign policy. But they must accept that the fundamental power to decide these questions rests in Trump's hands. Critics of the Trump presidency claim that he has unconstitutionally seized the power of a tyrant. But in this area, as in others, Trump can defend himself with the Constitution's text and structure, original understanding, and historical practice. Trump can call upon the example of past great presidents, such as George Washington, Abraham Lincoln, and FDR, to support his control over foreign policy.

The Constitution's text does not explicitly grant much to the president beyond the undefined executive power, the commander in chief role, and the right to receive ambassadors. He must share the treaty and appointment powers with the Senate, while Congress receives the powers to declare war and issue letters of marque and reprisal (government permission to privateers to conduct hostilities against an enemy), to raise and fund the military, and to regulate foreign commerce, among other powers. There have been periods where early presidents deferred to Congress's foreign policy leadership, though with poor results—witness President Adams and the 1798 Quasi-War with France, or President Madison and the War of 1812. Indeed, the conventional wisdom among many legal scholars is that the Constitution gives Congress control over foreign affairs.[31] As a practical matter, however, the president today can launch the nation into war without explicit congressional consent, enter or end international agreements, interpret international rules on behalf of the United States, and control diplomatic relations with other nations. These decisions, from President Truman's decision to wage the Korean War to Jimmy Carter's termination of the mutual defense treaty with Taiwan, have sparked political controversy and claims of presidential overreaching.

The spare constitutional text has led many scholars to conclude that Congress, not the president, controls foreign relations. They argue that the American Revolution rejected executive power and that the Framers designed the presidency as a limited, narrow office. Arthur Schlesinger Jr. famously attacked the Vietnam-era "Imperial Presidency" for seizing the power of foreign affairs from Congress.[32] Yale law professor Bruce Ackerman argues that constitutional "basics" require the president to carry out congressional foreign policy and that recent efforts by President Trump to use the military to guard the Mexican border or use force in Syria are illegal, and "if members of the armed forces obeyed his command, they would be committing a federal crime."[33] Recent work argues that foreign policy simply represents another domain for lawmaking, which obligates the president to carry out Congress's priorities.[34]

This argument exerts a superficial attraction because it assumes that foreign policy resembles domestic policy. With domestic affairs, the Constitution requires that a law pass both houses of Congress and receive the president's signature. The president then takes care to faithfully execute the law. But our eighteenth-century Founders understood foreign and domestic affairs to be fundamentally different, a concept embedded in the constitutional text by the grant of "the executive power" to the president. At the time of the Constitution's framing, the British and Americans believed that the executive power included the powers over war and peace, negotiation and communication with foreign nations, and control of the military. Parliament enjoyed control over domestic powers that could constrain executive foreign policy, primarily the power of the purse, the legislation to implement treaty commitments, internal regulation, and the raising of the army and navy. When the colonies declared their independence, the national government of the Articles of Confederation assumed the executive power over foreign relations, but it could not carry them into effect because it lacked the authority to tax or pass internal legislation. When the Framers vested the president with "the executive power" in the opening words of Article II, they would have understood that they had restored control over foreign policy to the chief executive.

Eighteenth-century Anglo-American constitutional thought distinguished between the foreign affairs power on the one hand and domestic legislation on the other. On foreign affairs, John Locke identified another power, the "federative" power. The federative power governed "the power

of war and peace, leagues and alliances, and all the transactions with all persons and communities without the commonwealth."[35] To separate the federative from the executive power would lead to "disorder and ruin," Locke predicted, because "the force of the public would be under different commands."[36]

Montesquieu closely followed Locke in maintaining a line between matters of war and peace on the one hand and domestic legislation on the other. His famous discussion of the English constitution in *Spirit of the Laws* begins, "In every government there are three sorts of powers: the legislative; the executive in respect to things dependent on the law of nations; and the executive in regard to matters that depend on the civil law."[37] Montesquieu adopted Locke's understanding of the executive power as composed of a foreign affairs power (Locke's federative power) and a domestic responsibility to execute the law. Under the foreign affairs power, Montesquieu observed, the executive "makes peace or war, sends or receives embassies, establishes the public security, and provides against invasions."[38] Legislative power, in contrast, sets the rules of conduct between citizens and checks the executive through its funding power.

Blackstone took Locke and Montesquieu a step further by declaring that the conduct of foreign affairs was always purely executive in nature. Initially, Blackstone had followed Locke on the functional superiority of the executive in foreign affairs. "It is impossible that the individuals of state, in their collective capacity, can transact the affairs of that state with another community equally numerous as themselves," Blackstone observed. "With regard to foreign concerns, the sovereign is the delegate or representative of his people."[39] Hence, the people vested the foreign affairs power in the Crown. "Unanimity must be wanting to their measures, and strength to the execution of their counsels."[40] Primacy in making war and peace required that the executive possess the lion's share of the war powers. Thus, Blackstone stated that the king is the "generalissimo, or the first in military command, within the kingdom." The Crown must possess the powers over both war and peace; as the sovereign representative and protector of the people, the monarch "united strength in the best and most effectual manner."[41]

In understanding whether the grant of "the executive power" would have included control over foreign affairs, the Framers would also have looked to the recent constitutional events of their own new nation. Upon independence, the new states wrote constitutions that disrupted the unity and

independence of the executive branch, such as replacing governors with committees or allowing for legislative selection of the governor. Despite the fragmentation of the executive as a unitary institution, the states left many of the executive's traditional powers in place, which suggests that the Framers did not wish to alter the allocation of constitutional authorities.[42]

To be sure, some leading revolutionaries hoped to restrict the executive's substance as well. Most Federalists, however, rejected this approach. Instead of declaring that the administrator could not wage war or make peace, most states maintained the governor's exclusive right to conduct foreign affairs and direct the military. In drafting their new constitutions, states generally favored John Adams. In his *Thoughts on Government*, Adams suggested that the states should adopt bicameral legislatures and create a governor "who, after being stripped of most of those badges of domination called prerogatives, should have a free and independent exercise of his judgment, and be made also an integral part of the legislature."[43] Adams considered the control of foreign affairs and national security not as "badges of domination" but as legitimate elements of the executive power. Adams advised the states to reproduce the forms and powers of the British constitution, after adjusting the branches of government to be more responsive to popular sovereignty. The revolutionaries decided to mimic the British forms of government, as recommended by Adams, rather than limit the executive.

States that married these substantive powers to a restored, unified executive served as the model for the federal Constitution. The Framers perhaps most admired New York's powerful executive.[44] Adopted in the spring of 1777, the New York constitution vested the office of the single, popularly elected governor with "the supreme executive power and authority of this State." No privy council checked his authority, nor did any limitation exist on the number of terms a governor could serve.[45] The constitution vested him with the position of "general and commander-in-chief of all the militia, and admiral of the navy of this State," and enumerated no foreign policy powers for the assembly. During the struggle for ratification, Hamilton expressed the thoughts of many when he declared that the New York constitution "has been justly celebrated both in Europe and in America as one of the best of the forms of government established in this country."[46]

Delegates came to Philadelphia in the summer of 1787 to repair the defects of the Articles of Confederation. Chief among them was its failure

to provide a sufficient defense against invasion and to negotiate treaties with potential allies. The weakness arose not because the Congress was unable to initiate war or conduct negotiations but because it had to rely on the good faith of the states to raise the military and to implement international agreements. The Framers quickly corrected this problem by expanding federal powers in foreign affairs at the expense of the states. The Constitution not only vested the federal government with the power to raise the military and to negotiate agreements, it also divested the states of the ability to wage war or to make peace.

When Edmund Randolph first proposed the Virginia Plan, he identified the chief problem with the Articles as the nation's inability to effectively conduct foreign relations. The United States could not "prevent a war nor [] support it by th[eir] own authority." To address these challenges, Randolph proposed a reconstituted national government. His Virginia Plan proposed a bicameral legislature elected by popular vote that would exercise all legislative power.[47] That legislature would choose the executive, which would enjoy the executive powers of government. A national judiciary would adjudicate controversies under federal law, but the job of reviewing the constitutionality of proposed legislation would fall to a council of revision. This new national government would exercise powers over foreign affairs, interstate commerce, areas in which the states were incompetent, and taxation. Randolph's proposal did not enumerate the national government's limited powers but instead resorted to broad grants of authority: the executive would "enjoy the Executive rights vested in Congress by the Confederation," and the "National Legislature" would exercise the "Legislative Rights" of the old Congress.[48] As the Articles had vested foreign affairs in the Congress, this language would have maintained control over this subject in the executive branch.

Drawing on their British experience, almost all of the delegates who spoke on this question agreed that the powers of war and peace were executive in nature. When the delegates discussed the executive power, several speakers protested the Virginia Plan's vesting of the complete powers over war and peace in the executive branch. Charles Pinckney declared that he "was for a vigorous Executive but was afraid the Executive powers of [the existing] Congress might extend to peace & war &c which would render the Executive a Monarchy, of the worst kind, to wit an elective one."[49] John Rutledge "was for vesting the Executive power in a single person, tho' he

was not for giving him the power of war and peace." Although James Wilson supported a single executive for its "energy dispatch and responsibility to the office," he too warned that the convention should not adopt the British division of executive and legislative powers. Wilson "did not consider the Prerogatives of the British Monarch as a proper guide in defining the Executive powers. Some of these prerogatives were of a Legislative nature. Among others that of war & peace &c."[50] Arguing that the model of the British constitution was ill suited to America, Wilson succeeded in limiting the president to executing the laws, appointing officers, and exercising powers delegated to him by Congress.[51]

These early stages of the Philadelphia Convention did not give rise to a change in the existing understanding of the foreign affairs power as executive in nature. On July 26, however, the convention sent specific resolutions to the Committee of Detail. The delegates retained the Virginia Plan's language that the national legislature would exercise the legislative powers of the old Congress, but they removed the vesting of executive power in the executive branch. In its place, they inserted an enumeration of the executive's power as extending only to executing the laws and appointing officers.[52] This draft of the Constitution vested much of the foreign affairs power in the Senate, which would act like the state councils that shared executive power with the governors. It vested the president with "the executive power of the United States," which would include the remaining foreign affairs powers, such as the conduct of diplomacy, not specifically vested in the Senate.[53]

As the Convention proceeded, it returned more of the foreign affairs power back to the executive. When the Convention changed the Senate into the representative of the states in Congress, for example, the Senate no longer made sense as a repository of the foreign affairs power.[54] Rather than the representative of the nation, the Senate might become a forum for sectional interests and disunion. Nationalists reconceptualized the presidency as not merely an executor of the laws but as the body that would represent the nation abroad.[55] Supporters of the executive diluted Congress's power from "making" war to "declaring" it, which expanded the president's authority to use force. They then transferred the power to make peace away from the Senate alone. Jack Rakove has laid out a strong case that once the Senate became the representative of the states, leading Framers moved the foreign affairs power to the popularly elected president instead.[56]

While the final Constitution did not follow the British model com-pletely, the Convention's changes did not fundamentally alter the nature of the foreign affairs power. Primary foreign affairs authority settled in the president, who had a national responsibility due to his election by the peo-ple, the means to act quickly due to his unitary control of the executive branch, and a longer-term perspective due to renewable four-year terms. The delegates still gave a role to the Senate, though its role in treaties was intended to protect the states. Congress had a role in declaring war, raising armies, and approving diplomats, but the Constitution gave all else to the president through its vesting of the executive power.

Hamilton and the other Federalists did not look to the executive to manage war and peace for tradition's sake. Congress's collective-action problems had hampered General Washington's ability to fight the Rev-olution. After independence, American leaders worried that they would lose in the peace what they had won in the war. The Framers learned the hard way that a single executive was functionally best matched in speed, unity, and decisiveness to the unpredictable, high stakes of foreign affairs. America's strategic position at the time demanded an energetic executive. Europe's great powers—Spain, France, and Great Britain—hemmed in the young democracy. Great Britain manned a long land border with the United States in Canada and refused to hand over key frontier strongholds as required by the 1783 peace treaty; Spain controlled New Orleans and hence the Mississippi River's access to the sea; France held key Caribbean islands and would reacquire the Louisiana Territory. All three sought to exacerbate divisions between the states, which split along sectional lines over foreign policy and trade. Congress had negligible armed forces at its command (barely 1,000 soldiers on the borders and no seafaring navy), the states could field only undistinguished militias, and no one had an interest in contributing resources or personnel to the national government. Under these precarious conditions, foreign relations loomed as desperately as do-mestic issues in the Framers' minds.[57]

Threats to the national security, Federalists argued during ratification, justified the centralization of foreign affairs in the executive. Article II gave the president the roles of commander in chief and chief executive. "Of all the cares or concerns of government, the direction of war most peculiarly demands those qualities which distinguish the exercise of power by a single hand," Hamilton wrote in *Federalist No. 74*. "The direction of war implies

the direction of the common strength," he continued, "and the power of directing and employing the common strength forms a usual and essential part in the definition of the executive authority." It was for this reason, Hamilton argued, that the Constitution vested executive authority in one person rather than fragmenting that authority among multiple executives as under the Articles of Confederation and the states.

Responding to Anti-Federalist accusations of monarchy, Federalists downplayed the president's powers in comparison with the British Crown. They emphasized the presidency's fixed term, its obedience to the laws, and its lack of funding. Hamilton observed that the British king was a permanent, hereditary monarch with an absolute veto and the right to raise armies and navies and declare war. In *Federalist No. 69*, he argued, the president's commander-in-chief role may nominally resemble the king's, "but in substance [is] much inferior to it." The former could not declare war or raise the military. Hamilton's rhetoric got the better of him here, as even in Britain by this time, Parliament exercised the power to raise armies. The only real difference between the king's and the president's military powers was Congress's power to declare war. Leading Federalists, however, did not argue that the Constitution deprived the president of the rest of the power over foreign affairs, even though they had every political incentive to do so during the ratification struggle.

Federalists referred to British history to explain the checks on executive power. In the Virginia ratifying convention, Patrick Henry, still famous for his "Give me liberty or give me death" speech, led the Anti-Federalist opposition. He claimed that the Constitution "squints toward monarchy" because the "President may easily become a King." "If your American chief be a man of ambition and abilities, how easy is it for him to render himself absolute!" Henry exclaimed. At the head of an army, the president "can prescribe the terms on which he shall reign master" and will violate the laws and "beat down every opposition."[58] The Senate and the president might conspire to impose an "absolute despotism."

Federalists countered that the other branches could stop him using their own constitutional powers. They did not respond with the traditional checks-and-balances approach of mixed government; instead, they argued that the separation of powers would rely on functionally defined branches of government—executive, legislative, and judicial—checking each other.[59] Federalists raised Parliament's funding powers as the most important

restraint. Madison agreed with Henry that "the sword and the purse are not to be given to the same member," but he disagreed that the American government combined the two. "The sword is in the hands of the British king; the purse in the hands of the Parliament. It is so in America, as far as any analogy can exist."[60] In another area of foreign affairs, for example, Federalists argued that Congress could contain the executive's treaty power (already conditioned by the Senate's advice-and-consent role) by refusing to enact laws or appropriate funds needed to bring the United States into compliance.[61] The ratification debates show that the Framers expected each branch to exercise its unique powers to block unconstitutional or mistaken decisions.

Immediate practice under Washington confirmed the vesting of foreign affairs in the president. Washington established from the beginning that the executive branch would assume the leading role in developing and carrying out foreign policy. Upon taking office, Washington moved quickly to take firm control over the nation's diplomatic relations. He immediately issued directions to the foreign minister and dictated diplomatic relations with other nations.[62] As Secretary of State Jefferson observed during the first Washington administration, "The constitution has divided the powers of government into three branches [and] has declared that 'the executive powers shall be vested in the president,' submitting only special articles of it to a negative by the senate." Due to this structure, Jefferson continued, "[t]he transaction of business with foreign nations is executive altogether; it belongs, then, to the head of that department, except as to such portions of it as are specially submitted to the senate. Exceptions are to be construed strictly."[63] Of diplomacy, Jefferson observed, "all this is left to the President; [the Senate] is only to see that no unfit persons be employed." Jefferson believed these decisions fell within Washington's authority because foreign affairs remained executive in nature, a view he would continue to hold during his own presidency.

But Jefferson would regret his views during the political controversies ignited by the French Revolution. Washington kept the United States out of the conflict based on his authority to set foreign policy, interpret and terminate treaties, and determine the nation's international commitments. The overthrow of the French monarchy and the subsequent invasion by the other European powers threw the American government into a quandary

over the 1778 treaties of alliance with France. At a minimum, those treaties promised that the United States would allow France to base warships in U.S. ports.[64] On April 18, 1793, Washington sent a list of 13 questions to Hamilton, Jefferson, Henry Knox, and Randolph.[65] Almost all of Washington's questions involved the interpretation of the 1778 treaties. When they transmitted their written advice, no one in the cabinet disputed that the president held the power over foreign affairs. Washington and his cabinet proceeded on the assumption that it was the province of the executive branch to interpret treaties, and so set foreign policy, on behalf of the United States. Although the Continental Congress had negotiated and ratified the 1778 treaties, Washington never asked about its intentions.[66] Both Hamilton and Jefferson grounded their appeals in the national interest, international law, and common sense. Neither expressed a belief that consultation with Congress or the Senate was necessary or advisable. They even agreed that the president had the authority to terminate the 1778 treaties.[67]

Jefferson and Randolph argued that international law did not permit the suspension or termination of a treaty because of a change in government.[68] Jefferson recommended that the administration do nothing. Hamilton and Knox responded that the civil war in France allowed the United States to suspend or even terminate the treaty.[69] Telling Jefferson that he "never had a doubt about the validity of the treaty," Washington decided against suspension.[70] But he also decided that the United States would stay out of the conflict.[71] He issued what would become known as the Neutrality Proclamation on April 22, 1793.[72]

The proclamation provoked one of the great constitutional debates in American history. In a series of newspaper articles in the summer of 1793, Hamilton adopted the pseudonym of "Pacificus" to defend Washington's proclamation. Hamilton began with the position that foreign policy was executive by its very nature. Congress was not the "organ of intercourse" with foreign nations, while the judiciary could only "decide litigations in particular cases." Declaring neutrality, therefore, must "of necessity belong to the Executive." It drew from the executive's authority as "the *organ* of intercourse between the Nation and foreign Nations," as "interpreter of the National Treaties in those cases in which the Judiciary is not competent," and as enforcer of the law, "of which treaties form a part." Hamilton argued

that treaties, as well as the rules of international law, were part of the laws to be carried out by the executive and that "[h]e who is to execute the laws must first judge for himself of their meaning."[73]

Presidential control over foreign affairs did not just arise from tradition and custom but from the constitutional text. Article II already made the president the commander in chief, maker of treaties with the advice and consent of the Senate, receiver of ambassadors, and executor of the laws. But "it would not consist with rules of sound construction to consider this enumeration of particular authorities as derogating from the more comprehensive grant contained in the general clause," Hamilton argued. Article II's enumeration of powers "ought . . . to be considered as intended . . . to specify and regulate the principal articles implied in the definition of Executive Power; leaving the rest to flow from the general grant of that power." For Hamilton, the Senate's role in making treaties was only a narrow exception from the general grant of executive power to the president and "ought to be construed strictly." When the Constitution transferred traditional executive powers away from the president, it did so specifically, as with the power to declare war. "The general doctrine then of our constitution is, that the Executive Power of the Nation is vested in the President," Hamilton concluded, "subject only to the exceptions and qualifications which are expressed in that instrument."

Under the pseudonym "Helvidius," Madison took issue with every one of Hamilton's points.[74] He dismissed Locke's and Montesquieu's classification of foreign affairs as executive in nature because they were "evidently warped by a regard to the particular government of England." Making treaties and declaring war were legislative powers because they had the force of law; therefore, the president could not exercise them. "The natural province of the executive magistrate is to execute laws, as that of the legislature is to make laws," Madison wrote. "All his acts therefore, properly executive, must presuppose the existence of the laws to be executed." To allow the president a share of the legislative power "is an absurdity—in practice a tyranny."[75] Congress, not the president, must have the power to make peace because it already had the power to make war. To place those powers in the executive would invite the dictatorial abuses of the past. "Those who are to conduct a war cannot in the nature of things be proper or safe judges whether a war ought to be commenced, continued,

or concluded."[76] Why? Because, according to Madison, "war is in fact the true nurse of executive aggrandizement."[77] Hamilton's reading of Article II's vesting clause, Madison argued, was nothing less than an effort to smuggle the British Crown into the Constitution.

History has looked more favorably on Hamilton's arguments than on Madison's. Helvidius claimed rather unpersuasively that foreign affairs were legislative in nature or shared between the branches, and he never directly addressed Hamilton's argument about Article II's vesting of the executive power in the president.[78] The proclamation set one of the most important precedents for executive power: presidents henceforth would exercise the initiative in foreign affairs. Jefferson and Madison wanted to limit the executive's powers in foreign affairs, where they were perhaps needed most. But the growth of the nation and its interests would place increasing pressure on their constitutional vision. As the effect of foreign affairs on the nation grew, the powers of the office would respond to keep pace. Still, Hamilton's view required no prerogative, no right to act beyond the Constitution when necessity demands. He believed that the Constitution gave the president, through the grant of "the executive power" of the government, all of the authority necessary to handle exigencies and unforeseen circumstances.

Contrary to critics, therefore, foreign affairs does not constitute simply another area subject to congressional regulation. Presidents ever since Washington have acted on the understanding that the Constitution gave them the right to set the nation's foreign policy. The Constitution, however, did not grant them the means to guarantee that America would live up to its promises or carry out its threats. Congress has its own constitutional powers with which to frustrate presidential foreign policy. Even if the president wishes to improve relations with a nation, such as Iran or North Korea, Congress can use its authority over foreign commerce to impose economic sanctions. Even if the president promises to protect allies abroad, Congress can deny foreign aid or refuse to build the necessary military forces. Even if the president wishes to reach a trade deal with China, Congress can refuse to approve a trade agreement or bring U.S. tariffs and taxes into accord with the pact. The president can make the promises, but he can neither construct nor maintain an international order without the active participation of Congress.

I V.

President Trump has succeeded in advancing his foreign policy because he has not needed the cooperation of the other branches. Trump is not building a new international order along the lines of NATO at the beginning of the Cold War. Rather, he is seeking to undo the entanglements of his predecessors. Unraveling foreign commitments requires no legislative consent. Even though the constitutional text remains silent, the best reading of the constitutional structure recognizes an executive ability to terminate treaties without congressional approval. But the president's power goes beyond the ability to terminate existing commitments. The president virtually enjoys an absolute veto over efforts to create new ones. By exercising both the power to end and the power not to begin, Trump has advanced his foreign policy agenda to reduce America's engagements abroad. His right to terminate agreements draws from the same constitutional roots as his authority to set foreign policy.

Since entering office, Trump has gone on a frenzy of agreement breaking. On May 8, 2018, the Trump administration announced that the U.S. would withdraw from the Joint Comprehensive Plan of Action, otherwise known as the Iran nuclear deal. Agreed upon by the United States, Iran, Russia, China, the United Kingdom, France, and Germany in 2015, the JCPOA required Iran to limit its nuclear energy research in exchange for a financial payment and the lifting of economic sanctions. Due to sharp political opposition in Congress, the Obama administration chose not to submit the JCPOA as a treaty or even as a congressional-executive agreement enacted by a statute. This made it all the easier for President Trump, once in office, to simply reverse Obama's unilateral policy. Declaring the agreement "one of the worst and most one-sided transactions the United States has ever entered into," Trump terminated the agreement despite the contrary advice of former secretary of defense Jim Mattis, former secretary of state Rex Tillerson, and our major NATO allies. Trump replaced the JCPOA with the restoration of tough economic sanctions on Tehran.[79] The president argued that Iran had failed to live up to its promises to disclose and end its nuclear weapons activity and that it had used the economic benefits of the deal to fund terrorism and aggression.

Obama's other landmark foreign policy achievement, a global agreement to reduce greenhouse gases, met a similar fate. Signed by the United

States and 187 other nations in 2016, the United Nations Framework Convention on Climate Change (known popularly as the Paris Agreement) had committed nations to reduce their carbon emissions in an effort to slow global warming.[80] As with the JCPOA, political controversy erupted over limiting U.S. economic activity and energy usage while China and India had taken on less demanding obligations. The Obama administration responded by not submitting the Paris Agreement for approval as a treaty or a statute. And as with the JCPOA, this lack of congressional support then gave Trump an opportunity to fulfill another campaign pledge. On June 1, 2017, President Trump announced that the United States would withdraw from the Paris Agreement. The accord "is simply the latest example of Washington entering into an agreement that disadvantages the United States to the exclusive benefit of other countries," Trump declared, "leaving American workers—who I love—and taxpayers to absorb the cost in terms of lost jobs, lower wages, shuttered factories, and vastly diminished economic production."[81]

But Trump's skeptical eye toward foreign commitments extended beyond simply reversing his predecessor's signal accomplishments. In perhaps the most significant, yet least controversial move, the United States withdrew from the Intermediate-Range Nuclear Forces Treaty on August 2, 2019. Entered into by President Reagan in 1987, the INF Treaty prohibited both the United States and the Soviet Union (now Russia) from deploying land-based ballistic and cruise missiles with a range of 500–5,500 kilometers. For the first time, two nations agreed on the destruction of an entire class of nuclear weapons, ones that threatened the strategic balance in Europe because of their short travel times to targets. National security leaders, such as former secretary of state George Shultz, former secretary of defense William Perry, and former senators Richard Lugar and Sam Nunn, urged President Trump to keep INF, which had "prevented the unchecked deployment of nuclear missiles in Europe, significantly reducing the risk of rapid escalation towards nuclear war."[82] The United States claimed that Russia had violated the treaty with its development and testing of a new intermediate-range cruise missile.[83] But more importantly, the Trump administration emphasized that INF only applied to the United States and Russia and did not limit the rising nuclear forces of China. "For too long, we have been held back by self-imposed limits while foreign competitors grow, and they advance more than we have over the

years," Trump said in a Pentagon speech shortly before announcing the termination of INF.[84]

Controversially, Trump has suggested withdrawing from other, even more important agreements. Press reports suggest that the Trump White House is considering termination of the New START agreement, which reduced the U.S. and Russian arsenals to roughly 1,550 nuclear warheads and 700–800 missile and bomber systems. Negotiated under the Obama administration, New START remains as the last strategic arms agreement between the United States and Russia. The administration apparently is also considering termination of the 1992 Open Skies agreement, which allows the United States, Russia, and other signatories to conduct unarmed surveillance flights over one another's territories to observe military movements. In October 2019, Democratic senators warned that U.S. withdrawal "would be yet another gift from the Trump administration to Putin."[85] But according to administration officials, Russia has refused to make all of its airspace available, as required under the treaty, and American satellite surveillance makes overflights unnecessary.

President Trump's efforts to reorder American commitments reached their heights in the economic realm. Free trade may have provided Trump with his first platform in politics; he initially appeared on television shows in the 1980s to rail against Japanese imports. During the campaign, Trump had declared that he would replace existing multilateral trade agreements, which he claimed had harmed the American economy, with one-on-one trade deals. In a January 2016 meeting with the *New York Times* editorial board, he promised to raise tariffs on Chinese goods to 45 percent.[86] In a widely covered June 2016 speech, the Republican nominee threatened to withdraw from NAFTA, launch a trade war with China, and pull out of the Trans-Pacific Partnership, which he called a "rape of our country." He attacked globalization for helping "the financial elite" while leaving "millions of our workers with nothing but poverty and heartache." With regard to China, Trump claimed that "we already have a trade war and we're losing badly."[87]

Upon entering office, Trump followed through on his campaign threats. He immediately terminated the Trans-Pacific Partnership, even though it created a free trade area in the Pacific to exclude China. The White House launched a trade war with China that has imposed tariffs of up to 25 percent on most Chinese imports, with China retaliating by imposing tariffs

on U.S. goods, halting the purchase of U.S. agricultural imports, and reducing its holdings of U.S. government bonds. Trump also imposed tariffs on Canada, Mexico, India, and the European Union, which also responded with retaliatory duties. These trade sanctions placed into doubt the fate of the 1993 World Trade Organization agreement, which generally requires that states levy the same duties and regulations on all imports.

Trump has also sought to reform the web of U.S. free trade agreements that go beyond the WTO. He threatened to terminate NAFTA in order to pressure Congress to approve his new U.S.-Mexico-Canada free trade agreement, the USMCA. Thanks to NAFTA, Canada and Mexico have risen in the last 25 years to become the United States' most important trading partners—one-third of all U.S. exports go to those two nations. While the USMCA only makes marginal changes to the basic features of NAFTA, President Trump seems intent on keeping his campaign promise to repeal the original agreement and then to use that threat to win on the replacement. Trump used similar moves to rewrite the U.S.–South Korea free trade agreement, which the Bush administration had originally signed in 2007 and the Senate ratified in 2011.

Without the Constitution's grant of presidential power, Trump's efforts to reorder the nation's security and foreign economic policies would come to naught. Critics have primarily attacked Trump's use of trade sanctions. But Congress delegated broad freedom to the executive branch to impose tariffs in the Trade Expansion Act of 1962, the Trade Act of 1974, and the International Emergency Economic Powers Act of 1977. Indeed, Congress has sought to pressure reluctant presidents into imposing trade sanctions far more often than the reverse. The real source of Trump's power to shake up American commitments lies in the president's power to terminate and interpret treaties.

Trump critics argue that Congress must consent to the ending or interpretation of an international agreement. Their logic runs thus. Article II creates a process for entering into treaties and Article VI declares that treaties enjoy supremacy above state law. Nowhere does the constitutional text explicitly grant the powers of interpretation or termination to the president. Statutes require the consent of both houses of Congress and the president, or two-thirds of Congress without the president, before their repeal. This makes sense as a formal matter, as the same process used to make a law should be applied to reverse it. Statutes can only be repealed by

subsequent statutes, Supreme Court decisions can overrule past decisions, and constitutional provisions can be nullified only by the ratification of a later constitutional amendment. Treaties, therefore, that have the force of law should only be terminated by the agreement of the president and the Senate, which had to consent to the agreement, or Congress, which had to implement it.

Even though the constitutional text does not specifically address the issue, however, the president has long exercised the power to terminate treaties unilaterally. This appears to have been the understanding of the framing generation, and it has received the support of historical practice. Although the United States has terminated treaties on relatively few occasions in its history, presidents have done so unilaterally at least half the time.[88] Lincoln, FDR, Carter, Reagan, and George W. Bush terminated treaties on their own. Bush displayed the executive branch's power over treaty termination when he withdrew the United States from the Anti-Ballistic Missile (ABM) Treaty in December 2001 without congressional or senatorial consent.[89] Because the federal courts have refused to adjudicate the merits of the dispute between the president and Senate, termination remains "as a practical matter," in the words of the Congressional Research Service, a power in the hands of the president.[90]

Vesting termination power in the president makes sense as a textual, structural, and functional matter. The constitutional text does not explicitly give the power to terminate to Congress or the judiciary, so, according to Article II's Vesting Clause, this unenumerated executive power must reside with the chief executive. As we saw with the earlier discussions of the removal and foreign affairs powers, leading Framers believed that Article II vested all of the federal government's executive power in the president, with the provisions of sharing appointments and treaties with the Senate only subtracting from that broader grant of authority. Recall Hamilton's defense of the Neutrality Proclamation. He argued that President Washington had the right to interpret the Treaty of Alliance with France as not requiring U.S. aid to the new revolutionary government, because the Vesting Clause gave all treaty powers to the president (other than the Senate's consent role): "The general doctrine then of our constitution is, that the Executive Power of the Nation is vested in the President," Hamilton argued, "subject only to the exceptions and qualifications which are expressed in that instrument."[91] Indeed, during the cabinet arguments over the

Proclamation, Hamilton had argued that Washington could choose to terminate the 1778 treaty rather than interpret it. Even Jefferson, who wished to assist his beloved France, did not question that the president had the power to withdraw from the agreement.

Recognizing in the president a power to terminate treaties would also make the best sense of the constitutional structure. Article II creates the inverse system for treaties that Article I creates for laws. While Congress governs the introduction and passage for statutes, the president controls the treaty process. The president alone decides whether to begin the treaty process, the president alone signs the agreement, the president alone chooses to submit it to the Senate, and the president alone makes the treaty after the Senate has given its advice and consent.[92] Congress cannot make a treaty over the objection of the president—it cannot negotiate one, it cannot give advice and consent to one, and it cannot complete the process; only the president can. Reserving to the president a unilateral power to terminate treaties maintains the harmony of the president's general authority over treaties and the unity of the executive power.

To be sure, the Constitution does not establish a pure separation of powers in which each branch solely exercises all functions peculiar to it. Nonetheless, the Senate's participation in treaty-making and appointments reflects the Framers' effort to dilute the unitary nature of the executive branch rather than to transform these functions into legislative powers. While the Constitution reduces executive power in favor of the legislature, it does not transfer what were considered legislative powers to Article II. When the Constitution grants the executive a legislative power, such as the veto over statutes, it does so in Article I, not in Article II, because Article I alone describes the finely balanced method for making federal laws. By its placement in Article II, therefore, treaty-making is clearly an executive power. Past actions of presidents remain subject to the unilateral reversal of their successors. Just as the president retains the power to remove executive branch officials, even though he shares the appointments power with the Senate, he also has the power to terminate treaties.

The Senate's participation does not change the treaty power into a *legislative* power, just as its role in appointments does not alter the nomination and confirmation of officers of the United States into a legislative authority. The Framers clearly understood the difference between the legislative power, which was seen as the authority to make rules to govern the private

conduct of citizens, and the executive power, which was seen as the power to execute the laws and employ the nation's strength in its foreign affairs. They embodied this understanding in the clear allocations of power between Articles I and II. In defining the line between the executive and legislative powers, the Court and prominent scholars, such as Professor Henry Monaghan, have defined the executive power by its very inability to make laws.[93] Reading the treaty power as establishing just another species of legislative power, which would require Congress to join in the termination of treaties, would directly violate this understanding of the separation of powers.

Recognizing an executive right to terminate treaties would also fit best with the overall conduct of foreign affairs. Courts and many scholars have long favored presidential control of foreign affairs because of the executive branch's clear structural superiorities in the conduct of international relations. According to Nobel Prize–winning economist Thomas Schelling, the successful conduct of national strategy depends on "the assumption of rational behavior—not just of intelligent behavior, but of behavior motivated by a conscious calculation of advantages, a calculation that in turn is based on an explicit and internally consistent value system."[94] The nation-state ideally creates a rational, unitary decision maker who can identify threats, develop responses, and evaluate the costs and benefits that arise from different policy options. The rational actor translates broad national security interests into more discrete goals, which it then seeks to achieve by adopting value-maximizing policies and actions. As Schelling writes, a nation-state would want "to have a communications system in good order, to have complete information, or to be in full command of one's own actions or of one's own assets."[95]

This idea exerted influence even before the appearance of political scientists. In *United States v. Curtiss-Wright Export Corp.*, the Supreme Court observed, "In this vast external realm, with its important, complicated, delicate and manifold problems, the President alone has the power to speak or listen as a representative of the nation."[96] Justice George Sutherland further explained that "[t]he nature of transactions with foreign nations . . . requires caution and unity of design, and their success frequently depends on secrecy and dispatch."[97] Sutherland could trace his view to Alexander Hamilton, who wrote in *Federalist No. 70* that "decision, activity, secrecy, and dispatch will generally characterize the proceedings of one man, in a

much more eminent degree, than the proceedings of any greater number; and in proportion as the number is increased, these qualities will be diminished."[98] Or, as future chief justice John Marshall declared, "[t]he President is the sole organ of the nation in its external relations, and its sole representative with foreign nations . . . The [executive] department . . . is entrusted with the whole foreign intercourse of the nation."[99]

Because of the executive branch's design, it could conduct foreign affairs in a superior manner to Congress or the courts. As a result, the Framers vested the president with the commander-in-chief power, the power to make treaties (with the advice and consent of the Senate), and the power to conduct diplomatic relations. The history of American foreign relations and the American presidency has been the story of the expansion of the executive's power thanks to its structural abilities to wield power quickly, effectively, and in a unitary manner.[100] The president therefore must retain the power to terminate treaties in order to give full effect to the Constitution's broader grant of the foreign affairs power to the executive branch. The president must have the ability to terminate international agreements when they conflict with the national interest or the executive's foreign policy goals, and he must at least be able to threaten to withdraw from treaties in order to procure better deals in international negotiations. Critics would divest the president of the flexibility needed to manage the nation's foreign affairs in order to transform treaties into a form of domestic lawmaking rather than a tool of foreign policy.

CONCLUSIONS

President Trump's effort to force a sea change in American foreign policy depends critically upon the Constitution. Article II's vesting of the executive power grants the president the right to develop foreign policy and conduct international relations. It extends even to the right to pull the United States out of treaties, if necessary. Criticism of the Trump Doctrine should focus on the policy of rebalancing American foreign commitments with military and financial resources rather than on claims of illegal tariffs or unconstitutional treaty termination.

Trump's control of the conduct of foreign relations, however, does not exclude Congress from any say over policy. The Framers remained relatively silent on the interaction between the branches over foreign affairs.

We can reach some inferences, however, from their views on the domestic implementation of treaties. As the Framers well knew from recent British history, treaties represented political agreements between sovereigns, which required legislation from Parliament before they could be implemented at home. This allowed Parliament to influence foreign policy by refusing to enact laws or vote supplies necessary for the Crown to make and execute treaty obligations. The Framers understood the Constitution to continue this distinction between the treaty and the legislative power, expressed in the location of the executive treaty power in Article II and its separation from the federal legislative power, which rests in Article I.[101] One implication of this separation is that treaties cannot directly regulate matters within Congress's Article I powers; another is Congress's freedom to frustrate presidential foreign policy and treaty initiatives through legislation and appropriations.

If Congress opposes presidential foreign policy, therefore, it has significant tools at hand. Its exclusive power over international commerce allows it to impose sanctions on nations toward which the president may have warmer feelings. Indeed, Congress has consistently imposed harsher economic penalties on Russia than have been sought by the Trump administration. Congress's plenary spending power also gives it the ability to help nations disfavored by the president. As the impeachment probe has made clear, Congress voted to send almost $400 million in military and foreign aid to Ukraine in 2019, even though President Trump bore deep suspicions about that nation's involvement in the 2016 elections. Congress can refuse to approve treaties and agreements, instead of approving the replacement of NAFTA with the USMCA, and it can decline to live up to our international promises by refusing to pass the necessary implementing laws. If Congress does not want to move the U.S. embassy in Israel to Jerusalem, it can zero out funding for new diplomatic facilities. If it believes the president has gone too far in deploying the military abroad, it can shrink the size and capabilities of the armed forces. As presidential scholar Edward Corwin once observed, the Constitution "is an invitation to struggle for the privilege of directing American foreign policy."[102]

But the Trump Doctrine clarifies a feature of the Constitution that had not mattered since the end of World War II. Permanent commitments of American aid and assistance depend on the cooperation of the president and Congress. Both branches had to work together to make the treaties

and agreements, build and deploy the militaries, and exercise the political leadership that contained the Soviet Union. The United States cannot maintain expeditionary forces abroad for long without the joint consent of the president, who orders their deployment, and the Congress, which pays for them. But getting America out of the world is far easier than getting it in. As commander in chief, President Trump can reduce American involvement abroad by moving troops or terminating treaties. Congress can refuse to fulfill executive promises and end alliances by cutting funding and downsizing the military. The American people elected Trump in part out of frustration with the overcommitments of U.S. foreign policy. Using the executive powers legitimately granted by the Constitution, the forty-fifth president is carrying out a doctrine that rebalances American ends and means.

FIRE AND FURY: TRUMP AT WAR

One minute, Iranian general Qasem Soleimani was leaving Baghdad International Airport in a caravan of vehicles after weeks of escalating attacks on American forces in the region. The next minute, he was dead. Trump's most spectacular act as commander in chief came on January 3, 2020, when U.S. forces killed the most influential military leader in Iran, a man who had exported the Iranian Revolution abroad, supported terrorist groups throughout the Middle East, and was responsible for the deaths of hundreds of American soldiers during the Iraq War. Trump's strike had followed a series of Iranian attacks on U.S. forces, including the shelling of a U.S. base in Iraq, which killed one defense contractor and injured several U.S. soldiers, and efforts by Iranian-backed militias to storm the U.S. Embassy in Baghdad. With access to extensive electronic and human intelligence, the Trump administration concluded that Soleimani and his associates were planning yet further attacks on American forces and embassies.

Trump boasted of the killing as revenge upon a bitter enemy. "Soleimani spread death, destruction, and mayhem across the Middle East and far beyond," Trump said at a campaign rally a week later. "He was a bad guy, he was a bloodthirsty terror, and he's no longer a terror. He's dead."[1] But he also suggested that killing Soleimani would deter further attacks on Americans. "If you dare to threaten our citizens, you do so at your own grave peril," the president warned.

Democrats responded by accusing the president of starting an illegal war. "The administration took this action without the consultation of Congress and without respect for Congress's war powers granted to it by the

171

Constitution," Speaker Pelosi said. Senator Chris Murphy of Connecticut charged the administration with "assassinat[ing], without any congressional authorization, the second most powerful person in Iran, knowingly setting off a potential massive regional war." Less than a week after the strike, the House passed a resolution "direct[ing] the President to terminate the use of United States Armed Forces to engage in hostilities against Iran."[2] According to the Democratic majority, the president could only use force in the event that Congress authorizes hostilities or if "necessary and appropriate to defend against an imminent armed attack."

Trump has made war central to his presidency, but like his other policies, his approach can seem impulsive. Even as he has tried to wind down U.S. involvement abroad, Trump opened 2020 with a startling strike that killed Iran's most influential military leader. But Trump's policies have made war a contradictory point of attack for his opponents too, who have criticized him both for inviting a broad conflict with Iran or North Korea and for refusing to keep fighting in the Syrian civil war. Regardless of which side has the policy calls right, the power to make war has become yet another arena where Trump's opponents would overthrow decades of constitutional practice in their zeal to stop him. For an alleged isolationist, Trump has become the most unlikely defender of the right of future presidents to protect the nation's security.

Critics of presidential power commonly claim that the executive has too much authority to launch destructive wars. But they also forget the reverse lesson of the 1930s: that the executive can keep the United States out of war too. It is this latter dimension of the president's war powers that has proven central to Trump's national security strategy. In contrast to Hillary Clinton and the Washington, D.C., foreign policy establishment, Donald Trump campaigned on ending foreign wars. In his view, conflicts wasted American lives and treasure for nothing. While President Obama had struggled over whether to intervene in the Syrian civil war, Trump tweeted: "We should stay the hell out of Syria." He asked, "WHAT WILL WE GET FOR OUR LIVES AND $BILLIONS? ZERO."[3]

Much to the dismay of the national security establishment and his own cabinet, Trump followed through. In December 2018, the White House announced that U.S. troops would withdraw from Syria.[4] After Jim Mattis resigned as secretary of defense in protest and Congress reacted in an uproar, Trump paused. But with John Bolton installed as national security advisor

and Mike Pompeo as secretary of state, Trump returned to his original plan. On October 6, 2019, following a phone call with Turkish president Recep Tayyip Erdogan, Trump redeployed 1,000 U.S. special forces away from the Turkey–Syria border. The Turkish military quickly invaded Syria and set up a buffer zone at the expense of the U.S.'s Kurdish allies.

Trump triumphantly tweeted: "COMING HOME! We were supposed to be there for 30 days—That was 10 years ago." He continued: "When these pundit fools who have called the Middle East wrong for 20 years ask what we are getting out of the deal, I simply say, THE OIL, AND WE ARE BRINGING OUR SOLDIERS BACK HOME, ISIS SECURED!"[5]

Syria symbolized Trump's broader campaign promise to rebalance American military strategy. He believes that the United States has spent too much protecting the free world while our allies have enjoyed a free ride. Afghanistan and Iraq symbolized for Trump the extreme costs of foreign entanglements. "We're rebuilding other countries while weakening our own," Trump said in his first major foreign policy speech. "I am the only person running for the presidency who understands this, and this is a serious problem."[6] Once in office, Trump set an end to U.S. involvement in Syria and began to wind down deployments in Afghanistan and Iraq. He raised doubts about whether the United States would honor Article 5 of the North Atlantic Treaty, which requires NATO members to treat any attack on one as an attack on all. He demanded that Japan and Korea pay more for the large U.S. military presences on their territory.

On the other hand, Trump followed a more activist course than at first appears. He continued the interventions of his predecessors in the Middle East. Trump ordered the strike that killed Soleimani and threatened Tehran with further escalation. He launched attacks on Syrian military facilities to punish the Assad regime for using chemical weapons. U.S. troops remained in Syria to fight ISIS and protect the Kurds. He kept the military in Afghanistan and authorized the spectacular use of heavy munitions.

Trump has introduced threats as a regular tool of foreign policy. In his 2017 speech to the United Nations, he promised the "total destruction" of North Korea if it continued to develop nuclear weapons. "Rocket man is on a suicide mission for himself and his regime," Trump said of Kim Jong Un. "If [the United States] is forced to defend itself or its allies, we will have no choice but to totally destroy North Korea."[7] Earlier that year, he had reacted to North Korean threats by declaring, "[T]hey will be met with fire and

fury like the world has never seen." Trump allowed the U.S. Navy to continue its challenges to China's fortified artificial islands in the South China Sea. Despite the Ukraine impeachment controversy, the United States sold lethal weapons to Kyiv to fight a Russian-backed separatist movement. Despite his isolationist instincts, Trump has kept the United States on the beat as the world's only policeman.

Nevertheless, both Democrats and Republicans have accused Trump of risking war. Trump used the United Nations "as a stage to threaten war," Senator Dianne Feinstein said, a threat that "further isolates the United States."[8] Trump, however, follows a long line of presidents who have used such threats to deter enemies, communicate resolve, and settle disputes.[9] Critics do not just attack the wisdom of these engagements. They accuse the White House of waging unconstitutional wars without congressional approval. American airstrikes on Syria or support for Saudi fighting in Yemen break the law, apparently, because Congress has not declared war. "Make no mistake: President Trump's airstrikes against Syria were unconstitutional," claimed Professor Michael Paulsen.[10] *National Review* columnist David French chimed in about U.S. support for Saudi Arabia: "It's now official: The president who ran for office pledging to reduce military entanglements abroad is involving American forces in a foreign war in direct defiance of the plain language of the Constitution."[11] Some conservatives, such as Senators Mike Lee of Utah and Rand Paul of Kentucky, proposed bills to declare that Trump's decisions as commander in chief had violated the Constitution. But these efforts failed in the face of a presidential veto.

Liberals have long proven inconsistent in their attitude toward presidents and war by claiming that Republicans wage unconstitutional wars while remaining silent under Democrats. Many sharply criticized George W. Bush (and George H. W. Bush, Reagan, and Nixon) for conducting wars without congressional approval. But few liberals claimed that Obama's war to overthrow Muammar al-Gaddafi in Libya violated the Constitution. When Obama launched attacks on Syria for its use of chemical weapons, liberals continued to keep quiet. They even accepted the Obama administration's implausible justification that the Libya and Syria interventions did not need authorization because they were not really wars at all.

But these critics gave full vent to their frustrations once Trump occupied the Oval Office. Senator Bernie Sanders asserted that Trump had "no legal

authority" to attack Syria, even though he had not criticized Obama's 2011 Libya intervention.[12] Democratic presidential candidate Tulsi Gabbard (D-Hawaii) took to the *Fox & Friends* TV program to criticize the Soleimani strike: "This was very clearly an act of war by this president without any kind of authorization or declaration of war from Congress, clearly violating the Constitution."[13] While questioning the killing of Soleimani, whom she described as a "senior foreign military official," Senator Elizabeth Warren called Trump "reckless" and "dangerous" and accused him of "marching toward war with Iran since his first days in office."[14] Sanders compared killing Soleimani to Putin's "assassinating dissidents."

This chapter will explain why these critics are wrong. The Constitution vests the president with the executive power and the role of commander in chief, which, in the words of *Federalist No. 70*, gives him the primary constitutional duty of "protection of the community against foreign attacks."[15] The Founders vested these powers in the president precisely because only a single man could act with sufficient "energy in the executive" to respond to the challenges of foreign policy and national security. Congress has an arsenal of authorities to block presidential war-making, such as control over the size and shape of the military. But the Constitution does not grant Congress, through its power to declare war, the sole right to decide whether to go to war. Instead, the Constitution divides the war power between the executive and legislative branches and encourages them to struggle for control. By refusing to concede an unprecedented veto to Congress over military operations, Trump preserves the constitutional right of future presidents to take the measures necessary to protect the nation's security.

I. THE TRUMP STRATEGY FOR WAR

President Trump took office in the midst of several wars. Almost two decades after the 9/11 attacks, the United States continues to fight the Taliban in Afghanistan. Although the United States had withdrawn from Iraq in 2010, the Obama administration had intervened in Syria to fight ISIS. President Trump won his greatest military victory by finishing off ISIS as a caliphate in control of territory, culminating in an October 27, 2019, operation that killed ISIS founder Abu Bakr al-Baghdadi.

Neither war raised a significant constitutional issue. Both could rely on the Authorization for Use of Military Force (AUMF) passed by Congress in

the wake of the September 11 attacks. In the broadest grant of war power by Congress since World War II, the AUMF recognized that "the President has the authority under the Constitution to take action to deter and prevent acts of international terrorism against the United States." It authorized him "to use all necessary and appropriate force against those nations, organizations, or persons he determines planned, authorized, committed, or aided the terrorist attacks."[16] It did not limit its approval for war by time or geography. As a young Justice Department lawyer during the Bush administration, I helped draft this language. I can attest that the administration sought to make sure that the AUMF would support the president no matter where the terrorists fled or how long it took to hunt them down.

The AUMF clearly authorized the wars that Trump inherited. The Taliban had provided al-Qaeda with a safe haven before the attacks and harbored it afterward. After the United States' lightning-quick victory over the Taliban in the weeks after 9/11, the Taliban fled to western Pakistan, regrouped, and returned. During the Bush years, troop deployments kept below 25,000. Obama ordered a temporary surge to 100,000 by 2011, but then drew down forces to about 8,000 by 2016.

Although Trump had campaigned on withdrawing from Afghanistan, he changed his mind once in office. In 2017, at the request of Defense Secretary Mattis, Trump agreed to boost the force level to about 14,000. But after firing Mattis in late 2018, the president announced that he would halve the deployment. Despite the investment in men and treasure, the Afghanistan war had reached a stalemate. By the end of the fighting season in 2019, the Taliban controlled about 12 percent of the country's districts, the U.S.-backed government controlled 53 percent, and 34 percent of the country remained contested.[17] Trump's frustration with the ongoing conflict revealed itself in the fall of 2019, with the leaked news that the president had planned to invite Taliban leaders to Camp David, *on September 11*, to sign an agreement for an end to the fighting and the withdrawal of U.S. troops. Trump canceled the event after public outcry, the resignation of John Bolton, and a Taliban car bomb attack in Kabul. Nevertheless, the Constitution gives the president as commander in chief the ability to order the U.S. Armed Forces to cease fighting. No doubt Trump will invoke this legal authority again to try to end the Afghanistan war.

Trump could also rely on the AUMF for what became the other war of his first term: Syria. Even before he had entered office, the United States

had already intervened in the civil war. In 2013, Obama called for regime change in Syria as a civil war erupted against the rule of Bashar al-Assad. As reports circulated that the Assad regime may have used chemical weapons against civilians, Obama declared that Syria had crossed "a red line." Obama went to Congress for authorization to intervene in Syria, but Congress refused. Russian president Putin came to a humiliating rescue, in which the United States refrained from war in exchange for Russian supervision of the Syrian removal of chemical weapons.

By 2014, Washington had shifted its attentions from chemical weapons to ISIS. An offshoot of al-Qaeda, ISIS seized vast swaths of territory in both Syria and Iraq during the civil war chaos. Its forces controlled major cities and significant population and resources in both nations; it had even threatened Baghdad before Iraqi forces had turned the tide. That fall, the Obama administration launched airstrikes against ISIS and soon deployed troops in Syria. Not only did Trump continue the war, he also loosened the rules of engagement so that U.S. forces could fight more aggressively. ISIS's last city, its capital of Raqqa, fell in 2018, and strikes killed al-Baghdadi and his number-two aide in summer 2019.

Like Obama before him, Trump could invoke Bush's AUMF. The September 11 law authorized the president to use forces against any "organization" that "committed or aided" the 2001 attacks. Although ISIS and al-Qaeda later became rivals, ISIS originally began as a franchise of the original terrorist group. Trump might also rely upon the 2002 AUMF that approved the Iraq invasion, which authorized the president to use the armed forces "as he determines to be necessary and appropriate" to "defend the national security of the United States against the continuing threat posed by Iraq" and "enforce all relevant United Nations Security Council resolutions regarding Iraq."[18] One of those Security Council resolutions authorized the United States to restore international peace and stability in the region. Ejecting ISIS from Iraqi territory and preventing ISIS from using Iraqi territory to attack Americans would qualify.

But Trump's use of force against the Syrian government would have to rely exclusively on the president's sole constitutional authority. Ending the Syrian civil war, stopping Assad's WMD use, or protecting Syrian civilians would not fall under either the 2001 or 2002 AUMF. And Trump willingly used force where Obama would not. In April 2017, Trump ordered a retaliatory strike against Syria for using chemical weapons against a rebel

village. The navy launched 59 Tomahawk cruise missiles against the Syrian air force base that had carried out the attack, damaged Syrian military facilities, and put 20 percent of the Syrian air force out of action. In a letter to Congress "consistent with the War Powers Resolution," Trump stated that he "acted in the vital national security and foreign policy interests of the United States, pursuant to my constitutional authority to conduct foreign relations and as Commander in Chief and Chief Executive."[19] Congressional Democrats criticized Trump for violating the Constitution, and public interest groups sued to stop the attacks.[20]

Trump ordered military strikes again when Damascus repeated its WMD use. According to U.S. intelligence, Assad ordered the use of chemical weapons at least 15 times between June 2017 and April 2018, including a lethal sarin gas attack in November 2017 on the outskirts of Damascus.[21] In April 2018, Trump joined British and French leaders in ordering airstrikes on three Syrian chemical weapons facilities. Thanks to Obama's deal with Putin, however, Russia had returned to the Middle East, and its air force and anti-aircraft defenses provided air cover for Assad's forces. Destruction was minimal.

Unlike Obama, Trump defended the legality of his attacks on Syria. While the Trump Justice Department claimed that the president had the authority to use force without congressional permission, it adopted a cramped theory of executive power developed by the Obama administration. A May 2018 opinion by DOJ's Office of Legal Counsel (OLC) began well enough. It argued that the Commander in Chief and Vesting Clauses gave him "the authority to direct U.S. military forces in engagements necessary to advance American national interests abroad." OLC repeated William Rehnquist's justification of Nixon's expansion of the Vietnam War to Cambodia: history plainly showed that "the Executive, under his power as Commander in Chief, is authorized to commit American forces in such a way as to seriously risk hostilities, and also to actually commit them to such hostilities, without prior congressional approval."

But then OLC imposed constraints on Trump. First, it maintained that the Syrian strikes had to advance the "national interest." According to OLC, the national interest had usually focused on the protection of American citizens and property abroad. It asserted that U.S. interests in the world meant that the president should have "wide latitude" to use force not just "to protect American interests" but to respond to "regional conflagrations

and humanitarian catastrophes," including, in Syria, regional stability, preventing humanitarian catastrophes, and deterring WMD use.

Despite its broad definition of "national interest," OLC proceeded to incorrectly cabin presidential power. It adopted the Clinton-Obama view that Congress's power to declare war gave it the sole authority to begin hostilities abroad. But to justify Trump's attack on Syria, like Obama's 2010 Libya attacks, OLC claimed that neither war was really a "war." Attacking Syria, OLC argued, did not rise to the level of a war because of the "anticipated nature, scope and duration" of the conflict. Military operations would cross the line into a constitutional war "when characterized by 'prolonged and substantial military engagements, typically involving exposure of U.S. military personnel to significant risk over a substantial period.'"[22] Trump's Syria strikes did not amount to war because the United States only used aircraft and missiles for a limited time and mission.

DOJ's conclusion cannot be taken seriously. Its distinction between small, short wars that the president may begin unilaterally and large, long wars that require prior congressional approval has no foundation in the Constitution's text. The Declare War Clause grants to Congress the power "To declare War, grant Letters of Marque and Reprisal, and make Rules concerning Captures on Land and Water." No mention of "small" versus "large" wars. OLC mistakenly defines a war based on the potential harm to U.S. troops regardless of the magnitude of the conflict. Suppose the United States launches a nuclear weapon against an enemy capital. No U.S. troops are at risk in a one-time attack that destroys the enemy's political and military leadership. Under OLC's test, a nuclear attack would not qualify as war. The magnitude of the destruction and the United States' object to change a foreign regime should meet the test for a war in the constitutional sense. During the Cold War, the United States and the Soviet Union arrayed tens of thousands of atomic weapons against each other. Under OLC's test, a nuclear exchange could have occurred and still no war would have taken place. Or suppose the United States used its overwhelming naval and air power to attack a weaker country that could not retaliate, such as Libya or Serbia. According to DOJ, the president can escape any constitutional limits on war by selecting some branches of the armed forces, but not others, to do the fighting.

It is unfortunate to see the Trump administration follow its Democratic predecessors in adopting an unprincipled approach to war powers. It may

make sense as a matter of political expediency but not as a matter of constitutional law. It also creates undesirable incentives. OLC's test would encourage the executive branch to choose air or sea forces, even when ground troops would more effectively protect American interests. The Balkan Wars, for example, ended not because of the air campaign against Serbia but because NATO threatened to send troops. DOJ's rule could encourage presidents to launch superficial attacks that may only defer challenges to our national security rather than solve them.

Trump would be better served, and he would better preserve the constitutional authority of the presidency, if he were to return to the original understanding of the Constitution. The next section will show that the Constitution does not prescribe a step-by-step method for beginning wars. It argues that the president can initiate hostilities abroad under executive power and his role as commander in chief. The president's power is not unilateral, but the check on it does not arise from the Declare War Clause. Instead, the legislature's main restraint on presidential power comes from the power of the purse. Congress can prevent presidential adventures by refusing to build, or continuing to supply, the armies and navies. Trump's use of force falls within the range of acceptable constitutional conduct because Congress has failed to use its readily available powers to stop him.

II.

Attacking Trump for violating the Constitution's division of war powers ignores both historical practice and the best reading of the document. Presidents have long initiated military conflict without specific congressional authorization. For large wars, this practice extends at least as far as the Korean War, if not earlier; for smaller conflicts, it begins with the origins of the Republic.[23] Congress has declared war only five times, the last more than 75 years ago. Meanwhile, presidents have committed military forces to combat without a declaration of war more than 130 times since the Constitution's ratification.[24] Since World War II, presidents have engaged in several significant military engagements without a declaration of war. When President Truman sent American troops to Korea in 1950, he did not seek congressional authorization, relying instead on his inherent executive and commander-in-chief powers. In Vietnam, President Johnson never obtained a declaration of war or an unambiguous congressional au-

thorization, although the Gulf of Tonkin Resolution expressed some level of congressional support. Congress never authorized Nixon's expansion of the war into Laos and Cambodia.

As the Supreme Court has recognized, governmental practice represents a significant factor in identifying the contours of the separation of powers. Even Justice Robert Jackson's *Youngstown* opinion, much beloved by Trump opponents, recognized that fact. "Congressional inertia, indifference or quiescence may sometimes, at least as a practical matter, enable, if not invite, measures on independent presidential responsibility," he wrote.[25] The importance of practice is heightened in the foreign affairs and national security areas, where an absence of judicial precedent gives a long history of interbranch interpretation and interaction more weight. Finally, practice shows that many government leaders throughout American history have read the constitutional text as providing presidents with the power to commence military hostilities without congressional authorization.

Practice demonstrates that the political branches have read the constitutional text to establish a stable, working system of war powers. The Constitution constructs a loose framework within which the president as commander in chief enjoys substantial discretion and initiative in conducting military hostilities. At the same time, Congress plays a significant role by controlling both the resources for war (through funding) and the legal status of hostilities (through declaring war). Unlike the legislative process, the constitutional text does not establish a specific procedure for going to war. Rather, it allocates different, potentially conflicting war powers to the two branches. This practical reading of the text better follows the original understanding of the commander-in-chief and executive powers. Throughout American history, these powers have given the president broad constitutional authority to respond to threats to the national security and foreign policy of the United States.[26]

Beginning with Vietnam, however, liberals turned against history and sought to enlist the Constitution in support. Leading liberal politicians, such as Senator Ted Kennedy, criticized the Reagan and Bush presidencies for their unconstitutional wars. Democrats even furiously attacked George W. Bush for the Afghanistan and Iraq wars, even though they had voted to authorize them. As antiwar candidate Barack Obama declared in 2008, "The President does not have power under the Constitution to unilaterally authorize a military attack in a situation that does not involve stopping an actual or imminent threat to the nation."[27] Future vice president Joe Biden even promised in 2007 that "I will move to impeach" President Bush if he were to attack Iran without congressional permission.[28]

While Obama swiftly dismissed constitutional principle when he assumed responsibility for national security, such inconsistency should disturb scholars. Yale law professors Bruce Ackerman and Harold Koh, for example, turn to the original understanding to claim that Congress's power to "declare war" gives it the exclusive right to decide whether to initiate military hostilities abroad. They usually only permit the president a small exception for self-defense.[29] This should produce some ideological discomfort, because liberal scholars would never consult the Framers' views on abortion, gay marriage, or the right to bear arms. Nevertheless, the leading lights of America's colleges and universities regularly accuse Republican presidents of violating the Framers' original understanding of war powers.

Once Democrats occupied the Oval Office, all that changed. Clinton displayed a willingness to use force in numerous situations and locations, including Haiti, Iraq, Sudan, Bosnia, and Afghanistan. When Clinton dispatched 20,000 troops to Bosnia in 1995 and launched an air war against Serbia in 1999, liberal critics were few and far between, even though Congress refused to authorize either deployment. Obama laid claim to executive power just as readily. In 2011, he ordered an air campaign to overthrow the regime in Libya, and in 2014, he launched attacks on Syria. No great debates erupted in Congress. Democrats who had attacked Reagan and the Bushes did nothing to stop Obama. Scholars who had kept silent under Clinton even went a step further. Many joined the Obama administration and facilitated his wars.

Of course, now those same liberals attack Trump's unconstitutional Syrian war, not to mention his threats against North Korea and Iran. These arguments are not just inconsistent, they also ignore the best reading of the Constitution and the history of its adoption. Because they accept that practice runs contrary to their view that Congress must declare all wars first, liberals (and some conservatives) plead the original understanding. There is a "clarity of the Constitution on this question," writes John Hart Ely, one of the great constitutional theorists of the twentieth century. Often "the 'original understanding' of the document's framers and ratifiers can be obscure to the point of inscrutability"; but "[i]n this case, it isn't." Accord-

ing to Ely, "all wars, big or small, 'declared' in so many words or not . . . ,
had to be legislatively authorized."[30]

Critics of presidential power believe everything turns on Congress's
power to declare war. Conservative professor Michael Ramsey makes the
argument concisely. He argues that the Framers understood the power to
"declare war" as giving Congress the sole power to decide on whether to
commence military hostilities against other nations. Under international
and domestic law at the time of the ratification, "declare war" must have
been shorthand for "begin war" or "commence war" or "authorize war."[31]
Another conservative, Professor Sai Prakash, also claims that the diplomatic, political, and legal elites of the eighteenth century used "declare
war" to mean "start war." The president cannot activate his commander-
in-chief authority and fight a war until Congress gives its blessing first—
though they, and virtually all scholars, concede that the president can use
force immediately to repel attacks on the United States. As Professor Michael Glennon writes, the clause not only "empowers Congress to declare
war" but also "serves as a limitation on executive war-making power, placing certain acts off limits for the President."[32]

These critics make an initial argument based on the text, but they fail
to carefully read the full constitutional text and structure. First, the Constitution does not treat "declare war" as synonymous with the power to
begin military hostilities. While Congress has the power to declare war, the
president also possesses significant war powers. Article II, Section 2 states
that the "President shall be Commander in Chief of the Army and Navy
of the United States, and of the Militia of the several States, when called
into the actual Service of the United States." He is further vested with all of
"the executive Power" and the duty to execute the laws. These provisions
have long been recognized to give the president absolute command over
the armed forces of the United States, to the point of ordering their use in
hostilities abroad. Nowhere does the constitutional text provide that the
commander-in-chief power must wait for a declaration of war before its
use.

The Framers significantly decided to place the Commander in Chief
Clause in Article II rather than in Article I's listing of legislative powers. It
shows that the Framers did not see the president as an adjunct of the legislative process, as he is with the right to veto bills. Instead, it shows that

the Framers chose to divide the war power, which was once unified in the British Crown, into legislative and executive components. The president and Congress can use their authorities to compete and fight over control. For example, Article II gives the president the power to make treaties and appoint officers, with the advice and consent of the Senate. But Congress can refuse to pass the laws needed to live up to the treaty, and it can refuse to fund the officers appointed by the president.

Neglecting the president's Article II powers amounts to a critical error. These provisions allow the president to deploy military forces and to use them both to protect the national security and to advance American interests. To be sure, in the wake of Vietnam, Congress enacted the War Powers Resolution (WPR), which limits foreign military interventions to 60 days without congressional authorization. Critics of presidential activism often invoke the WPR, and some have even brought lawsuits under it, though to no avail. Presidents have refused to accept its legality, and neither Congress nor the courts have shown any interest in enforcing it. Bush's Persian Gulf War, Clinton's Kosovo air campaign, and Obama's interventions in Libya and Syria breached the WPR's time limits without suffering any consequences.

A.

Trump's critics reject historical practice because they assume that "declare war" must have the colloquial meaning to begin hostilities. But the Constitution nowhere defines or uses the phrase "declare" in this way. If the liberal view were correct, the Constitution should consistently repeat the phrase when addressing war-making. It does not. When discussing war in other provisions, the Constitution employs phrases that indicate that declaring war refers to something less than the sole power to send the nation into hostilities.

Article I, Section 10, which limits the ability of states to wage war, contains the clearest example. It prohibits states "without the Consent of Congress" from "engag[ing] in War, unless actually invaded, or in such imminent Danger as will not admit of delay." If we take a written Constitution seriously, we must give the same words in the Constitution the same meaning throughout. If liberals were correct, the Framers intended to duplicate Article I, Section 10's system of war-making when they gave Con-

gress the power to declare war. Section 10 even sets out the exception for automatic self-defense that liberals must concede lies within the executive power. Why didn't the Framers simply copy the exact language and replace "states" with "the President"? Or, if "declare war" meant "start hostilities," then Article I, Section 10 should have only said, "No state shall, without the consent of Congress, declare war." Instead, the Framers clearly thought "engage in war"—not "declare war"—meant starting hostilities.

Two additional provisions similarly reject the "declare war" theory. Article III defines the crime of treason as consisting of "levying War" against the United States. Why not "declare" here too? "Levying," like "engage," conveys starting hostilities. Congress's power to declare war also does not stand alone but instead is part of a clause that includes the power to "grant Letters of Marque and Reprisal" and to "make Rules concerning Captures on Land and Water." Placement of the power to declare war alongside these other two is significant, because they clearly involved the power of Congress to recognize or declare the legal status and consequences of certain wartime actions and not the power to authorize those actions. Letters of marque and reprisal allowed a sovereign nation to extend the protections of the laws of war to private forces acting in coordination with its armed forces.[33] Rules concerning captures determine the law that applies to prizes seized by American forces. In both cases, these powers did not act to authorize hostilities as much as they determined the legal status and consequences of those hostilities.

Other foundational documents of the period demonstrate that beginning hostilities and declaring war were not the same thing. Article IX of the Articles of Confederation vested Congress with "the sole and exclusive right and power of determining on peace and war." Again, no "declare war." If the Framers had intended to grant Congress the power to commence military hostilities, they could easily have borrowed the phrase for the new Constitution, as they did with many other powers. Critics also fail to take into account the next most important documents of the time: the state constitutions. Most of the state constitutions did not explicitly grant the power to initiate hostilities to the legislature.[34] One state, however, chose to create exactly the type of arrangement contemplated by presidential critics. In its first 1776 constitution, South Carolina vested in its chief executive the power of commander in chief, but then declared that "the president and

commander-in-chief shall have no power to make war or peace . . . without the consent of the general assembly and legislative council."[35] In 1778, South Carolina amended the provision to say that "the governor and commander-in-chief shall have no power to commence war, or conclude peace" without legislative approval. South Carolina used "make" or "commence" war, but not "declare." Both constitutions provided an example of constitutional language that clearly and explicitly created the very legislature-dominated war-making system for which presidential critics wish.

When the Framers employed "declare," they usually used it in a juridical manner, in the sense that courts "declare" the state of the law or the legal status of a certain event or situation. The Framers' thoughts on declaring war would have turned to their most significant national legal act, the Declaration of Independence. The Declaration did not begin war with Great Britain. When the Continental Congress met at Philadelphia in 1776, hostilities had already existed for more than a year. The Declaration instead transformed the legal status of the hostilities from an insurrection to a war between equals. As historian David Armitage observes, "[I]n order to turn a civil war into a war between states, and thus to create legitimate corporate combatants out of individual rebels and traitors, it was essential to declare war and to obtain recognition of the legitimacy of such a declaration."[36] As a nation-state, the United States could make alliances and conduct commerce with other nations, which were critical steps in winning independence. The Declaration of Independence was the nation's first declaration of war.

Declarations do simply what they say they do: they declare. They make public and show openly the state of legal relations with another nation. During the eighteenth century, declarations often took the form of a legal complaint in which a nation identified the grounds for waging war, explained the new rules that would apply, and outlined the remedy. Declarations are also important for domestic purposes. A declaration of war triggers enhanced powers on the part of the federal government. Congress has recognized the distinction between declared wars and non-declared hostilities by providing the executive branch with expanded domestic powers such as seizing foreign property, conducting warrantless surveillance, arresting enemy aliens, and taking control of transportation systems only when war is declared.

B.

The Constitution does not establish a set process for going to war but instead allows the president and Congress to compete for primacy. What happens if a president disagrees with Congress on the merits of a war or on the methods dictated by Congress? Suppose Congress had ordered FDR to ignore the Pacific theater entirely, to leave Italy alone, or to avoid a direct invasion of France. It seems obvious that the president as commander in chief can block congressional decisions, just as Congress can block the president through the funding power. The president can refuse to carry out congressional orders to implement a particular strategy or tactic, or even to conduct hostilities against another nation. But under the presidential critics' reading of the text, a president would have to carry out Congress's demands that the nation wage war, just as he would any other statute.

Constitutional structure, furthermore, requires that ambiguities in the allocation of an executive power be resolved in favor of the president. Article II, Section 1 provides that the "executive Power shall be vested in a President of the United States." As we have seen earlier, Hamilton famously argued that: "The general doctrine of our Constitution, then is, that the executive power of the nation is vested in the President; subject only to the exceptions and qualifications which are expressed in the instrument."[37] The Framers may have altered the process for exercising some executive powers, such as treaties and appointments, by including Senate consent. But this only redirects some elements of executive power to Congress, or divides some functions between the president and the Senate. The Vesting Clause grants all other executive powers to the president.

There can be little doubt that deploying military force is executive. It calls for action and energy in execution rather than the enactment of legal rules to govern private conduct. "The direction of war implies the direction of the common strength," wrote Hamilton, "and the power of directing and employing the common strength forms a usual and essential part in the definition of the executive authority." Because the constitutional text does not explicitly transfer the power to start hostilities to Congress, Article II's Vesting Clause requires that it remain with the president. Indeed, two of the most prominent conservative critics of the president's war powers, Professors Prakash and Ramsey, make exactly this argument to claim that the president exercises virtually all of the nation's foreign affairs powers.[38]

Yet, on the question of war powers, they reverse the polarity of the constitutional structure to claim that the text hems in the president. A consistent
approach finds presidential authority both to initiate military hostilities and
to conduct foreign policy. From the beginning of the Republic, as we saw
in the last chapter, the vesting of the executive, commander-in-chief, and
treaty powers in the president has given him control over foreign relations. A
"declare war" reading of the Constitution would allow the president to make
threats and promises while depriving him of the ability to back them up.

Presidential critics claim that granting control over war to Congress will
lead to greater responsibility and accountability. But it is not clear that
a Congress-based system would advance those goals or that they should
preempt other important considerations. The Framers believed that giving authority to the president, rather than Congress, would increase government accountability because of the concentration of responsibility in a
single official elected by the nation as a whole. As Hamilton wrote, "[t]he
sole and undivided responsibility of one man will naturally beget a livelier
sense of duty and a more exact regard to reputation."[39]

The Framers also believed that a single president would make the executive branch more effective. "Good government" requires "energy in the
executive," Hamilton wrote in *Federalist No. 70*. A vigorous president was
"essential to the protection of the community against foreign attacks."[40] In
Federalist No. 74, Hamilton was even more explicit about the executive
branch's superior ability in war. "Of all the cares or concerns of government, the direction of war most peculiarly demands those qualities which
distinguish the exercise of power by a single hand." Hamilton believed that
the power of "directing and employing the common strength" of society
in war "forms a usual and essential part in the definition of the executive
authority."[41] The branch of government most functionally suited to act in
a dangerous foreign environment is the executive. As Hamilton observed,
"[d]ecision, activity, secrecy, and dispatch will generally characterise the
proceedings of one man, in a much more eminent degree, than the proceedings of any greater number."[42] Presidential critics cannot explain why the
abstract values of accountability and responsibility, or other interests such
as effectiveness and speed, favor transferring war powers to Congress.

Critics worry about placing unlimited power in presidential hands. But
that worry is misplaced. Even if the Framers had struck the Declare War
Clause from the Constitution, Congress would have ample ability to check

presidential war-making. In *Federalist No. 58*, Madison states that Parliament's use of "the engine of a money bill" had secured for centuries its "continual triumph . . . over the other branches of the government."[43] Congress can refuse to create units necessary to carry out the executive's plans, limit funding for the military, and restructure the military to counter aggressive executive designs. As one eighteenth-century student of the British constitution wrote, the king's power to wage war "is like a ship completely equipped but from which the Parliament can at pleasure draw off the water, and leave it aground,—and also set it afloat again, by granting subsidies."[44]

In funding the military, Congress has a full and fair opportunity to consider the merits of a war. At the time of the founding of the Republic, the United States had no navy and an army of about 1,000 troops.[45] Although the state militias might have provided an alternative fighting force, Congress controls when it comes under presidential control. To fight the Quasi-War with France, the Wars of 1812 and 1848, and the Civil War, Congress had to create a military before presidents could fight. Congress easily could have prevented the commencement of hostilities by refusing to appropriate any funds. As Walter Russell Mead writes, the president loses much of his power to accomplish his military and political objectives without congressional funding and "must govern like a Stuart king."[46]

The United States did not have a large standing military in peacetime until after 1945. Critics argue that this allows presidents to launch quick wars that evade the power of the purse. There are two main reasons to doubt this argument. First, the high cost of modern warfare requires presidents to seek congressional support. Even during the Kosovo War, Clinton had to seek special appropriations for his limited air strikes. Second, Congress has chosen to allow presidents to act quickly. If it wanted to limit the president, it could leave aside the carrier groups, strike bombers, and armored divisions. Congress acquiesces because it would rather have the president take the risk for unpredictable and dangerous wars. A lack of congressional opposition reveals no flaw in the constitutional structure. It only reflects long-term cooperation between the executive and legislature.

C.

Some honest critics will concede that recent practice, and even the Constitution's structure, support presidential initiative. Instead, they claim that eighteenth-century English speakers used "declare war" colloquially

to mean "commence hostilities." James Wilson, for example, asserted in the Pennsylvania convention that "[i]t will not be in the power of a single man" to involve the nation in war, "for the important power of declaring war is vested in the legislature at large."[47] In *Federalist No. 69*, Hamilton sought to downplay the presidency by contrasting it with the broader powers of the British king. Hamilton argued that the commander-in-chief power "would amount to nothing more than the supreme command and direction of the military and naval forces, as first General and Admiral of the confederacy." Meanwhile, he observed, the power "of the British King extends to the *declaring* of war and to the *raising* and *regulating* of fleets and armies; all which by the Constitution under consideration would appertain to the Legislature."[48]

Other than these two key statements, presidential critics generally draw on passages from seventeenth- and eighteenth-century sources. Several leading founders at times used "declare war" to mean commencing hostilities. Writing as Pacificus, for example, Hamilton noted in 1793 that "the Legislature can alone declare war, can alone actually transfer the nation from a state of peace to a state of hostility."[49] Responding as Helvidius, Madison agreed that "those who are to *conduct a war* cannot in the nature of things, be proper or safe judges, whether *a war ought* to be *commenced, continued, or concluded.*"[50]

This evidence cannot overcome the constitutional text, structure, and history. First, it does not adequately account for the history of the Constitution's ratification. Second, it ignores the language that Americans actually used in constitutional texts of the time. Eighteenth-century Americans could use the phrase "declare war" to mean beginning military hostilities. But "declare war" also held the narrower legal meaning of setting international legal relations.

Developments between the Declaration of Independence and the Constitution favored broadening executive power.[51] In the burst of constitution-making after Independence, the Framers adopted a national charter, the Articles of Confederation, that lacked an organized and effective executive. Congress inherited the Crown's imperial powers in the colonies, such as "the sole and exclusive right and power of determining on peace and war," to enter into treaties, and to conduct foreign relations.[52] Article IX required the approval of nine states before the nation could "engage in a war." Article VI made clear that "[n]o state shall engage in any war" without the consent

of Congress, unless under threat of invasion or imminent danger. Here
again, the Framing generation used the word "engage" rather than "declare"
to clearly refer to the beginning of military hostilities. As with the Constitution, "engage" in war contained the broadest grant of power to begin
hostilities; "declare" refers to a narrower subset of the war power that does
not even make an appearance in our nation's first constitution.

Congress's problem was not a lack of formal executive power but its organization and support. With Congress composing the executive branch,
government by committee proved disastrous. The government lacked
"method and energy," observed young Alexander Hamilton.[53] The states
refused to supply revenue to the national government or comply with its
requests. Once peace arrived, Congress proved utterly unable to handle
its executive duties. It could not establish even a small military to protect
forts along the Canadian border. Britain and France imposed harmful trading rules against American commerce, while Spain closed the critical port
of New Orleans to American shipping. Congress had no authority over
commerce to threaten retaliatory sanctions.[54]

Experimentation with the executive power went even further in the new
state constitutions. In all but one state, the assembly elected the governor,
making clear who worked for whom. Some states created councils of state
to restrain the governor. Most states limited the governor's term and eli-
gibility. Most states provided for the annual election of the governor, restricted the number of terms a governor could serve, or both. Pennsylvania
even replaced the governor with a twelve-man executive council chosen
annually by the legislature. As historian Gordon Wood has observed, the
states often made the governors "little more than chairmen of their executive boards."[55]

Federalists rejected the progressive weakening of the executive. During
the Philadelphia Convention, initial drafts of the Constitution proposed
vesting in the president "the Executive rights vested in Congress by the
Confederation," which were presumably those over war and peace. Even
the well-known but confused August 1787 debate over the Declare War
Clause supports the broad approach to executive war power. Delegates
rejected a proposal to grant Congress the power "to make war" because its
"proceedings were too slow" and the House would know too little about
foreign affairs. Pierce Butler argued for "vesting the power [to make war]
in the President, who will have all the requisite qualities, and will not make

war but when the Nation will support it." Madison and Elbridge Gerry moved to replace "make war" with "declare," "leaving to the Executive the power to repel sudden attacks."[56]

Confusion over the Madison-Gerry amendment suggests that the Convention did not share a consensus about the war power. Roger Sherman, for example, believed the original draft "stood very well. The Executive shd. be able to repel and not to commence war." He thought that reducing Congress's power to that of declaring war would permit the executive to commence wars unilaterally. He favored leaving "make" war as it was, because it was "better than 'declare' the latter narrowing the power too much." Gerry rose to proclaim that he "never expected to hear in a republic a motion to empower the Executive alone to declare war." George Mason differentiated between war and peace: he "was for clogging rather than facilitating war; but for facilitating peace." He "was agst giving the power of war to the Executive, because not safely to be trusted with it; or to the Senate because not so constructed as to be entitled to it," but then curiously backed the change from "make" to "declare." Mason may have supported the change to "declare" war because it limited the executive's ability to plunge the nation into a total war. The Convention approved the Madison amendment by 8 states to 1.

Delegates approved the change from "make" to "declare" to prohibit Congress from encroaching on the executive's right to conduct war. The Framers understood that a reduction in congressional authority would produce a corresponding expansion in executive authority. Adopting the amendment made clear that the president could not unilaterally take the nation into a total war, but it also suggested that he could engage the nation in hostilities short of that. The August 17 debate also shows that the delegates did not envision the executive as a magistrate charged only with executing the laws. Some Framers believed that the president enjoyed a "protective power," as Henry Monaghan has described it, that permitted him to guard the nation from attack even in the absence of congressional consent.[57]

When the Constitution went to the states for ratification, Federalists had every incentive to downplay presidential power. Yet, they did not mention the Declare War Clause as a check on executive war-making. Neither Federalists nor Anti-Federalists bestowed upon the Declare War Clause the broad sweep that liberal critics want today. The closest they came was

Hamilton's effort in *Federalist No. 69*, to contrast the new president's powers with the British king's. Even there, Hamilton never defined the power to declare war, nor did he raise it as a legislative check on the executive. Hamilton does not argue that the president had to seek congressional permission before deploying troops and ships as he thought best.

Rather than the Declare War Clause, Federalists predicted that Congress's power over funding would serve as the primary check on the president's military ambitions. The most direct confrontation occurred in Virginia, probably the most politically significant state in the ratification struggle. Patrick Henry, leader of the Anti-Federalists, argued in the Virginia convention that the president would use his command over the military to centralize his power.[58] Federalists responded by invoking the British Parliament's power of the purse to control war-making. "[N]o appropriation of money, to the use of raising or supporting an army, shall be for a longer term than two years," Federalist delegate George Nicholas said. "The President is to command. But the regulation of the army and navy is given to Congress. Our Representatives will be a powerful check here. The influence of the Commons in England in this case is very predominant."[59] Madison followed not with the Declare War Clause but with the maxim "that the sword and purse are not to be given to the same member." Madison observed that "[t]he sword is in the hands of the British King. The purse is in the hands of the Parliament. It is so in America, as far as any analogy can exist."[60] Although Madison would attack the constitutionality of the Neutrality Proclamation in 1793, here he made no claims that Congress could constrain presidential war-making because of the Declare War Clause.

Critics may argue that this dialogue has limited relevance because it centers on concerns of a domestic military tyranny rather than foreign military adventures. But the Federalists would have had every incentive to raise the Declare War Clause in response to Virginian concerns over executive adventurism. No Federalists invoked the Declare War Clause to assuage fears of an aggrandizing executive. A few offhand comments in which "declaring" war is used to refer to beginning war have much less relevance to the question at hand than Federalist explanations of the separation of powers in practice. Federalists carefully explained that the checks on war-making under the new American Constitution would resemble practices under the British. While the executive would have command of the army and navy,

only the legislature could bring them into existence. While the president could conduct military operations, they would continue only while Congress chose to fund them.

And what to make of the Declare War Clause? By granting Congress the power to declare war, the Framers enabled it to serve notice to American citizens, neutral nations, and intended or actual foreign enemies of the existence of a state of war. Congress had the authority to set forth the grievances that impelled the United States to war and to define the United States' peace terms and strategic objectives. These functions—giving notice, providing justification, stating war aims—are found in the United States' first declaration of war—the Declaration of Independence.[61] The Declaration of Independence served notice of a change in the legal relations between the United States and Great Britain, but it didn't authorize the beginning of the war—the battles of Lexington and Concord occurred on April 19, 1775. The Declaration of Independence transformed the ongoing American Revolution from a mere civil war or rebellion into a public war between two states.

Critics of presidential power also place great store in the practice of the executive branch after the Framing. In arguing that Trump's actions in Syria were unconstitutional, Fox News commentator Andrew Napolitano claimed that "Madison himself argued that if the president could both declare and wage wars, he'd not be a president but a prince."[62] The weight that practice deserves is unclear, as subsequent practice could not inform the understanding of those who had ratified the Constitution. Nevertheless, critics believe that the post-ratification statements of presidents reflect a consistent understanding of the power to declare war that extends back several decades. Examples from America's early wars, however, do not support the claim that Congress had authorized every early conflict. While presidents sought congressional approval for military hostilities on some occasions during this period, such as the Quasi-War with France and the War of 1812, presidents did not seek legislative authorization for other conflicts. Washington's war against the Indians of the Ohio Valley and Jefferson's war against the Barbary States lacked any formal declaration.

Critics portray presidential uses of force, from Washington to Trump, as violations of the Constitution. Only a declaration of war from Congress, according to this account, can cure the problem. But the Declare War Clause cannot bear this heavy responsibility. Even if English speakers

in 2020 or in 1789 used "declare war" colloquially to refer to starting hostilities, the clause did not concentrate the authority to begin a conflict in Congress. Careful scrutiny of the Constitution's text, structure, and history establishes that the clause had a narrower and more precise meaning. The most plausible interpretation of the clause reads it as conferring on Congress the power to create a variety of legal regimes under international and domestic law suitable to various kinds of conflicts. Rather than regulating the relations between the president and Congress, the Declare War Clause enables Congress to regulate the relations between the United States and other states. The Framers countered the risk of executive aggrandizement in war-making in other ways—most notably by vesting in Congress the power to raise and fund armies and navies. The long and successful history of Parliament's struggle against the Crown demonstrated to the Framers that the funding power was the most certain and effective check against executive abuse.

CONCLUSIONS

An obvious attraction of the Congress-first, president-second approach is that it is familiar. It is identical to the process that governs the enactment of legislation. We expect Congress to hold the initiative in passing laws, and that its collective representation of the American electorate will achieve deliberation, consensus, and clarity of legislative purpose. Furthermore, the "Declare War" approach seeks to "clog" the rush toward war by requiring both the Congress and the president to agree before risking American lives and treasure abroad. Reducing the amount of war draws upon deeply ingrained American notions that, as the exceptional nation, the United States can either withdraw from the conflict-torn affairs of the Old World or change the world as to render war itself obsolete.

But these assumptions do not rest on any tested truths. A Congress-first approach does not always generate a sufficient deliberation that produces fewer wars. The Mexican-American War of 1846–1848, for example, did not result from extensive deliberation but rather a rush to war after an alleged attack on Sam Houston's forces along the Rio Grande. Congress did not declare war against Spain in 1898 after long discussion but rather after the destruction of the U.S.S. *Maine* in Havana harbor. Both wars resulted in quick victory and large territorial conquests, but it is not clear

whether the defenders of congressional prerogatives today would have considered either as "good" wars.

Nor does congressional deliberation ensure consensus. Even though Congress passed the Gulf of Tonkin Resolution, the Vietnam War still provoked some of the most divisive politics in American history. Congress authorized the war in Afghanistan in 2001 and the invasion of Iraq in 2002, but both wars lost their consensus as well. Conversely, a process without congressional declarations of war does not necessarily result in less deliberation or consensus, or poor and unnecessary wars. Perhaps the most important example is the long struggle between the United States and the Soviet Union from 1946 through 1992. Presidents waged war against Soviet proxies in Korea and Vietnam, the Soviet Union fought in Afghanistan, and the two almost came into direct conflict during the Cuban Missile Crisis. Despite the division over Vietnam, a significant bipartisan consensus agreed on the overall strategy (containment) and the goal (defeat of the Soviet Union, protection of Europe and Japan). Congress consistently devoted significant resources to the standing military to achieve them. Presidents bore the heavy responsibility and potential blame for war alone.

Presidential initiative and responsibility, sometimes accompanied by a reluctant Congress, remains the basic operating procedure for war today. Congress does not want the accountability for decisions on war. Instead, it provides the executive branch with a military designed to conduct offensive wars abroad, without any conditions. If the wars go well, Congress can take credit for providing the troops; if the wars go badly, it blames the president. The duty to protect the nation's security and advance its foreign interests falls upon the president, whether it be Bush, Obama, or Trump. Congress can criticize Trump for withdrawing from Syria too early or staying in Afghanistan too long, but the last thing it wants to do is take political responsibility for war. Presidents will take up the sword paid for by Congress, whether they want to or not, because the electorate will hold them responsible.

Syria and Afghanistan underscore one last truth about the American way of war. Critics conceive of war as presidential adventurism unchecked by congressional fecklessness. But they cannot understand the Trump quandary of a Congress that is more warlike than the president. Trump withdrew U.S. troops from the Syrian-Turkish border and abandoned our Syrian Kurdish allies. While his decision triggered howls of complaint from

the military, members of Congress, and the national security establishment, the legislature cannot force the president to fight a war he doesn't
want to fight. Congress can pay for the military and even declare war, but
it cannot decide tactics, strategy, or the deployment of the armed forces.
Only the president has the authority as commander in chief to make those
fundamental decisions. While Trump's critics may want U.S. troops to remain in Syria or Afghanistan, they cannot prevent a president from withdrawing from a fight abroad. And in keeping true to his campaign promise
to end these wars, regardless of their strategic benefits or costs, Trump is
defending the power of future presidents to lead the nation in war.

CHAPTER 8

"SEE YOU IN THE SUPREME COURT": THE TRUMP JUDICIARY

In September 2019, a year after the fight over his appointment to the Supreme Court, Justice Brett Kavanaugh again took incoming fire. During his fall 2018 confirmation hearings, Christine Blasey Ford, a California psychologist, claimed that a drunken teenaged Kavanaugh had sexually assaulted her at a house party in the Washington, D.C., area. Kavanaugh testified under oath that the assault never happened, and he denied other claims of drunkenness and sexual misconduct. Kavanaugh won confirmation when Republican senators sent the FBI to investigate and ultimately concluded that the accusations were uncorroborated.

A year later, two *New York Times* articles reignited the controversy with a fresh attack. This time, they claimed that as a freshman at Yale, Kavanaugh had committed sexual misconduct toward a fellow student while both were drunk at a party.[1] But the story turned against the *Times* when the reporters revealed, in a book, that the alleged victim said she had no memory of the event and no witnesses came forward to confirm the accusation by Democratic Washington, D.C., lawyer Max Stier, who claimed he had seen the event. Opponents had raised a similar story in 2018, but it too crumbled when no witness could corroborate the alleged drunken sexual abuse and the victim herself apparently spent days asking others whether Kavanaugh had even been present at the same party. The *Times* had to print a humiliating correction that neither the alleged victim nor Stier would confirm the story.

Nevertheless, within a day of the release of the *Times* story, three of the four leading contenders for the Democratic presidential nomination immediately called upon Congress to impeach Kavanaugh. Senators Elizabeth

Warren, Bernie Sanders, and Kamala Harris demanded that the House begin impeachment proceedings. "These newest revelations are disturbing," Warren tweeted. "Like the man who appointed him, Kavanaugh should be impeached,"[2] she wrote. Harris declared: "He was put on the Court through a sham process and his place on the Court is an insult to the pursuit of truth and justice."[3] Everyone's favorite socialist, Representative Alexandria Ocasio-Cortez, further explained: "It is unsurprising that Kavanaugh, credibly accused of sexual assault, would lie under oath to secure a Supreme Court seat. Because sexual assault isn't a crime of passion—it's about the abuse of power. He must be impeached."[4] Her fellow freshman progressive, Representative Ayanna Pressley, immediately introduced articles of impeachment. "Sexual predators do not deserve a seat on the nation's highest court," the Massachusetts Democrat said.[5] House Judiciary Committee chair Jerry Nadler, however, said he was too busy impeaching Trump to include Kavanaugh too! "We have our hands full with impeaching the president right now, and that's going to take up our limited resources and time for a while," Nadler said on WNYC radio.[6]

Democrats have brought the judicial confirmation process to a new low. They began by launching a campaign of character assassination against Kavanaugh, a distinguished appeals court judge and former Bush White House official (in the interests of full disclosure, I overlapped with Kavanaugh in law school and in the Bush administration). While Democrats had mounted opposition to Samuel Alito and John Roberts for their past writings and official actions, they had not raised claims of sexual harassment since their failed effort to stop the nomination of Clarence Thomas (another disclosure—I served as a law clerk for Justice Thomas). Democrats are using the allegations to discredit Kavanaugh, who they suspect will vote to overturn *Roe v. Wade*, or to threaten him into moving toward the middle. They crossed another line by continuing the attacks on Kavanaugh after his confirmation to the Supreme Court. Our political system had discarded the idea of using impeachment to remove judges on ideological grounds ever since President Jefferson's effort to remove Supreme Court Justice Samuel Chase had failed in 1804.

Democrats may honestly believe that Congress should move forward to impeach Justice Kavanaugh. Or they may imagine instead an effort to influence him or even delegitimize his votes. Debra Katz, Christine Blasey Ford's attorney, declared in April 2019 that "[h]e will always have an

asterisk next to his name. When he takes a scalpel to *Roe v. Wade*, we will know who he is, we know his character, and we know what motivates him, and that is important. It is important that we know, and that is part of what motivated Christine."[7] Katz's revealing statement suggests that Ford had a pro-abortion agenda that motivated her controversial appearance in the confirmation hearings. Critics may hope that the continuing drumbeat of attacks will push Kavanaugh to moderate his views, or that they will spark efforts to dismiss his votes on the Court as the work of a sexual abuser.

I.

Attacks on the judiciary, however, will not stop with efforts to influence Justice Kavanaugh. Democratic presidential candidates have proposed a fundamental change to the Supreme Court. If Democrats cannot stop Trump from appointing conservative judges, then they can promise to create more judgeships when they return to power. Former Texas congressman and presidential candidate Beto O'Rourke, for example, has proposed expanding the size of the Supreme Court from 9 to 15 justices and imposing a limit of 18 years on their terms.[8] Agreeing with the idea, Mayor Pete Buttigieg declared that increasing the number of justices to 15 would "prevent the Supreme Court from continuing on this trajectory to become basically ruined by being a nakedly political institution."[9] Kamala Harris warned that "we are on the verge of a crisis of confidence in the Supreme Court" and that "everything is on the table" to "take this challenge head on."[10] Warren also threatened, "If Republicans are going to try to block us on key legislation or judges that we're trying to move forward, then you better believe all the options are on the table."[11] At another point, Warren explained that "[i]t's not just about expansion, it's about depoliticizing the Supreme Court."[12]

These comments would spark howls of outrage if a Republican Congress had made them during the reign of a Democratic president. But legal academics and leaders of the bar, who normally should oppose blatant efforts to interfere with the independence of the judiciary, fell into line. Instead, they believe that political payback for the failed Merrick Garland nomination and Trump's appointments of Neil Gorsuch and Kavanaugh justify court-packing. "The time is overdue for a seriously considered plan of action by those of us who believe that [Sen. Mitch] McConnell Republicans,

abetted by and abetting the Trump Movement, have prioritized the expansion of their own power over the safeguarding of American democracy and the protection of the most vulnerable among us," declared liberal Harvard law professor Laurence Tribe. Tribe announced a campaign to increase the size of the Court by four justices.[13] Another prominent liberal legal scholar, Erwin Chemerinsky, defended political retaliation in the judicial wars. "If a Democrat wins the presidency in 2020, and Democrats take control of Congress, I think Democrats need to think seriously about increasing the size of the court as a way of offsetting the stolen seat with regard to Merrick Garland," he said.[14]

Liberals also defend changing the Court's size as necessary to alter the path of constitutional law in a liberal direction. Chemerinsky, for example, defends court-packing as "the only way to keep there from being a very conservative Court for the next 10–20 years."[15] Other scholars were shocked to discover that the Court had rendered political decisions. Only now that Trump had appointed the justices would liberals support an increase in the Court's size. "Here to stay is the sea-change the Republican party has forced onto a once-proud institution. No longer a 'check' or 'balance,' it is now—and will henceforth be seen by both sides as—simply another lever of power," writes noted constitutional scholar Garrett Epps. "And on the day the Democrats hold power to alter the makeup of the court by bare-knuckle means, they will do it. And they should."[16]

Why have Democrats launched such a destructive attack on Kavanaugh and the independence of the federal judiciary? It is because their fears have come true: Trump indeed has launched a conservative makeover of the federal courts, which may finally undo the liberal remaking of society through judicial fiat. "The Democrats and their allies in the media are obviously getting desperate," Vice President Mike Pence said in a Heritage Foundation speech in the midst of the Kavanaugh controversy. "The calls by Democrat candidates for the president to remove Justice Kavanaugh from the court are a disgrace and nothing short of an attack on our independent judiciary," Pence said. Trump's very success has set off the extreme, anticonstitutional response that has liberals attacking the independence of the Supreme Court and, perhaps, sparking a cycle of retribution that will make the judiciary a political body.

In speeches, of course, Trump is given to exaggeration about his achievement. He claims that he has appointed more judges than any president

except one. "We have many appeals court judges—many—that we'll have appointed. The courts are a whole different thing," Trump said at a Turning Point USA conference in July 2019. He asked teenagers, "I will be up to 147, not including the two Supreme Court justices. Now, percentage-wise, I blow everybody away except one person. One person I'll never beat. You know who the one person is?" "George Washington!" the teen audience shouted, the correct answer.[17] Washington, however, had the unfair advantage of being the first president, thus having to fill every federal judgeship.

Trump still has every right to trumpet his success with judicial appointments. He may well owe his election to the Supreme Court. Or, more precisely, he may owe it to the prospect of Hillary Clinton filling an open seat on the Supreme Court. After Justice Antonin Scalia's untimely death in January 2016, the Court remained divided between four liberal justices and four conservatives (some more so than others). Central constitutional concerns, including religious freedom, voting rights, property rights, the death penalty, and gun control, remained up for grabs depending on the next president's appointment of Scalia's replacement. A plurality of Republican voters said that they voted for Trump because of his promise to appoint conservative judges. In campaign events, Trump himself gloated over the leverage he wielded on Republican voters. "They have no choice," Trump said. "Even if you can't stand Donald Trump, you think Donald Trump is the worst, you're going to vote for me. You know why? Justices of the Supreme Court."

If Trump has kept one campaign promise, it has been his commitment to appoint conservative judges. But Trump did more than make the same promises that past Republicans had made to appoint justices who interpret, not make, the law. After all, these same Republican presidents had appointed in recent memory Justices Harry Blackmun, John Paul Stevens, and David Souter, who had become reliable members of the Court's liberal wing, as well as Justices Sandra Day O'Connor and Anthony M. Kennedy, who had become swing votes in the middle and had provided the key votes to uphold *Roe v. Wade* and create a right to gay marriage in *Obergefell v. Hodges*. During a critical point in the Republican primary race, when Trump and Ted Cruz emerged as the leaders, Trump made an unprecedented promise. Not only would he pick conservative judges but, to prove it, he also released a list of at first ten, then of twenty names from which he would select his Supreme Court justices. Conservatives greeted the list

with acclaim: many were leaders of the conservative movement on federal and state benches from around the country. The Trump campaign happily told the press that they had received the names from the Federalist Society and the Heritage Foundation. No nominee had ever issued a short list of Supreme Court nominees. Many conservatives made peace with Trump because of his promise to appoint a justice "like a Scalia or Clarence Thomas" who would "overturn *Roe v. Wade.*"

On this promise, Trump has come through for conservatives. In 2017, he filled Scalia's seat with Neil Gorsuch, who had served on the federal appellate court in Denver for about a decade. Gorsuch had written a book defending natural law, clerked for Justice Anthony Kennedy, served in the Bush Justice Department, and, as a lower court judge, had held that the Free Exercise Clause exempted Catholic nuns and religious companies from Obamacare's birth control mandate. The following year, Trump elevated Kavanaugh when Kennedy retired in the summer of 2018. Kavanaugh had checked off similar boxes as Gorsuch: he too had clerked for Kennedy, worked on the Clinton Whitewater investigation, served as a high-ranking official in the Bush White House, and served with distinction as an appeals judge in Washington, D.C.

In just two years, Trump changed the trajectory of constitutional law. Before the appointments of Gorsuch and Kavanaugh, conservatives and liberals both contended for the fifth vote of Justice Kennedy, whose libertarian instincts had led him to uphold *Roe v. Wade* and find a constitutional right to gay marriage, but also to uphold affirmative action in college admissions and limit religion in the public square. While the jury is still out on the appointments, Gorsuch gives every sign of assuming a position near that of Justice Thomas. They appear to share a healthy respect for the Founders, an interest in their natural law thinking, and a disdain for past Supreme Court precedent—all a recipe for a more activist review of congressional and executive acts. Kavanaugh, however, may not end up as far to the conservative end of the spectrum (thus, the efforts to influence him). But as a lower court judge, he followed a generally conservative approach and took originalism seriously, though Supreme Court precedent hemmed in how far he could go. While Kavanaugh may have been the most moderate judge on Trump's list of potential Supreme Court nominees, he tried to prevent the Obamacare case from reaching the Supreme Court (which upheld it), and voted to strike down the agencies created in the

wake of the financial crisis for violating the separation of powers. He seems to seek clear principles rather than deciding cases based on the facts and developing the law slowly.

If these predictions on Gorsuch and Kavanaugh prove accurate, then their appointments should provide the fourth and fifth conservative votes to undo the most liberal Supreme Court decisions of the last few decades. Without the need to attract a moderate fifth vote, the conservative majority can cast aside the incrementalism and fear of broad principles that has deprived conservative decisions of much of their impact. The Trump Court could overturn the abortion and gay marriage cases, end affirmative action in schools, allow greater scope for religion in the public square, expand Second Amendment rights, and generally narrow the reach of federal power. Should a liberal justice retire, the White House would have the opportunity to cement a more secure six-justice conservative majority. Trump will have changed the arc of constitutional law for the next quarter century at least.

After Justice Kennedy's departure, the most liberal member of the Republican-appointed majority on the Court becomes Chief Justice John Roberts. Roberts has disappointed conservatives, first in his two decisions upholding Obamacare from constitutional and statutory challenges, and then during the Trump years with a ruling that forbade inclusion of a question about citizenship on the 2020 census forms.[18] Nevertheless, the chief justice has led the Court in a more conservative direction, such as restoring limits on the federal government, particularly its powers to spend, regulate commerce, and enforce racial distinctions. If the Supreme Court doesn't reach these and other long-held conservative goals, it will only be because Chief Justice Roberts sees his role as limiting the political consequences of a conservative counterrevolution on the Court.

II.

The Supreme Court has not held the president's attention alone. Trump has pursued an equally aggressive campaign to remake the lower courts. While Supreme Court battles attract the political attention, presidents may achieve equally lasting influence through their appointments to the appeals courts, where 99 percent of all federal cases end.[19] In his first three years in office, Trump had successfully appointed a record 50 judges to the U.S.

circuit courts of appeals. For comparison purposes, by the same point in their first terms, President Obama had appointed just 19 out of 32 nominations to the appeals courts (59 percent), while President George W. Bush had appointed 26 out of 44 nominations (59 percent). With the cooperation of the Republican Senate, Trump also pushed the judges through far faster than his predecessors, in 151 days, compared with 249 days under Obama and 260 days under Bush. After three years in office, Trump had already set a modern record for the appointment of appeals court judges.

Trump's judicial juggernaut could not have succeeded by itself. It required the cooperation of a Republican Senate majority. Mitch McConnell not only held open the Scalia seat in Obama's last year and eliminated the Senate filibuster for Supreme Court nominees, but he also made the confirmation of appellate judges a Senate priority. By the end of three years in office, Trump and McConnell had confirmed enough federal appeals judges to ensure that Republican presidents had appointed a bare majority of all federal appeals judges in the nation.[20] Unlike the House elections in 2018, when Republicans lost their control by a decisive margin, they grew their majority by 2 seats to 53 senators. The increase in the size of the Republican Senate majority has allowed Republicans to accelerate the passage of their nominees through the confirmation process to unprecedented speeds.

But Trump's campaign to remake the federal courts can only accomplish so much in one term. Sixty percent of his picks replaced judges whom Republican presidents had already appointed. About half of Trump's choices went to four appellate courts, primarily those stretching from Texas to the upper Midwest, where conservative judges already held strong majorities. Only one appeals court, the Third Circuit covering Pennsylvania, New Jersey, and Delaware, has switched from a majority of Democratic-appointed judges to Republican-appointed judges during Trump's presidency. But five other appeals courts, covering some of the most important cities, such as Washington, D.C., and its northern Virginia suburbs (where many challengers file suit against the federal government), New York (the nation's financial capital), Los Angeles (the entertainment capital), San Francisco (the tech capital), and Boston, would switch to Republican-appointed majorities with a change of just two seats. If Trump were to win reelection, he would probably succeed in flipping most, if not all, appellate courts to conservative control. Even if he were not to win, the White House has selected

judges of such youth and energy that they could easily serve 15 to 25 years each until another Republican president could choose their successors.

Trump's success with judicial appointments came about through the normal constitutional process. He may have chosen younger, more conservative judges. But here he followed closely the example set by President Reagan (indeed, some of Reagan's most conservative picks are still serving on the appeals courts today). He may have openly relied upon the Federalist Society or the Heritage Foundation for nominees. But he only made transparent what both Republicans and Democrats have done for decades: turning to organized groups with expertise for suggestions on personnel and policy. Trump may have taken advantage of the end of Senate filibuster for appeals court judges. But the filibuster met its death at the hands of Senator Harry Reid in 2013 to allow the Obama administration to fill several seats on influential circuit courts. Trump's accomplishment owes more to a White House counsel office that has focused on filling judicial vacancies as quickly as possible, perhaps to the exclusion of other important national priorities. However, any president could have devoted more resources to judicial selection if they believed it to be as politically important as Trump.

But here, as in other areas discussed in this book, Democrats have responded with such a blind fury at Trump that they are willing to overthrow constitutional norms and principles to oppose him. Court-packing provides a startling example. The Constitution does not set the number of justices. Article III only creates a Supreme Court and the office of chief justice; it leaves all other details up to Congress. In the Judiciary Act of 1789, Congress created a Court with six justices—apparently the Founders' command of math did not match their understanding of politics. Jefferson's allies in Congress increased the number to seven in 1807, and then Andrew Jackson and his Democratic Party increased the figure to nine in 1837. Between 1863 and 1869, the Republicans in Congress increased the Justices to ten and then down to seven, but then returned the Court back to nine members. While there is nothing magic about the number nine, the Supreme Court has functioned with the same number of justices for most of our history and the last 150 years.

A tradition has lasted since the Reconstruction Era that presidents should not attempt to change the size of the Supreme Court because of disagreement with its decisions. We accept, of course, that presidents may

seek to alter the Court's outcomes when filling vacancies. That process is as old as Jefferson, who became the first opposition party leader to win the presidency. He made his first appointment to the Supreme Court to dilute the nationalizing influence of Chief Justice John Marshall. Lincoln appointed his secretary of treasury, Salmon Chase, to replace the pro-slavery Roger Taney as chief justice, which effectively ended the Supreme Court's skeptical attitude toward the Civil War.

But expanding the size of the Court to change its decisions seems to more directly threaten judicial independence than gradual change through the replacement of retiring justices. Altering the size of the Court can have an immediate effect on the Court's decisions. If conservatives succeed in overturning *Roe v. Wade* with the Kavanaugh appointment, it will have taken them almost a half century to succeed. If court-packing became part of the regular political arsenal, conservatives could have reached their goal more immediately by adding Court seats in the periods when they controlled both the presidency and Congress, such as during the George W. Bush administration, or even when they had a working coalition of Republicans and conservative Democrats during the Reagan years. To supercharge his promise to make the courts more conservative, Trump and the Republican Congress of 2016–18 could have simply added five justices to the Supreme Court and doubled the number of appellate judges.

But Trump, like his predecessors, did not. Trump respected the existing norms protecting judicial independence. Expanding the number of justices to retaliate against the Court would effectively put the power of decision in the hands of the political branches. It could also launch a spiraling escalation where each party adds seats to the Court when it wins the next election. While some majorities have changed the appellate courts to either introduce or preserve their power—notably Jefferson's elimination of the Adams administration's creation of new judges, and the Carter administration's expansion of appellate seats in 1980—they have never changed the size of the Supreme Court for that purpose.

Court-packing would simply make the judiciary a direct consequence of winning an election, much as we expect a president to replace cabinet officers and other top officials of the agencies with officers who will follow his agenda. For that reason, efforts to change the size of the Supreme Court have always ended up as crank proposals or glorious failures. FDR's 1937 proposal to increase the Supreme Court from 9 to 15 justices provoked a

broad bipartisan opposition that ended up not just killing his court-packing plan but also stalling the New Deal altogether (although it did persuade the justices to stop striking down New Deal laws).

Trump is defending constitutional norms by opposing those who would pack the Court. His stalwart defense of Justice Kavanaugh also reinforces judicial independence against partisan attack. Here again, history provides a guide. When Jefferson entered office in 1801, his political opponents had filled the judiciary for the first twelve years of the Republic. "They have retired into the judiciary as a stronghold," Jefferson wrote. "There the remains of federalism are to be preserved and fed from the treasury, and from that battery all the works of republicanism are to be beaten down and erased."[21] Jefferson felt no unease in having his allies in Congress repeal new judgeships, postpone Supreme Court terms to influence decisions, and, in his most ambitious effort, remove judges in an effort to change the direction of the law. But when Jeffersonians impeached Justice Samuel Chase, a signer of the Declaration of Independence, who had engaged in several political outbursts on the bench, the Senate refused to convict. Chase's acquittal established the understanding that Congress would not use impeachment to overturn judicial decisions. By threatening to impeach Justice Kavanaugh, Democratic leaders are resurrecting a threat that would undermine the judicial independence that has helped stabilize democracy and defend the minority rights that they claim to hold so dear.

Trump critics would argue, however, that they do not seek to use impeachment for ideological reasons but to remove a justice for sexual assault committed in high school and college. They would say that Congress could remove Kavanaugh because he lied about the allegations during the confirmation process. It is hard to believe that the Democratic presidential candidates are invoking a neutral principle that they would apply equally to liberal justices. Indeed, when Republicans cited similar grounds to impeach Bill Clinton, no Senate Democrats voted to remove him.

Even if Trump critics were pursuing a principle in good faith, it would violate the Constitution. Article III guarantees the lifetime tenure of judges "during good behavior." Democratic candidates seek to remove Kavanaugh for his alleged conduct as a teenager, long before he ever became a Supreme Court justice. Even if the claim were that Kavanaugh lied during his confirmation, that too took place before he joined the Supreme Court. The Appointments Clause vests the Senate with this "check" on the president

"to prevent the appointment of unfit characters," as Hamilton put it in *Federalist No. 76*. Senators had their opportunity to review Kavanaugh's fitness in the face-to-face hearings themselves. The Senate, and only the Senate, can decide how much the allegations should affect Kavanaugh's confirmation. When senators voted 50–48 to confirm Kavanaugh, they judged the credibility of the nominee and the witnesses against him not for purposes of criminal guilt or innocence but for purposes of fitness for office.

III.

Trump's defense of the Constitution comes not just through his fight to defend the integrity of the judicial appointments process but also through the judicial philosophy of those he placed on the bench. Democrats launched their scorched-earth war against Kavanaugh, an outstanding judge and distinguished public servant, precisely because his appointment promised a reliable fifth vote for a conservative majority. There's a good argument to make that conservatives have not had such a working majority on the Court since 1936. Even though Republican presidents have appointed the majority of justices since 1968, when Richard Nixon won on a law-and-order platform, their appointments have often "grown in office" and drifted leftward. These justices based their decisions not in the original understanding of the Constitution when ratified but in their own modern visions of equality, justice, and social good.

Choosing Kavanaugh and Gorsuch rejects this freewheeling attitude to constitutional interpretation. During both sets of confirmation hearings, Democratic senators advanced a view of a judge as simply the enabler of a political party's policy goals. They cross-examined the judges on the specific outcomes they had reached in cases relating to minorities, women, labor, and environmental organizations. In their view, the only difference between a judge and a congressman is that the former wears a robe. These Democrats believe judges exercise raw and unchecked political power to determine winners and losers.

This view mistakenly appeals to the way state judges make the common law, which governs garden-variety subjects such as property, contract, and torts. Common-law judges are free to create the rules as they see fit. They exercise the equivalent of legislative power—they are the lawgivers in these areas governed by the states. Importing that model into the federal judi-

ciary creates judges who will not feel themselves bound by the written Constitution or the text of an act of Congress. Supreme Court justices will find themselves tempted to lead the people to where they "should be" rather than where they are. There is nothing to limit a justice but his imagination.

Trump and Republican senators, however, rejected this approach. Their view requires judges to be indifferent to the demographics of the parties before them. In Chief Justice Roberts's metaphor, judges are umpires who call balls and strikes, but do not promote personal preferences or prejudices. Even liberal nominees pay homage to this ideal. As Justice Elena Kagan put it in her confirmation hearings, "[T]he question is not, 'Do you like this party or do you like that party? Do you favor this cause or do you favor that cause?' . . . The question is what the law requires." Conservatives view the judge as an umpire who is as constrained as the judge-as-philosopher-king is free. They seek judges who interpret the words of the law based on their meaning at the time of enactment—in other words, "originalism." Originalism is the only legitimate way for a Supreme Court justice to approach the job, because it respects the will of the people who made and continue to accept the Constitution and it limits the ability of their personal views to interfere. As Hamilton famously explained in *Federalist No. 78*, "courts must declare the sense of the law; and if they should be disposed to exercise WILL instead of JUDGMENT, the consequence would equally be the substitution of their pleasure to that of the legislative body."[22]

Non-originalist justices ignore Hamilton's caution. They may seek, as does Justice Stephen Breyer, to use their discretion to choose the most efficient result for society, or, as do Justices Ruth Bader Ginsburg and Sonia Sotomayor, to promote a contemporary vision of equality or social justice. But these liberal justices are elevating their own preferences above those established by the Constitution's adopters, who often had to choose political stability or compromise over today's notions of a just society. Such judging transfers sovereignty from the people to the hands of five justices who, by design, enjoy independence from politics. Allowing a majority of the Supreme Court to read the Constitution at odds with the original understanding effectively allows it to amend the Constitution. A supermajority of the original 13 states had to adopt the Constitution to bring it into force; amending the Constitution requires a similar fraction of Congress

and the states. Allowing five justices to overrule the will of the overwhelming majority of the people turns our constitutional system on its end. With
the confirmation of Justice Kavanaugh, there is a majority of justices on the
Supreme Court for the first time in generations who, to varying degrees,
practice originalism and textualism. Trump's justices can begin to restore
the Constitution to its original meaning and reject liberal justices' efforts
to substitute instead their visions of the good society.

IV.

A new conservative majority, unhindered by Justice Kennedy's swing vote,
could restore constitutional law to the Framers' original vision in areas
ranging from privacy to race, religion, guns, and free speech. This section
will provide a flavor of the type of change that the Trump justices may
bring by examining three of the most important areas: abortion, federal
versus state power, and the powers of the administrative state.

ABORTION AND PRIVACY

Before it devolved into a degrading abuse of the confirmation process, Kavanaugh's fiercest opponents came from the usual source: abortion supporters. Some protesters interrupted his hearing with screams to defend
abortion, while others dressed as characters from feminist dystopian
TV shows. Pro-choice groups spent hundreds of thousands of dollars on
television ads warning of *Roe v. Wade*'s death. With characteristic sub-
tlety, activists sent over a thousand hangers, symbols of self-administered
abortions, to Senator Susan Collins (R–Maine), one of the critical confirmation votes. But the pro-choice effort may have backfired. In the 2018
midterm elections, Democratic senators in North Dakota, Indiana, and
Missouri who voted against Kavanaugh lost reelection bids, while the sole
Democrat who voted for him barely held on in West Virginia.

The left understandably considered the fight against Kavanaugh to be a
final stand, because the fate of *Roe v. Wade* may well rest in the new justice's hands. Liberal justices Ginsburg, Breyer, Kagan, and Sotomayor have
voted in lockstep to strike down virtually any effort by the states to regulate
abortion. But only Kennedy could give them the majority they desperately
needed. Kennedy's strained efforts to conjure forth a right to abortion
from a spare constitutional text had resulted in confused, even mystical,

definitions of privacy. "At the heart of liberty is the right to define one's own concept of existence, of meaning, of the universe, and of the mystery of human life," Kennedy notoriously wrote in *Casey v. Planned Parenthood*, the critical 1992 case that upheld *Roe*. Kennedy's self-defining aspirations created a new jurisprudence of subjectivity, wherein the Court would find rights wherever it so chose if some favored group felt its "own concept of existence" was threatened.

While many on the left loved *Roe*'s result, some of its more serious thinkers worried about the Court's reasoning and its embrace of a political role. Future Justice Ginsburg, for example, criticized the *Roe* Court, arguing that the right to abortion should be grounded in equal protection, not privacy, and that abortion would be better protected in the long term by state-by-state adoption rather than the Court imposing its will from on high. The great liberal legal scholar John Hart Ely called *Roe* "a very bad decision," but not because he disagreed with it on policy grounds. Rather, he viewed *Roe* as "bad because it is bad constitutional law, or rather because it is *not* constitutional law and gives almost no sense of an obligation to try to be."

Roe was the case that launched a thousand flights of jurisprudential fancy. Gay rights soon joined Kennedy's strange mysticism in *Casey*. In *Lawrence v. Texas*, the Court struck down a Texas law criminalizing homosexual relations between consenting adults. As Justice Thomas noted in dissent, the law was "uncommonly silly," but it was constitutional. Instead of relying on the political process and the states to regulate sex, as our nation had for two centuries, Kennedy invented a new constitutional right to intimate relations. He wrote, "[L]iberty presumes an autonomy of self that includes . . . certain intimate conduct." *Lawrence* itself involved "liberty of the person both in its spatial and in its more transcendent dimensions." In *Lawrence*, *Roe* gave rise to amateur poetry masquerading as constitutional analysis.

All of this led up to gay marriage, with Justice Kennedy once again holding the reins. Citizens may support or oppose gay marriage (or abortion, or the criminalization of sodomy) at the ballot box, but our policy preferences should not bear on the proper interpretation of the Constitution. In *Obergefell*, however, the Court elevated the demands of the gay rights movement over more than two centuries of state control over marriage. Relying on *Griswold v. Connecticut* and *Lawrence*, Kennedy wrote for the majority that "substantive" due process produced a constitutional

right to marry someone of the opposite sex, regardless of state or federal law. His vacuous reasoning did not disappoint: "The Constitution promises liberty to all within its reach, a liberty that includes certain specific rights that allow persons, within a lawful realm, to define and express their identity." Who determines that "lawful realm," and who decides which identities count? The Supreme Court.

Who needs a written constitution when five justices can just rewrite it whenever they see fit? As Scalia wrote in dissent, "This practice of constitutional revision by an unelected committee of nine, always accompanied (as it is today) by extravagant praise of liberty, robs the People of the most important liberty they asserted in the Declaration of Independence and won in the Revolution of 1776: the freedom to govern themselves." If we are to return to the rule of law rather than the rule of the Supreme Court, conservative justices must restore the Constitution by removing the Court from these policy debates. If the people want to constitutionalize legal abortion or same-sex marriage, it can choose to do so.

With Trump's appointment of two new justices, the era of constitutional mysticism has come to a close. Narrowing and ultimately overruling *Roe* will provide the common ground for the five conservative justices to finally define the Roberts Court. In 1992, Thomas dissented from *Casey* when Kennedy joined O'Connor and Souter to uphold *Roe*. Thomas, moreover, has long made clear that he pays no heed to incorrect precedent. Alito has become a reliable, even stalwart defender of traditional values and conservative jurisprudence. Gorsuch's writings on natural law, assisted suicide, and euthanasia suggest that he would defend the state's interest in preserving the life of the fetus. As a young lawyer in the George H. W. Bush Justice Department, Roberts drafted briefs asking the justices to overturn *Roe*. As chief justice, he has voted to uphold most state restrictions on abortion. If Roberts were to vote his beliefs rather than worry about the political standing of the Supreme Court (a big "if" after his vote to uphold Obamacare in 2012), Kavanaugh's appointment should establish a 5–4 majority to end the regime of *Roe*.

The Trump justices do not simply create a majority to overturn *Roe*. Their arrival could trigger a wholesale reconsideration of the Supreme Court's misguided adventure into the world of unwritten, non-textual, judicially created rights. For the last half century, the left has used the Supreme Court to win what it could not gain with normal politics. The Court

has embedded the sexual revolution into the Constitution and "found" new progressive rights for privacy and dignity in a document that mentions neither. The Trump Court will not overturn *Roe* because it shares the left's obsession with abortion; it will reverse the case because *Roe* and its progeny short-circuit constitutional democracy in the service of the latest left-wing ideals.

The Court's new conservative majority might shy away from such a radical restructuring of privacy. But these first steps would make a great contribution to our constitutional and political system well beyond the narrow issues of abortion or gay marriage. Pulling the Court out of privacy would rejuvenate our politics. Under the baleful influence of the Warren years, the Supreme Court has steadily added more and more important social issues to its docket. Every time it claims power over another constitutional issue, it deprives the people's elected representatives in our statehouses or in Congress of the ability to determine the policies that govern them. As it assumes the jurisdiction of a legislature, the Court has steadily become more political. It is no surprise that the Kavanaugh nomination took on the character of an electoral campaign. Anyone who cares deeply about abortion, gay marriage, race, religion, or speech can achieve policy changes only by influencing the appointment of justices to the Supreme Court, rather than working to win elections and appealing to our elected representatives. They will view the decisions of the justices on these issues as political, rather than legal, in nature.

Restoring these issues to the political process will result in a diversity of policies on many issues. Our federal system already allows such difference on matters of life and death, as it does on the death penalty or euthanasia. The states, and the people, will become more responsible—leading to a more robust democracy rather than the increasingly fragile one we have today. It may be asking too much for the Court to clip its own wings, but with Kavanaugh and Gorsuch now there, it might just have the moxie to make the hard choice of correcting its indefensible privacy jurisprudence. The best way for the Court to stay out of politics is for the Court to stay out of politics.

FEDERALISM

States have become the battleground for some of our nation's most contentious political controversies during the Trump years. Resistance to the

administration's immigration policies has arisen primarily in cities and states. Hawaii sued to prevent Trump from imposing a "Muslim ban," later rejected by the Supreme Court, while "sanctuary cities" such as San Francisco refuse to cooperate with ICE agents. Efforts to reverse the Trump administration's environmental deregulation proceed in state capitals, as do attempts to legalize marijuana at odds with federal law.

Ironically, progressives have only conservative justices to thank for these forums of resistance. While restoring the proper balance between the powers of the federal and state government became *the* major achievement of the Rehnquist Court, federalism has suffered setbacks under the Roberts Court, especially the 2012 decision upholding Obamacare. The new Trump justices can help get the "federalism revolution" back on track. Their presence provides the first real opportunity since the New Deal to restore the federal–state balance to something resembling that of the original Constitution.

Federalism does not just benefit liberals. Texas led a group of states that blocked Obamacare in court on the ground that it violated limits on federal power. A similar coalition of states sued the Obama administration over the DAPA and DACA programs. Federalism will not inevitably slant toward one party or the other, but instead promotes decentralized government. States serve as the "laboratories of democracy," as Justice Louis Brandeis famously observed.[23] They allow the nation to experiment with a variety of policies to solve pressing national problems, with the bad effects of poor choices limited to a state and the good ideas able to spread. Federalism further can tailor national programs to local conditions and different communities. Environmental policy should not impose the same mandates in states with different weather and geographic conditions. Smaller governments can also better regulate subjects—such as crime and family policy—that depend on more responsive government closer to the people. Finally, federalism promotes state competition over regulation and taxes to attract residents, much as the market efficiently forces producers to compete for consumers.

The Constitution creates a two-dimensional separation of power. The horizontal separation creates three branches of the national government, which exercise distinct national powers. They limit each other through overlapping powers and other checks and balances. A second separation of powers also stands sentinel over government power: a vertical separation

that limits national government to enumerated fields and reserves the rest for the states. By dividing power in both ways, the Constitution provides what Madison called a "double security" for liberty. Influenced by European writers such as Locke and Montesquieu and affected by their revolutionary history, the Framers believed that the concentration of power otherwise would bring tyranny.

Unfortunately, the Court has allowed the federal government to acquire vast powers and turn our constitutional system upside down. One of its weapons? Money. Most federal policy in education, environment, health, and welfare arrives through the imposition of federal rules on states as the price for receiving federal funds. With the passage of the Sixteenth Amendment in 1913—the dreaded personal income tax—the national government tapped into vast wealth. But Washington, D.C., needed the Supreme Court to turn a blind eye to the extension of the Taxing and Spending Clauses to subjects beyond the enumeration of federal powers. Jefferson and Madison believed that these clauses did not provide Congress with any authorities beyond the enumerated powers described elsewhere in the Constitution. Congress could only tax and spend to exercise its enumerated powers—such as providing an army and navy—and not for whatever end it desired. Hamilton disagreed. He argued that the Constitution only required that spending and taxes advance the general welfare and common defense.

Under the pressure of Franklin Roosevelt's court-packing plan, the Supreme Court ultimately agreed with Hamilton. Congress and the president could claim that every law fell under the general welfare, and after losing the New Deal confrontation with FDR, the Court has never second-guessed them. With this authority to spend on virtually any subject, coupled with the ability to raise huge amounts of money through personal and corporate income taxes, Congress gained an enormous advantage over the states. What governor or legislature isn't willing to trade some of its state's abstract independence and sovereignty for immediate cash? Very few, it seems, as we have seen in the number of states that expanded their healthcare programs in exchange for Obamacare funds.

Spending is not the only encroachment on federalism that should gain the attentions of the new Trump justices. Congress's other major weapon against the states comes through the Commerce Clause. Article I, Section 8 authorizes Congress "[t]o regulate Commerce . . . among the several states." At the founding, commerce appeared to refer to the trading, bartering,

selling, and incidental transportation of goods. The Framers sensibly gave Congress this authority to prevent the trade wars and protectionism that had broken out among the states under the Articles of Confederation. But the Court, again under the pressure of FDR's attacks, reinvented the Commerce Clause to give the federal government an almost limitless regulatory power. The most infamous example of the Court's surrender was *Wickard v. Filburn* (1942), which allowed the government to prohibit a farmer from growing 260 bushels of wheat, because aggregating the conduct of all farmers in the nation would affect the market price for wheat. Under this logic, Congress could control virtually any economic or commercial activity, no matter how small, no matter if it never crossed state lines. And for the next sixty years, Congress did exactly that.

Only in the last two decades have the justices hesitantly placed boundaries on federal power. In the Obamacare case, *National Federation of Independent Business v. Sebelius*, Congress required Americans to purchase health insurance or pay a fine to the IRS. And Congress claimed the authority for this unprecedented law under the Commerce, Spending, and Taxing Clauses. Ultimately, the Court split the baby. Chief Justice Roberts, joined in principle by four conservatives (Scalia, Kennedy, Thomas, and Alito), found that the Commerce Clause could not support a mandatory duty to purchase health insurance. The power to regulate commerce does not include the power to create commerce to regulate—a market must preexist exercise of the Commerce Clause. Seven justices also agreed that Congress's spending power cannot "coerce" states to participate in a federal program by threatening to cut off large amounts of federal dollars. Obamacare had cut off all existing Medicaid funding to states that refused to expand their healthcare programs to the administration's desired levels. The Court refused to countenance that bullying.

Sebelius, however, contained nationalizing elements too. Roberts and the four liberal justices concluded that Congress could force all Americans to purchase health insurance by levying a fine on the unwilling. Even though Congress considered the fine a "penalty," and even though Congress did not rely on its taxing power to pass the law, Roberts held that it was indeed a tax. This grants Congress a nearly limitless ability to tax that could be federalism's ultimate death knell. Take the so-called Green New Deal put forth by congressional Democrats and endorsed by several presidential candidates. It would impose $7 trillion in new taxes to switch all

national energy production to clean sources, provide a job with the national government for anyone looking for work, and purchase a comfortable and environmentally friendly home for all.

To restore federalism to its proper place in our constitutional order, the new Trump justices will likely lead the Court to the original understanding of both the Taxing and Spending Clause and the Commerce Clauses. They can begin by adopting Madison and Jefferson's approach to the taxing and spending powers: Congress can tax and spend, as long as it does it on something that rests otherwise within the enumerated powers of the federal government. With regard to the Commerce Clause, they could return Congress to regulating the sale, trade, or transportation of goods across state lines.

Restoring a robust federalism does not mean that every issue where the states and the national government clash will be resolved in favor of the states. Defense, foreign policy, and regulating the interstate markets will remain prerogatives of the national government. But many national–state disputes would tip in the states' favor once the national government lacked authority to spend and act in that area. Or at least the national government's ability to act would be severely curtailed. But federalism would once again allow the United States to capture the benefits of decentralized policymaking that brings the government closer to the people, permits more experimentation and tailored federal programs, and provides citizens with choice.

THE ADMINISTRATIVE STATE

Before his confirmation, Kavanaugh had no clear views on privacy, race, or sexuality, the constitutional holy trinity of the left. Instead, his real threat to modern liberalism came from his hostility to the progressive vision of technocratic government run by insulated bureaucrats and protected by deferential judges. While the administrative state has always been with us in some form, it has metastasized into a progressive perpetual motion machine. It calls on Congress to delegate broad swaths of its legislative power to federal agencies, insulates the bureaucrats who exercise that regulatory power from the president's political control, and demands that courts defer to officials' policy choices and even readings of the law.

The modern state distorts the original constitutional design, which sought to use federal power sparingly. As Madison described it in *Federalist No. 51*, the Framers deliberately created a difficult obstacle course for

any new law. Identical bills must pass two separate houses of the legislature, each one elected by different constituents at different times. A president could veto the law, which would then require two-thirds agreement by both houses to override. The Constitution imposed enumerated limits on the subjects of federal law, with the states providing most of the direct rules for daily life. "In the compound republic of America, the power surrendered by the people is first divided between two distinct governments, and then the portion allotted to each subdivided among distinct and separate departments," Madison argued. "Hence a double security arises to the rights of the people. The different governments will control each other, at the same time that each will be controlled by itself."[24]

But during the Progressive Era at the turn of the last century, American political leaders decided that the Constitution had become obsolete. The Constitution's antiquated structures of federalism and the separation of powers, Woodrow Wilson believed, could not provide the expert, scientific regulation demanded by a modern industrialized economy and nationalized society. Wilson's experiments, later cemented into our government by FDR's New Deal, replaced the Framers' system of the rare, specialized federal law with a supercharged bureaucratic engine that issues an inexhaustible stream of regulations unencumbered by the limits on Congress's powers.[25]

Trump's judges may now supply the fifth vote to undo this Teutonic transplant (Wilson had studied and admired the German theory and practice of administration) into the American system of decentralized, cautious government. In *Federalist No. 51*, Madison argued that people need constitutions because men are not angels. Despite progressive faith to the contrary, bureaucrats are not angels either. An independent agency can go rogue by pursuing its own agenda or seeking to help favored parties or even political leaders. Because agencies often deal with technical regulatory matters, courts tiptoe lightly when it comes to reviewing agency decisions. We don't want generalist judges weighing in with their less-than-scientific opinions on outright policy choices.

But there is one area in which judges are experts—interpreting the law. Nevertheless, under the *Chevron* and *Auer* doctrines, when an agency appears before a court, judges will defer to that agency's interpretation of relevant statutes and regulations if the court deems these laws ambiguous. This outsources the judge's job to the agency. This is bad enough when

dealing with acts of Congress, but it is even worse when a court defers to an agency's interpretation of its own regulations. The agency truly is then judge, jury, and executioner—resembling the tyranny against which Montesquieu and Madison warned.

Trump's justices will likely lead the Court to jettison the deference doctrines without second-guessing legitimate areas for scientific and technical expertise. Agencies can continue to use their expertise to come up with clean air or seatbelt safety standards within the reasonable and limited boundaries Congress has set for them. But the courts should not defer when it comes to interpreting the law itself, which is an exercise where the courts, not agencies, are the constitutionally designated experts. As Chief Justice John Marshall famously declared, the role of the judiciary is "to say what the law is," meaning to interpret the law (not to make the law), in order to apply it to the case or controversy before the court. While courts ferociously guard this duty by refusing to defer to the views of the president or Congress, they undergo a strange crisis of confidence when confronted by unelected bureaucrats.

Justices Gorsuch and Kavanaugh can begin with the *Chevron* doctrine, which requires judges to accept an administrative agency's reading of any ambiguous words in its governing statutes, including those defining the extent of its own powers. *Chevron* has allowed the administrative state to not only set policies as it wishes but also to steadily expand the reach of agencies' mandates at the expense of Congress and the states. Even as a lower court judge, Kavanaugh attacked the *Chevron* doctrine, which requires judges to defer to an agency's "reasonable" interpretation of the statutes it enforces, as "an atextual invention by courts."[26] As a lower court judge, Gorsuch called for *Chevron*'s rejection,[27] and as a Supreme Court justice, he has steadily narrowed it. The two would join Justice Thomas, who has criticized *Chevron* because it "precludes judges from exercising [independent] judgment, forcing them to abandon what they believe is 'the best reading of an ambiguous statute' in favor of an agency's construction." Ultimately *Chevron* deference allows agencies to expand their powers at the expense of the judiciary and the separation of powers. According to Thomas, *Chevron* "thus wrests from Courts the ultimate interpretative authority to 'say what the law is,' and hands it over to the Executive."[28]

The Supreme Court's 2018 term put the agencies on notice that the conservatives intend to wage war on *Chevron*. *Kisor v. Wilkie* challenged the

judicial practice of accepting an agency's interpretation of its own regulations, known as the *Auer* doctrine. *Auer* added to the unfair advantage
enjoyed by agencies, which already transform vague statutory commands
to advance their preferred policies. Yet courts, which bear the constitutional responsibility to say what the law is and who do not defer to what
other parties think the law is, including Congress or the president, lie down
and play dead before agencies. In *Kisor*, the Court refused to overturn the
Auer doctrine. But the four liberal justices had to so narrow *Auer* to attract
Roberts's surprising fifth vote that it will now apply to very few cases in the
real world. And the case planted the seeds for a much greater change. The
four conservative dissenters not only rejected the *Auer* doctrine but also
called for the reversal of *Chevron*. Despite voting to uphold *Auer*, Roberts
declared that he would leave the door open to overrule *Chevron*. As with
non-delegation, there may now be five votes to kill *Chevron* and require
judges—not bureaucrats—to interpret the law.

Overruling *Chevron* would presage an even more direct attack on the
agencies. The administrative state draws its sustenance from Congress's
broad, vague delegations of its lawmaking powers. Due to a combination
of increasing societal complexity and congressional cowardice, Congress
has punted more and more of its legislative power to agencies. In the Clean
Air Act, for example, Congress gave the Environmental Protection Agency
the power to regulate any and all air pollutants, even, according to the
Court, carbon dioxide.[29] The consequence of this delegation is easy to see.
Agencies have been only too happy to assume vast legislative powers, such
as deciding the gas mileage requirements for cars or how much energy
should come from coal or natural gas, without answering to the voters. In
the last year of the Obama administration, agencies published 95,894 pages
of regulations. By contrast, in the last two years of the Obama administration, Congress averaged only 165 new federal laws per year. A "non-
delegation doctrine" that prohibits the excessive transfer of legislative
power to executive agencies has lain dormant since 1937, another casualty
of the Court's switch in time during its fight with FDR.

For conservatives committed to the original understanding of the Constitution, such broad transfers of legislative power violate the separation of
powers. The Framers granted executive power to the presidency, legislative
power to Congress, and judicial power to the courts rather than allow their
combined exercise as in parliamentary systems. They worried, as Madison

wrote in *Federalist No. 47*, that the "accumulation of all powers, legislative, executive, and judiciary, in the same hands, whether of one, a few, or many, . . . may justly be pronounced the very definition of tyranny." Despite the separation of powers, federal agencies now exercise all three types of power—making laws, enforcing laws, and adjudicating disputes over these laws. Conservatives once tried to make peace with the administrative state by centralizing control in the White House, which could demand that regulation survive a cost-benefit test. But these broad delegations of power have allowed our elected representatives to escape responsibility for difficult decisions and have prevented the president and the courts from controlling an increasingly ideological bureaucracy. The Founders' nightmare has come to pass.

In the Court's first full term with Justices Gorsuch and Kavanaugh on board, the conservative justices signaled their intent to end this game. In *Gundy v. United States*, a law authorized the attorney general to determine whether certain sex offenders have to publicly register as such. By a 5–3 vote, the Court found no violation of the non-delegation doctrine. But beneath the surface, a conservative majority declared its intent to restore limits on Congress. Roberts, Thomas, and Gorsuch voted to strike down the sex offender law. Kavanaugh recused himself, but his record as a lower court judge displays a strong hostility to independent agencies. Tellingly, Alito, who provided the fifth vote to uphold the law, nevertheless appended a one-page statement: "If a majority of this Court were willing to reconsider the approach we have taken [to non-delegation] for the past 84 years, I would support that effort." Kavanaugh and Gorsuch could well provide the votes to restore the separation of powers and prevent Congress from handing off hard decisions—and great power—to the agencies.

Even the Trump administration's most politically damaging defeat at the Court, the census case, shows that the justices intend to bring the welfare state under tighter control. In *Department of Commerce v. New York*, the Court found that Commerce had manufactured a pretext for asking about citizenship on the census. Commerce's real reason may well have been to benefit Republican states in the 2020 census by undercounting aliens, who group more highly in blue states such as New York and California. Chief Justice Roberts, joined by the four liberal justices, declared that "the evidence tells a story that does not match the explanation the Secretary gave for his decision." He declared that the "sole state reason" for adding the

citizenship question to the census "seems to have been contrived." Federal agencies must "offer genuine justifications for important decisions, reasons that can be scrutinized by courts and the interested public." Otherwise, judicial review becomes "an empty ritual."

In dissent, Justice Thomas, joined by Gorsuch and Kavanaugh (Alito filed a separate dissent), correctly called the opinion "an unprecedented departure from our deferential review of discretionary agency decisions." Courts generally only examine the facial rationale provided by the government for regulation and do not search for any hidden "real" reason that might involve political purposes. Subjecting agency regulation to more searching scrutiny in the future rather than accepting their purported reasons will slow bureaucrats in their ability to flex their power and demand that they satisfy searching judicial scrutiny before they do so. Thomas observed that "if taken seriously as a rule of decision, this holding would transform administrative law."

In their quest to hand Trump a defeat in the census case, the four liberals agreed to lay the groundwork for a new world in which agency actions receive a strict examination from federal judges. This change alone would be significant. But couple it with *Gundy* and *Kisor* and it augurs a conservative judicial majority that will soon attack the foundations of the administrative state. Presidents may regain full control of the executive branch, Congress may no longer outsource lawmaking, and courts will no longer defer to agency rules. The Trump Court may produce a slimmer administrative state with thousands fewer regulations and smaller agencies that focus more on enforcement than lawmaking. While we will still have clean water and air and safe highways, Congress will have to enact and take responsibility for the policies. We might start to live in a republic that once again resembles the Framers' original design.

CHAPTER 9

"YOU'RE FIRED!": IMPEACHING
THE PRESIDENT

I t's impeachment or bust. That could have been the campaign slogan
of congressional Democrats from day one of the Trump presidency.
For progressives, a heady brew of Russian election interference, criminal conspiracies, and shady lawyers and lobbyists had inflated hopes that
Special Counsel Robert Mueller would yield indictments not just of high-
ranking officials but also of the president himself. But Mueller refused to
do the Democrats' job for them.

Disappointed Democrats next seized on a fraught phone call between
Trump and the president of Ukraine as evidence of an abuse of power.
Even though they mustered enough to impeach on a party-line vote, they
utterly failed in the Senate. Only Senator Mitt Romney of Utah joined 47
Democratic senators in voting to remove Trump from office, far short of
the two-thirds required by the Constitution. The exercise may prove to be
more than political theater, however. It could augur the partisan misuse of
impeachment to control future presidents, which would undo the original
Constitution's greatest innovation: an independent executive.

House Democrats set a speed record in investigating the Ukraine affair.
Reports emerged only in late August 2019 that Trump had asked Ukraine's
president to open a corruption investigation into former vice president
and current Democratic primary presidential candidate Joe Biden and his
son Hunter Biden. Within two months, a parade of civil servants testified
that the White House had delayed almost $400 million in aid until Ukraine
launched the probe.

Democrats were immediately convinced that Trump's quid pro quo justified a rushed process to force his removal from office. The House Intelligence

Committee started deposing witnesses in October 2019; the House voted out articles of impeachment a mere two months later on December 18, 2019. For comparison purposes, the probe into Nixon's abuses began in October 1973 and ended only with the president's resignation on August 9, 1974. "The president's actions have seriously violated the constitution, especially when he says and acts upon the belief 'Article 2 says I can do whatever I want.' No," House Speaker Nancy Pelosi declared in calling for impeachment. "His wrongdoing strikes at the very heart of our constitution. A separation of powers, three co-equal branches, each a check and balance on the other. A republic, if we can keep it, said Benjamin Franklin."[1]

Pelosi and her Democratic majority correctly read the Constitution's standard for impeachment. Article II allows the House to impeach a president for "Treason, Bribery, or other high Crimes and Misdemeanors." Although the constitutional text alone might suggest that Congress can only impeach a president for committing crimes, as Trump's defense lawyer Alan Dershowitz famously argued in the January 2020 Senate trial, the history shows "other high Crimes and Misdemeanors" includes more serious, noncriminal conduct. In borrowing the concept from their eighteenth-century British cousins, the American Founders believed that removing a president in between elections should only occur if the occupant committed a grave abuse of power. But they also did not want Congress to remove presidents over simple policy disputes or partisan rivalry. They rejected including "maladministration" as a ground for impeachment and instead linked "other high Crimes and Misdemeanors" to treason and bribery to show the seriousness of the offenses.

Impeachment does not require a crime. Impeachable offenses are those that "proceed from the misconduct of public men, or, in other words, from the abuse or violation of some public trust," Alexander Hamilton explained in *Federalist No. 65*. "They are of a nature which may with particular propriety be dominated POLITICAL, as they related chiefly to injuries done immediately to the society itself." The Framers had in mind a president's abuse of the foreign affairs power. During the struggle over the Constitution's adoption, supporters provided two cases of impeachable conduct involving foreign affairs. First, thanks again to their shared British heritage, the Framers agreed that Louis XIV of France's payments to Charles II to stay out of the wars on the Continent would have met the standard for impeachment. Even though Charles II had committed no crime, he had

abused the power of his office for personal benefit. Second, the Constitution's defenders suggested that Congress could remove a president who entered into a treaty that benefited him, his party, or even his region at the expense of the national interest.

The haste of the House of Representatives' inquiry, however, doomed it. In their rush to conclude the investigation before an artificial Christmas deadline, Democrats did not create a bipartisan staff to carefully and thoroughly investigate accusations of presidential abuse of power. They did not question the figures who directly discussed Ukraine with Trump: Vice President Mike Pence, Secretary of State Mike Pompeo, and former national security advisor John Bolton. Instead, they built their case on the testimony of career officials who never discussed a quid pro quo with the president in person. As a result, House Democrats could not nail down whether Trump really wanted Joe Biden investigated for political dirt to use in the 2020 campaign or whether the Bidens had become Trump shorthand for the political corruption that has beset Ukraine.

That case proved enough for Democrats to impeach by a party-line vote, but the weak facts guaranteed acquittal in the Senate. While abuse of the foreign affairs power could provide the grounds of impeachment, the Founding arguments show that the offense must be as serious as treason or bribery. A failed effort to trade foreign aid—which the White House ultimately released—for political dirt did not rise to the level of the bribery of Charles II or treaties that give away territory or other national interests. Trump may have acted inappropriately or even abused the executive power over foreign affairs, but Democrats could not show that the Ukraine affair had seriously harmed the nation. Indeed, when all was said and done, the Trump administration had provided greater aid and support to Ukraine than the Obama administration.

Trump critics lay blame instead on the requirement of a two-thirds Senate vote to remove the president. The one-third of the Senate necessary to acquit could represent as little as 18 percent of the population. But as Hamilton explained during the ratification fight, the Constitution sets the bar so high for conviction as to guarantee that an impeachment does not arise solely from "factions" (today's political parties) and "all their animosities, partialities, influence, and interest." The House's party-line vote to impeach Trump met Hamilton's definition of a partisan impeachment effort that predictably failed in the Senate.

Democrats should have followed the Framers' advice. They believed that elections, not impeachment, should render the ultimate verdict on a president's conduct in office. "At the end of four years, [the president] may be turned out of his office," Edmund Randolph said during the 1788 Virginia ratifying convention. Otherwise, Federalists worried, Congress would use impeachment to transform an independent presidency into its servant. As the election season got into full swing, Democratic presidential candidates joined the House in demanding Trump's removal from office. But they, not impeachment, are the Framers' primary remedy for abuse of presidential power. The Constitution trusts the American people, acting through the ballot box, to decide whether to remove Trump.

This chapter will argue that House Democrats erred in impeaching Trump rather than allowing the American people to render their verdict through the electoral process. It will first discuss the facts of the Mueller investigation and whether prosecution can replace impeachment. It will return to the original understanding of the Constitution to unearth the purposes behind impeachment. It will conclude by examining the Ukraine controversy and whether it justified Trump's removal from office.

I. THE MUELLER REPORT

After an expensive, damaging two-year probe, Robert Mueller unintentionally did Trump a great favor. The special counsel definitively cleared Trump, his campaign, and his administration of conspiring with Russia to break federal law. Mueller's investigation found significant Russian efforts to harm Hillary Clinton's candidacy. The special counsel indicted multiple Russian hackers and concluded that the "Russian government interfered in the 2016 presidential election in sweeping and systematic fashion." But it found no cooperation by the Trump campaign. "The investigation did not establish that members of the Trump Campaign conspired or coordinated with the Russian government in its election interference activities," the Mueller report found. Mueller put to rest the claim that Trump had conspired with Russian agents to win the 2016 elections.

But Mueller refused to clear Trump of obstruction of justice. The report identified 10 separate incidents where, it suggested, Trump may have tried to interfere with the investigation. Some of the incidents included the picayune, such as candidate Trump declaring publicly, "Russia, if you're listening,

I hope you're able to find the 30,000 [Clinton] emails that are missing."[2] But some of the incidents had a more serious cast, such as Trump's decision to fire FBI director Comey, which, he explained on national television, "when I decided just to do it, I said to myself—I said, you know, this Russia thing with Trump and Russia is a made-up story."[3] Trump also considered firing Mueller and Attorney General Jeff Sessions because of the special counsel investigation, but White House staff did not follow up, and the president ultimately dropped the idea.[4]

Mueller's theory of obstruction did not take traditional form. Trump did not destroy evidence or threaten witnesses. Instead, Mueller detected more subtle forms of interference, such as firing FBI director Comey. But these acts could also have represented the president's exercise of his constitutional authority over law enforcement. Mueller also could not nail down the critical element of obstruction: did Trump have the "corrupt" mental state to impede the special counsel probe? Rather than seek a live interview with the president, the special counsel allowed Trump to submit written answers that placed off limits any questions about obstruction. Mueller could not have reached any definitive conclusions about Trump's mental state and, therefore, whether he had committed obstruction.

Instead, Mueller punted on obstruction. Mueller decided "not to make a traditional prosecutorial judgment" and reach "ultimate conclusions about the President's conduct."[5] He explicitly declared that his report did not exonerate the president. Instead, Attorney General William Barr reviewed the report and decided, as the nation's top federal prosecutor, that "the evidence developed by the Special Counsel is not sufficient to establish that the President committed an obstruction-of-justice offense." In a March 2019 press conference summarizing the Mueller report's findings, Barr argued that he had worked within Mueller's "legal framework," despite his disagreements with it, and simply found that the evidence did not meet the standard for a prosecution. Both Mueller and Barr properly concluded that Justice Department legal opinions prohibited them from charging a sitting president with a federal crime. As the Clinton DOJ ruled in 2000, "the indictment or criminal prosecution of a sitting President would impermissibly undermine the capacity of the executive branch to perform its constitutionally assigned functions."[6]

But the Mueller report, and Barr's declination to prosecute, did not end the matter. Mueller appears to have thought his investigation of obstruction

could provide the grounds for impeachment. He made clear that he had "conducted a thorough factual investigation in order to preserve the evidence when memories were fresh and documentary materials were available." Preserving evidence and memories makes no sense if Mueller had already decided he could not bring a case against a sitting president. The Justice Department does not play the role of national historian. Instead, Mueller explained that DOJ does not prosecute sitting presidents so as not to "potentially preempt constitutional processes for addressing presidential misconduct." The Constitution lists only two "processes" for addressing "presidential misconduct." One is elections—the American people can punish an abusive president by voting him out of office at the next ballot. The second is impeachment. There are no others.

II. IMPEACHMENT: THE ORIGINAL UNDERSTANDING

Whether Congress could constitutionally impeach and remove Trump raises questions as old as the Republic and facts as new as social media. The Constitution uses language to define the grounds for impeachment, such as "high Crimes and Misdemeanors," that remain a mystery today. Does impeachment require a federal crime? Does impeachment apply only to crimes but not disgraceful acts? Can members of Congress consider politics as well as law? Can Congress remove a president because of a good-faith disagreement over the scope of executive power or the meaning of the Constitution itself? Because the Supreme Court has decided that impeachment qualifies as a "political question" left up to the other branches, these questions have no legal answers from traditional sources, such as judicial opinions.

Historical practice also provides little help. The House of Representatives has impeached only two presidents in American history. In the wake of Abraham Lincoln's assassination, Republicans in Congress found their plans for a radical reconstruction of the South frustrated by President Andrew Johnson, a Southern Democrat who favored a more lenient peace.[7] In 1868, the House impeached Johnson for conducting himself in office in a disgraceful, yet not illegal, manner. Johnson broke prevalent norms by speaking directly to the people to lobby for legislation and attacking Congress as "traitors." Congress responded by including an article of impeachment for

his unacceptable rhetoric.[8] To strengthen their case, congressional Republicans made it a crime for the president to fire his cabinet officers without their consent—a law that the Supreme Court would later find an unconstitutional infringement of the executive power. The Senate fell one vote short of removal. Johnson's trial suggests that Congress cannot impeach over simple policy disputes or presidential exercise of legitimate executive powers.

Exactly 130 years later, the House flexed its impeachment powers for only the second time, but over the sordid and banal rather than the high and mighty. Bill Clinton's impeachment asked whether the president had committed perjury about his affair with an intern. The president had committed a crime, but independent counsel Kenneth Starr concluded that he could not indict a sitting president, much as Mueller would two decades later. Instead, Starr referred the case to Congress. While the House impeached, the Senate refused to convict. Clinton's argument that he had only lied about sex and had not caused any serious national harm carried the day. The partisan nature of the Senate vote also suggested that impeachment would become a test of party discipline; presidents would survive so long as they could maintain the support of 34 senators of their party.

A third president, Richard Nixon, likely would have faced impeachment and removal had he not resigned on August 9, 1974. Both a special counsel and the House had launched probes into the burglary of the Democratic Party offices at the Watergate Hotel during the 1972 elections. After the Supreme Court ordered Nixon to obey a subpoena for White House tapes, the House Judiciary Committee reported three articles of impeachment. Nixon resigned before the House could vote. While the committee had considered a wide variety of charges, such as bombing Cambodia without congressional authorization and IRS abuse, in the end it recommended impeachment only for obstruction of the special counsel investigation and impeding the House's probe, and violating the individual rights of his political enemies. While there are parallels between the allegations against Nixon and those against Trump, the Nixon case never came to a vote in the House, not to mention a full trial in the Senate. It is difficult to conclude that Nixon's resignation creates some kind of precedent in the way that the 1868 and 1998 examples might.

It is not even clear that the Nixon case or the Johnson and Clinton

impeachments should create any precedent at all. In both the Johnson and Clinton cases, the Senate refused to convict. It could have found that the House had not "proved" its case, though in both cases the facts were clear. Johnson had indeed fired his secretary of war without the consent of Congress; Clinton had lied to prosecutors. The Senate must have acquitted because Johnson's and Clinton's acts did not amount to high crimes and misdemeanors as defined by the Constitution. But the Senate leaves behind no written opinion to explain its decision, because it acts much as a jury in a criminal trial. Therefore, we can draw no firm legal precedents from these earlier impeachments. Nor could a past Senate bind a future Senate to its understanding of impeachment.

Without any binding precedent, the Constitution's original understanding becomes magnified in importance. The Constitution does not provide for the trial or punishment of a sitting president by prosecutors or a regular court. Instead, the Impeachment Clause vests the power to impeach in the House. Impeachment amounts to an indictment in a criminal case, where prosecutors decide they have enough evidence to bring a prosecution before a jury. Vesting the power in the House alone already suggests that impeachment will not fall solely within the preserve of law but will involve politics as well.

While recognizing that both law and politics would infuse impeachment, the Constitution also tries to prevent Congress from removing the president for purely political ends. Article I seeks this goal by dividing impeachment from the trial itself. Article I gives the duty of conducting the trial to the Senate. Unlike the decision to impeach, the Constitution requires a two-thirds vote for conviction. If the one-third smallest states banded together, roughly 9 percent of the nation could prevent the other 91 percent from removing a president. The Constitution sets such a high bar to convict to ensure that removal represents a broad consensus across the nation's geography and population.[9]

Yet a third provision declares that the punishment "shall not extend further than to removal from Office, and disqualification to hold and enjoy any Office of honor, Trust or Profit under the United States." This provision effectively limits impeachment to the same punishment as that possible at the next quadrennial election: being voted out of office. It also states that after conviction, the removed officer "shall nevertheless be liable and subject to Indictment, Trial, Judgment and Punishment, according to

Law."[10] Thus, impeachment only addresses removal from office, and that prosecution for violating federal law must wait. The Constitution provides no right to appeal a conviction, and the Supreme Court ruled in 1993 that it considers impeachment to pose a "political question" beyond judicial review.[11] The Constitution prevents a president from enjoying complete immunity from lawbreaking by allowing prosecution once he leaves office.

Only two constitutional provisions address the standard for impeachment. Article II states that Congress can remove the president and other executive branch officers for "Treason, Bribery, or other high Crimes and Misdemeanors." Article III states that "The Judges, both of the supreme and Inferior Courts, shall hold their Offices during good Behavior." Read together, these two provisions suggest that "Treason, Bribery, or other high Crimes and Misdemeanors" includes a more serious set of offenses than a violation of "good Behavior." Reading the text carefully also suggests that "high Crimes and Misdemeanors" must be as serious as "Treason" and "Bribery" because they are included in the same list and the key inclusion of "other." If the clause had read "Treason, Bribery, and high Crimes and Misdemeanors" instead, without the "other," impeachment might have a much broader scope. Other parts of the Constitution reinforce the idea that "high Crimes and Misdemeanors" limits impeachment to serious offenses. Article I immunizes members of Congress from arrest when attending a session except for "Treason, Felony, and Breach of the Peace." It seems that felonies or breaches of the peace do not amount to "high" crimes. Article IV requires states to extradite fugitives charged with "Treason, Felony, or other Crime." This approach does not answer the question of what treason, bribery, and other high crimes and misdemeanors should have in common, only that we should read the catchall as including only offenses of a similar gravity.

A. DRAFTING THE IMPEACHMENT CLAUSE

At the time of the Constitutional Convention, the delegates would have had experience with the British practice and the impeachment mechanisms of the state constitutions. The Framers borrowed impeachment from Great Britain, where it had existed for several centuries, but modified it to suit America. At the time of the Framing, Great Britain was evolving from the Crown-dominated system of past centuries into the parliamentary democracy of today. The monarch, rather than the leader of

the majority party, appointed the cabinet. Parliament could oppose Crown policies by impeaching and removing its ministers. Offenses included what the Framers would describe as "political offenses" against the nation or even "mal-administration." Unlike the American system, however, British impeachment had become a criminal process. Parliament held a criminal trial and could impose a criminal punishment.[12]

While the newly independent states kept impeachment, they moderated its reach. Even though the state constitutions gave the legislature far greater powers, they did not do away completely with the separation between the executive and legislative branches. Because executive officers did not represent the majority in the legislature, as in modern parliamentary systems, the assemblies wished to retain some way to remove them. While keeping impeachment as a tool, the state constitutions did not follow the British practice of limiting impeachment to criminal acts while in office.[13] The leading models at the Philadelphia Convention, the constitutions of New York and Massachusetts, included policy differences as well as criminal acts as impeachable conduct. In the former, the legislature could impeach for "mal and corrupt conduct" in office, while in the latter, the legislature could impeach "for misconduct and maladministration."[14]

These precedents inspired the Constitutional Convention. Early proposals agreed that the judiciary would hold the power to impeach federal officers.[15] The New Jersey Plan created a special process for removal of the president by Congress upon the request of a majority of state governors. Hamilton first set out a definition of an impeachable offense as "mal[administration] and corrupt conduct."[16] The delegates started on draft language that allowed the president "to be removable on impeachment and conviction [for] malpractice or neglect of duty."[17]

On July 19, 1787, the Convention first debated presidential impeachment. Some delegates opposed impeachment altogether because the president would already have the incentive to seek approval from the people by reelection. "If he be not impeachable whilst in office, he will spare no efforts or means whatever to get himself re-elected," said William Davie. "He considered this as an essential security for the good behavior of the Executive."[18] Gouverneur Morris argued further that periodic elections would allow the people to decide whether to remove the president. "In case he should be re-elected, that will be sufficient proof of his innocence." Rufus King agreed that the president would fall subject to trial by the electorate

at every election. "Like them, therefore, he ought to be subject to no intermediate trial, by impeachment."[19]

These delegates worried that impeachment would clip the wings of the
new presidency. Morris warned that impeachment would undermine the
executive's independence, vigor, and energy. If the Constitution vested
the power to remove the president in another branch of government, it
"would render the Executive dependent on those who are to impeach."[20]
Charles Pinckney agreed that the legislature would hold impeachment "as
a rod over the Executive" and "effectually destroy his independence."[21] King
worried that impeachment by Congress would "be destructive of his independence and of the principles of the Constitution."[22]

A majority of the delegates, however, believed the Constitution should
provide a mechanism to remove a president midstream. "Shall any man
be above Justice? Above all shall that man be above it, who can commit
the most extensive injustice?"[23] George Mason asked. Mason raised the
prospect of a president who used bribery to secure his election. Madison
argued for grounds that went beyond criminal conduct. "Some provision
should be made for defending the Community [against] the incapacity,
negligence or perfidy of the chief Magistrate," he declared. He did not believe that coming up for election every four years would provide enough
of a safeguard. "He might lose his capacity after his appointment," Madison worried. Or worse yet, "[h]e might pervert his administration into a
scheme of peculation or oppression. He might betray his trust to foreign
powers."[24] Edmund Randolph supported Madison because "the Executive
will have great opportunities of abusing his power; particularly in time of
war when the military force, and in some respects the public money will
be in his hands."[25]

These concerns about interference by a foreign power persuaded the
Convention. Morris changed his mind in favor of impeachment. Unlike
a hereditary monarch, the president "may be bribed by a greater interest
to betray his trust," Morris observed. "No one would say that we ought
to expose ourselves to the danger of seeing the first Magistrate in foreign
pay without being able to guard [against] it by displacing him."[26] Even the
British king had gone on the payroll of Louis XIV. "The Executive ought
therefore to be impeachable for treachery," Morris agreed. "Corrupting his
electors, and incapacity were other causes for impeachment." After Morris
spoke, the Convention approved impeachment by eight states to two.[27]

As the Constitution moved through different drafts, the definition of impeachable offenses changed. In August, the Committee on Detail defined impeachment for "neglect of duty, malversation, or corruption."[28] By September 4, a second committee proposed to limit the offenses to "treason or bribery."[29] This provoked a reaction from Mason, who argued that "Treason as defined in the Constitution will not reach many great and dangerous offenses."[30] He moved to add "maladministration" too, but Madison responded that "so vague a term will be equivalent to a tenure during pleasure of the Senate." Morris argued that "an election of every four years will prevent maladministration." Mason withdrew his amendment and proposed instead "other high crimes and misdemeanors" in addition to treason and bribery, which passed by eight states to three.[31] Professor Michael Gerhardt reads "other high crimes and misdemeanors" to merely amount to a restatement of "bribery or maladministration."[32] But Yale law professor Charles Black Jr. just as easily concludes that the Convention raised the standard for impeachment above "maladministration."[33]

One other important debate occurred on impeachment at this time. By the end of the first debates, it appeared that the Convention had not come to a final view on where to locate the trial. When drafts had given Congress the right to select the president, delegates worried about giving Congress the power to remove him too. By the September 4 debate, the creation of the Electoral College caused the Convention to vest the trial role in the Senate. Madison proposed locating the trial in the Supreme Court because Congress would use the lower standard of impeachment to control the president. He complained that "the President under these circumstances was made improperly dependent."[34] Pinckney agreed. "If he opposes a favorite law," he argued, "the two Houses will combine against him, and under the influence of heat and action throw him out of office."[35] A majority of delegates, however, thought it better to remove the Supreme Court, which could become "warped or corrupted" by the political pressures. While "he was against a dependence of the Executive on the Legislature, considering the Legislative tyranny the greater danger," Morris argued that the Senate was too numerous to corrupt, that senators would live up to their oaths of office, and that a guilty president "can be turned out" every four years by election.[36] The Convention voted down Madison's proposal by nine states to two, and then it approved the Impeachment Clauses we have today by 10–1.[37]

While the Convention drafted the Constitution, the critical act of adopting it fell to the state ratifying conventions. In *Federalist No. 65*, Hamilton explained to the public the need for impeachment. Impeachment exists for "offenses which proceed from the misconduct of public men, or, in other words, from the abuse or violation of some public trust," Hamilton wrote. "They are of a nature which may with particular propriety be denominated POLITICAL, as they related chiefly to injuries done immediately to the society itself."[38] Impeachable offenses had to rise to the level of a harm to the nation, and they would include political offenses rather than just crimes. Impeachment served the function "as a bridle in the hands of the legislative body upon the executive servants of the government." But he also warned against "the greatest danger, that the decision will be regulated more by the comparative strength of the parties, than by the real demonstration of innocence or guilt."

The process of impeachment, Hamilton predicted, would be intensely political rather than legal. Such cases "will seldom fail to agitate the passions of the whole community" and will enlist factions and "all their animosities, partialities, influence, and interest" on both sides. While there was no perfect place to locate such a politically fraught role, Hamilton argued that the Senate would have large enough numbers to reduce the influence of politics. "The awful discretion which a court of impeachments must necessarily have, to doom to honour or to infamy the most confidential and the most distinguished characters of the community," Hamilton wrote, "forbids the commitment of the trust to a small number of persons."[39] The Constitution wisely chose not to vest the trial in the courts, Hamilton further explained, because judges could well see a disgraced president in their courts after his removal, and they might also engage in self-dealing if they too came up for impeachment.

Hamilton addressed two further issues that bear directly on Trump. The Mueller investigation turned on whether the Justice Department could prosecute a sitting president. Hamilton explained that judges should not sit on impeachment trials because they would also sit on any subsequent criminal case. After his removal, Hamilton wrote, the president "will still be liable to prosecution and punishment in the ordinary course of law."[40] Judges would find a strong incentive to uphold the earlier impeachment verdict and so would effectively undermine the Constitution's limit on impeachment only to removal from office. In comparing the British king

with the American executive in *Federalist No. 69*, Hamilton again made clear that criminal prosecution could only follow an impeachment. "The president of the United States would be liable to be impeached, tried, and, upon conviction of treason, bribery, or other high crimes or misdemeanors, removed from office," he explained.[41] The Federalists could not have made themselves clearer that impeachment would come first, and criminal proceedings would only come second.

A second issue is impeachment's political nature. House Democrats complain that impeachment was futile because of the Republican majority in the Senate.[42] After the Senate rejected a motion to hear from John Bolton and other witnesses, Nancy Pelosi even accused Republican senators of being "accomplices to the President's cover-up."[43] Anti-Federalists made a somewhat similar attack on impeachment for excessively increasing the power of Congress generally, and that of the Senate in particular, over the president. In a contradiction, other Anti-Federalists argued that the Senate could use its power to shield the officials that it had confirmed or to protect presidents with whom it had conspired. Answering the first critique, Hamilton argued that the division of impeachment between the House and Senate would make it difficult for Congress to exploit its power for political gain. "Assigning to one the right of accusing, to the other the right of judging, avoids the inconvenience of making the same persons both accusers and judges; and guards against the danger of persecution, from the prevalency of a factious spirit in either of those branches," Hamilton explained in *Federalist No. 66*.[44]

Responding to the second critique, Hamilton found it unlikely that the Senate would protect a president just because of shared policies or partisan interests. He believed that the Senate would have little incentive to ignore the facts that would justify impeachment. Human experience "must destroy the supposition, that the Senate, who will merely sanction the choice of the executive, should feel a bias, towards the objects of that choice, strong enough to blind them to the evidences of guilt so extraordinary, as to have induced the representatives of the nation to become its accusers."[45] He pressed the point even further in taking up the possibility that the Senate would never impeach a president for betraying the nation in a treaty, to which it would have given its approval earlier. While the two-thirds requirement for treaties made such a prospect difficult to imagine, Hamilton conceded that the same issue would arise if the House

cooperated with the president to "sacrific[e] the interests of the society by an unjust and tyrannical act of legislation." Again, Hamilton claimed that Americans could count on the senators, and "upon their pride, if not upon their virtue," in order "to punish the abuse of their confidence, or to vindicate their own authority" in response to an abuse of executive power. At the very least, he predicted, senators would "divert the public resentment from themselves, by a ready sacrifice of the authors of their mismanagement and disgrace."[46] Hamilton believed that the political nature of impeachment might just as easily lead senators to punish a president to protect their own institutional prerogatives or even personal careers, as well as to shield him.

B. IMPEACHMENT AND THE RATIFICATION DEBATES

Only two state ratifying conventions, Virginia and North Carolina, discussed impeachment at any length. Virginia's convention was perhaps the most important to ratification. As the home of Washington and Jefferson, Virginia was critical, along with Massachusetts, Pennsylvania, and New York, for the success of the Revolution. It brought together leading critics of the Constitution who had been prominent figures in the Revolution, such as Patrick Henry and George Mason, and the younger generation of nationalists who would play important roles under the new Constitution, such as James Madison and John Marshall. The Constitution passed by only 89–79 in the Virginia convention; it is difficult to imagine the government succeeding had six votes switched and Virginia remained outside the new nation. As a result, Virginia provided the ultimate forum for the contest over the Constitution, and its debates over the document's meaning should take second place only to *The Federalist* itself.

Virginia Federalists promised that impeachment would encompass more than only crimes. George Nicholas responded to criticism of the aristocratic nature of the Constitution by arguing that the Congress had ample powers to control the executive. The most important power was funding. A second "source of superiority is the power of impeachment."[47] According to Nicholas, "this power must have much greater force in America, where the President himself is personally amenable for his mal-administration." Edmund Randolph, governor of Virginia and a future attorney general and secretary of state, agreed that impeachment covered more than crime. "At the end of four years, [the president] may be turned out of his office," he

said in response to Anti-Federalists who claimed that the executive held too much power. "If he misbehaves he may be impeached, and in this case he will never be reelected."[48]

Anti-Federalists, however, charged that presidents might conspire with senators to betray the public trust to foreign powers. Henry suggested that countries might bribe the president and the Senate to give away valuable trading rights or territory. "Yes, you can impeach [the president] before the Senate," Henry admitted. But "a majority of the Senate may be sharers in the bribe. Will they pronounce him guilty?"[49] John Tyler agreed that impeachment even made the Senate "too dangerous" when combined with the treaty power.[50] Mason, who had refused to sign the Constitution, agreed that senators would be a serious problem. "The senators were to try themselves," Mason said. "If a majority of them were guilty of the crime, would they pronounce themselves guilty?"[51] Under the Constitution, he predicted, "The Senate and President will form a combination that cannot be prevented by the representatives." Impeachment only allows "the guilty [to] try themselves. The President is tried by his counsellors. He is not re-moved from office during his trial."[52]

Abuse of the treaty power rose to become one of the most important issues in the Virginia convention. Anti-Federalists appealed to delegates from the west by raising the prospect of a treaty that gave up trading and navigation rights in New Orleans, the city that controlled access to the Mississippi. Control of the great river itself was the key to unlocking western expansion, because of the speed and low cost of shipping by sail rather than over land. The Continental Congress had almost approved the Jay-Gardoqui Treaty, which would have surrendered American rights to navigation of the Mississippi in exchange for generous trading privileges with the Spanish Empire (which would have benefited the northeastern states). Anti-Federalists charged that the new Constitution would allow the president and Senate to make similar treaties against the national interest without any check by the popular House of Representatives.[53]

Federalists conceded that in Great Britain, bad treaties could provide the grounds for impeachment. But they argued that more than mere dis-agreement over policy justified removal of a president. "In England, those subjects which produce impeachments are not opinions," Madison said in response to Henry. "No man ever thought of impeaching a man for an opinion. It would be impossible to discover whether the error in opinion

resulted from a willful mistake of the heart, or an involuntary fault of the head."[54] Madison, however, argued that a president who conspired with the smallest states to approve a treaty against the larger national interest could fall subject to impeachment. "Were the President to commit anything so atrocious as to summon only a few states [to approve a treaty], he would be impeached and convicted," Madison declared, "as a majority of the states would be affected by his misdemeanor."[55] Nicholas added that the British Parliament could use impeachment "for the punishment of such ministers as, from criminal motives, advise or conclude any treaty which shall afterwards be judged to derogate from the honor and interest of the nation."[56]

Randolph further argued that if a president received a bribe for a treaty, he would be "receiving emoluments from foreign powers. If discovered, he may be impeached. If he be not impeached, he may be displaced at the end of the four years."[57] Madison added that impeachment could extend not just to enforcement of the Emoluments Clause but also to punishment for abuse of the pardon power. "If the President be connected, in any suspicious manner, with any person, and there be grounds to believe he will shelter him, the House of Representatives can impeach him; they can remove him if found guilty," Madison declared in response to Mason.[58]

Henry remained unconvinced and continued to call impeachment "a mere sham—a mere farce."[59] Arguing that Henry misunderstood impeachment, Madison claimed that the Constitution would impose a tighter limit on abuse of the treaty power than in England. "If there be an abuse of this royal prerogative, the minister who advises [the king] is liable to impeachment," Madison began.[60] But not, Madison emphasized, the king himself. "Now, sir, is not the minister of the United States under restraint? Who is the minister? The President himself, who is liable to impeachment. He is responsible in person." Virginia then approved the Constitution without seeking any changes to impeachment.

North Carolina, which did not ratify the Constitution in its first try, raised many of the same arguments about impeachment. North Carolina's delegates extensively parsed the meaning of "high Crimes and Misdemeanors." Anti-Federalists in the state waged war against the impeachment clauses with outlandish hypotheticals, such as the prospect of Congress using impeachment to punish state officials, minor employees, or even private citizens for innocent conduct. Or they repeated the argument that senators would never remove a president with whom they conspired to abuse

the treaty and appointments powers. "What can the Senate try him for?" Samuel Spencer asked. "For doing that which they have advised him to do, and which, without their advice, he would not have done."[61] He predicted that the Senate would never convict a president "with any effect, or to any purpose, for any misdemeanor in his office, unless it should extend to high treason," or unless it wished to shift political blame.

Federalists responded by distinguishing between regular crimes and impeachable offenses. "If an officer commits an offence against an individual, he is amenable to the courts of law," Samuel Johnson said. "If he commits crimes against the state, he may be indicted and punished. Impeachment only extends to high crimes and misdemeanors in a *public office*. It is a mode of trial pointed out for great misdemeanors against the public."[62] Richard Spaight, a signer of the Constitution, even suggested that misuse of the military could qualify. Congress "alone had the means of supporting armies, and . . . the President was impeachable if he in any manner abused his trust."[63] James Iredell, who would become one of the first Supreme Court justices, emphasized that impeachment involved the violation of the public trust. "If the President does a single act by which the people are prejudiced, he is punishable himself," Iredell observed. "If he commits any misdemeanor in office, he is impeachable, removable from office, and incapacitated to hold any office of honor, trust, or profit."[64] Iredell acknowledged that impeachment created a "punishment for crime which it is not easy to describe, but which everyone must be convinced is a high crime and misdemeanor against the government."[65] Nevertheless, the Constitution had to vest the power in Congress "because the occasion for its exercise will arise from acts of great injury to the community, and the objects of it may be such as cannot be easily reached by an ordinary tribunal."[66]

Federalists sought to make clear that impeachment went beyond mere mistakes in policy. Anti-Federalists claimed that the Senate would not remove a president for a treaty to which it had consented. Spaight repeated the Federalist argument that the Senate could remove a president for a poor treaty. "He may be impeached and punished for giving his consent to a treaty, whereby the interest of the community is manifestly sacrificed," he told the delegates.[67] Iredell, however, drew a finer line between policy errors and decisions driven by unworthy motives. "When any man is impeached, it must be for an error of the heart, and not of the head," he told delegates. "God forbid that a man, in any country in the world, should be

liable to be punished for want of judgment."[68] Iredell maintained that if a "treaty should be deemed unwise, or against the interests of the country, yet if nothing could be objected against it but the difference of opinion," impeachment would not apply.[69] He worried that if impeachment reached differences over policy alone, the best leaders would refuse to serve in government and those that did would "act from a principle of fear." Accordingly, impeachment should only apply to a president "where he had received a bribe, or had acted from some corrupt motive or other." As an example, Iredell proposed a president "giving false information to the Senate" and with it "induced them to enter into measures injurious to their country," which the Senate would "not have consented to had the true state of things been disclosed."[70]

C. LESSONS FROM THE FOUNDING

The history of the drafting and ratification of the Constitution left important markers that not only made Trump's acquittal, but gave the president every incentive to fight the charges and refuse to compromise. First and foremost, the Framers believed that the political process should impose the primary restraint on the executive. A president intent on bribery, treason, or other high crimes and misdemeanors would need the cooperation of the House and Senate to succeed in his plans, either through funding, legislation, or the approval of treaties and appointees. The separation of powers would make it difficult for the president to execute any nefarious designs. "[T]he great security against a gradual concentration of the several powers in the same department, consists in giving to those who administer each department, the necessary constitutional means, and personal motives, to resist encroachments of the others," Madison wrote in *Federalist No 51*. "Ambition must be made to counteract ambition. The interest of the man, must be connected with the constitutional rights of the place."[71] By pursuing their own self-interest, the other branches of government should check any undue aggrandizement of power by the president.

Congressional Democrats, of course, took to the newspapers, airwaves, and blogs to accuse Trump of violating the Constitution. But this is just cheap talk. A president's opponents should deploy their own constitutional authority to stop abuses of power. House Democrats, for example, can hold oversight hearings and probe executive misdeeds. Voters can consider the scandals at the next congressional or presidential elections. Democrats can

go even further and refuse to enact the administration's legislative agenda. If the Trump administration wants tax cuts, a trade deal with Canada and Mexico, or tougher immigration laws, it needs the cooperation of the House. Speaker Pelosi could prevent any of these items from becoming reality simply by refusing to schedule a vote. At a minimum, she could have refused to invite the president to deliver the State of the Union address, not just on the day before the Senate's impeachment vote, but at all.

House Democrats could go even further. They enjoy the ultimate control over the government, the power of the purse. As Madison argued in *Federalist No. 58*, the "power over the purse may, in fact, be regarded as the most complete and effectual weapon, with which any constitution can arm the immediate representatives of the people, for obtaining a redress of every grievance, and for carrying into effect every just and salutary measure."[72] If Democrats truly believe that Trump has violated the Constitution and has committed high crimes and misdemeanors, they can block administration spending priorities or simply refuse to fund the government. Trump critics can wield the Constitution's most effective check on executive power simply by doing nothing at all.

Second, the Founders expected that elections could constrain abusive chief executives. The Framers understood that a president still might commit a corrupt act that could escape impeachment. Anti-Federalists made arguments remarkably similar to those made against Republican senators today. Critics claimed that Republicans voted to protect President Trump out of political survival, just as Democrats shielded President Clinton two decades ago.[73] But that is nothing new. Critics at the time of the Framing worried that senators might have a political incentive to block impeachment when they had already blessed executive conduct. Federalists responded that impeachment would impose enormous political pressures on senators to try a president in good faith. Even if the Senate failed in its duty, the people would still have their say. By rejecting a president's campaign for reelection, the people would render their own verdict. While the constitutional amendment limiting presidents to two terms may mute this judgment, it underscores the faith that the Founders put in elections to constrain executive power.

The Framers' electoral check revealed the hollowness of Trump's impeachment. It makes little sense to conduct an impeachment inquiry when the next presidential election is just months away. House Democrats could

claim that the Mueller report had missed some vital fact or had leaped to an incorrect legal conclusion. They could call all the same witnesses and demand all the same documents. But they are unlikely to uncover facts missed by the Mueller team, which had millions of dollars and dozens of experienced prosecutors and investigators. The White House waived executive privilege, ordered administration officials to fully cooperate, and provided millions of pages of documents. House Democrats could say that they reached a different legal conclusion about Russian collusion or obstruction of justice based on the Mueller report. But then such a truncated impeachment proceeding should take weeks and could have wrapped up easily in 2019. Conducting an impeachment that stretches into 2020 not only creates a wasteful constitutional redundancy but also only seems designed to politically damage an incumbent president during an election year.

Third, the Framers tried to strike a delicate balance between checking executive abuses while preventing impeachment from becoming a tool for legislative control of the executive. Congress could become too dominant due to its control over spending, taxes, and laws. "The legislative department is everywhere extending the sphere of its activity, and drawing all power into its impetuous vortex," Madison observed in *Federalist No. 48*.[74] The Founders sought to give the president independence by providing for his election by the people rather than by the legislature. They deliberately divided impeachment between the House and the Senate to prevent Congress from using removal as a tool to control the executive. Impeachment would have to represent the views of two bodies elected at different times and representing different constituencies. A president need only keep one-third of the Senate, which even then could represent a small fraction of the people (in the 1790 census, the smallest one-third of the states represented a mere 11.7 percent of the population). A supermajority requirement makes it almost impossible for Congress to remove a president over mere differences over policy.

Fourth, the Founders remained acutely aware of the possibility of executive wrongdoing. But they created a two-track approach to safeguard against it. While they knew that a president might commit a crime, they wanted prosecutors to wait until a president left office before bringing a case. A president subject to the criminal law could be dragged from "pillar to post" by lawsuits, wrote Jefferson.[75] The criminal justice system would have little effect on a sitting president anyway. A president could simply order any federal charges dropped, and if any officials refused to carry out his orders, he could remove them. Impeaching a president for crimes would represent something akin to double jeopardy, because it would essentially predetermine the results of any criminal case against the president after he left office. Federal judges would likely suppress any state prosecutions for violating the Supremacy Clause.

The second track, impeachment, does not depend on criminal law. High crimes and misdemeanors might become vague on the margins, but they do not simply incorporate all crimes. Impeachment would not reach conduct that amounted to minor crimes or did not involve the performance of executive duties. While such acts might be crimes and misdemeanors, they would not be "high." This is not to say that impeachable offenses could not be crimes themselves. Treason and bribery are both impeachable offenses and crimes. But if "other high Crimes and Misdemeanors" are to rise to the level of treason and bribery, they must involve a similar level of corruption or harm to the public interest. Bill Clinton may have lied, but it was not about any great matter of state. In such cases, the federal justice system will punish a president for such misdeeds after office.

This principle readily disposes of criminal and congressional investigations into Trump for his alleged payments of "hush money" to cover up past affairs. In August 2018, Trump's personal lawyer, Michael Cohen, pled guilty to tax evasion, campaign finance violations, and making false financial statements. Cohen confessed that he had arranged payments in 2016 to two women "for the principal purpose of influencing the election."[76] According to Cohen, these payments violated the federal limits on campaign contributions at the direction of then-candidate Trump. As election law scholar Bradley Smith argued, however, the payments would not have violated campaign contributions limits if Trump would have made them even if he were not a candidate—if they were just part of the regular course of business for him.[77] A candidate's spending on clothes and daily expenses does not qualify as campaign expenditures, even though they might help him or her succeed in a campaign, because the candidate would have spent the money anyway. More importantly, the payments do not rise to the same level of criminal conduct as treason or bribery. Even if Cohen and Trump had conspired to make any illegal campaign expenditures, they should just pay a fine—albeit a large one. The Mueller investigation did not pursue Cohen's claims, which it likely believed fell outside its mandate. Federal prosecutors declined to bring charges against Trump.

Impeachment is both narrower and broader than the criminal law. The impeachment clauses overlap with the criminal law in cases of treason and bribery. But impeachment punishes political offenses against the people. The Constitutional Convention debates could have supported the opposite reading; when Mason replaced "mal-administration" with "high Crimes and Misdemeanors," he could have thought that they carried the same meaning. But several leading scholars, such as Black and Amar, believe that choosing "high crimes and misdemeanors" amounted to a rejection of simply poor policies or administration.[78] The Federalists clearly conceded during the state ratification debates that impeachment would punish more than criminal acts.

Several examples will illustrate. The Framers agreed that Congress could impeach a president who signed a treaty that sacrificed the national interest to advance a personal, partisan, or regional goal. A president who aligned U.S. foreign policy to curry favor with a foreign power for his personal or family benefit, rather than to advance the public interest, could be impeached. Both Federalists and Anti-Federalists referred to Louis XIV's bribes of Charles II. Federalists also suggested that a president who misused his power as commander in chief might fall subject to impeachment, as had British ministers who had lost grievous wars or had worked with other nations against the national interest.[79]

Suppose a president were to react to a foreign invasion by refusing to order the military to fight the enemy. Surrender would not violate the criminal law, in that he received nothing in exchange (bribery), nor did he directly "adhere[] to [the] enemy, giving them Aid and Comfort." Perhaps he believed that losing the war was in the best interest of the American people. Surrender would seem to be grounds for impeachment. Misuse of the commander in chief power might also include cases where the president leads the United States into utterly disastrous wars that advance no plausible national interest, and for which he displays egregious lack of judgment. Attacking longtime allies, for example, might qualify, or invading lands in the face of stiff resistance for little discernable strategic gain.

Consider another possible abuse of executive power that would not violate the criminal law. President Nixon had used the IRS and the FBI to investigate members of his "political enemies list." Even though it does not appear that Nixon's orders violated any criminal law at the time, they provided the grounds for his second article of impeachment. Suppose that the

Obama administration had refused to grant tax-exempt status to conservative nonprofits (which it did), not because of the schemes of IRS official Lois Lerner but because of White House orders. Using the power of the government to punish political or ideological opponents could form the basis for impeachment.

The lessons from the Founding support DOJ's brief legal opinion that it cannot prosecute the chief executive. Criminal laws cannot bar a president's exercise of his constitutional power. Otherwise, Congress could pass laws that deprive the executive branch of its independent authorities. For example, it could make it a criminal offense to fire a subordinate executive official even though all three branches have historically agreed that the president enjoys a removal power. Congress did exactly this to prevent Andrew Johnson from firing members of his cabinet, most of whom were holdovers from the Lincoln administration. When Johnson fired the secretary of war, Congress used his violation of the law as the principal ground for impeachment. As we saw in chapter 2, the Supreme Court made clear that the act had violated the president's removal authority.[80]

Broad powers would accrue to Congress if it could pass criminal laws that applied to executive conduct. It could enact broad laws, such as obstruction of justice, which makes anyone who "corruptly" alters and destroys evidence for use in an official proceeding or "otherwise obstructs, influences, or impedes any official proceeding" guilty of obstruction.[81] Obstruction of justice formed the basis for Nixon's first article of impeachment. Suppose a president impedes an investigation not by corruptly interfering with witnesses or destroying evidence but by wasting time and resources. He uses his pardon power to immunize targets. He orders the case dropped and fires investigators who disobey. All of these actions could meet the plain text of the obstruction statute.

But Congress cannot use a statute, even a criminal law, to alter the Constitution's allocation of powers between the president and Congress. As William Barr argued in a June 8, 2018, memo, the broad terms of the obstruction statute could arguably constrict the president's ability to exercise prosecutorial discretion.[82] A president could decide for any number of reasons to drop a case, which would normally take immediate effect without question; indeed, the courts long ago recognized that such decisions lie outside their review.[83] But should prosecutors disagree, DOJ or Congress could accuse him of corruptly obstructing justice. In order to prove such a

claim, the judiciary would have to delve into the president's state of mind to judge whether he acted "corruptly." This not only would place a heavy burden on the executive's ability to perform its constitutional functions, but it would also allow Congress to expand its control over the executive branch.

According to the Mueller report, Trump separately ordered the stopping of the probe, demanded the removal of the special counsel and the attorney general, and publicly encouraged witnesses and targets not to cooperate. But each of these acts would have involved Trump's exercise of a core executive power. Trump has the inherent executive power to fire subordinate officials, including both the attorney general and the special counsel. Trump has the authority to order the beginning or end of any federal investigation. The president has the unlimited power to issue pardons, subject only to the exceptions for impeachment or state crimes. Reading the obstruction of justice statute to criminalize the use of these powers, even if under the suspicion of Oval Office self-dealing, would violate the Constitution's grant of these authorities to the president in the first place.

It turns out that Trump had good reason to end the Mueller probe. He knew that his campaign had not conspired with the Russian government in 2016. While Mueller found that Russia had conducted serious cyber operations to attempt to affect the elections, he did not find that the Trump campaign had ever coordinated with Russian officials. Mueller's successful prosecutions amounted primarily to "process crimes," such as lying to FBI agents. It is theoretically possible to commit obstruction of justice even when no substantive crime has occurred, just as an innocent person can lie to federal agents. But the president's knowledge that his campaign was innocent makes it difficult to conclude that he held a corrupt motive.

But suppose that President Trump had actually committed the elements of a crime. Trump could have halted the special counsel to cover up campaign misdeeds. Or he could have directed the acting attorney general, Rod Rosenstein, or Mueller to curtail the probe. Or he could have even fired Sessions, Rosenstein, and Mueller, as he had apparently considered. Trump could have contacted potential witnesses and targets and encouraged them not to cooperate. Perhaps he did more than just implicitly dangle the possibility of pardons; he could have offered them to everyone subjected to the Mueller investigation, as some conservative commentators recommended. Trump could have blocked White House officials from interviewing with the special counsel or providing documents.

Even so, Congress would need more to prove obstruction of justice sufficient to meet the standard for impeachment. The hypothetical actions mentioned above fall within the executive power of the president and could have plausible, independent reasons behind them. President Trump might have fired Sessions because, after his recusal, he could no longer effectively lead the Justice Department. Trump could have lost confidence in Rosenstein after news broke that Rosenstein had considered wearing a wire in his Oval Office meetings. He could have fired Mueller or closed the investigation because of the waste in money and resources.

To find these acts impeachable, Congress would have to go beyond finding that they had factually occurred. It would have to find that Trump had used his constitutional powers for corrupt purposes on a par with those that characterize treason and bribery. The need for a showing of motive becomes even more critical if the House were to seek to impeach Trump because of an alleged bias in favor of Putin and the Russians. Some of the most fevered commentators, including Obama's director of national intelligence, James Clapper, have claimed that Trump acts like a Russian intelligence "asset." Obama's CIA director, John Brennan, claimed that Trump's behavior toward Putin "rises to & exceeds the threshold of 'high crimes & misdemeanors'" and "was nothing short of treasonous."[84] But finding such a malign state of mind would prove near impossible. Trump could adopt a friendlier posture toward Russia because the national interest requires the United States to seek allies to counterbalance the greater threat posed by a rising China. Trump and his advisors might conclude in good faith that closer relations with Russia require reducing tensions in Eastern Europe and the Middle East. Making such foreign policy choices lies within the executive branch's constitutional authority to set foreign policy.

Or consider the overheated charges of treason. Trump could have had several reasons to discourage any investigation into behavior that, while perhaps not the most wholesome in nature, would not meet the constitutional standard. It is possible that Trump benefited from Russians hacking into the Clinton email server or planting social media misinformation. Trump may even have received past favors while a private citizen, but without any overt agreement. Recalling the way that the British government had used accusations of treason to suppress political opposition, the Framers made treason the only crime defined in the Constitution: "Treason against the United States, shall consist only in levying War against

them, or in adhering to their Enemies, giving them Aid and Comfort."[85] Further, the Constitution requires that conviction cannot stand "unless on the Testimony of two Witnesses to the same overt Act, or on Confession in open Court." Even if Russia meddled in the 2016 elections, the United States is not at war with Russia. If Congress could find evidence to support the existence of such corrupt or treasonous motives, it might have grounds to impeach President Trump. But without them, it cannot remove him.

Focus on obstruction of justice obscures the broader uses of impeachment that could present themselves. Tying "other high Crimes and Misdemeanors" to treason and bribery suggests that impeachment includes only conduct that implies a certain corruption or similar abuse of office. But the ratification debates make clear that the Framers believed impeachment would sweep more broadly. They appeared to reject the idea that "maladministration," or disagreements over policy and values, could constitute grounds for impeachment. But the Federalists also understood that the nation would face crises where an individual had failed in the duties and responsibilities of the office, even if they had committed no crime. Dereliction of duty must constitute grounds for impeachment. If Congress could impeach a president for a bad treaty, for example, it should have the power to remove him for its opposite, a bad war. As some Federalists cautioned, however, Congress should not use its power to punish bad judgment alone, but something more serious, whether it be cowardice, indifference, or even the elevation of family, social, economic, or regional interests over the public interest.

House Democrats who truly believe that Trump has conducted foreign affairs to advance himself rather than the United States have an avenue open to them. If they conclude in good faith that Trump moved the U.S. embassy in Israel from Tel Aviv to Jerusalem for religious or ethnic reasons, they could launch impeachment proceedings. If congressional critics think that Trump bombed targets in Syria or elsewhere to distract attention from his political troubles—as they once suggested of both Bill Clinton and George W. Bush—they could investigate. If Democrats find that Trump eased U.S. sanctions toward Russia because he feared blackmail or owed Moscow favors, Congress could seek to remove him. If they believe that Trump has sparked a disastrous trade war with China, or even imposed sanctions on European imports, to advance his personal finances, or even to gain reelection, they could start impeachment. And, of course, House

Democrats believed that Trump had held up foreign aid to Ukraine to gather political dirt on the Bidens, so they did impeach.

But with foreign policy, as with obstruction, Trump's state of mind makes all the difference. For most every decision, Trump has a plausible, if not compelling, reason that could explain his choices. The president could argue that he believed, as did several U.S. Congresses, that the United States should support Israeli nationhood. Trump could have bombed Syria to punish the Assad regime for using chemical weapons on his own people, as had President Obama. He could seek improved relations with Moscow to balance China. He could maintain that his mention of the Bidens in the July 25, 2019, phone call with the Ukrainian president was meant to ensure that he was not sending taxpayer money to a corrupt foreign government.

Similar problems beset impeachment for domestic dereliction of duty. If the Constitution should establish any noncriminal impeachable offenses, it should punish an intentional refusal to perform the duties and responsibilities of the office of the presidency. A good example comes from President Obama's DACA and DAPA programs. Even though he enjoys prosecutorial discretion, a president cannot decline to enforce a law because he disagrees with its policies. Obama did not promulgate his DACA and DAPA policies because he believed that the immigration laws violated the Constitution or that there were insufficient resources to enforce the immigration laws. Obama created DAPA and DACA because he believed that the current immigration law unfairly required the removal of alien children who had entered the United States illegally through no fault of their own. Proving that a president sought to suspend a law, however, rather than simply exercise prosecutorial discretion might come down to intention as well as numbers. Obama could claim that he continued to enforce the immigration laws overall. His administration used its discretion to concentrate ICE and DOJ resources on removing felons and others more dangerous to public safety than Dreamers.

Suppose President Trump had tried something similar. Like Nixon, Ford, Carter, and Reagan before him, Trump may have concluded that over-regulation was throttling the economy. Where previous presidents had responded by imposing a cost-benefit test on new regulations, Trump could have gone further by suspending enforcement of any existing regulations that failed cost-benefit analysis. Where Obama could claim that he did not enforce parts of the immigration laws because he disagreed with

the effects on aliens, Trump could argue that he disagreed with inefficient and ineffective regulations that suppressed economic growth. To impeach, Congress would have to reject the prosecutorial discretion traditionally granted to the executive and conclude instead that the president had deliberately refused to enforce the laws.

These examples show the difficulty of impeaching President Trump for the conduct set out in the Mueller report or the Ukraine affair. First, the Framers intended impeachment to remove presidents for serious abuses of power on a par with treason and bribery rather than for policy disagreements or partisan opposition. The Constitution set the vote to remove at two-thirds to prevent impeachment from becoming a partisan tool. With the Republican Party holding a majority in the Senate, Congress would not remove Trump unless the evidence was so overwhelming that 40 percent of Republican senators would vote against their party. This is not to say that the impeachment and trial must take the form of a courtroom proceeding. The Framers rejected the involvement of the federal judiciary in impeachment and clearly understood that they had given the power to political actors. But members of Congress must still obey the Constitution in their political actions, and they should not convict unless the proof exceeds a simple more likely than not standard.

Second, the Framers sought to narrow the scope of impeachment so that its use would not inflict permanent harm on the Constitution's structures. Chief among those structures was the executive branch. They did not want Congress to use impeachment to undermine the president's independence or to sap the executive power of its vigor. Trump's removal of James Comey constituted a valid use of his executive power to fire subordinates. Without that power, presidents could not ensure that agencies would follow their directives in carrying out federal law. Indeed, Trump would have had an obligation to fight any obstruction of justice charges as hard as possible, not just for his own political survival but to ensure that future presidents would not fall into a state of congressional dependency.

III. THE UKRAINE MESS

Even as the Mueller probe ended, House Democrats seized on a second controversy to launch a real impeachment proceeding. Just days after the Mueller report came to a finish, President Trump made a July 25, 2019,

phone call to Ukrainian president Volodymyr Zelensky. Democrats claim that beginning with the July 25 call, Trump sought a quid pro quo from Ukraine. Trump allegedly would release almost $400 million in U.S. foreign and military aid already earmarked by Congress for Ukraine. In exchange, Kyiv would investigate Hunter Biden's lucrative board seat with Burisma, a Ukrainian natural gas company, and Joe Biden's role in pressuring a previous Ukrainian government to protect it.

As discussed in chapter 3, the call set off impeachment hearings within a month of the first news reports of the call. The House Intelligence Committee completed its investigation in about two months, the Judiciary Committee voted out articles of impeachment in two weeks, and the House impeached before Christmas. Even though the Constitution did not require the House to provide due process, its hasty and incomplete proceedings suggest that Democrats decided not to pursue a serious inquiry. Speaker Pelosi only underscored the irregularity of the House investigation by refusing to transmit the articles of impeachment for a month in a failed effort to pressure Senate Majority Leader McConnell into allowing the presentations of new witnesses and evidence in the Senate trial. Following existing impeachment trial rules, the Senate held a proceeding that essentially consisted only of prepared statements by the House impeachment managers and Trump's defense team, with a few days of questions passed through the presiding judge, Chief Justice John Roberts. The Senate could have based its February 5, 2020, decision to acquit solely on the ground that the House had failed to conduct a fair, thorough investigation before exercising its most awesome constitutional power.

Congress has never removed an American president from office. The House had impeached only two presidents, Andrew Johnson in 1868 and Bill Clinton in 1998, but the Senate acquitted them both. Trump's impeachment in 2019 and his trial in 2020 followed the same pattern. Only Nixon would likely have been removed in the Watergate scandal if the House had impeached and the Senate held a trial.

By fighting his impeachment, Trump stood for more than just maintaining the constitutional legacies of his predecessors. Johnson sought to frustrate Congress's post–Civil War plans by ending Reconstruction early. Even though he survived, Johnson failed to alter the course of Reconstruction. Clinton sought to conceal a sordid affair with a young White House intern, among other scandals. He remained in office, with little effect on

the nation's system of governance. Trump's struggle with House Democrats was not just about self-preservation. His successful defense had the effect of preserving the right of future presidents to conduct foreign policy and to manage the executive branch.

The 2019 impeachment first raised the question of procedure. Even as they rushed headlong into their unavoidable constitutional crash, Trump and Pelosi might have agreed on the impeachment inquiry's process. Contrary to the president's claims, the Constitution does not require the House to be "fair" in its probe. But House leaders should still have furnished the president with due process. Otherwise, the impeachment proceedings could not persuade the Senate or the American people of the case against Trump. That is ultimately what happened.

Both sides staked out extreme constitutional positions from the start. In an October 8, 2019, letter, White House counsel Pat Cipollone declared that the president would refuse to cooperate with the inquiry or even recognize its legality. Cipollone accused the House of "acting contrary to the Constitution of the United States and all past bipartisan precedent" and of designing an inquiry that "violates fundamental fairness and constitutionally mandated due process." Claiming that any allegations against Trump were "baseless," Cipollone informed Pelosi that neither the president nor his administration "would participate in your partisan and unconstitutional inquiry."[86] Trump's private counsel, Rudy Giuliani, was equally critical of the House. "You look at all the irregularities, you can come to the conclusion that this is an illicit hearing," he said the next day. "This is the first time that a president hasn't had the ability to have his party to call witnesses in the preliminary phase. It sounds like they're singling him out for unfair treatment."[87]

Even while adopting an absolutist constitutional position, Trump still signaled an openness to compromise. Even though he attacked the House for running a "kangaroo court," the president said a week later that he might cooperate if the House voted to approve the impeachment inquiry and provided some procedures. "Yeah, that sounds O.K.," he told reporters. "We would if they give us our rights. It depends."[88] Trump and Cipollone had half a point. The House acted at odds with the Nixon and Clinton precedents. Rather than hold a House vote to launch impeachment, Pelosi simply gave her public blessing to ongoing committees' probes into President Trump's Ukraine machinations. She did not have the House vote

to authorize the impeachment inquiry until a month after the impeachment inquiry began.[89] Unlike Watergate, the Democratic House committee
chairs did not create a bipartisan staff, nor did they grant the president (or
the Republican minority) the right to have counsel present, cross-examine
witnesses, call their own witnesses, subpoena evidence, or present competing arguments and facts. Democrats threatened to ignore any executive
privilege raised by administration witnesses. "Any failure to appear," one
committee chair informed a career State Department official, "shall constitute evidence of obstruction."

Despite these hardball tactics, Pelosi had the Constitution on her side.
Article I gives the House "the sole Power of Impeachment" and the right
to "determine the Rules of its Proceedings." It does not place any limits on
the power. Because of this sparse text, the House may run its impeachment
inquiry in whatever manner it wishes. In 1868, the House voted to impeach
Johnson only three days after he unilaterally fired the secretary of war.[90] If
the Watergate or Whitewater hearings provided presidents with any rights,
they came as a matter of legislative grace, not constitutional right.

Supreme Court precedent affirms the House's broad discretion. In *Nixon
v. United States* (1993), the justices considered parallel constitutional language that gives the Senate "the sole Power to try all Impeachments." A
federal judge argued that his removal violated the Constitution and that
he had not received a real trial with due process rights. Writing for a 9–0
Court, Chief Justice Rehnquist held that the word "sole" ousted the judiciary's right of review. The Senate was to operate "independently and
without assistance or interference."[91] The House's "sole" power to impeach
excludes judicial review of impeachment too.

The White House, however, had institutional politics on its side. If the
House had sought seriously to remove the president, it should have granted
Trump more rights. Holding a vote of the House to authorize the investigation held only symbolic value. The real benefits would have come in the
day-to-day conduct of the probe. Democrats should have invited the White
House and the Republican minority to witness interviews and to review
all documentary evidence. They should have provided all witnesses with
the right to counsel. They should have recognized all valid privileges. They
should have bent over backward to give Trump and House Republicans the
opportunity to participate, such as by cross-examination. A defendant's
right to confront his or her accusers traces to the very beginnings of West-

ern civilization. In a 1988 case, Justice Scalia quoted St. Paul in Acts 25:16: "It is not the manner of the Romans to deliver any man up to die before the accused has met his accusers face to face, and has been given a chance to defend himself against the charges."[92]

Pelosi could argue that Trump's demands go beyond anything required by Article II's Impeachment Clause. The House plays the role of a prosecutor, who does not bring defendants along to meet witnesses and see evidence. That comparison does not fit, however, because prosecutors also do not hold hearings to air their evidence in public, nor do they engage in majority and minority questioning of witnesses. The division of authority between the House and Senate creates an even weightier responsibility. Under the existing rules, the Senate holds only a pale imitation of a trial. Individual senators cannot speak, question witnesses, or test evidence. They never debate the meaning of "high crimes and misdemeanors." House managers present their case in speeches, the president's lawyers make closing statements, and the senators vote. Treating senators as silent jurors, a Senate trial creates no forum for the testing of the witnesses or the evidence.

Because of the Senate's obsolete rules, the House impeachment process provided the only opportunity for the American people to weigh the factual evidence and the legal arguments against President Trump. That magnified the importance of providing Trump with due process rights, which would have given the public greater faith in a decision to impeach. Even if the Senate acquitted, the House's bulletproofed judgment that Trump committed a "high crime or misdemeanor" would surely affect the looming November 2020 election, which the Framers expected to make the ultimate decision to remove a president.

Trump's impeachment also gave the Senate the opportunity to reform its antiquated rules for the trial. Under existing Senate procedures, the trial produced the worst of both worlds. When the House has a flimsy case, the Senate must still put the country through a wrenching, divisive trial without any opportunity to immediately dismiss the case. When the House has a strong case, senators must sit silently by without any chance to participate directly in the trial. Allowing a real trial would have improved the decision-making over whether to fire Trump and would have made the Congress more responsive and accountable to the American people.

With House Democrats swiftly marching to impeachment in the course

of just three months, senators could have attended to the defects revealed by Clinton's 1998 trial. Those rules give senators a passive role: they cannot reject the House's decision to send an impeachment over, they must sit and listen to House prosecutors and White House defense lawyers without making a peep, they never directly see or examine witnesses or documents, and they never reach a conclusive judgment about the meaning of "high Crimes and Misdemeanors."[93]

As early as October 2019, Senate majority leader Mitch McConnell properly recognized that existing Senate rules automatically required a trial if the House impeached. Some conservative commentators argued that Senate Republicans should slow-walk the process. They may have hoped for a repeat of their success in holding open the seat of Supreme Court Justice Antonin Scalia by refusing to schedule a vote for Obama's nominee, Merrick Garland. If Republicans could have delayed a trial indefinitely, or at least until after the 2020 elections, Trump would never face removal from office at all.

Nothing in the constitutional text required the Senate to consider a House impeachment promptly, or even at all. The Senate could have postponed consideration of a House impeachment indefinitely—say, until after the 2020 presidential election. Just as a court need not schedule a trial upon a prosecutor's wishes, so the Senate could suit its own convenience, not just that of the House. Or the Senate could simply have voted to reject the case, much as a court can find that a plaintiff has no legal case even if all the facts are accepted as true. The House may have proven that Trump had indeed asked Ukraine for a favor that would have benefited him personally, but the Senate could conclude that the facts did not rise to the level of treason, bribery, or other high crime and misdemeanor.

Under its own rules, the Senate gave up its constitutional flexibility. Upon receiving the House's articles of impeachment, the Senate had to "proceed to the consideration" of the articles.[94] It had to remain in session every day "until final judgment shall be rendered." These rules senselessly required the Senate to move immediately to a trial no matter how meritless or partisan the House's case for impeachment. Suppose the House impeached Trump for a difference over foreign policy where the president had done nothing wrong, as the White House argued throughout. Even then, the Senate had to go to a trial that consumed all of the air in our nation's political system.

Trump critics should also have supported reform. Under the existing rules, individual senators could not debate the substance of impeachment at any length. They never questioned witnesses, never tested documentary evidence, and never reached an interpretation of "high Crimes and Misdemeanors." While senators played the role of impartial jurors, their silence curbed debate and diminished political accountability. A real trial would have allowed the American people not just to see Trump's impeachment but to judge it as well. Under current Senate rules, the trial only became a trailer for the main show of the House impeachment hearings.

Trump's impeachment, of course, did not turn on process. Many Republican senators, such as Tennessee senator Lamar Alexander, acquitted because they concluded that the facts claimed by the House—even if true—did not justify removal. Because impeachment ended without removal by the Senate—following the pattern of Johnson and Clinton—Democrats could be blamed for dragging the nation through a futile ordeal. Trump could claim the acquittal proved his innocence, which he immediately proclaimed the day after the Senate's verdict. The waste of the people's time and the diversion of attention and resources from other national problems might well bring about Democrats' worst nightmare: Trump's reelection.

Overall, the hearings were relatively monotonous and made little progress on substance. Few people changed their minds after watching weeks of testimony. In the televised hearings in the House Intelligence Committee, distinguished U.S. diplomats—such as acting ambassador to Ukraine William Taylor and Deputy Assistant Secretary of State George Kent—carefully and unemotionally described what they witnessed. Intelligence Committee chairman Adam Schiff (D–Calif.) fought with Republican committee members who questioned his exclusion of their witnesses and lines of questioning.

But the facts remained the same. On July 25, President Trump made a phone call to Ukrainian president Volodymyr Zelensky. In the course of the conversation, Trump asked for "a favor," according to a rough transcript released by the White House. The favor? That Zelensky investigate why Ukrainian prosecutors had not investigated the appointment of the unqualified Hunter Biden (son of then vice president Joe Biden) to a cushy spot on the board of the Burisma natural gas firm—reportedly at a salary of about $50,000 per month. The White House temporarily delayed nearly $400 million in U.S. foreign and military aid to Ukraine until the public

announcement of the investigations. But the Ukrainians never announced or conducted any investigations, and the White House eventually released the funds. As a result, Trump provided far more effective assistance for Ukraine's struggle against Russian aggression than President Obama did.

Most of this story was already widely known, thanks to Democratic legislative malpractice. House Democrats had conducted depositions of Kent, Taylor, Alexander Vindman, Gordon Sondland, Fiona Hill, and others behind closed doors, with little participation by the minority Republicans. But Democrats then released the witnesses' written testimony, after earlier leaking the high points of the questioning. With no new testimony, and civil servants doing their best to be bland and nonpartisan (which, after all, is their job), the hearings only repeated what the news media had already broadcast weeks before. The televised hearings also provided few critical facts because of the White House's decision weeks before to release the rough transcript of the July 25 Trump–Zelensky call. The White House's move reduced much of the public testimony to providing color and context to facts already known.

The speed of the House impeachment proceedings prevented the thorough investigation demanded by a decision of such constitutional magnitude. Democrats had difficulty showing that Trump had demanded a true quid pro quo. The July 25 transcript showed that Trump had asked Ukraine for the "favor" of looking into whether a Ukrainian-linked cybersecurity company had anything to do with interference in the 2016 elections. While this conspiracy theory of Ukrainian meddling makes no sense and does not square with the facts, a request for further investigation seems within the national interest and not just to Trump's personal benefit. If Trump had asked Ukraine to help with a U.S. investigation into Russian meddling in the 2016 election, it seems beyond doubt that such a favor would have equally fallen within the scope of U.S. national interests. Just because information might benefit Trump does not mean that it does not benefit the nation as well.

But Democrats faced even more difficult challenges in showing a quid pro quo for looking into the Bidens' Ukraine activities. The July 25 transcript does not even make Trump's request clear. "There's a lot of talk about Biden's son, that Biden stopped the prosecution," Trump said on the call. "A lot of people want to find out about that so whatever you can do with

the Attorney General would be great." He finished by telling Zelensky that "Biden went around bragging that he stopped the prosecution so if you can look into it . . . It sounds horrible to me."[95] Viewed in a fair light, Trump seems to be rambling here, and it is unclear what Trump wants Zelensky to do—whatever it is, it does not seem to take the form of a demand. But more importantly, Trump never mentions in the phone call that he has ordered a hold on foreign and military aid for Ukraine, and it appears that Ukraine did not even learn about the delay until more than a month later. Ukraine's president has said that he did not feel any coercion had occurred, and he never publicly announced an investigation into the Bidens or Burisma. It is hard to pull off a quid pro quo if the holder of the quo doesn't know about the quid.

We do not know whether Trump was pursuing corruption in the national interest or seeking information on Biden for his own political advantage. This is where the House Democrats failed in their constitutional duty. They limited their investigation to the questioning of career Foreign Service and National Security Council staff, plus a few midlevel political appointees and ambassadors. None of them apparently had ever discussed Ukraine with President Trump or had direct evidence of a corrupt quid pro quo. A thorough investigation should have sought the testimony of those who would have directly spoken with the president about Ukraine. The list of indispensable witnesses includes former acting White House chief of staff Mick Mulvaney, former national security advisor John Bolton, and Secretary of State Mike Pompeo. While these officials initially claimed executive privilege, Congress has many tools at its disposal to overcome such obstacles or to persuade presidents to waive their right to secrecy. In past impeachment inquiries, not to mention regular oversight hearings, Congress has managed to convince presidents to allow their subordinates to cooperate with Congress.

House Democrats would not wait for the courts or for political negotiations. Instead, they followed a political schedule of concluding impeachment by Christmas and starting a trial in the new year. Some clearly feared that Trump would be reelected if they did not remove him swiftly, while others may have calculated that drawing impeachment out into 2020 could help Trump win reelection. House Democrats could offer no good, nonpolitical reason to halt the impeachment investigation before Congress

had a chance to hear from the most important, relevant witnesses. Putting these calculations before investigatory thoroughness betrayed the politics behind Trump's impeachment.

The Framers understood that impeachment would cause political disruption. Because of impeachment's effect on the body politic, it should only occur when the Constitution truly calls for it. Carrying out a truncated impeachment investigation guaranteed that the Senate would acquit and that the nation's political time and energy would go to waste. The Constitution creates impeachment for extraordinary circumstances, and it accordingly calls on the House and the Senate to conduct their roles with seriousness and diligence. The Framers would have seen the use of impeachment simply to satisfy a partisan interest or to engage in a symbolic protest as a misuse of an awesome power. By not taking their time, calling all of the relevant witnesses, and undertaking a careful review of the facts and the law, House Democrats saw impeachment as a political weapon, rather than as a constitutional duty.

The public hearings and the news coverage also ignored the central question of whether the facts justified President Trump's impeachment and removal from office. By the end of the hearings, Democrats were accusing Trump of committing bribery rather than of seeking a quid pro quo. This chapter's review of the founding history, however, indicates that any exchange of benefits between Trump and Zelensky would not have risen to the level of bribery contemplated by the Impeachment Clause.

To be sure, the *type* of conduct at issue involving President Trump and Ukraine could provide the grounds for impeachment. But House Democrats focused instead on bribery. While the writers of the Constitution thought bribery occurred when a foreign nation paid off the president, it seems unlikely that they had in mind the opposite case where the United States bribed a foreign official. Under the Washington and Adams administrations, the United States made payments to the Barbary States to allow U.S. shipping to ply the Mediterranean free from seizure.[96] Today, the CIA bribes foreign officials for information all the time. The Framers clearly believed that the bribery of the Impeachment Clause occurred when a foreign nation bribed a U.S. official, but not vice versa.

House Democrats' claim that Trump violated the federal bribery statute missed the point. Federal law does make it a crime if someone "corruptly gives, offers, or promises anything of value to any public official" to influ-

ence their decisions.[97] The law also makes it a crime when a public official "corruptly demands, seeks, receives, accepts, or agrees to receive or accept anything of value." As recently interpreted by the Supreme Court, the federal bribery statute does not even prohibit all quid pro quos between donors and politicians. Unless the latter performs a specific "official act" in exchange for the bribe, it is doubtful that the quid pro quo with Ukraine, even if true, would meet the Court's heightened standard.[98] And at the time of the Constitution's drafting and ratification, the federal bribery statute did not even exist—Congress would not pass one until 1962. Congress could not alter the meaning of bribery in the Impeachment Clause by passing its own bribery statute. As Chief Justice Marshall explained in *Marbury v. Madison*, Congress cannot enact laws that seek to change the meaning of terms in the Constitution. Here Congress could not expand the Constitution's definition of "bribery" for purposes of impeachment.

Applying the lessons of history indicates that Trump's conduct would not rise to the level of bribery as used in the Impeachment Clause. Impeachable bribery must rise to a level of serious abuse of power similar to that of treason. Hamilton explained that treason, bribery, or other high crime and misdemeanor must amount to an offense against the whole body politic. Federalists illustrated their argument with the example of a foreign state bribing a U.S. president to go to war or not go to war. They would have had difficulty finding the Trump–Zelensky phone call to have risen to the same level of seriousness as the annual payments from Louis XIV to Charles II.

Democrats would have had more success in arguing that Trump's conduct qualified as a "high crime or misdemeanor." The Framers openly worried about a president who might use his foreign affairs powers for personal or political gain. Recall that Federalists illustrated "high crimes and misdemeanors" with the example of a president who negotiated a treaty that sacrificed the national interest for personal, partisan, or regional advantage. It is on this point where the House impeachment hearings proved so disappointing. House Democrats did not convincingly explain why a quid pro quo that never succeeded (assuming the facts in the worst light for the White House) and that involved a distant country at the border of Eastern Europe justified impeachment.

House Democrats never successfully rebutted the White House's defenses of Trump's conduct. While the administration delayed foreign aid

to Ukraine, it eventually released the funds in September 2019. Trump justified the delay on the government's right to withhold funds that would fall prey to foreign corruption. The White House argued that in referring to the Bidens, Trump had merely resorted to shorthand in his own mind for Ukrainian government corruption. House Democrats had to show why Trump's true motive was to seek dirt on his likely opponent in the 2020 presidential race, with evidence that at least was clear and convincing, if not beyond a reasonable doubt (the standard required in criminal jury trials). Instead, House Democrats impeached based on shaky inferences of the president's state of mind based on no direct testimony by the president or, indeed, by any witness who had directly and credibly discussed Ukraine with him.

This is not to argue that Trump deserved no blame for the Ukraine affair or that he might have had ulterior political motives in mind. This chapter instead only underscores that impeachment cannot serve as the catchall remedy for all executive misdeeds. Our nation's founders believed that impeachment should only come as a last resort. They expected that the American people would hold a president accountable for any abuses of power at the ballot box. Defenders of the Constitution designed impeachment to be a rare event, especially by making the requirement for removal a two-thirds vote of the Senate for treason, bribery, or other high crimes or misdemeanors rather than "maladministration," in their words. The Federalists worried that the president otherwise would become too dependent on a Congress eager to use impeachment to fight political and partisan disputes. Trump's successful defeat of impeachment may well have preserved the independence of the presidency for his successors, even as it involved such political damage that it could lead to his loss on the November 2020 ballot.

CONCLUSIONS

Before we launched special counsels, criminal probes, and impeachment proceedings, we should have considered the long-lasting damage to the presidency. The Framers learned all too well the failures brought by a lack of independence and energy in the executive. In Article II of the Constitution, they sought to cure the disease by vesting "the executive power" in the president, which they understood to include the power over national

security and foreign affairs as well as the execution of the laws. Both the Mueller probe and the Ukraine impeachment may have lowered Trump in the minds of the public, but they could not lead to the president's removal from office.

Critics might have felt satisfaction in the political symbolism of Trump's impeachment, but it could come at the cost of the independence and vigorousness necessary for a successful president. Watergate may have properly forced Nixon's resignation, but it also led to a period of congressional supremacy that contributed to the failed Ford and Carter presidencies. The nation would have to wait for Ronald Reagan to use a rejuvenated executive branch to jump-start the economy and to restore America's standing in the world. Here, Trump's critics risk the same harm to the presidency, but all for the prize of inflicting political harm on a president within a year of a presidential election. Trump properly fought impeachment as hard as he did in order to prevent Congress from undermining presidential independence and sapping it of executive energy. Only the 2020 presidential elections will tell whether his defense of constitutional principle helped the nation avoid the mistakes of past impeachments.

EPILOGUE

On February 6, 2020, Donald Trump strode confidently into the East Room of the White House to give a remarkable speech in a presidential term already filled with them. He reigned at the height of his political fortunes. He had fought off an impeachment that had ended the day earlier with his acquittal. Two days before, he had given a well-received State of the Union address. Its optimistic reelection themes had so unbalanced the Democratic opposition that Nancy Pelosi visibly ripped up her copy of the speech from behind the rostrum. According to Gallup, about half of all Americans—49 percent—approved of Trump's job performance, the highest rating of his presidency.[1]

Trump spent the day celebrating his acquittal and attacking his enemies (with an emphasis on the latter). Two decades earlier, Bill Clinton had marked his own survival of impeachment by apologizing to the American people. "I want to say again to the American people how profoundly sorry I am for what I said and did to trigger these events, and the great burden they have imposed on the Congress and on the American people," Clinton said on February 12, 1999. Trump would have none of this. "We had the witch hunt that started from the day we came down the elevator," Trump said after his acquittal. "And it never really stopped. We've been going through this now for over three years. It was evil. It was corrupt. It was dirty cops. It was leakers and liars."[2]

The East Room had probably never witnessed such a raw president venting his anger in public. After insisting that the July 25 phone call was "perfect," Trump apologized only to his family for the "phony, rotten" ordeal that they were put through "by some very evil and very sick people." Of

the Mueller investigation, Trump declared that "it's all bullshit." Of Nancy Pelosi, who said that she prays for the president and the nation's leaders, he said: "I doubt she prays at all." Trump called Pelosi a "horrible person," Adam Schiff "a vicious, horrible person," James Comey "a sleazebag," and former FBI officials Peter Strzok and Lisa Page "two lowlifes." Of the Comey FBI, Trump said: "These are the crookedest, most dishonest, dirtiest people I've ever seen." Of Senator Mitt Romney, the sole Republican to vote to convict, Trump said: "The only one that voted against was a guy that can't stand the fact that he ran one of the worst campaigns in the history of the presidency." Trump finished by thanking his defense lawyers, cabinet members, and particularly Senate Majority Leader Mitch McConnell and House Minority Leader Kevin McCarthy.

But Trump left out the most important people, without whom he would not have survived. It was not the Republican senators who voted to acquit. It was not his defense team members, such as Pat Cipollone, Alan Dershowitz, Ken Starr, and Pam Bondi. It wasn't even the Fox News hosts who presented Trump's defense every night.

Trump forgot to thank the Founders. They were the ones who gave Trump a built-in constitutional advantage in any impeachment trial. With 53 Republicans holding the Senate majority, the House had to persuade 20 Republicans to vote to convict. They convinced only one. But the Founders didn't impose the two-thirds vote requirement in the Senate to protect future Trump. They did it to defend the presidency and all of its future occupants. The Framers rejected a parliamentary system in which Congress selects a prime minister who both leads the legislative majority and heads the executive branch. Their great experiment in the separation of powers took the form of a presidency with independent constitutional powers and responsibilities and separate election by the people. They feared that impeachment by simple majority vote in the House and Senate would render the president dependent on Congress, and thus deprive him of the energy, speed, and decisiveness needed for good government. The two-thirds vote requirement ensured that Democrats could not remove Trump due to partisanship, or even policy disputes. The Constitution became Trump's great shield, and in winning the impeachment battle, Trump repaid the favor by reinforcing the independence of the executive.

House Democrats knew they had little chance of winning a conviction, but proceeded with impeachment anyway. In their eagerness to bring down

Trump, Democrats transformed impeachment from a remedy for serious crimes and abuses of power into a tool of political criticism and opposition. While no doubt he was obeying every instinct for self-preservation, Trump had the institutional incentive to fight and win to prevent future Congresses from subordinating future presidents. Defeating the Mueller investigation, while also in Trump's personal self-interest, similarly defended the institution. In both the special counsel probe and impeachment, the permanent law enforcement and foreign policy bureaucracies attacked a president that they considered a threat to the national security. In overcoming their challenges, Trump did not just escape charges of wrongdoing, he also fought for the essential principle of the constitutional unity of the executive branch. If the bureaucratic resistance had succeeded, it would not just have forced Trump from office, it would also have encouraged the FBI, foreign service, and other national security staff to consider themselves independent from the elected president.

Trump critics similarly have sought to stretch or even break other important constitutional understandings in order to defeat the president. Democratic candidates have proposed to eliminate the Electoral College, even though it represents a careful melding of popular majoritarianism with a more deliberate state-based process. They seek to use personal attacks to block Trump appointments to the Supreme Court, and if they fail, propose to pack the Court with new justices. Opposition has not just followed partisan battle lines. Republicans have joined Democrats in attacking the constitutionality of Trump's immigration policies, even though they rely upon the same system of congressional delegation, executive regulation, and judicial deference that governs the administrative state. Members of both parties have also sought to counter Trump's exercise of powers, which his predecessors have long used, such as the powers to use force abroad (in Iraq and Iran) and conduct foreign policy. Even though Trump may have succeeded in defending these powers, future presidents may also learn the lesson from his travails that they can no longer trust their NSC, State Department, or Justice Department to carry out the policies upon which they won election.

In order to win reelection, Trump will have to draw even more deeply upon the Constitution. So far, his political success has depended on using the Constitution as a shield to preserve the presidency's historic prerogatives. To make the case for another term, he will have to use the Constitution

more as a sword to advance his positive agenda. Consider the economy. The day after Trump's East Room celebration, government statistics reported that the U.S. economy continued its steady growth, even as the world around us stalled. In the same month that his trial began, Trump presided over an economy that added 225,000 jobs (economists had expected only 158,000), with the unemployment rate rising slightly to 3.6 percent only because more people joined the labor force looking for work. Labor force participation hit highs unseen since before the Great Recession of 2008, with more jobs than job seekers and unemployment at 50-year lows. The Trump economy closed 2019 by adding two million new jobs and driving faster wage gains for those at the bottom than at the top. For an economy already operating beyond earlier estimates of full employment, inflation remained modest at 2.3 percent, interest rates stayed low, and the Dow Jones Industrial Average and the S&P 500 were at all-time highs.[3] In January 2020, Gallup found that Americans' confidence in the economy had tied with its record high from 2000, when the nation was in the midst of the dot-com bubble.

To foster even more favorable economic conditions, Trump must continue to call upon the powers of the presidency. With Democrat control of the House making further tax cuts unlikely, the White House will have to push its deregulatory agenda further and faster to incite more growth. Trump will have to exercise his power of reversal to repeal burdensome regulations and replace them with more business-friendly rules. He will also have to stand down in his trade wars. Using his constitutional authority to negotiate with foreign nations, he has already started making rather than breaking trade agreements. On January 29, 2020, he signed legislation approving the new U.S.–Mexico–Canada trade deal, which introduced some minor protectionism into NAFTA but kept its fundamental free trade principles intact. Just two weeks earlier, Trump agreed to a first phase trade deal with China, which called a halt to the escalating economic war with Beijing and set the stage for more serious negotiations over intellectual property theft and trade barriers next year. These two agreements reduced the uncertainty inflicted by Trump's trade wars, which had depressed investment and business activity. Trump could use his authority in foreign relations to improve economic relations with Europe and Asia as a prelude to a more unified front against China.

International economic power so far has provided the foundation for

Trump's foreign policies as well. If the American people judge Trump as they have his predecessors, they will vote based on the performance of the economy and the nation's security. While Trump has promised to wind down America's military involvement abroad, he has elevated economic sanctions into the United States' primary weapon in foreign affairs. Using powers delegated by Congress, he has tightened sanctions on Russia, Iran, North Korea, Cuba, and Venezuela to strike back at regional competitors, hostile regimes, and disruptive threats. But economic sanctions can only go so far. With Iran, for example, Trump had to resort to the president's executive and commander-in-chief powers to order the strike against General Soleimani. While critics predicted a regional conflagration, the attack appears to have stopped a series of Iranian provocations and attacks on American forces abroad. Trump may yet have to use military force in Syria, Venezuela, or North Korea to promote other foreign policy and security goals. In that case, Trump will have to draw upon the deepest sources of executive power to act with energy and speed to protect the nation.

Finally, presidential power may provide a glimpse of the political and constitutional change that Trump may have triggered. Political analysts have observed that Trump represents a realignment in American politics. Republicans may come to represent a populist nationalism suspicious of globalization, foreign entanglements, and immigration, while Democrats may evolve away from their working-class constituents to represent the cosmopolitan, educated elites in coastal cities and suburbs. Trump is already using his constitutional powers to pursue an agenda appealing to the non-college-educated middle- and lower-class families in the center of the country. But the deeper change that Trump's election may have triggered is a revolution in the nature of government. At certain periods in our history, government can become ossified and overgrown by rules and bureaucracy that have grown too distant from the wishes of the people. Jefferson, Jackson, Lincoln, FDR, and Reagan led popular movements that swept away old political orders and replaced them with new, spartan forms of government more responsive to the political times.

Trump's election may augur a similar seismic shift in government, one that extends far beyond his own personal political interests. The basic form of today's federal government can trace its origins to the New Deal. Large, expert federal bureaucracies exercising broad powers delegated by Congress continue to govern an economy and society that have evolved far

from the world of the 1930s through the 1960s. Even as America races into a twenty-first-century post-industrial society, where information has become the foundation of the most valuable goods and services, it continues to govern itself with forms suited for large, continent-spanning GMs and IBMs and their matching labor unions. Even while he recalls America to an older, more stable society, Trump may have shaken up the political system enough to allow it to adapt to the new economy of social media, networks, and AI. Presidential power provides the critical leverage to spark such significant government change, and it may be Trump's most unlikely legacy to have preserved the constitutional authorities of his office that could make such reform happen.

ACKNOWLEDGMENTS

Writing this book has proven both easier and harder than earlier ones. It has come easier because several friends and colleagues loved to debate me over Trump's every exercise of presidential power. During frequent lunches, drinks, and dinners, Jesse Choper, Jack Citrin, and Peter Schuck—no Trump lovers they—robustly challenged my views on the presidency. Their critiques of Trump forced me to respond with the arguments that became this book. They unwittingly enlisted in the Greek chorus for *Defender in Chief*; I cannot thank them enough for their patience and advice. I should give similar thanks to the liberal Berkeley students in my classes on the separation of powers, the presidency, and the Constitution. They may not agree that Trump has kept mostly within constitutional boundaries, but I hope they concede that we must preserve executive power in order for his successors to succeed.

Writing has come harder because this book will appear to defend Trump, rather than the office of the presidency. Some readers may even treat it as a brief for the Republican Party. I have attempted to explain that the controversies over Trump are more important than the man, his movement, or our partisan divides. I have never met Trump and, from all I have read and seen, I do not find him personally appealing. Philadelphians instinctively dislike brash New Yorkers. Nevertheless, in my three decades of studying the presidency, I've found much truth in Alexander Hamilton's statement that "[e]nergy in the executive is a leading character in the definition of good government." In order to achieve that energy, Hamilton observed, the executive branch must have unity, which enables "decision, activity, secrecy, and despatch." I think that protecting these qualities in the office,

273

which have brought much good to the nation and the world, outweigh the passing harm from any single individual or moment.

Several friends—Brad Barber, Victor Davis Hanson, and Steve Hayward—helped me understand the Trump presidency in this way. I thank them for many valuable conversations, made possible by right-of-center programs at Berkeley and Stanford, of all places. I also must thank two co-authors, Robert Delahunty and James Phillips, with whom I have collaborated on writing for both academic and popular audiences. I have had the honor of working with Robert since the 9/11 attacks, when we both served in the Department of Justice and saw an energetic executive in action. I am glad that we have continued to work together in academia on the presidency. I first met James as a law student at Berkeley, and I am happy to see him enter the world of law-school teaching. I hope this book shows them both their influence on my thinking. I must also thank Erwin Chemerinsky at Berkeley Law, Robert Doar at the American Enterprise Institute, and Tom Gilligan at the Hoover Institution of Stanford University for creating the most hospitable circumstances for research and writing.

I must thank many people who shepherded this book from vague ideas to the printed text. Keith Urban, Dylan Colligan, and Jonathan Bronitsky of Javelin transformed a series of debates into an organized proposal with a focused theme. My editors Adam Bellow, Kevin Reilly, and George Witte of St. Martin's Press transformed an outline into a book; they especially helped slim down a weighty manuscript into a trim, readable work. Jennifer Fernandez at St. Martin's went over the manuscript with an eagle's eye. I received outstanding research help from Helena Gu, Mitchell Horn, Min Soo Kim, Florence Liu, Allison Murray, and Dee Pugh. Drew Kloss ably kept all the trains on time. They saved me from many errors; the remaining ones are mine alone. I reserve my deepest thanks for my family. I am grateful to my wife, Elsa, who supported me in this endeavor as she has in all others for more than three decades. I thank my brother, Christopher Yoo, and his family and my mother, Sook Hee Yoo, M.D., who should enjoy this book more than anyone.

NOTES

INTRODUCTION

1. Read Nancy Pelosi's Remarks on Articles of Impeachment, N.Y. Times, Dec. 5, 2019.

2. Schumer Floor Remarks on the Announcement of a Formal House Impeachment Inquiry of President Trump, Sept. 25, 2019.

3. Hillary Clinton: Trump is an "illegitimate president," Wash. Post, Sept. 26, 2019.

4. Kaine Statement on Syria Airstrikes, Apr. 13, 2018.

5. Annie Linskey, A Critic's Guide: Five Ways Trump May Have Violated the Constitution, Boston Globe, Jan. 31, 2017.

6. John Yoo, Crisis and Command: A History of Executive Power from George Washington to the Present xvii–xviii (2011).

7. John Yoo, Executive Power Run Amok, N.Y. Times, Feb. 6, 2017.

8. Alexandra Ocasio-Cortez (@AOC), Twitter (Oct. 6, 2018), https://twitter.com/aoc/status/1048667886527627265.

9. John Dingell, I Served in Congress Longer Than Anyone. Here's How to Fix It, The Atlantic, Dec. 4, 2018; Parker Richards, The People v. the U.S. Senate, The Atlantic, Oct. 20, 2018.

CHAPTER 1: "YOU'RE HIRED!"

1. State and County QuickFacts: Wyoming, California Census Bureau (2010), https://www.census.gov/quickfacts/fact/table/WY,CA/POP010210.

2. Federal Elections Commission, Federal Elections 2016: Election Results for the U.S. President, the U.S. Senate and the U.S. House of Representatives 6 (2017).

3. Time to End the Electoral College, N.Y. Times, Dec. 19, 2016.

4. Sarah D. Wire, California Sen. Barbara Boxer Files Long Shot Bill to Scrap the Electoral College System, L.A. Times, Nov. 15, 2016.

5. Donald J. Trump (@realDonaldTrump), Twitter (Nov. 6, 2012), https://twitter.com/realdonaldtrump/status/266038556504494082.

6. Let the People Pick the President, N.Y. Times, Nov. 7, 2017.

7. George Will, The President Who Knew Too Little About the Electoral College, National Review Online (May 3, 2018), https://www.nationalreview.com/2018/05/president-trump-electoral-college-complaints-unfounded/.

8. Akhil Amar, The Troubling Reason the Electoral College Exists, Time, Nov. 10, 2016.

9. Paul Finkelman, The Proslavery Origins of the Electoral College, 23 Cardozo L. Rev. 1145, 1147 (2002).

10. Akhil R. Amar, Some Thoughts on the Electoral College: Past, Present, and Future, 33 Ohio N. Univ. L. Rev. 467, 470 (2007).

11. Finkelman, supra note 9, at 1155.

12. Amar, supra note 10, at 471.

13. Federalist No. 68, at 351 (George W. Carey & James McClellan eds. 2001) (Alexander Hamilton).

14. Shlomo Slonim, The Electoral College at Philadelphia: The Evolution of an Ad Hoc Congress for the Selection of a President, 73 J. Am. Hist. 35, 37 (1986).

15. 1 Records of the Federal Convention of 1787, at 21 (Max Farrand ed. 1911) [hereinafter Farrand's Records] .

16. Id. at 68.

17. Id.

18. See Gordon Wood, The Creation of the American Republic 1776–1787, at 403–25 (1969).

19. Slonim, supra note 14, at 37–38.

20. 1 Farrand's Records, supra note 15, at 77.

21. John Yoo, Crisis and Command: A History of Executive Power from George Washington to George W. Bush 24 (2010); see also Jack Rakove, Original Meanings: Politics and Ideas in the Making of the Constitution 263 (1996).

22. 2 Farrand's Records, supra note 15, at 29.

23. Id. at 29–30.

24. Id. at 31.

25. See, e.g., George Mason, Objections to the Constitution (Oct. 7, 1787), reprinted in 13 Documentary History of the Ratification of the Constitution 349 (John P. Kaminski & Gaspare J. Saladino eds. 1986).

26. 2 Farrand's Records, supra note 15, at 32.

27. Id. at 32.

28. Id. at 52.

29. Id. at 56.

30. Id.

31. Id. at 58.

32. 1 Farrand's Records, supra note 15, at 561.

33. 2 Farrand's Records, supra note 15, at 101.

34. Slonim, supra note 14, at 44–45.

35. 2 Farrand's Records, supra note 15, at 109.

36. Id. at 111.

37. Id. at 112.

38. Id.

39. Rakove, supra note 21, at 263.

40. 2 Farrand's Records, supra note 15, at 500.

41. See Rakove, supra note 21, at 268–75.

42. Federalist No. 68, supra note 13, at 352.

43. Id. at 353.

44. Id. at 354.

45. Martin Diamond, The Electoral College and the American Idea of Democracy 6 (1977).

46. Bradford R. Clark, Separation of Powers as a Safeguard of Federalism, 79 Tex. L. Rev. 1321, 1329 (2001).

47. See John McGinnis & Michael Rappaport, Our Supermajoritarian Constitution, 80 Tex. L. Rev. 703 (2002); John McGinnis & Michael Rappaport, Originalism and the Good Constitution (2013).

48. See generally Elmer Griffith, The Rise and Development of the Gerrymander (1907); Samuel Issacharoff et al., The Law of Democracy: Legal Structure of the Political Process (5th ed. 2016).

49. See Sai Prakash & John Yoo, People ≠ Legislature, 39 Harv. J. L. & Pub. Pol'y 342 (2017).

50. Judith Best, The Case Against Direct Election of the President: A Defense of the Electoral College 55–57 (1971).

51. Wood, supra note 18, at 550–52.

52. Federalist No. 68, supra note 13, at 354.

53. James W. Ceaser, Presidential Selection: Theory and Development 1–40 (1979).

54. Id. at 32–33.

CHAPTER 2: "THE END OF MY PRESIDENCY"

1. Aaron Blake, The Justice Department's case against James B. Comey, annotated, Wash. Post, May 9, 2017.

2. Joshua Barajas et al., How lawmakers are reacting to FBI director Comey's firing, Pub. Broad. Serv., May 9, 2017.

3. PBS NewsHour, Senate Minority Leader Schumer news conference on FBI Director Comey's dismissal (May 9, 2017), https://www.youtube.com/watch?v=Fa_If1qrxIw.

4. Office of the Inspector General, U.S. Department of Justice, Report of Investigation of Former Bureau of Investigation Director James Comey's Disclosure of Sensitive Investigative Information and Handling of Certain Memoranda (August 2019).

5. Devlin Barrett et al., Comey: White House lied about me, FBI, Wash. Post, June 8, 2017.

6. Andrew C. McCarthy, Ball of Collusion: The Plot to Rig an Election and Destroy a Presidency 29 (2019).

7. Office of the Deputy Att'y Gen., Order No. 3915–2017, Appointment of Special Counsel to Investigate Russian Interference with the 2016 Presidential Election and Related Matters (May 17, 2017)

8. 2 Robert S. Mueller III, U.S. Dep't of Justice, Report on the Investigation into Russian Interference in the 2016 Presidential Election 78 (2019).

9. Id. at 84–87.

10. Id. at 90–96.

11. Special Counsel Independence and Integrity Act, S. 2644, 115th Cong., 2d Sess. (2018).

12. Chris Megerian, Republicans avoid confronting Trump over whether he can fire special counsel, L.A. Times, April 27, 2018.

13. Id.

14. Donald Trump, Remarks by President Trump Before Meeting with Senior Military Leadership (April 9, 2018).

15. Bradley Smith, Those Payments to Women Were Unseemly. That Doesn't Mean They Were Illegal, Wash. Post, Aug. 22, 2018.

16. United States v. Paul J. Manafort Jr. & Richard W. Gates III, United States District Court for the District of Columbia, Case 1:17-cr-00201, Indictment, Document No. 13, filed Oct. 30, 2017.

17. Myers v. United States, 272 U.S. 52, 118 (1926).

18. Morrison v. Olson, 487 U.S. 654, 690 (1988).

19. Id. at 699 (Scalia, J., dissenting).

20. Id.

21. Brett Samuels, Trump lashes out at Mueller for alleged conflicts of interest, The Hill, July 29, 2018.

22. 487 U.S. 654, 705 (Scalia, J., dissenting). These textual arguments are more fully explored in Steven G. Calabresi & Saikrishna Prakash, The President's Power to Execute the Laws, 104 Yale L.J. 541 (1994); Steven G. Calabresi & Kevin H. Rhodes, The Structural Constitution: Unitary Executive, Plural Judiciary, 105 Harv. L. Rev. 1153 (1992); Gary Lawson, The Rise and Rise of the Administrative State, 107 Harv. L. Rev. 1231 (1994); Lee S. Liberman, Morrison v. Olson: A Formalist Perspective on Why the Court Was Wrong, 38 Am U. L. Rev. 313 (1989); Thomas W. Merrill, The Constitutional Principle of Separation of Powers, 1991 Sup. Ct. Rev. 225.

23. Federalist No. 75, at 388 (George W. Carey & James McClellan eds. 2001) (Alexander Hamilton).

24. See Robert J. Delahunty & John Yoo, Dream On: The Obama Administration's Nonenforcement of Immigration Laws, the DREAM Act, and the Take Care Clause, 91 Tex. L. Rev. 781, 798–800 (2013).

25. 30 The Writings of George Washington 334 (John C. Fitzpatrick ed. 1939).

26. Myers v. United States, 272 U.S. 52, 163–64 (1926).

27. See generally Michael Stokes Paulsen, The Most Dangerous Branch: Executive Power to Say What the Law Is, 83 Geo. L.J. 217 (1994).

28. Saikrishna B. Prakash & John C. Yoo, The Origins of Judicial Review, 70 U. Chi. L. Rev. 887, 914 (2003).

29. See Griffin B. Bell & Ronald J. Ostrow, Taking Care of the Law 28 (1982).

30. Ethics in Government Act of 1978, Pub. L. No. 95–521, 92 Stat. 1824.

31. Morrison v. Olson, 487 U.S. 654, 691 (1988).

32. Id. at 691–92.

33. See, e.g., Lawrence Lessig & Cass R. Sunstein, The President and the Administration, 94 Colum. L. Rev. 1, 15–16 (1994).

34. See, e.g., Martin S. Flaherty, The Most Dangerous Branch, 105 Yale L.J. 1725 (1996); A. Michael Froomkin, The Imperial Presidency's New Vestments, 88 Nw. U. L. Rev. 1346 (1994).

35. Lessig & Sunstein, supra note 33, at 48–50.

36. Id. at 67.

37. See John Yoo, Crisis and Command: A History of Executive Power from George Washington to George W. Bush 81–91 (2010).

38. Alexander Hamilton, Pacificus No. 1, June 28, 1793, reprinted in The Pacificus–Helvidius Debates of 1793–94, at 13 (Morton J. Frisch ed. 2007).

39. See John Yoo, The Powers of War and Peace: The Constitution and Foreign Affairs After 9/11, at 215–92 (2005).

40. See Delahunty & Yoo, supra note 24, at 802.

41. INS v. Chadha, 462 U.S. 919 (1983).

42. Federalist No. 70, at 362 (George W. Carey & James McClellan eds. 2001) (Alexander Hamilton).

43. Id. at 363.

44. 2 Documentary History of the Ratification of the Constitution 495 (Merrill Jensen, John P. Kaminski, & Gaspare J. Saladino eds. 1976).

45. Id. at 579.

46. Federalist No. 70, supra note 42, at 366–69.

47. Federalist No. 71, at 369 (George W. Carey & James McClellan eds. 2001) (Alexander Hamilton).

48. Federalist No. 73, at 379 (George W. Carey & James McClellan eds. 2001) (Alexander Hamilton).

49. Federalist No. 75, at 388 (George W. Carey & James McClellan eds. 2001) (Alexander Hamilton).

50. Federalist No. 73, at 380 (George W. Carey & James McClellan eds. 2001) (Alexander Hamilton).

51. Akhil Reed Amar, America's Constitution: A Biography 184 (2005).

52. Federalist No. 73, at 381 (George W. Carey & James McClellan eds. 2001) (Alexander Hamilton).

53. See, e.g., Michael Rappaport, The Unconstitutionality of "Signing and Not-Enforcing," 16 Wm. & Mary Bill of Rights J. 113 (2007).

54. See Prakash & Yoo, supra note 28.

55. 2 Documentary History, supra note 44, at 450–51; Amar, supra note 51 at 179.

56. Federalist No. 74, at 385–86 (George W. Carey & James McClellan eds. 2001) (Alexander Hamilton).

57. Myers v. United States, 272 U.S. 52, 132 (1926).

58. Id. at 134.

59. Printz v. United States, 521 U.S. 898 (1997).

60. Id. at 922.

61. Federalist No. 15, at 72 (George W. Carey & James McClellan eds. 2001) (Alexander Hamilton).

62. Harvey C. Mansfield Jr., Taming the Prince: The Ambivalence of Modern Executive Power 142, 144 (1989).

63. John Locke, The Second Treatise of Civil Government, in Two Treatises of Government § 143–44, at 194–95 (Thomas Cook ed. 1965) (1690).

64. Charles Louis de Secondat, Baron Montesquieu, Spirit of the Laws, bk. 11, ch. 6 (Thomas Nugent trans. 1949) (1748).

65. Id. at 70.

66. 1 William Blackstone, Commentaries on the Laws of England *160.

67. Id. at *249–50.

68. See Evarts B. Greene, The Provincial Governor in the English Colonies of North America 139 (1898); Oliver W. Hammonds, The Attorney General in the American Colonies, in 2 Anglo-American Legal History Series 1–20 (1939); Julius Goebel Jr. & T. Raymond Naughton, Law Enforcement in Colonial New York: A Study in Criminal Procedure 367–78 (1944).

69. Saikrishna Prakash, The Essential Meaning of Executive Power, U. Ill. L. Rev. 701, 757–58 (2003).

70. The Essex Result, in 1 American Political Writings 1760–1805, at 480, 494, 501 (Charles S. Huneman & Donald S. Lutz eds. 1983).

71. 1 Records of the Federal Convention of 1787, at 21 (Max Farrand ed. 1911) [hereinafter Farrand's Records].

72. Id. at 244.

73. Id. at 66.

74. Id. at 67.

75. Prakash, Essential Meaning, supra note 69, at 771–72.

76. 2 Farrand's Records, supra note 71, at 35.

77. Id. at 34.

78. Federalist No. 44, at 235 (George W. Carey & James McClellan eds. 2001) (James Madison).

79. 4 The Debates in the Several State Conventions of the Adoption of the Federal Constitution 58–59 (Jonathan Elliot ed. 1836).

80. The Federalist No. 70, supra note 42, at 362 (Alexander Hamilton).

81. The Federalist No. 75, supra note 49, at 388 (Alexander Hamilton).

82. Glenn A. Phelps, George Washington and American Constitutionalism 145 (1993); see also Leonard D. White, The Federalists 27 (1948).

83. 1 Cong. Register 354 (May 19, 1789).

84. Jerry Mashaw, Creating the Administrative Constitution: The Lost One Hundred Years of American Administrative Law (2012); Lessig & Sunstein, supra note 33; Martin S. Flaherty, The Most Dangerous Branch, 105 Yale L.J. 1725 (1996).

85. Lessig & Sunstein, supra note 33, at 71–74.

86. Abraham Lincoln, First Debate with Stephen A. Douglas, Aug. 21, 1858, 3 Collected Works of Abraham Lincoln 27 (Roy P. Basler ed. 1953).

CHAPTER 3: "I NEED LOYALTY!"

1. H.R. Rep. No. 116–346, at 124 (2019).

2. McCarthy, Ball of Collusion: The Plot to Rig an Election and Destroy a Presidency xvi (2019).

3. Letter to Richard Burr, Chairman, Select Committee on Intelligence, United States Senate, and Adam Schiff, Chairman, Permanent Select Committee on Intelligence, United States House of Representatives, Aug. 12, 2019.

4. Letter to the Honorable Richard Burr, Chairman, Select Committee on Intelligence, U.S. Senate et al., From: Jason Klitenic, General Counsel, Office of the Director of National Intelligence, Sept. 13, 2019.

5. Memorandum of Telephone Conversation, Telephone Conversation with President Zelensky of Ukraine, July 25, 2019.

6. John Yoo, Crisis and Command: Executive Power from George Washington to George W. Bush 382–83 (2010).

7. United States v. Nixon, 418 U.S. 683, 703–13 (1974).

8. Laurence H. Silberman, Toward Presidential Control of the State Department, 57 Foreign Aff. 872 (1979).

9. Permanent Select Committee on Intelligence & Committee on Oversight and Reform & the Committee on Foreign Affairs, U.S. House of Representatives, Deposition of Lieutenant Colonel Alexander S. Vindman, Oct. 29, 2019, at 16.

10. Permanent Select Committee on Intelligence & Committee on Oversight and Reform & the Committee on Foreign Affairs, U.S. House of Representatives, Deposition of William B. Taylor, Oct. 22, 2019, at 18.

11. Vindman deposition, supra note 9, at 18.

12. Permanent Select Committee on Intelligence & Committee on Oversight and Reform & the Committee on Foreign Affairs, U.S. House of Representatives, Deposition of Marie "Masha" Yovanovitch, Oct. 11, 2019, at 24.

13. Chicago & S. Air Lines v. Waterman S.S. Corp., 333 U.S. 103, 111 (1948).

14. McCarthy, supra note 2, at 121–24.

15. 1 Robert S. Mueller III, U.S. Dep't of Justice, Report on the Investigation into Russian Interference in the 2016 Presidential Election 95 (2019).

16. 1 id. at 80–94.

17. 1 id. at 14–65.

18. John Yoo, The Terrorist Surveillance Program and the Constitution, 14 Geo. Mason L. Rev. 565, 572–82 (2007).

19. William McGurn, Mueller Exposes Spy Chiefs, Wall St. J., Mar. 25, 2019.

20. 50 U.S.C. § 1805(a)(2).

21. Victor Davis Hanson, The Case for Trump (2019).

22. David E. Bernstein more fully describes the Obama administration's failure to enforce the law in Lawless: The Obama Administration's Unprecedented Assault on the Constitution and the Rule of Law (2015).

23. Office of the Inspector General, U.S. Department of Justice, Report of Investigation of Former Federal Bureau of Investigation Director James Comey's Disclosure of Sensitive Investigatory Information and Handling of Certain Memoranda, August 2019, at 17.

24. Andrew C. McCarthy, Trump Was Always the Target of the Russia Investigation, National Review, Aug. 30, 2019.

25. DOJ OIG Report, supra note 23, at 31–32.

26. Id. at 39.

CHAPTER 4: DRAINING THE SWAMP

1. These figures come from Council of Economic Advisors, The Economic Report of the President 2019, Mar. 2019, https://www.whitehouse.gov/wp-content/uploads/2019/03/ERP-2019.pdf.

2. Id. at 3.

3. Exec. Order 13,771, 82 Fed. Reg. 9339 (Jan. 20, 2017).

4. Council of Economic Advisers, The Economic Effects of Federal Deregulation Since January 2017: An Interim Report, June 2019, at 1. https://www.whitehouse.gov/wp-content/uploads/2019/06/The-Economic-Effects-of-Federal-Deregulation-Interim-Report.pdf.

5. Whitman v. American Trucking Association, 531 U.S. 457 (2001).

6. See, e.g., Commonwealth of Pa. v. Lynn, 501 F.2d 848, 855–56 (D.C. Cir. 1974).

7. See John Yoo & Todd Gaziano, Presidential Authority to Revoke or Reduce National Monument Designations, 35 Yale J. Reg. 617 (2018).

8. See Antonin Scalia & Bryan A. Garner, Reading Law: The Interpretation of Legal Texts 278 (2012).

9. Federalist No. 64, at 336 (George W. Carey & James McClellan eds. 2001) (John Jay).

10. Brown v. Board of Education of Topeka, 347 U.S. 483 (1954).

11. Plessy v. Ferguson, 163 U.S. 537 (1896).

12. Immigration and Naturalization Serv. v. Chadha, 462 U.S. 919, 957 (1983).

13. Exec. Order No. 11,821, 39 Fed. Reg. 41,501 (1974); Exec. Order No. 12,044, 43 Fed. Reg. 12,661 (1978); Exec. Order No. 12,291, 46 Fed. Reg. 13,193 (1981); Exec. Order No. 12,866, 58 Fed. Reg. 51,735 (1993); Exec. Order No. 13,258, 67 Fed. Reg. 9385 (2002); Exec. Order No. 13,422, 72 Fed. Reg. 2,763 (2007); Exec. Order No. 13,497, 74 Fed. Reg. 6,113 (2009).

14. Myers v. United States, 272 U.S. 52 (1926).

15. See Bowsher v. Synar, 478 U.S. 714 (1986).

16. Humphrey's Executor v. United States, 295 U.S. 602 (1935); Morrison v. Olson, 487 U.S. 654 (1988).

17. See John Yoo, Globalism and the Constitution: Treaties, Non-Self-Execution, and the Original Understanding, 99 Colum. L. Rev. 1955 (1999).

18. Federalist No. 64, supra note 9, at 336.

19. An Act to Declare the Treaties Heretofore Concluded with France, No Longer Obligatory on the United States, 1 Stat. 578 (July 7, 1798).

20. For a discussion of the ABM Treaty, see John Yoo, Politics as Law: The Anti-Ballistic Missile Treaty, the Separation of Powers, and Treaty Interpretation, 89 Cal. L. Rev. 851 (2001).

21. See Goldwater v. Carter, 617 F.2d 697 (D.C. Cir.), vacated by Goldwater v. Carter, 444 U.S. 996 (1979); see also Kucinich v. Bush, 236 F. Supp. 2d 1 (D.D.C. 2002). For a summary of the academic discussion on treaty interpretation and termination, see John Yoo, The False Sirens of Delegation: Treaty Interpretation and Separation of Powers, 90 Cal. L. Rev. 1305 (2002). See also Louis Henkin, Foreign Affairs and the United States Constitution 214 (2d ed. 1996).

22. Tamara Keith, Wielding a Pen and a Phone, Obama Goes It Alone, NPR, Jan. 20, 2014.

23. See generally David E. Bernstein, Lawless: The Obama Administration's Unprecedented Assault on the Constitution and the Rule of Law (2015).

24. See Memorandum from Janet Napolitano, Sec'y of Homeland Sec., to David Aguilar, Acting Comm'r, U.S. Customs and Border Protection, Alejandro Mayorkas, Dir., U.S. Citizenship and Immigration Servs., and John Morton, Dir., U.S. Immigration and Customs Enforcement (June 15, 2012).

25. Remarks by the President in Address to the Nation on Immigration (Nov. 20, 2014); see also U.S. Department of Homeland Security, Fixing Our Broken Immigration System Through Executive Action—Key Facts, Aug. 19, 2015.

26. Texas v. United States, 809 F.3d 134 (5th Cir. 2015), aff'd, 136 S. Ct. 2271 (2016).

27. Robert J. Delahunty & John Yoo, Dream On: The Obama Administration's Nonenforcement of Immigration Laws, the DREAM Act, and the Take Care Clause, 91 Tex. L. Rev. 781 (2013).

28. Department of Homeland Security v. Regents of the Univ. of Calif., 908 F.3d 476 (9th Cir. 2018).

29. Heckler v. Chaney, 470 U.S. 821 (1985).

30. Thomas Jefferson to Spencer Roane, Sept. 6, 1819, https://founders.archives.gov/documents/Jefferson/98 -01-02-0734.

31. 8 U.S.C. § 1227 (2006).

32. Department of Homeland Security, Immigration and Customs Enforcement, Enforcement and Removal Operations, https://www.ice.gov/features/ERO-2018. At the time of DACA's announcement, apprehending, detaining, and removing all illegal aliens in the nation would have required an ICE budget of $135 billion. Letter from Nelson Peacock, Assistant Sec'y for Legislative Affairs, U.S. Dep't of Homeland Sec., to Senator John Cornyn (Dec. 3, 2010). ICE's appropriation for 2013 ran to just under $6 billion. William L. Painter, Cong. Research Serv., R42557, Department of Homeland Security

Appropriations: A Summary of the House-Passed and Senate-Reported Bills for FY 2013 at 6 (2012). President Trump requested an increase in 2019 to $9 billion.

33. Delahunty & Yoo, supra note 27, at 789.

34. Memorandum from Janet Napolitano to David Aguilar et al., supra note 24.

35. Cass R. Sunstein, Problems with Rules, 83 Cal. L. Rev. 953, 1008 (1995).

36. Lincoln v. Vigil, 508 U.S. 182 (1993); Massachusetts v. EPA, 549 U.S. 497, 527 (2007).

37. Arizona v. United States, 567 U.S. 387 (2012).

38. President George Washington, Proclamation Regarding the Cessation of Violence and Obstruction of Justice in Protest of Liquor Laws, Sept. 15, 1792.

39. Heckler v. Chaney, 470 U.S. 821, 832–33 n.4 (1985).

40. Federalist No. 63, at 327 (George W. Carey & James McClellan eds. 2001) (James Madison).

41. Cf. Byrd v. Raines, 521 U.S. 811, 817 (1997).

42. Federalist No. 70, at 362–63 (George W. Carey & James McClellan eds. 2001) (Alexander Hamilton).

43. Saikrishna B. Prakash & John C. Yoo, The Origins of Judicial Review, 70 U. Chi. L. Rev. 887, 914 (2003).

44. 2 The Debates in the Several State Conventions on the Adoption of the Federal Constitution 445–46 (Jonathan Elliot ed. 1836). See also Akhil Reed Amar, America's Constitution: A Biography 179 (2005).

45. 3 The Records of the Federal Convention of 1787, at 171 (Max Farrand ed. 1911) [hereinafter Farrand's Records].

46. Id. at 185.

47. Id. at 597, 600.

48. 2 James Wilson, Lectures on Law Pt. II, in Collected Works of James Wilson 829, 878 (Kermit L. Hall ed. 2007).

49. See Vt. Const. of 1786, ch. 1, art. XVII; Md. Const. of 1786 sec. VII. See also Saikrishna Prakash, The Essential Meaning of Executive Power, U. Ill. L. Rev. 701, 726 n.113 (2003).

50. See Christopher N. May, Presidential Defiance of "Unconstitutional" Laws 16, 160 n.58 (1998).

51. Dennis Dixon, Godden v Hales Revisited—James II and the Dispensing Power, 27 J. Legal Hist. 129, 134–36 (2006).

52. John Locke, Two Treatises of Government § 145 (J. W. Gough ed. 3d ed. 1966) (1690). See M.J.C. Vile, Constitutionalism and the Separation of Powers 60–61 (1967); W. B. Gwyn, The Meaning of the Separation of Powers: An Analysis of the Doctrine from Its Origin to the Adoption of the United States Constitution 82–99 (1965).

53. Locke, supra note 52, at § 146.

54. Id. at § 147.

55. Id.

56. Id. at § 276.

57. John Yoo, Crisis and Command: A History of Executive Power from George Washington to George W. Bush 106–107 (2010).

58. Jefferson to Dickinson, Aug. 9, 1803, 10 The Writings of Thomas Jefferson 262 (Andrew A. Lipscomb ed. 1903–1904).

59. Id. at 242.

60. Id. at 279.

61. Jeremy D. Bailey, Thomas Jefferson and Executive Power 15–22 (2007); Gary J. Schmitt, Thomas Jefferson and the Presidency, in Inventing the American Presidency 326–46 (Thomas E. Cronin ed. 1989).

62. See, e.g., Arthur M. Schlesinger Jr., The Imperial Presidency 59 (1973); Clinton Rossiter, Constitutional Dictatorship: Crisis Government in the Modern Democracies (1948); Edward S. Corwin, The President: Office and Powers, 1787–1957, at 20 (4th ed. 1957).

63. 7 Collected Works of Abraham Lincoln 282 (Roy P. Basler ed. 1953).

64. 4 id. at 429.

65. 4 id. at 224. See also Michael Stokes Paulsen, Review: The Civil War as Constitutional Interpretation, 71 U. Chi. L. Rev. 691, 706–707 (2004) (explaining Lincoln's belief in a duty to defeat secession).

66. Edward J. Corwin, supra note 62, at 201.

67. Barack Obama, Exclusive: A Nation of Laws and a Nation of Immigrants, Time Ideas, June 17, 2012, http://ideas.time.com/2012/06/17/A-NATION-OF-LAWS-AND-A-NATION-OF-IMMIGRANTS/.

68. Memorandum from Denise A. Vanison, Debra A. Rogers & Donald Neufeld to Alejandro N. Mayorkas 10 (undated).

69. Arizona v. United States, 567 U.S. 387, 434 (2012) (Scalia, J., concurring in part and dissenting in part).

70. TVA v. Hill, 437 U.S. 153 (1978).

71. Erwin Chemerinsky et al., Law Professor Letter on President's Article II Powers (June 4, 2018), https://protectdemocracy.org/law-professor-article-ii/.

72. Ex parte Garland, 71 U.S. 333, 380 (1866).

73. Chairman Nadler Statement for Subcommittee Hearing on Examining the Constitutional Role of the Pardon Power, March 27, 2019.

74. Id.

75. Adam Schiff (@RepAdamSchiff), Twitter (April 13, 2018, 7:14 AM), https://twitter.com/RepAdamSchiff/status/984796875780915200.

76. 2 Robert S. Mueller III, U.S. Dep't of Justice, Report on the Investigation into Russian Interference in the 2016 Presidential Election 124 (2019).

77. 2 id. at 127.

78. Brian C. Kalt, Note, Pardon Me: The Constitutional Case Against Self-Pardons, 106 Yale L.J. 779, 779–80 (1996).

79. 2 Farrand's Records, supra note 45, at 500–501.

80. Id. at 501–502.

81. Id. at 626.

82. Id.

83. Id. at 627.

84. George Mason, Objections to the Constitution, Oct. 7, 1787, reprinted in 13 Documentary History of the Ratification of the Constitution 349 (John P. Kaminski & Gaspare J. Saladino eds. 1981).

85. 3 The Debates in the Several State Conventions on the Adoption of the Federal Constitution 496–98 (Jonathan Elliot ed. 1836).

86. Federalist No. 74, at 385 (George W. Carey & James McClellan eds. 2001) (Alexander Hamilton).

87. Josh Delk, Pelosi: Libby pardon shows that "obstructing justice will be rewarded" by Trump, The Hill (April 13, 2018).

88. James P. Pfiffner, The Scope of the President's Pardon Power (Mar. 31, 2019), https://www.ssrn.com /abstract=3363187.

89. Federalist No. 10, at 44 (George W. Carey & James McClellan eds. 2001) (James Madison).

90. Jed Shugerman and Ethan J. Leib, This overlooked part of the Constitution could stop Trump from abusing his pardon power, Wash. Post (March 14, 2018).

91. Mary C. Lawton, Memorandum Opinion for the Deputy Attorney General, Presidential or Legislative Pardon of the President, 1 Supp. Op. O.L.C. 370, 370 (1974), https://www.justice.gov/file/20856 /download.

92. Kalt, supra note 78, at 795; Akhil Amar, The Bill of Rights as a Constitution, 100 Yale L.J. 1131, 1133 (1991).

93. City of Boerne v. Flores, 521 U.S. 507 (1997).

94. Cooper v. Aaron, 358 U.S. 1 (1958).

95. David Gray Adler, "The President's Pardon Power," in Thomas E. Cronin, ed., Inventing the American Presidency (1989).

96. Kalt, supra note 78, at 808.

97. James Pfiffner and Justin Florence, Using the pardon power to encourage law breaking, The Hill (July 31, 2019).

CHAPTER 5: "WE HAVE TO HAVE BORDERS"

1. Here's Donald Trump's Presidential Announcement Speech, Time, June 16, 2015.

2. Richard Wolf, Travel Ban Lexicon: From Candidate Donald Trump's Campaign Promises to President Trump's Tweets, USA Today, Apr. 24, 2018.

3. Aside from a single poll from February 14–16, 2016, which showed Ted Cruz ahead by 2 points, Trump led every single poll of Republican voters from Nov. 1, 2015, until he won the nomination. Real Clear Politics, Polls, 2016 Republican Presidential Nomination, https://www.realclearpolitics.com/epolls /2016/president/us/2016_republican_presidential_nomination-3823.html#polls.

4. See Trump v. Hawaii, No. 17–965, Joint Appendix, 160–227 (U.S. 2018).

5. Presidential Candidate Donald Trump Rally in Miami, Florida, C-SPAN (Nov. 2, 2016), https://www .c-span.org/video/?417864-1/donald-trump-campaigns-miami-florida&start=2330.

6. Executive Order No. 13769, Protecting the Nation from Foreign Terrorist Entry into the United States, 82 Fed. Reg. 8977 (2017).

7. The White House, President Donald J. Trump Restores Responsibility and the Rule of Law to Immigration, Sep. 5, 2017.

8. See, e.g., Office of Public Affairs, U.S. Department of Justice, Department of Justice Announces New Immigration Compliance Requirements for FY 2018 Grants (June 28, 2018).

9. The White House, Remarks by President Trump on the Illegal Immigration Crisis and Border Security, Nov. 1, 2018; Julie Hirschfeld Davis, President Wants to Use Executive Order to End Birthright Citizenship, N.Y. Times, Oct. 30, 2018.

10. Nancy Pelosi & Chuck Schumer, Pelosi, Schumer Joint Statement on the President's Unlawful Emergency Declaration (Feb. 15, 2019), https://www.speaker.gov/newsroom/21519-2.

11. Max Boot, Trump Is Trashing the Rule of Law to Stay in Power, Wash. Post, Apr. 9, 2019.

12. John Yoo, Executive Power Run Amok, N.Y. Times, Feb. 6, 2017.

13. Gustavo Lopez et al., Key Findings About U.S. Immigrants, Pew Foundation (Sept. 14, 2018).

14. Pew reports about 11 million in 2018, while the Department of Homeland Security's most recent figure, for 2014, is 12.1 million. See id., Department of Homeland Security, Office of Immigration Statistics, Estimates of the Unauthorized Immigrant Population Residing in the United States: January 2014.

15. Jeffrey S. Passel et al., Number of U.S.-born babies with unauthorized immigrant parents has fallen since 2007, Pew Research Center (Nov. 1, 2018).

16. See Peter Schuck, One Nation Undecided: Clear Thinking About Five Hard Issues That Divide Us 116–17 (2017); Aristide R. Zolberg, A Nation by Design: Immigration Policy in the Fashioning of America 1 (2006).

17. Immigration and Nationality Act of 1952, Pub. L. No. 82–414, 66 Stat. 163 (1952).

18. Immigration and Nationality Act of 1965, Pub. L. No. 89–236, 79 Stat. 911 (1965).

19. Immigrants, 1991 Yearbook of Immigration Statistics 15, 19–20 (1991).

20. Pew Research Center, More Mexicans Leaving Than Coming to the U.S. (Nov. 19, 2015), http://www .pewhispanic.org/2015/11/19/more-mexicans-leaving-than-coming-to-the-u-s/.

21. Pew Key Findings, supra note 13.

22. Chae Chan Ping v. United States (Chinese Exclusion Case), 130 U.S. 581 (1889); Kleindienst v. Mandel, 408 U.S. 753, 766 (1972).

23. 8 U.S.C. § 1182(a)(1)–(a)(3).

24. See Adam B. Cox & Cristina M. Rodriguez, The President and Immigration Law, 119 Yale L.J. 458, 461– 62 (2009).

25. Knauff v. Shaughnessy, 338 U.S. 537, 542 (1950).

26. Cox & Rodriguez, supra note 24, at 463–64.

27. 8 U.S.C. § 1182(f).

28. U.S. Customs and Border Protection, Southwest Border Migration FY2019.

29. Illegal Immigration Reform and Immigrant Responsibility Act of 1996, Pub. L. No. 104–208, Secure Fence Act of 2006, P.L. 109-367; See generally Michael J. Garcia, Congressional Research Service, Barriers Along the Borders: Key Authorities and Requirements (Jan. 27, 2017).

30. Executive Order No. 13767, Jan. 25, 2017.

31. Presidential Proclamation Declaring a National Emergency Concerning the Southern Border of the United States, Feb. 15, 2019.

32. Peter Baker, Trump Declares a National Emergency, and Provokes a Constitutional Clash, N.Y. Times, Feb. 15, 2019.

33. Emily Cochrane & Glenn Thrush, Senate Rejects Trump's Border Emergency Declaration, Setting Up First Veto, N.Y. Times, Mar. 14, 2019.

34. Federalist No. 23, at 113 (George W. Carey & James McClellan eds. 2001) (Alexander Hamilton).

35. Federalist No. 70, at 363 (George W. Carey & James McClellan eds. 2001) (Alexander Hamilton).

36. The Prize Cases, 67 U.S. (2 Black) 635, 668 (1862).

37. National Emergencies Act, Sept. 14, 1976, Pub. L. No. 94–412, 90 Stat. 1255.

38. Youngstown Sheet & Tube Co. v. Sawyer, 343 U.S. 579 (1952).

39. Id. at 587.

40. Ramesh Ponnuru and Yuval Levin, Democrats and Republicans Threaten the Constitution, National Review, Apr. 8, 2019.

41. Dames & Moore v. Regan, 453 U.S. 654 (1981).

42. Id. at 674.

43. Id. at 678.

44. 10 U.S.C. § 2808.

45. 33. U.S.C. § 2293.

46. Federalist No. 23, at 113 (George W. Carey & James McClellan eds. 2001) (Alexander Hamilton).

47. Hera Mir, Immigrant Advocates Condemn Supreme Court Decision to Uphold Muslim Ban, New Jersey Alliance for Immigrant Justice (June 26, 2018).

48. Exec. Order No. 13,769, 82 Fed. Reg. 8,977 (Feb. 1, 2017).

49. Michael D. Shear & Helene Cooper, Trump Bars Refugees and Citizens of 7 Muslim Countries, N.Y. Times, Jan. 27, 2017.

50. Trump v. Hawaii, 138 S. Ct. 2392, 2436 (2018) (Sotomayor, J., dissenting).

51. Id.

52. Washington v. Trump, 847 F. 3d 1151 (9th Cir. 2017).

53. See Executive Order 13,780; Trump v. Hawaii, 138 S. Ct. 2392 (2018).

54. Washington v. Trump, No. C17-0141-JLR, 2017 WL 462040 (W.D. Wash. Feb. 3, 2017).

55. Chae Chin Ping v. United States, 130 U.S. 581, 603 (1889).

56. 8 U.S.C. § 1182(f).

57. Executive Order No. 12,324, 46 Fed Reg. 48109 (1981). See also Sale v. Haitian Centers Council, 509 U.S. 155 (1993).

58. United States ex rel. Knauff v. Shaughnessy, 338 U.S. 537, 542–43 (1950).

59. Executive Order No. 13,780, 82 Fed. Reg. 13,209 (Mar. 6, 2017).

60. International Refugee Assistance Project v. Trump, 857 F.3d 554 (4th Cir. 2017).

61. Id. at 572.

62. Id. at 592.

63. Proclamation No. 9645, 82 Fed. Reg. 45,161 (Sept. 24, 2017).

64. Trump v. Hawaii, 138 S. Ct. 2392, 2408–10 (2018).

65. Id. at 2408.

66. Id. at 2415.

67. Id. at 2420 n.5.

68. Id. at 2424 (Thomas, J., concurring).

69. Federalist No. 70, at 363 (George W. Carey & James McClellan eds. 2001) (Alexander Hamilton).

70. Lujan v. Defenders of Wildlife, 504 U.S. 555, 577 (1992).

71. Trump v. Hawaii, 138 S. Ct. at 2433 (Sotomayor, J., dissenting).

72. Id. at 2440 (Sotomayor, J., dissenting).

73. Jonathan Swan & Stef W. Kight, Exclusive: Trump targeting birthright citizenship with executive order, Axios, Oct. 30, 2018.

74. John C. Eastman & Edwin Meese III, Brief of Amicus Curiae, The Claremont Institute Center for Constitutional Jurisprudence, Hamdi v. Rumsfeld, No. 03–6696; See also H.R. 698; H.R. 3700, § 201; H.R. 3938, § 701; Dual Citizenship, Birthright Citizenship, and the Meaning of Sovereignty: Hearing Before the Subcomm. on Immigration, Border Security, and Claims of the H. Comm. on the Judiciary, 109th Cong. (2005).

75. Oforji v. Ashcroft, 354 F.3d 609, 620–21 (7th Cir. 2003) (Posner, J., concurring); Charles Wood, Losing Control of America's Future, 22 Harv. J.L. & Pub. Pol'y 465, 503–22 (1999); Peter Schuck & Rogers Smith, Citizenship Without Consent (1985).

76. Immigration, Poll, Gallup, https://news.gallup.com/poll/1660/immigration.aspx.

77. Michael Anton, Citizenship Shouldn't Be a Birthright, Wash. Post, July 18, 2018.

78. Inglis v. Trustees of the Sailor's Snug Harbor, 28 U.S. 99, 164 (1830) (Story, J.). See also James C. Ho, Defining "American": Birthright Citizenship and the Original Understanding of the 14th Amendment, 9 Greenbag 2d 367, 368 (2006).

79. For the background, see Don Fehrenbacher, The Dred Scott Case: Its Significance in American Law and Politics (2001); Mark Graber, Dred Scott and the Problem of Constitutional Evil (2006).

80. Dred Scott v. Sanford, 60 U.S. 393 (1857).

81. Edward J. Erler, Trump's Critics Are Wrong About the 14th Amendment and Birthright Citizenship, National Review, Aug. 19, 2015; John C. Eastman, We Can Apply the 14th Amendment While Also Reforming Birthright Citizenship, National Review, Aug. 24, 2015.

82. 14 Stat. 27 § 1.

83. Cong. Globe, 39th Cong., 1st Sess. 498 (1866).

84. Id. at 2890–91.

85. Id. at 2891.

86. 169 U.S. 649, 652–53.

87. 457 U.S. 202, 211 n.10 (1982).

CHAPTER 6: AMERICA FIRST

1. Donald Trump, The White House, Statement by President Trump on Jerusalem (Dec. 6, 2017).

2. Zivotofsky v. Kerry, 576 U.S. 1059 (2015).

3. Donald J. Trump, Presidential Proclamation No. 9852, Recognizing the Golan Heights as Part of the State of Israel, 2019 Daily Comp. Pres. Doc. No. 172, at 3 (Mar. 25, 2019). See also Palestine Brings Case Against the U.S. in the International Court of Justice at a Fraught Time for U.S.-Palestinian Relations, 113 Am. J. Int'l L. 143, 147–79 (2019).

4. Tulsi Gabbard (@TulsiGabbard), Twitter (Nov. 19, 2019), https://twitter.com/TulsiGabbard/status /1196958345065684994.

5. Amy Klobuchar (@amyklobuchar), Twitter (Nov. 18, 2019), https://twitter.com/amyklobuchar/status /1196611715661733888.

6. Bernie Sanders (@SenSanders), Twitter (Nov. 19, 2019), https://twitter.com/SenSanders/status /1196527568704458752.

7. Jacob Poushter, U.S. International Relations Scholars, Global Citizens Differ Sharply on Views of Threats to Their Country, Pew Research Center, (May 9, 2018), https://www.pewresearch.org/fact-tank/2018

/05/09/u-s-international-relations-scholars-global-citizens-differ-sharply-on-views-of-threats-to-their -country/.

8. Bernie Sanders, By Ending the Iran Deal, Trump Has Put America on the Path to War, The Guardian, May 14, 2018.

9. Al Gore, Statement by Former Vice President Al Gore on Today's Decision by the Trump Administration to Withdraw from the Paris Agreement (June 1, 2017).

10. Max Boot, Trump crosses the DMZ, but his diplomacy is on the road to nowhere, Wash. Post, June 30, 2019.

11. Eliot A. Cohen, America's Long Goodbye: The Real Crisis of the Trump Era, Foreign Affairs, December 11, 2018.

12. White House, National Security Strategy of the United States 1 (December 2017) [hereinafter NSS].

13. The World Bank, Data, Military Expenditures (% of GDP), https://data.worldbank.org/indicator/MS.MIL .XPND.GD.ZS.

14. Center for Strategic and International Studies, China Power Project, How Much Trade Transits the South China Seas?

15. See John Yoo, Point of Attack: Preventive War, International Law, and Global Welfare (2014).

16. President Barack Obama, Address by President Obama to the 71st Session of the United Nations General Assembly (September 20, 2016).

17. A transcript of Donald Trump's meeting with the Washington Post editorial board, Wash. Post, Mar. 21, 2016.

18. President Donald Trump, Remarks by President Trump to the 73rd Session of the United Nations General Assembly (September 25, 2018).

19. Michael R. Pompeo, Restoring the Role of the Nation-State in the Liberal International Order, Dec. 4, 2018.

20. Michael R. Pompeo, Remarks at the Claremont Institute's 40th Anniversary Gala: "A Foreign Policy from the Founding."

21. NSS, supra note 12, at 2.

22. Id. at 25.

23. Id. at 26.

24. Countering America's Adversaries Through Sanctions Act of 2017, 22 U.S.C. §§ 9501, 8909, 8910, 9221, 9225, 9241, 1232 (2017); U.S. Dep't of State, Sanctions Announcement on Russia (December 19, 2018), https://www.state.gov/sanctions-announcement-on-russia/; U.S. Dep't of State, Sanctions Under Section 231 of the Countering America's Adversaries Through Sanctions Act of 2017 (September 20, 2018), https://www.state.gov/sanctions-under-section-231-of-the-countering-americas-adversaries -through-sanctions-act-of-2017-caatsa/.

25. Anderson Cooper 360°: Keeping Them Honest (CNN television broadcast, Jul. 1, 2019).

26. Rosie Gray, Trump Declines to Affirm NATO's Article 5, Atlantic, May 25, 2017; Peter Baker, Trump Says NATO Allies Don't Pay Their Share. Is That True? N.Y. Times, May 26, 2017.

27. Robin Emmott, Jeff Mason & Alissa de Carbonnel, Trump Claims NATO Victory After Ultimatum to Go It Alone, Reuters (July 11, 2018), https://www.reuters.com/article/us-nato-summit/trump-claims-nato -victory-after-ultimatum-to-go-it-alone-idUSKBN1K135H.

28. Donald Trump (@realDonaldTrump), Twitter (Mar. 18, 2017), https://twitter.com/realdonaldtrump /status/843090516283723776?.

29. Choe Sang-Hun, U.S. and South Korea Sign Deal on Shared Defense Costs, N.Y. Times, Feb. 10, 2019.

30. Mornings with Maria (Fox Business Network television broadcast, June 26, 2019).

31. See, e.g., Louis Henkin, Foreign Affairs and the U.S. Constitution (2d ed. 1996); Harold Hongju Koh, The National Security Constitution: Sharing Power After the Iran-Contra Affair (1990); Michael J. Glennon, Constitutional Diplomacy (1990).

32. Arthur Schlesinger Jr., The Imperial Presidency (1973).

33. Bruce Ackerman, No, Trump Cannot Declare an "Emergency" to Build His Wall, N.Y. Times, Jan. 5, 2019.

34. See, e.g., Julian Mortenson, The Executive Power Clause, 167 U. Pa. L. Rev. ___ (forthcoming); Julian Mortenson, Article II Vests Executive Power, Not the Royal Prerogative, 109 Colum. L. Rev. 1169 (2019); John Harrison, Executive Power, https://papers.ssrn.com/sol3/papers.cfm?abstract_id=3398427 (2019).

35. John Locke, Two Treatises of Government § 146 (J. W. Gough ed., 3d ed. 1966) (1690).

36. Id. § 148.

37. Charles Louis de Secondat, Baron Montesquieu, Spirit of the Laws, bk. 11, ch. 6 (Thomas Nugent trans. 1949 [1748]).

38. Id.

39. 1 William Blackstone, Commentaries on the Laws of England *252.

40. Id. at *245.

41. Id. at *254.

42. Charles C. Thatch Jr., The Creation of the Presidency, 1775–1789: A Study in Constitutional History 29 (1922).

43. John Adams, Thoughts on Government (1776), reprinted in 4 Papers of John Adams 65, 89 (Robert J. Taylor ed. 1979).

44. See Thatch, supra note 42, at 34–35.

45. N.Y. Const. arts. VIII, XVII (1777), reprinted in 5 Francis N. Thorpe, ed., The Federal and State Constitutions, Colonial Charters, and Other Organic Laws 2632 (1909).

46. The Federalist No. 26, at 129 (George W. Carey & James McClellan eds. 2001) (Alexander Hamilton).

47. See 1 Records of the Federal Convention of 1787, at 20–21 (Max Farrand ed. 1911) [hereinafter 1 Farrand's Records].

48. Id. at 21.

49. Id. at 64–65; see also id. at 65 (Rutledge); id. at 65–66 (Wilson).

50. Id. at 65–66.

51. Id. at 67.

52. 2 The Records of the Federal Convention of 1787, at 131–32 (Max Farrand ed. 1911) [hereinafter 2 Farrand's Records].

53. See Saikrishna B. Prakash & Michael D. Ramsey, The Executive Power over Foreign Affairs, 111 Yale L.J. 231, 284 (2001).

54. See 2 Farrand, supra note 52, at 15–16. The politics and consequences of the Great Compromise are retold in Jack Rakove, Original Meanings: Politics and Ideas in the Making of the Constitution 62–70 (1996).

55. See Jack N. Rakove, Solving a Constitutional Puzzle: The Treatymaking Clause as a Case Study, 1 Persp. Am. Hist. 233, 240–41 (1984).

56. Id. at 240–41.

57. See, e.g., Frederick Marks, Independence on Trial: Foreign Affairs and the Making of the Constitution 52–95 (1986).

58. 3 Jonathan Elliot, The Debate in the Several State Conventions on the Adoption of the Federal Constitution 59–60 (1836) [hereinafter Elliot's Debates].

59. Rakove, supra note 55, at 276–77.

60. 3 Elliot's Debates, supra note 58, at 383.

61. See John Yoo, Globalization and the Constitution, 99 Colum. L. Rev. 1955 (1999).

62. See Prakash & Ramsey, supra note 53, at 299–300.

63. Thomas Jefferson, Opinion on the Powers of the Senate (Apr. 24, 1790), in 5 The Writings of Thomas Jefferson 161 (Andrew A. Lipscomb & Albert E. Bergh eds. 1923).

64. Treaty of Amity and Commerce, Feb. 6, 1778, U.S.-Fr., 8 Stat. 12., art. XVII.

65. Letter from Washington to Hamilton, Jefferson, Knox, and Randolph (Apr. 18, 1793), in 14 The Papers of Alexander Hamilton, 326–27 (Harold Syrett ed. 1969).

66. See Jack N. Rakove, The Beginnings of National Politics: An Interpretive History of the Continental Congress 113–18 (1979); and Samuel F. Bemis, The Diplomacy of the American Revolution 58–69 (1957).

67. Prakash & Ramsey, supra note 53, at 325–27.

68. Opinion on the Treaties with France (Apr. 28, 1793), in 25 The Papers of Thomas Jefferson 608–18 (John Catanzariti ed. 1993).

69. Letter from Hamilton & Knox to Washington, May 2, 1793, in 14 The Papers of Alexander Hamilton, supra note 65, at 367–96.

70. Notes on Washington's Questions on Neutrality and the Alliance with France (1793), reprinted in 25 The Papers of Thomas Jefferson, supra note 68, at 666.

71. 1 Compilation of the Messages and Papers of the Presidents: 1789–1897 156 (James D. Richardson ed. 1900).

72. Neutrality Act, 1 Stat. 381 (June 5, 1794).

73. See Pacificus No. 1, reprinted in 15 Papers of Hamilton, supra note 65, at 33–43.

74. See Helvidius Nos. 1–5, reprinted in 15 The Papers of James Madison 66–120 (Thomas Mason ed. 1985).

75. Helvidius No. 1, in 15 id. at 69.

76. Id.

77. Helvidius No. 4, in 15 id. at 108.

78. See Stanley Elkins & Eric McKitrick, The Age of Federalism 362 (1995).

79. President Donald J. Trump Is Ending United States Participation in an Unacceptable Iran Deal, White House Fact Sheet, May 8, 2018.

80. United Nations Framework Convention on Climate Change, Paris Agreement Status of Ratification.

81. Donald Trump, The White House, Statement by President Trump on the Paris Climate Accord (June 1, 2017).

82. Letter from Susan Berk et al. to Donald Trump, President (Nov. 7, 2018).

83. Michael R. Pompeo, Secretary of State, Press Statement, Withdrawal from the INF Treaty (August 2, 2019).

84. Remarks by President Trump and Vice President Pence Announcing the Missile Defense Review, Jan. 17, 2019.

85. Arshad Mohammed & Jonathan Landay, Democrats Alarmed About Possible U.S. Withdrawal from Open Skies Treaty, Reuters, Oct. 8, 2019.

86. Maggie Haberman, Donald Trump Says He Favors Big Tariffs on Chinese Exports, N.Y. Times, Jan. 7, 2016.

87. Nick Corasaniti et al., Donald Trump Vows to Rip Up Trade Deals and Confront China, N.Y. Times, June 28, 2016.

88. See David Gray Adler, The Constitution and the Termination of Treaties 161 (1986).

89. George W. Bush, Remarks Announcing the United States Withdrawal from the Anti-Ballistic Missile Treaty, Weekly Comp. Pres. Docs. 1783 (Dec. 13, 2001).

90. Senate Comm. on Foreign Relations, S. Prt. 106–71, Treaties and Other International Agreements: The Role of the United States Senate 201 (Comm. Print 2001); see also Goldwater v. Carter, 444 U.S. 996 (1979).

91. See Pacificus No. 1, reprinted in 15 Papers of Hamilton, supra note 65, at 33–43.

92. See Henkin, supra note 31, at 184; Goldwater v. Carter, 617 F.2d 697, 705 (D.C. Cir.), vacated as moot, 444 U.S. 996 (1979).

93. See Youngstown Sheet & Tube v. Sawyer, 343 U.S. 579, 587 (1952); Henry P. Monaghan, The Protective Power of the Presidency, 93 Colum. L. Rev. 1 (1993).

94. Thomas C. Schelling, The Strategy of Conflict 4 (1960).

95. Id. at 18.

96. 299 U.S. 304, 319 (1936).

97. Id.

98. The Federalist No. 70, at 363 (George W. Carey & James McClellan eds. 2001) (Alexander Hamilton).

99. 10 Annals of Cong. 613–14 (1800).

100. See, e.g., Koh, supra note 31, at 118–23; Arthur M. Schlesinger Jr., The Imperial Presidency (1972).

101. See generally John Yoo, Globalism and the Constitution: Treaties, Non-Self-Execution, and the Original Understanding, 99 Colum. L. Rev. 1955 (1999).

102. Edwin S. Corwin, The President: Office and Powers 171 (4th rev. ed., 1957).

CHAPTER 7: FIRE AND FURY

1. Toluse Olorunnipa & Ashley Parker, As Congress Votes to Limit His War Powers, Trump Supporters Offer Their Full-Throated Support for His Iran Strategy, Wash. Post, Jan. 9, 2020.

2. H. Con. Res. 83, 116th Cong., 2d Sess. (Jan. 9, 2020).

3. Donald Trump (@realDonaldTrump), Twitter (June 15, 2013), https://twitter.com/realdonaldtrump/status/346063000056254464.

4. Dion Nissenbum, Nancy Youssef & Vivian Salama, In Shift, Trump Orders U.S. Troops out of Syria, Wall St. J., Nov. 27, 2018.

5. Donald Trump (@realDonaldTrump), Twitter (Oct. 25, 2019), https://twitter.com/realDonaldTrump /status/1187708412685107200.

6. Transcript: Donald Trump's Foreign Policy Speech, N.Y. Times, Apr. 27, 2016.

7. Remarks by President Trump to the 72nd Session of the United Nations General Assembly, Sept. 19, 2017.

8. Dianne Feinstein, Feinstein Statement on Trump UN Speech (Sept. 19, 2017).

9. See Matthew C. Waxman, The Power to Threaten War, 123 Yale L.J. 1626 (2014).

10. Michael Stokes Paulsen, Trump's First Unconstitutional War, Nat'l Rev., April 11, 2017.

11. David French, America's War in Yemen Is Plainly Unconstitutional, Nat'l Rev., April 27, 2019.

12. Bernie Sanders, Sanders Statement on Trump's Authority to Go to War in Syria (Apr. 11, 2018); Michael Crowley, Bernie's Foreign Policy Deficit, Politico, Jan. 30, 2016.

13. Asher Stockler, Tulsi Gabbard Calls Soleimani Strike "Act of War," Says Trump Violated the Constitution, Newsweek, Jan. 3, 2020.

14. Chris Cillizza, What Elizabeth Warren's Statements on Qasem Soleimani Really Tell Us, CNN.com, Jan. 6, 2020, https://www.cnn.com/2020/01/06/politics/elizabeth-warren-quasem-soleimani-trump-2020 /index.html.

15. Federalist 70, at 362 (George W. Carey & James McClellan eds. 2001) (Alexander Hamilton).

16. Authorization to Use Military Force, Pub. L. No. 107–40, 115 Stat. 224 (2001).

17. Congressional Research Service, Afghanistan: Background and U.S. Policy in Brief (May 1, 2019).

18. Authorization for Use of Military Force Against Iraq Resolution of 2002, H.R.J. Res. 114, 107th Cong. § 3, 116 Stat. 1498 (2002).

19. Secretary of Defense Jim Mattis, Briefing by Secretary Mattis on U.S. Strikes in Syria (Apr. 13, 2018), https://www.defense.gov/News/Transcripts/Transcript-View/Article/1493658/briefing-by-secretary -mattis-on-us-strikes-in-syria/.

20. Charlie Savage, Watchdog Group Sues Trump Administration, Seeking Legal Rationale Behind Syria Strike, N.Y. Times, May 8, 2017; Charlie Savage, Was Trump's Syria Strike Illegal? Explaining Presidential War Powers, N.Y. Times, April 7, 2017.

21. See Memorandum Opinion for Counsel to the President, April 2018 Airstrikes Against Syrian Chemical-Weapons Facilities (May 31, 2018).

22. Id.

23. See John C. Yoo, The Powers of War and Peace: The Constitution and Foreign Affairs After 9/11 (2005).

24. Congressional Research Service, Instances of Use of United States Armed Forces Abroad, 1798–2018 (Dec. 28, 2018).

25. Youngstown Sheet & Tube v. Sawyer, 343 U.S. 579, 637 (1952) (Jackson concurring); see also Mistretta v. United States, 488 U.S. 361, 393 (1989); United States v. Midwest Oil Co., 236 U.S. 459, 474 (1915).

26. See Loving v. United States, 517 U.S. 748, 776 (1996) (Scalia concurring); Johnson v. Eisentrager, 339 U.S. 763, 789 (1950); The Prize Cases, 67 U.S. (2 Black) 635, 670 (1862); Fleming v. Page, 50 U.S. (9 How) 603, 614 (1850).

27. Charlie Savage, Barack Obama's Q&A, The Boston Globe, Dec. 20, 2007.

28. Mike Memoli, Biden Once Warned a President: War with Iran Without Congressional Approval Is Impeachable, NBC News, June 20, 2019.

29. See, e.g., Harold Hongju Koh, The National Security Constitution: Sharing Power After the Iran-Contra Affair 158–61 (1990); Bruce Ackerman, Trump Can't Make War Whenever He Likes, N.Y. Times, Apr. 16, 2018.

30. John Hart Ely, War and Responsibility: Constitutional Lessons of Vietnam and Its Aftermath 3–5 (1993).

31. See, e.g., Michael D. Ramsey, Textualism and War Powers, 69 U. Chi. L. Rev. 1543, 1590–1609 (2002).

32. Michael J. Glennon, Constitutional Diplomacy 17 (1990).

33. See John C. Yoo, The Continuation of Politics by Other Means: The Original Understanding of War Powers, 84 Cal. L. Rev. 167, 250–52 (1996).

34. Willi Paul Adams, The First American Constitutions: Republican Ideology and the Making of the State Constitutions (2001).

35. SC Const Art XXVI (1776), reprinted in Francis N. Thorpe, ed., 6 The Federal and State Constitutions, Colonial Charters, and Other Organic Laws 3247 (1909).

36. See David Armitage, The Declaration of Independence and International Law, 59 William & Mary Q (3d ser.) 39 (2002).

37. Pacificus No. 1, in The Helvidius-Pacificus Debates of 1793–94, at 13 (Morton J. Frisch ed. 2007).

38. See Saikrishna B. Prakash and Michael D. Ramsey, The Executive Power over Foreign Affairs, 111 Yale L.J. 231, 252–53 (2001).

39. Federalist No. 76, at 392 (George W. Carey & James McClellan eds. 2001) (Alexander Hamilton).

40. Federalist No. 70, at 362 (George W. Carey & James McClellan eds. 2001) (Alexander Hamilton).

41. Federalist No. 74, at 385 (George W. Carey & James McClellan eds. 2001) (Alexander Hamilton).

42. Federalist No. 70, supra note 40, at 363.

43. Federalist No. 58, at 303 (George W. Carey & James McClellan eds. 2001) (James Madison).

44. J. L. De Lolme, The Constitution of England; Or, an Account of the English Government 71 (N.Y., Hodge & Campbell 1792).

45. See Morris J. MacGregor, The Formative Years, 1783–1812, in American Military History 101 (Maurice Matloff ed. 1969).

46. Walter Russell Mead, Special Providence: American Foreign Policy and How It Changed the World 202 (2001).

47. 2 Jonathan Elliot, ed., Debates in the Several State Conventions on the Adoption of the Federal Constitution 528 (1836).

48. Federalist 69, at 357 (George W. Carey & James McClellan eds. 2001) (Alexander Hamilton).

49. Pacificus No. 1, supra note 37, at 16.

50. Helvidius No. 1, in The Helvidius-Pacificus Debates of 1793–94, at 62 (Morton J. Frisch ed. 2007).

51. Forrest McDonald, The American Presidency: An Intellectual History 98–153 (1994); Gordon S. Wood, The Creation of the American Republic 1776–1787, at 138, 393–429, 434 (1967).

52. Articles of Confederation art. IX (1777).

53. 1 The Works of Alexander Hamilton 219 (Henry Cabot Lodge ed., 2d ed. 1904).

54. See Frederick W. Marks III, Independence on Trial: Foreign Affairs and the Making of the Constitution 52–95 (1973); McDonald, supra note 51, at 143–53.

55. Wood, supra note 51, at 138.

56. 2 The Records of the Federal Convention of 1787, at 318–19 (Max Farrand ed. 1911).

57. Cf. Henry P. Monaghan, The Protective Power of the Presidency, 93 Colum. L. Rev. 1, 67 (1993).

58. 9 Documentary History of the Ratification of the Constitution 964 (John P. Kaminski & Gaspare J. Saladino eds. 1990).

59. 10 id. at 1281.

60. 10 id. at 1282.

61. See David Armitage, The Declaration of Independence and International Law, 59 Wm. & Mary Q. 39, 46–47 (2002).

62. Andrew P. Napolitano, The Presidency, War Powers, and the Constitution, Wash. Times, October 9, 2019.

CHAPTER 8: "SEE YOU IN THE SUPREME COURT!"

1. Robin Pogrebin & Kate Kelly, Brett Kavanaugh Fit In with the Privileged Kids. She Did Not, N.Y. Times, Sept. 14, 2019.

2. Elizabeth Warren (@ewarren), Twitter (Sept. 15, 2019), https://twitter.com/ewarren/status /1173290967773982722.

3. Kamala Harris (@KamalaHarris), Twitter (Sept. 15, 2019), https://twitter.com/KamalaHarris/status /1173250953103007745.

4. Alexandria Ocasio-Cortez (@AOC), Twitter (Sept. 16, 2019), https://twitter.com/AOC/status /1173609907033116672.

5. Represenatative Ayanna Pressley, Press Release, Rep. Pressley calls for Brett Kavanaugh Impeachment Inquiry (Sept. 17, 2019), https://pressley.house.gov/media/press-releases/rep-pressley-calls-brett -kavanaugh-impeachment-inquiry.

6. Kyle Cheney, Nadler Throws Cold Water on Kavanaugh Impeachment, Politico, Sept. 16, 2019.

7. William McGurn, Pin the Asterisk on Kavanaugh, Wall St. J., Sept. 16, 2019.

8. Rachel Frazin, O'Rourke Says Adding SCOTUS Justices Is Worth Exploring, The Hill (Mar. 14, 2019), https://thehill.com/homenews/campaign/434119-orourke-says-adding-scotus-justices-is-worth -exploring.

9. Pod Save America, 2020: Pete Buttigieg on Freedom and Farting Cows (Mar. 1, 2019).

10. Burgess Everett & Marianne Levine, 2020 Dems Warm to Expanding Supreme Court, Politico, Mar. 18, 2019.

11. Kevin Urmacher, Kevin Schaul & Jeff Stein, Where 2020 Democrats Stand on Democratic Changes, Wash. Post (Updated Jan. 31, 2020), https://www.washingtonpost.com/graphics/politics/policy-2020 /voting-changes/?.

12. Everett & Levine, supra note 10.

13. Mark Sherman, New Campaign Seeks Support for Expanded Supreme Court, Boston Globe, Oct. 16, 2018.

14. Sean Illing, Why the Constitution Is an Inherently Progressive Document, Vox (Dec. 18, 2018), https:// www.vox.com/2018/12/18/18127273/american-constitution-erwin-chemerinsky-we-the-people.

15. Michael Hiltzik, Opinion, How a New Court-Packing Scheme Could Save the Supreme Court from Right-Wing Domination, L.A. Times, July 2, 2018.

16. Dahlia Lithwick, The Case for Court Packing, Slate (Apr. 5, 2019), https://slate.com/news-and-politics/2019/04/court-packing-has-become-a-litmus-test-left.html.

17. Remarks by President Trump at Turning Point USA's Teen Student Action Summit 2019, June 23, 2019, https://www.whitehouse.gov/briefings-statements/remarks-president-trump-turning-point-usas-teen-student-action-summit-2019/.

18. See, e.g., NFIB v. Sebelius 567 U.S. 519 (2012); King v. Burwell, 135 S. Ct. 2480 (2015); Department of Commerce v. New York, 588 U.S. ___ (2019).

19. While the White House has left large numbers of vacancies in the district courts, which conduct the trials, it has filled virtually all the openings on the appellate courts, which exercise the greater policy-making power in the federal judicial system.

20. See Russell Wheeler, Trump's Judicial Appointments Record at the August Recess: A Little Less Than Meets the Eye, Brookings, Aug. 8, 2019.

21. Jefferson to Dickinson, Dec. 19, 1801, 10 The Writings of Thomas Jefferson 302 (Andrew A. Lipscomb ed. 1903–04).

22. Federalist No. 78, at 405 (George W. Carey & James McClellan eds. 2001) (Alexander Hamilton).

23. New State Ice Co. v. Liebmann, 285 U.S. 262, 311 (1932).

24. Federalist No. 51, at 270 (George W. Carey & James McClellan eds. 2001) (James Madison).

25. See generally Ronald J. Pestritto, Woodrow Wilson and the Roots of Modern Liberalism (2005).

26. Brett M. Kavanaugh, Fixing Statutory Interpretation, 129 Harv. L. Rev. 2118, 2150 (2016).

27. Gutierrez-Brizuela v. Lynch, 834 F.3d 1142, 1151 55 (10th Cir. 2016) (Gorsuch, J., dissenting).

28. Michigan v. EPA, 135 S. Ct. 2699, 2712 (2015) (Thomas, J., concurring) (citations omitted).

29. See Massachusetts v. EPA, 549 U.S. 497 (2007).

CHAPTER 9: "YOU'RE FIRED!"

1. Read Nancy Pelosi's Remarks on Articles of Impeachment, N.Y. Times, Dec. 5, 2019, https://www.nytimes.com/2019/12/05/us/politics/pelosi-impeachment-trump.html.

2. 2 Robert S. Mueller III, U.S. Dep't of Justice, Report on the Investigation into Russian Interference in the 2016 Presidential Election 18 (2019).

3. Id. at 73.

4. Id. at 77–98.

5. Id. at 182.

6. A Sitting President's Amenability to Indictment and Criminal Prosecution, 24 Op. O.L.C. 222 (2000).

7. See Michael Les Benedict, The Impeachment and Trial of Andrew Johnson (1973).

8. Jeffrey K. Tulis, Impeachment in the Constitutional Order, in The Constitutional Presidency 229, 232 (Joseph M. Bessette & Jeffrey K. Tulis eds. 2009).

9. Akhil Amar, America's Constitution: A Biography 202 (2006).

10. U.S. Const. art. I, § 2, cl. 5. (House impeachment); id., art. I, § 3, cl. 6 (Senate trial); id., art. I, § 3, cl. 7 (punishment).

11. Nixon v. United States, 506 U.S. 224 (1993).

12. 1 Blackstone's Commentaries *244.

13. See Peter Charles Hoffer & N.E.H. Hull, Impeachment in America, 1635–1805, at 96 (1974).

14. Const. of N.Y., 1777, art. XXXIII, 5 The Federal and State Constitutions 2533, 2635 (Francis Newton Thorpe ed. 1909); Const. of Mass., 1780, ch. I, § III, art. VIII, 3 id. at 1263, 1897.

15. 1 Records of the Federal Convention of 1787, at 22 (Max Farrand ed. 1911) (Virginia Plan) [hereinafter 1 Farrand's Records]; id. at 244 (New Jersey Plan).

16. Id. at 292.

17. Id. at 64.

18. Id.

19. Id. at 67.

20. Id. at 65.

21. Id. at 66.

22. Id. at 67.

23. 2 id. at 65.

24. Id. at 65–66.

25. Id. at 67.

26. Id. at 68.

27. Id. at 69.

28. 2 The Records of the Federal Convention of 1787, at 337 (Max Farrand ed. 1911) [hereinafter 2 Farrand's Records].

29. Id. at 493–95.

30. Id. at 550.

31. Id.

32. Michael J. Gerhardt, The Federal Impeachment Process: A Constitutional and Historical Analysis 9 (3d ed. 2019).

33. Charles L. Black Jr. & Philip Bobbitt, Impeachment: A Handbook New Edition 27 (2018).

34. 2 Farrand's Records, supra note 29, at 551.

35. Id.

36. Id.

37. Id. at 551–52.

38. Federalist No. 65, at 338 (George W. Carey & James McClellan eds. 2001) (Alexander Hamilton).

39. Id.

40. Federalist No. 65, supra note 38, at 340.

41. Federalist No. 69, at 356 (George W. Carey & James McClellan eds. 2001) (Alexander Hamilton).

42. Felicia Sonmez, House Democratic Leaders Face Pressure to Impeach Trump Post-Mueller Hearings, Wash. Post, July 31, 2019.

43. Pelosi Calls Senate Republicans "Accomplices to the Cover-Up," Wash. Post, Jan. 31, 2020, https://www .washingtonpost.com/politics/impeachment-trial-live-updates/2020/01/31/9a853bbe-4415-11ea-b5fc -eefa848cde99_story.html.

44. Federalist No. 66, at 342 (George W. Carey & James McClellan eds. 2001) (Alexander Hamilton).

45. Id. at 345.

46. Id. at 347.

47. 3 The Debates in the Several State Conventions on the Adoption of the Federal Constitution 17 (Jonathan Elliot ed. 1836).

48. Id. at 201.

49. Id. at 355.

50. Id. at 366.

51. Id. at 402.

52. Id. at 494.

53. John Yoo, Globalism and the Constitution: Treaties, Non-Self-Execution, and the Original Understanding, 99 Colum. L. Rev. 1955, 2061–68 (1999) (Virginia debate on treaties).

54. 3 Elliot's Debates, supra note 47, at 401.

55. Id. at 500.

56. Id. at 506.

57. Id. at 486.

58. Id. at 498.

59. Id. at 512.

60. Id. at 516.

61. 4 id. at 117.

62. 4 id. at 48.

63. 4 id. at 114.

64. 4 id. at 109.

65. 4 id. at 113.

66. 4 id. at 114.

67. 4 id. at 124.

68. 4 id. at 125–26.

69. 4 id. at 126.

70. 4 id. at 127.

71. Federalist No. 51, at 268 (George W. Carey & James McClellan eds. 2001) (Alexander Hamilton).

72. Federalist No. 58, at 303 (George W. Carey & James McClellan eds. 2001) (Alexander Hamilton).

73. "Out on a Limb": Inside the Republican Reckoning over Trump's Possible Impeachment, Wash. Post, Oct. 6, 2019.

74. Federalist No. 48, at 256–57 (George W. Carey & James McClellan eds. 2001) (James Madison).

75. Letter from Jefferson to Hay, 10 The Works of Thomas Jefferson 404 (Paul Leicestor Ford ed. 1904–5).

76. United States of America v. Michael Cohen, 1:18-cr-00602-WHP (S.D.N.Y. Aug. 21, 2018).

77. Bradley Smith, Those Payments to Women Were Unseemly. That Doesn't Mean They Were Illegal, Wash. Post, Aug. 22, 2018.

78. Black & Bobbitt, supra note 33, at 27–28; Amar, supra note 9, at 200.

79. See John C. Yoo, The Continuation of Politics by Other Means: The Original Understanding of War Powers, 84 Cal. L. Rev. 167, 214 (1996).

80. Myers v. United States, 272 U.S. 52 (1926)

81. 18 U.S.C. § 1512(c)(1)–(2).

82. Memorandum from Bill Barr to Deputy Attorney General Rod Rosenstein & Assistant Attorney General Steve Engel, Re: Mueller's "Obstruction" Theory (June 8, 2018).

83. See United States v. Armstrong, 517 U.S. 456 (1996).

84. Sonam Sheth, Former Director of National Intelligence James Clapper: Putin Is Handling Trump Like a Russian "Asset," Bus. Insider (Dec. 18, 2017), https://www.businessinsider.com/james-clapper-putin -trump-russia-asset-2017-12; Maegan Vazquez, Former Intel Chiefs Condemn Trump's News Conference with Putin, CNN (July 17, 2018), https://www.cnn.com/2018/07/16/politics/john-brennan-donald -trump-treasonous-vladimir-putin/index.html.

85. U.S. Const. art. III, § 3.

86. Letter from Pat A. Cipollone, Counsel to the President, to Nancy Pelosi, Speaker of the House of Representatives (Oct. 8, 2019).

87. Peter Baker, Trump's Sweeping Case Against Impeachment Is a Political Strategy, N.Y. Times, Oct. 9, 2019.

88. Id.

89. Nicholas Fandos & Sheryl Gay Stolberg, A Divided House Endorses Impeachment Inquiry into Trump, N.Y. Times, Oct. 31, 2019.

90. See generally Michael Les Benedict, The Impeachment and Trial of Andrew Johnson (1972).

91. 506 U.S. 224 (1993).

92. Coy v. Iowa, 487 U.S. 1012, 1015–16 (1988).

93. See generally Rules of Procedure and Practice in the Senate When Sitting on Impeachment Trials, Senate Manual, S. Doc. 113–1.

94. Id. at § III, at 223.

95. Memorandum of Telephone Conversation, Telephone Conversation with President Zelensky of Ukraine, July 25, 2019.

96. See discussion in John Yoo, Crisis and Command: A History of Executive Power from George Washington to George W. Bush 111–15 (2010).

97. 18 U.S.C. § 201.

98. McDonnell v. United States, 136 S. Ct. 2355 (2016).

EPILOGUE

1. Gallup, Trump Job Approval, Jan. 29, 2020, https://news.gallup.com/poll/203207/trump-job-approval -weekly.aspx.

2. David Nakamura, Trump Celebrates End of Impeachment with Angry, Raw and Vindictive 62-Minute White House Rant, Wash. Post, Feb. 6, 2010, https://www.washingtonpost.com/politics/trump -celebrates-end-of-impeachment-with-angry-raw-and-vindictive-62-minute-white-house-rant/2020 /02/06/78cd95ee-4914-11ea-b4d9-29cc419287eb_story.html.

3. Sarah Chaney, U.S. Economy Added 225,000 Jobs in January, Wall. St. J., Feb. 7, 2020, https://www.wsj .com/articles/january-jobs-report-11581076802?.

INDEX